D0461180

Taste of Home
quick
COOKING
ANNUAL RECIPES

RDA ENTHUSIAST BRANDS, LLC • MILWAUKEE, WI

Taste of Home
quick
COOKING
ANNUAL RECIPES

■ EDITORIAL
Editor-in-Chief **Catherine Cassidy**
Creative Director **Howard Greenberg**
Editorial Operations Director **Kerri Balliet**

Managing Editor/Print & Digital Books **Mark Hagen**
Associate Creative Director **Edwin Robles Jr.**

Editor **Michelle Rozumalski**
Art Director **Maggie Conners**
Layout Designer **Courtney Lovetere**
Editorial Production Manager **Dena Ahlers**
Editorial Production Coordinator **Jill Banks**
Copy Chief **Deb Warlaumont Mulvey**
Copy Editor **Mary-Liz Shaw**
Contributing Copy Editors **Valerie Phillips,
Kristin Sutter**

Food Editors **Gina Nistico; James Schend;
Peggy Woodward, RD**
Recipe Editors **Sue Ryon (lead); Mary King;
Irene Yeh**
Business Analyst, Content Tools **Amanda Harmatys**
Content Operations Assistant **Shannon Stroud**
Editorial Services Administrator **Marie Brannon**

Test Kitchen & Food Styling Manager
Sarah Thompson
Test Cooks **Nicholas Iverson (lead),
Matthew Hass, Lauren Knoelke**
Food Stylists **Kathryn Conrad (lead),
Shannon Roum, Leah Rekau**
Prep Cooks **Bethany Van Jacobson (lead),
Megumi Garcia, Melissa Hansen**
Culinary Team Assistant **Megan Behr**

Photography Director **Stephanie Marchese**
Photographers **Dan Roberts, Jim Wieland**
Photographer/Set Stylist **Grace Natoli Sheldon**
Set Stylists **Melissa Franco, Stacey Genaw,
Dee Dee Jacq**

Editorial Business Manager **Kristy Martin**
Editorial Business Associate **Samantha Lea Stoeger**

Editor, *Taste of Home* **Jeanne Ambrose**
Associate Creative Director, *Taste of Home*
Erin Burns
Art Director, *Taste of Home* **Kristin Bowker**

■ BUSINESS
Vice President, Group Publisher **Kirsten Marchioli**
Publisher, *Taste of Home* **Donna Lindskog**
General Manager, Taste of Home Cooking School
Erin Puariea
Executive Producer, Taste of Home Online
Cooking School **Karen Berner**

■ TRUSTED MEDIA BRANDS, INC.
President & Chief Executive Officer
Bonnie Kintzer
Chief Financial Officer/Chief Operating Officer
Howard Halligan
Chief Revenue Officer **Richard Sutton**
Chief Marketing Officer **Leslie Dukker Doty**
Chief Digital Officer **Vince Errico**
Senior Vice President, Global HR &
Communications **Phyllis E. Gebhardt, SPHR;
SHRM-SCP**
Vice President, Digital Content & Audience
Development **Diane Dragan**
Vice President, Brand Marketing **Beth Gorry**
Vice President, Financial Planning & Analysis
William Houston
Publishing Director, Books **Debra Polansky**
Chief Technology Officer **Aneel Tejwaney**
Vice President, Consumer Marketing Planning
Jim Woods

Cover Photography
Taste of Home Photo Studio

© 2016 RDA Enthusiast Brands, LLC
1610 N. 2nd St., Suite 102, Milwaukee WI 53212-3906

International Standard Book Number:
978-1-61765-502-9

International Standard Serial Number: 1522-6603

Component Number: 117800053H

All rights reserved.

Taste of Home is a registered trademark of
Trusted Media Brands, Inc.

Printed in China
1 3 5 7 9 10 8 6 4 2

Easy
MEALS for BUSY
FAMILIES

PICTURED ON FRONT COVER Simple Tomato Soup (p. 272), Rich Buttercream Frosting (p. 310),
Chicken & Waffles (p. 84), Bow Tie & Spinach Salad (p. 21) and Root Beer Pulled Pork Sandwiches (p. 168).
PICTURED ON PAGE 1 Pizza in a Bowl (p. 63).
PICTURED AT LEFT Mint Twist Meringues (p. 220), Taco Stew (p. 40) and Breakfast Spuds (p. 161).
PICTURED ON BACK COVER Easy Asian Chicken Slaw (p. 118), Chipotle Turkey Club Sandwich (p. 45),
Beef & Noodle Casserole (p. 138), Cherry Cream Cheese Dessert (p. 121) and Balsamic-Glazed Pork Tenderloin (p. 76).

contents

LIKE US
facebook.com/tasteofhome

TWEET US
@tasteofhome

FOLLOW US
pinterest.com/taste_of_home

SHARE A RECIPE
tasteofhome.com/submit

SHOP WITH US
shoptasteofhome.com

E-MAIL US
bookeditors@tasteofhome.com

VISIT tasteofhome.com *for* MORE!

HOME-COOKED MEALS HAVE NEVER BEEN EASIER

SWEET & SPICY ASIAN
CHICKEN PETITES (p. 13)

THAI-STYLE COBB
SALAD (p. 25)

BERRY-BASIL
LIMEADE JAM
(p. 302)

COLA CAKE WITH
STRAWBERRIES & CREAM (p. 227)

The pros at *Taste of Home* have gathered hundreds of super-quick but delicious dishes for you. They're all here in this sensational new edition of *Quick Cooking Annual Recipes*!

TODAY'S HOME COOKS KNOW

how to fit family-pleasing food into a hectic schedule. That's why they rely on *Quick Cooking Annual Recipes* time and again for fast mealtime solutions their families love.

Inside this exciting cookbook from *Taste of Home,* you'll discover a full year's worth of recipes featured in *Simple & Delicious* magazine. What's more, you get 100+ bonus recipes! Shared by cooks like you, each tasty dish uses basic ingredients, is simple to assemble and comes together in a snap. With these recipes, you're sure to have sweet success every time.

ICONS IN THIS BOOK

FAST FIX
Recipes that are table-ready in 30 minutes or less.

⑤INGREDIENTS
Recipes that use five or fewer ingredients (they may also call for water, salt, pepper, and canola or olive oil).

EAT SMART
Dietitian-approved recipes that are lower in calories, fat and sodium.

FREEZE IT
Freezer-friendly recipes that include directions for freezing and reheating.

SLOW COOKER 🍲
Recipes that use a slow cooker.

BANANA SUNDAE
DESSERT (p. 228)

ZUCCHINI & SAUSAGE
STOVETOP CASSEROLE (p. 92)

Serve up simply sensational food with
650+ RECIPES & TIPS!

FRESH IN THIS EDITION
Finished in 15
When your busy schedule leaves only 15 minutes to spend in the kitchen, these super-fast recipes will save the day.

Quick-Read Recipes
Check for colorful boxes that contain recipes summed up in just one short paragraph. How easy is that?

Effortless Entertaining
This sparkling chapter features speedy but special favorites that are ideal when you want to host family and friends.

30-Minute Menus
Choose any quick main course you prefer. Each one includes a complementary side, beverage or dessert to round out your menu perfectly.

Express Entrees
This extra-big chapter is full of hearty dishes that are ready to serve in half an hour—or less. Just take your pick and enjoy!

More Icons Than Ever
Love using your slow cooker? Be on the lookout for a new icon that identifies slow-simmered favorites families crave.

Festive Parties
Celebrate with a New Year's Eve brunch at midnight, a make-ahead Christmas dinner, sweet treats for a Halloween bash, a Thanksgiving feast and more.

Special Sections
These bonus sections give you dozens of extra recipes, from dinnertime solutions for last night's leftovers to bright desserts for birthdays.

PLUS...
Discover lightened-up comfort foods, fun dishes for kids, hearty casseroles, cookout favorites, breakfast delights and more!

Ashley Lecker's
Warm Feta Cheese Dip
PAGE 10

Appetizers & Beverages

After-school snacks, holiday beverages, tailgating munchies...the small bites and drinks in this chapter will suit any occasion. They're so easy to make, even the busiest cook can whip them up with time to spare.

Colleen Vrooman's
Brat & Bacon Appetizer
Pizza PAGE 8

Chris Runyan's
Warm & Cozy Spiced Cider
PAGE 15

Ariane McAlpine's
Jalapeno Popper Spread
PAGE 9

BEST-EVER STUFFED MUSHROOMS

FAST FIX

Brat & Bacon Appetizer Pizza

Chopped bratwurst and maple bacon are a great way to start a pizza. I jazz it up even more with apricot preserves and honey mustard. The snack-size slices win over even the toughest critics.

—**COLLEEN VROOMAN** WAUKESHA, WI

START TO FINISH: 25 MIN.
MAKES: 24 SERVINGS

- 1 tube (11 ounces) refrigerated thin pizza crust
- 4 maple-flavored bacon strips, chopped
- ¼ cup finely chopped onion
- 3 fully cooked beer bratwurst links, finely chopped
- ⅓ cup apricot preserves
- 2 teaspoons honey mustard
- 2 cups (8 ounces) shredded white or yellow cheddar cheese

1. Preheat oven to 400°. Unroll and press the pizza dough onto bottom and ½ in. up sides of a greased 15x10x1-in. baking pan. Bake 8-10 minutes or until edges are lightly browned.
2. Meanwhile, in a large skillet, cook the bacon and onion over medium heat until the bacon is crisp, stirring occasionally. Remove with a slotted spoon; drain on paper towels. Discard the drippings. Add the bratwurst to same pan; cook and stir 2-3 minutes or until browned.
3. In a small bowl, mix the preserves and honey mustard. Spread over crust; top with the bratwurst, bacon mixture and cheese. Bake 8-10 minutes or until the cheese is melted.

Best-Ever Stuffed Mushrooms

Every Christmas Eve, I bring out a platter of my fresh-from-the-oven mushrooms. When you want a change, consider fixing the sausage filling all by itself—it's good spread on baguette slices and crackers.

—**DEBBY BEARD** EAGLE, CO

PREP: 20 MIN. • **BAKE:** 15 MIN.
MAKES: 2½ DOZEN

- 1 pound bulk pork sausage
- ¼ cup finely chopped onion
- 1 garlic clove, minced
- 1 package (8 ounces) reduced-fat cream cheese
- ¼ cup shredded Parmesan cheese
- ⅓ cup seasoned bread crumbs
- 3 teaspoons dried basil
- 1½ teaspoons dried parsley flakes
- 30 large fresh mushrooms (about 1½ pounds), stems removed
- 3 tablespoons butter, melted

1. Preheat oven to 400°. In a large skillet, cook sausage, onion and garlic over medium heat 6-8 minutes or until sausage is no longer pink and onion is tender, breaking up sausage into crumbles; drain. Add cream cheese and Parmesan cheese; cook and stir until melted. Stir in bread crumbs, basil and parsley.
2. Meanwhile, place mushroom caps in a greased 15x10x1-in. baking pan, stem side up. Brush with butter. Spoon the sausage mixture into mushroom caps. Bake, uncovered, 12-15 minutes or until mushrooms are tender.

Ginger Pear Sipper

A refreshing treat for brunch or cocktail hour, this nonalcoholic drink will please just about any palate. In a tall glass, combine 3 ounces each chilled ginger ale and pear nectar; garnish with a fresh pear slice for an elegant accent. *Makes 1 serving.*

—**SUSAN WESTERFIELD** ALBUQUERQUE, NM

POMEGRANATE
PISTACHIO CROSTINI

> With honey-brightened cream cheese and shaved dark chocolate, Pomegranate Pistachio Crostini makes a delightfully sweet choice on an appetizer buffet.
> —ELISABETH LARSEN PLEASANT GROVE, UT

FAST FIX
Pomegranate Pistachio Crostini

START TO FINISH: 30 MIN.
MAKES: 3 DOZEN

- 36 slices French bread baguette (¼ inch thick)
- 1 tablespoon butter, melted
- 4 ounces cream cheese, softened
- 2 tablespoons orange juice
- 1 tablespoon honey
- 1 cup pomegranate seeds
- ½ cup finely chopped pistachios
- 2 ounces dark chocolate candy bar, finely shaved

1. Preheat oven to 400°. Place the French bread slices on an ungreased baking sheet; brush one side with the melted butter. Bake 5-7 minutes or until light brown. Remove from the pan to a wire rack to cool.
2. Meanwhile, in a small bowl, beat the cream cheese, orange juice and honey until blended; spread over the toasts. Top with the pomegranate seeds, chopped pistachios and shaved dark chocolate.

Jalapeno Popper Spread

Partygoers tell me that this tastes exactly like a jalapeno popper. I love the fact that the recipe requires only 10 minutes of prep work before baking.
—**ARIANE MCALPINE** PENTICTON, BC

PREP: 10 MIN. • **BAKE:** 25 MIN.
MAKES: 16 SERVINGS

- 2 packages (8 ounces each) cream cheese, softened
- 1 cup mayonnaise
- ½ cup shredded Monterey Jack cheese
- ¼ cup canned chopped green chilies
- ¼ cup canned diced jalapeno peppers
- 1 cup shredded Parmesan cheese
- ½ cup panko (Japanese) bread crumbs
  Sweet red and yellow pepper pieces and corn chips

In a large bowl, beat the first five ingredients until blended; spread into an ungreased 9-in. pie plate. Sprinkle with Parmesan; top with bread crumbs. Bake at 400° for 25-30 minutes or until lightly browned. Serve with peppers and corn chips.

EAT SMART
Homemade Ranch Dressing & Dip Mix

Keep a versatile mix on hand to use for stirring together either a dip or a salad dressing. They're both delicious!
—*TASTE OF HOME TEST KITCHEN*

START TO FINISH: 5 MIN.
MAKES: 16 SERVINGS PER BATCH

- ⅓ cup buttermilk blend powder
- ¼ cup dried parsley flakes
- 2 tablespoons dried minced onion
- 2 teaspoons salt
- 2 teaspoons garlic powder

ADDITIONAL INGREDIENTS FOR SALAD DRESSING
- 1 cup reduced-fat mayonnaise
- 1 cup plus 6 tablespoons buttermilk

ADDITIONAL INGREDIENTS FOR DIP
- 2 cups (16 ounces) reduced-fat sour cream

Combine the first five ingredients. Store the mix in an airtight container in a cool, dry place for up to 1 year. Yield: 4 batches (about ¾ cup).
FOR SALAD DRESSING In a small bowl, whisk mayonnaise, buttermilk and 3 tablespoons mix. Refrigerate for at least 1 hour. Yield: about 2 cups.
FOR DIP In a small bowl, combine the sour cream and 3 tablespoons mix. Refrigerate for at least 2 hours. Serve with crackers and fresh vegetables.
PER SERVING *Ranch Salad Dressing: 2 tablespoons equals 62 cal., 5 g fat (1 g sat. fat), 7 mg chol., 219 mg sodium, 3 g carb., trace fiber, 1 g pro. Ranch Dip: 2 tablespoons equals 42 cal., 3 g fat (2 g sat. fat), 10 mg chol., 73 mg sodium, 2 g carb., trace fiber, 2 g pro.*

HOMEMADE RANCH DRESSING & DIP MIX

Antipasto Cups

Experience Italian antipasto in a whole new way! Put it inside little cups of salami for deliciously different finger food.

—**MELISSA BEYER** UTICA, NY

PREP: 20 MIN. • **BAKE:** 10 MIN./BATCH
MAKES: 2 DOZEN

- 24 slices Genoa salami (3½ inches)
- 1 can (14 ounces) water-packed artichoke hearts
- 1 jar (8 ounces) marinated whole mushrooms
- 1 jar (8 ounces) roasted sweet red peppers
- ½ pound fresh mozzarella cheese, cut into ½-inch cubes
- 3 tablespoons olive oil
- 2 tablespoons red wine vinegar
- ½ teaspoon garlic salt
- ⅛ teaspoon pepper

1. Preheat oven to 400°. Press half of the salami into 12 muffin cups. Loosely crumple aluminum foil to form twelve 2-in. balls; place in the cups to keep salami from sliding. Bake 6-8 minutes or until the edges begin to brown. Using tongs, remove from pans and invert onto paper towels to drain. Wipe muffin cups clean. Repeat with remaining salami, reusing foil balls.
2. Meanwhile, drain and coarsely chop artichoke hearts, mushrooms and red peppers; transfer to a small bowl. Stir in cheese. In another bowl, whisk the oil, vinegar, garlic salt and pepper until blended. Drizzle over the vegetable mixture; toss to coat. Using a slotted spoon, fill salami cups with vegetable mixture.

MARINATED CHEESE WITH PEPPERS AND OLIVES

ANTIPASTO CUPS

(5) INGREDIENTS FAST FIX

Warm Feta Cheese Dip

We're huge fans of appetizers, and this super-easy baked dip is a mashup of some of our favorite ingredients. It goes so well with a basket of crunchy tortilla chips or slices of a French bread baguette.

—**ASHLEY LECKER** GREEN BAY, WI

START TO FINISH: 30 MIN.
MAKES: 2 CUPS

- 1 package (8 ounces) cream cheese, softened
- 1½ cups (6 ounces) crumbled feta cheese
- ½ cup chopped roasted sweet red peppers
- 3 tablespoons minced fresh basil or 2 teaspoons dried basil
  Sliced French bread baguette or tortilla chips

1. Preheat oven to 400°. In a small bowl, beat cream cheese, feta cheese, roasted sweet red peppers and basil until blended.
2. Transfer the dip to a greased 3-cup baking dish. Bake 25-30 minutes or until bubbly. Serve with French bread baguette slices or tortilla chips.

Marinated Cheese with Peppers and Olives

In only 10 minutes, I can have chunks of cheddar and veggies soaking in a tangy marinade full of garlic, oregano and basil. The next day, I just remove the bowl from the fridge and set out toothpicks.

—**POLLY BRUNNING** THAXTON, VA

PREP: 10 MIN. + CHILLING
MAKES: 15 SERVINGS

- 12 ounces cheddar cheese, cut into ¾-inch cubes
- 2 medium sweet red peppers, cut into ¾-inch pieces
- 2 cans (6 ounces each) pitted ripe olives, drained
- ¼ cup canola oil
- 1 tablespoon white vinegar
- 1 garlic clove, minced
- ½ teaspoon dried basil
- ½ teaspoon dried oregano

In a large bowl, combine all ingredients. Refrigerate, covered, at least 4 hours or overnight.

FREEZE IT
Mushroom Bundles

I love creating my own party starters. When I made these crispy bundles for New Year's Eve, they were gone in a flash.
—**TINA COOPMAN** TORONTO, ON

PREP: 30 MIN. • **BAKE:** 15 MIN.
MAKES: 1 DOZEN

- 1 tablespoon olive oil
- 1 cup chopped fresh mushrooms
- 1 cup chopped baby portobello mushrooms
- ¼ cup finely chopped red onion
- 2 garlic cloves, minced
- ¼ teaspoon dried rosemary, crushed
- ⅛ teaspoon pepper
- 4 sheets phyllo dough (14x9-inch size)
- 3 tablespoons butter, melted
- 2 tablespoons crumbled feta cheese

1. Preheat oven to 375°. In a large skillet, heat the oil over medium-high heat. Add mushrooms and onion, cook and stir 4-5 minutes or until tender. Add garlic, rosemary and pepper; cook 2 minutes longer. Remove from heat.
2. Place one sheet of phyllo dough on a work surface; brush with butter. (Keep the remaining phyllo covered with plastic wrap and a damp towel to prevent it from drying out.) Layer with three additional phyllo sheets, brushing each layer. Using a sharp knife, cut the layered phyllo sheets into twelve 3-in. squares. Carefully press each stack into an ungreased mini muffin cup.
3. Stir feta into mushroom mixture; spoon 1 tablespoon into each phyllo cup. Form into bundles by gathering edges of phyllo squares and twisting centers to close. Brush tops with the remaining butter. Bake 12-15 minutes or until golden brown. Serve warm.
FREEZE OPTION *Freeze the cooled pastries in resealable plastic freezer bags. To use, reheat pastries on a greased baking sheet in a preheated 375° oven until crisp and heated through.*

MUSHROOM BUNDLES

FESTIVE HOLIDAY SLIDERS

FAST FIX
Festive Holiday Sliders

My mini turkey sandwiches with cranberry sauce, horseradish and ginger keep well in the refrigerator. I like to have a batch on hand for Christmastime get-togethers, when we bake gifts and wrap presents.
—**PAMELA MILLER** BIG RAPIDS, MI

START TO FINISH: 30 MIN.
MAKES: 2 DOZEN

- 1 package (8 ounces) cream cheese, softened
- ½ cup mayonnaise
- ¼ cup Creole mustard
- 2 tablespoons minced fresh gingerroot
- 1 tablespoon grated orange peel
- 1½ teaspoons prepared horseradish
- 1 cup whole-berry cranberry sauce
- 4 green onions, sliced
- 2 packages (12 ounces each) Hawaiian sweet rolls or 24 dinner rolls
- 1½ pounds thinly sliced cooked turkey

1. In a small bowl, beat the cream cheese and mayonnaise until smooth. Beat in the Creole mustard, minced ginger, orange peel and horseradish. In another bowl, mix the cranberry sauce and green onions.
2. Spread the cream cheese mixture on the bottoms of rolls. Top with the cranberry mixture and sliced turkey; replace the tops of rolls.

Using crescent roll dough, Sriracha and chili sauce, I came up with Sweet & Spicy Asian Chicken Petites. Freeze a batch to reheat when you have drop-in guests.
—**JEANETTE NELSON** BRIDGEPORT, WV

SWEET & SPICY
ASIAN CHICKEN PETITES

We prefer
homemade
cocoa over
store mixes.
Kahlua Hot
...real treat.
...OLLYWOOD, CA

GINGER PORK
LETTUCE WRAPS

FREEZE IT | FAST FIX

Ginger Pork Lettuce Wraps

I prepare my Asian wraps as an appetizer. But with the way my family gobbles them up, I should serve them for supper!
—**MARY KISINGER** MEDICINE HAT, AB

START TO FINISH: 30 MIN.
MAKES: 2 DOZEN

- 1 **pound lean ground pork**
- 1 **medium onion, chopped**
- ¼ **cup hoisin sauce**
- 4 **garlic cloves, minced**
- 1 **tablespoon minced fresh gingerroot**
- 1 **tablespoon red wine vinegar**
- 1 **tablespoon reduced-sodium soy sauce**
- 2 **teaspoons Thai chili sauce**
- 1 **can (8 ounces) sliced water chestnuts, drained and finely chopped**
- 4 **green onions, chopped**
- 1 **tablespoon sesame oil**
- 24 **Bibb or Boston lettuce leaves**

1. In a large skillet, cook the pork and onion over medium heat 6-8 minutes or until the pork is no longer pink and the onion is tender, breaking up pork into crumbles.

2. Stir in hoisin sauce, garlic, ginger, red wine vinegar, soy sauce and chili sauce until blended. Add the water chestnuts, green onions and sesame oil; heat through.

3. To serve, place the pork mixture in lettuce leaves; fold the lettuce over the pork mixture.

FREEZE OPTION *Freeze the cooled meat mixture in freezer containers. To use, partially thaw in refrigerator overnight. Heat through in a saucepan, stirring occasionally and adding a little water if necessary.*

FREEZE IT

Sweet & Spicy Asian Chicken Petites

PREP: 25 MIN. • **BAKE:** 10 MIN.
MAKES: 16 APPETIZERS

- 4 **teaspoons olive oil, divided**
- ⅓ **cup finely chopped sweet red pepper**
- 3 **green onions, finely chopped**
- 2 **garlic cloves, minced**
- 1 **cup finely chopped cooked chicken breast**
- 2 **tablespoons island teriyaki sauce**
- 1 **tablespoon white grapefruit juice or water**
- 1 **tablespoon sesame oil**
- 1 **teaspoon Sriracha Asian hot chili sauce**
- 1 **tube (8 ounces) refrigerated crescent rolls**
- 2 **teaspoons sesame seeds**
  Sweet chili sauce

1. Preheat oven to 375°. In a large skillet, heat 2 teaspoons olive oil over medium-high heat. Add the sweet red pepper, onions and garlic; cook and stir 3-5 minutes or until the vegetables are tender. Stir in the chicken, teriyaki sauce, grapefruit juice, sesame oil and hot chili sauce. Remove from the heat; cool slightly.

2. Unroll the crescent roll dough into one long rectangle; press perforations to seal. Roll dough into a 12-in. square; cut into sixteen 3-in. squares. Place 1 tablespoon chicken mixture in the center of each square of dough. Bring the edges of the dough over the chicken mixture, pinching the seams to seal; shape into a ball.

3. Place balls on ungreased baking sheets, seam side down. Brush the tops with the remaining olive oil; sprinkle with the sesame seeds. Bake 10-12 minutes or until golden brown. Serve warm with sweet chili sauce for dipping.

FREEZE OPTION *Freeze the cooled appetizers in resealable plastic freezer bags. To use, reheat the appetizers on a baking sheet in a preheated 375° oven until heated through.*

⑤ INGREDIENTS FAST FIX

Raspberry-Lemon Spritzer

For your next summertime get-together, go beyond the usual lemonade. This tangy thirst-quencher is so refreshing on warm days. It's not too sweet, and the beautiful pink color makes it even more appealing. Garnish each glass with a lemon slice.
—**MARGIE WILLIAMS** MOUNT JULIET, TN

START TO FINISH: 15 MIN.
MAKES: 2 SERVINGS

- ½ **cup fresh or frozen raspberries, thawed**
- ⅓ **cup sugar**
- 2½ **cups club soda, chilled**
- ¼ **cup lemon juice**
  Ice cubes
- 2 **lemon slices**

1. Place the raspberries and sugar in a food processor; cover and process until pureed. Strain, reserving juice and discarding seeds.

2. In a small pitcher, combine the club soda, lemon juice and raspberry juice. Serve in tall glasses over ice. Garnish with lemon slices.

draine
1 tables
½ cup p
crumb
¾ cup r
1 table
or cl
Ass

1. In a s
lemon p
desired
Shape i
Refrige
2. Mea
oil ove
crumb
until g
crum
3. Ur
bread
Spoo
cilan

Slim Deviled Eggs

Want a lighter option? Cut 6 hard-cooked eggs in half lengthwise. Remove the yolks; set aside the whites. Mash 4 yolks (save the remaining yolks for another use). Stir in 3 tablespoons reduced-fat mayonnaise, ½ teaspoon each garlic powder and ground mustard and ⅛ teaspoon each salt and pepper. Stuff the mixture into egg whites; sprinkle with paprika. *Makes 1 dozen.*
—*TASTE OF HOME* TEST KITCHEN

Mini Mac & Cheese Bites

When young relatives were coming for a party, I wanted to make something fun. I'm not sure who liked these cheesy bites more—the kids or the adults!
—**KATHERINE MAINIERO** POUGHKEEPSIE, NY

PREP: 35 MIN. • **BAKE:** 10 MIN.
MAKES: 3 DOZEN

- 2 cups uncooked elbow macaroni
- 1 cup seasoned bread crumbs, divided
- 2 tablespoons butter
- 2 tablespoons all-purpose flour
- ½ teaspoon onion powder
- ½ teaspoon garlic powder
- ½ teaspoon seasoned salt
- 1¾ cups 2% milk
- 2 cups (8 ounces) shredded sharp cheddar cheese, divided
- 1 cup (4 ounces) shredded Swiss cheese
- ¾ cup biscuit/baking mix
- 2 large eggs, lightly beaten

1. Preheat oven to 425°. Cook the macaroni according to the package directions; drain.
2. Meanwhile, sprinkle ¼ cup bread crumbs into 36 greased mini muffin cups. In a large saucepan, melt the butter over medium heat. Stir in the flour and seasonings until smooth; gradually whisk in the milk. Bring to a boil, stirring constantly; cook and stir 1-2 minutes or until thickened. Stir in 1 cup cheddar cheese and Swiss cheese until melted.
3. Remove the cheese sauce from the heat; stir in the biscuit mix, eggs and ½ cup bread crumbs. Add the cooked macaroni; toss to coat. Spoon about 2 tablespoons macaroni mixture into prepared mini muffin cups; sprinkle with the remaining cheddar cheese and bread crumbs.
4. Bake 8-10 minutes or until golden brown. Cool appetizers in pans for 5 minutes before serving.

⑤ INGREDIENTS FAST FIX

Warm & Cozy Spiced Cider

During our freezing Minnesota winters, we take comfort food seriously. This nicely spiced cider warms us up body and soul.
—**CHRIS RUNYAN** MONTEVIDEO, MN

START TO FINISH: 30 MIN.
MAKES: 10 SERVINGS (¾ CUP EACH)

- 2 quarts unsweetened apple cider
- 1 cup orange juice
- 1 can (5½ ounces) apricot nectar
- 1 teaspoon ground cinnamon
- ⅛ teaspoon ground cloves

In a 6-qt. stockpot, combine all ingredients. Bring to a boil. Reduce heat; simmer, uncovered, 15 minutes to allow flavors to blend. Serve warm.

MINI MAC & CHEESE BITES

LOADED BAKED
POTATO DIP

Sparkling Cranberry Kiss

Pour ginger ale into a pitcher of orange and cranberry juices, and you'll have a sparkling nonalcoholic punch that's perfect for holidays. We use cranberry juice cocktail, but feel free to stir in cran-apple or another blend instead.

—SHANNON ARTHUR
CANAL WINCHESTER, OH

START TO FINISH: 5 MIN.
MAKES: 14 SERVINGS (¾ CUP EACH)

- 6 cups cranberry juice
- 1½ cups orange juice
- 3 cups ginger ale
  Ice cubes
  Orange slices, optional

In a pitcher, combine the cranberry juice and orange juice. Just before serving, stir in the ginger ale; serve punch over ice. If desired, serve with orange slices.

TOP TIP

Have leftover tortilla chips from a party or other get-together? Here are simple ways to give those extra munchies a second life. Sprinkle coarsely crushed chips on a bowl of Mexican-style soup, on a casserole as a topping or on a salad in place of croutons. Use finely crushed chips instead of dry bread crumbs as a coating for chicken or fish.

Loaded Baked Potato Dip

I never thought of using waffle-cut fries as scoops for dip until one of my friends presented it that way at a baby shower. What a great idea! Try this lightened-up but irresistible recipe—the combination tastes just like a loaded baked potato, but reduced-fat ingredients make it guilt-free.

—BETSY KING DULUTH, MN

START TO FINISH: 10 MIN.
MAKES: 2½ CUPS

- 2 cups (16 ounces) reduced-fat sour cream
- 2 cups (8 ounces) shredded reduced-fat cheddar cheese
- 8 center-cut bacon or turkey bacon strips, chopped and cooked
- ⅓ cup minced fresh chives
- 2 teaspoons Louisiana-style hot sauce
  Hot cooked waffle-cut fries

In a small bowl, mix the first five ingredients until blended; refrigerate until serving. Serve with waffle fries.
PER SERVING ¼ cup (calculated without fries) equals 149 cal., 10 g fat (6 g sat. fat), 38 mg chol., 260 mg sodium, 4 g carb., trace fiber, 11 g pro.

Zippy Tortilla Chips

For homemade chips, combine ½ teaspoon brown sugar with ¼ teaspoon each garlic powder, onion powder, ground cumin and paprika. Season with cayenne pepper. Cut a stack of 4 corn tortillas into 6 wedges; arrange them in a single layer on a baking sheet coated with cooking spray. Spritz them with cooking spray; sprinkle with the seasoning mixture. Bake at 375° for 9-10 minutes or until lightly browned. Cool for 5 minutes. *Makes 2 dozen.*

—KIM SUMRALL APTOS, CA

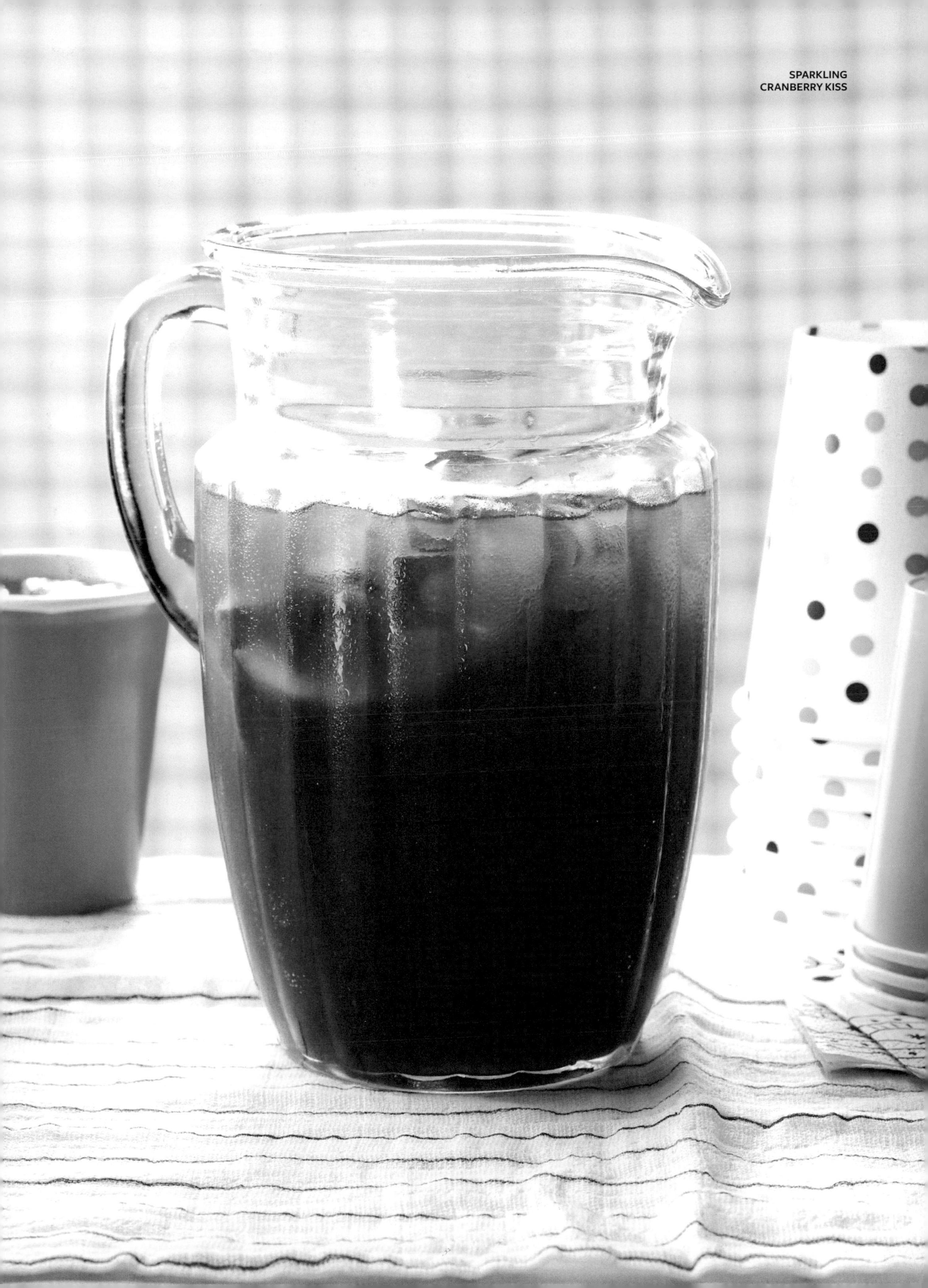

SPARKLING
CRANBERRY KISS

**Julie Kirkpatrick's
Bow Tie & Spinach Salad**
PAGE 21

Side Dishes & Salads

From refreshing pasta medleys to roasted veggies and salad entrees, the special selections in this chapter will take your menu to a whole new level. Just choose your favorites and enjoy!

**Melissa Jelinek's
Chicken and Asian Slaw**
PAGE 22

**Joan Hallford's
Patio Pintos**
PAGE 23

**Elisabeth Larsen's
Thai-Style Cobb Salad**
PAGE 25

LAYERED CORN
BREAD SALAD

⑤ INGREDIENTS

Marinated Asparagus with Blue Cheese

Asparagus marinated in a tangy vinaigrette and sprinkled with blue cheese makes an exceptional side. Feel free to substitute Parmesan or feta if you prefer.

—**SUSAN VAITH** JACKSONVILLE, FL

PREP: 20 MIN. + MARINATING
MAKES: 4 SERVINGS

- 1 **pound fresh asparagus, trimmed**
- 4 **green onions, thinly sliced**
- ¼ **cup olive oil**
- 2 **tablespoons white wine vinegar**
- 1 **garlic clove, minced**
- ½ **teaspoon salt**
- ¼ **teaspoon pepper**
- ½ **cup crumbled blue cheese**

1. In a large saucepan, bring 6 cups water to a boil. Add asparagus; cook, uncovered, 2-3 minutes or just until crisp-tender. Remove asparagus and immediately drop into ice water. Drain and pat dry.

2. In a large resealable plastic bag, combine green onions, olive oil, white wine vinegar, garlic, salt and pepper. Add the asparagus; seal bag and turn to coat. Refrigerate at least 1 hour.

3. Drain the asparagus, discarding the marinade. Place the asparagus on a serving plate; sprinkle with crumbled blue cheese.

MARINATED ASPARAGUS
WITH BLUE CHEESE

Layered Corn Bread Salad

When our vegetable garden is bursting with fresh delights, we layer them with corn bread and relish for this snappy dish. Everyone wants a second scoop.

—**REBECCA CLARK** WARRIOR, AL

PREP: 45 MIN. + CHILLING
MAKES: 14 SERVINGS (¾ CUP EACH)

- 1 **package (8½ ounces) corn bread/ muffin mix**
- 1 **cup mayonnaise**
- ½ **cup sweet pickle relish**
- 2 **cans (15 ounces each) pinto beans, rinsed and drained**
- 4 **medium tomatoes, chopped**
- 1 **medium green pepper, chopped**
- 1 **medium onion, chopped**
- 10 **bacon strips, cooked and crumbled**

1. Preheat oven to 400°. Prepare the corn bread batter according to the package directions. Pour the corn bread batter into a greased 8-in. square baking pan. Bake 15-20 minutes or until a toothpick inserted in the center comes out clean. Cool completely in the pan on a wire rack.

2. Coarsely crumble the cooled corn bread into a large bowl. In a small bowl, mix the mayonnaise and sweet pickle relish.

3. In a 3-qt. trifle bowl or glass bowl, layer a third of the corn bread and half of each of the following: pinto beans, tomatoes, green pepper, onion, bacon and mayonnaise mixture. Repeat the layers. Top with the remaining corn bread. Refrigerate, covered, 2-4 hours before serving.

My green-thumb neighbors frequently share their homegrown produce with me. I return the favor by baking them an **Heirloom Tomato Pie.**
—**ANGELA BENEDICT** DUNBAR, WV

HEIRLOOM TOMATO PIE

Heirloom Tomato Pie

PREP: 45 MIN. • **BAKE:** 35 MIN. + COOLING
MAKES: 8 SERVINGS

- 1¼ **pounds heirloom tomatoes (about 4 medium), cut into ¼-inch slices**
- ¾ **teaspoon salt, divided**
- 1½ **cups (6 ounces) shredded extra-sharp cheddar cheese**
- ¾ **cup all-purpose flour**
- ¼ **cup cold butter, cubed**
- 1 **to 2 tablespoons half-and-half cream**
- 5 **bacon strips, cooked and crumbled**

FILLING
- 1 **package (8 ounces) cream cheese, softened**
- ½ **cup loosely packed basil leaves, thinly sliced**
- 2 **tablespoons minced fresh marjoram**
- 1½ **teaspoons minced fresh thyme**
- ½ **teaspoon garlic powder**
- ⅛ **teaspoon coarsely ground pepper**

1. Preheat oven to 350°. Place the tomato slices in a single layer on paper towels; sprinkle with ½ teaspoon salt. Let stand 45 minutes. Pat dry.
2. Meanwhile, place the cheddar cheese, flour and remaining salt in a food processor; pulse until blended. Add butter; pulse until butter is the size of peas. While pulsing, add just enough cream to form moist crumbs.
3. Press the dough onto bottom and up sides of an ungreased 9-in. fluted tart pan with a removable bottom. Gently press the bacon into dough. Bake 20-22 minutes or until light brown. Cool on a wire rack.
4. In a large bowl, beat cream cheese, herbs and garlic powder until blended. Spread over the crust. Top with the tomato slices; sprinkle with pepper. Bake 35-40 minutes longer or until edges are golden brown and tomatoes are softened. Cool on a wire rack. Refrigerate leftovers.

Bow Tie & Spinach Salad

It's often easy to vary the ingredients in pasta salad recipes. When the mood strikes, we alter this one by using black beans instead of chickpeas or by tossing in grilled chicken and pine nuts.
—**JULIE KIRKPATRICK** BILLINGS, MT

START TO FINISH: 30 MIN.
MAKES: 6 SERVINGS

- 2 **cups uncooked multigrain bow tie pasta**
- 1 **can (15 ounces) garbanzo beans or chickpeas, rinsed and drained**
- 6 **cups fresh baby spinach (about 6 ounces)**
- 2 **cups fresh broccoli florets**
- 2 **plum tomatoes, chopped**
- 1 **medium sweet red pepper, chopped**
- ½ **cup cubed part-skim mozzarella cheese**
- ½ **cup pitted Greek olives, halved**
- ¼ **cup minced fresh basil**
- ⅓ **cup reduced-fat sun-dried tomato salad dressing**
- ¼ **teaspoon salt**
- ¼ **cup chopped walnuts, toasted**

1. Cook the bow tie pasta according to package directions. Drain; transfer to a large bowl.
2. Add beans, vegetables, cheese, olives and basil to pasta. Drizzle with the dressing and sprinkle with salt; toss to coat. Sprinkle with walnuts.
NOTE *To toast nuts, bake in a shallow pan in a 350° oven for 5-10 minutes or cook in a skillet over low heat until lightly browned, stirring occasionally.*
PER SERVING 2 cups equals 319 cal., 13 g fat (2 g sat. fat), 6 mg chol., 660 mg sodium, 39 g carb., 7 g fiber, 14 g pro. *Diabetic Exchanges: 2 starch, 2 fat, 1 lean meat, 1 vegetable.*

TOP TIP

To quickly cut fresh basil, stack several leaves and roll them into a tight tube. Slice the leaves widthwise into narrow pieces to create long thin strips. If you need smaller pieces, chop the strips again.

EAT SMART FAST FIX
Avocado Fruit Salad with Tangerine Vinaigrette

On long summer days when we just want to relax, I make a fruit salad with avocado and drizzle on a tangerine vinaigrette.
—**CAROLE RESNICK** CLEVELAND, OH

START TO FINISH: 25 MIN.
MAKES: 8 SERVINGS

- 3 **medium ripe avocados, peeled and thinly sliced**
- 3 **medium mangoes, peeled and thinly sliced**
- 1 **cup fresh raspberries**
- 1 **cup fresh blackberries**
- ¼ **cup minced fresh mint**
- ¼ **cup sliced almonds, toasted**

DRESSING

- ½ **cup olive oil**
- 1 **teaspoon grated tangerine or orange peel**
- ¼ **cup tangerine or orange juice**
- 2 **tablespoons balsamic vinegar**
- ½ **teaspoon salt**
- ¼ **teaspoon freshly ground pepper**

Arrange the avocados and fruit on a serving plate; sprinkle with the mint and almonds. In a small bowl, whisk dressing ingredients until blended; drizzle over salad.

NOTE *To toast nuts, bake in a shallow pan in a 350° oven for 5-10 minutes or cook in a skillet over low heat until lightly browned, stirring occasionally.*

PER SERVING *1 cup with about 1 tablespoon dressing equals 321 cal., 23 g fat (3 g sat. fat), 0 chol., 154 mg sodium, 29 g carb., 8 g fiber, 3 g pro.*

AVOCADO FRUIT SALAD WITH TANGERINE VINAIGRETTE

PARMESAN-ROMANO POTATO WEDGES

Parmesan-Romano Potato Wedges

I taught my nieces to prepare these easy, cheesy oven-baked potatoes. When the whole family comes over, we triple the recipe—and never have leftovers!
—**ANN BROWN** NILES, MI

PREP: 15 MIN. • **BAKE:** 40 MIN.
MAKES: 6 SERVINGS

- 3 **large potatoes (about 2½ pounds)**
- ¼ **cup olive oil**
- 3 **garlic cloves, minced**
- ½ **teaspoon dried thyme**
- ½ **teaspoon seasoned salt, divided**
- ¾ **cup grated Parmesan and Romano cheese blend, divided**
- ¼ **cup minced fresh parsley**

1. Preheat oven to 425°. Cut each potato lengthwise into eight wedges; place in a large bowl. Add oil, garlic, thyme and ¼ teaspoon seasoned salt; toss to coat.
2. With a slotted spoon, transfer the potatoes to two greased baking sheets. Set oil mixture aside.
3. Roast 30 minutes, turning once. Return the potatoes to oil mixture. Sprinkle with ½ cup cheese and parsley; toss to coat. Return potatoes to baking sheets. Roast 10-15 minutes longer or until golden brown and tender. Sprinkle with remaining cheese and seasoned salt.

EAT SMART ⑤INGREDIENTS
Chicken and Asian Slaw

We enjoy sampling new foods but keep going back to this one-bowl meal again and again. The zing comes from our favorite sesame ginger dressing.
—**MELISSA JELINEK** APPLE VALLEY, MN

START TO FINISH: 20 MIN.
MAKES: 4 SERVINGS

- 2 **cups cubed fresh pineapple**
- 2 **cups sliced bok choy**
- 2 **cups shredded red cabbage**
- ⅓ **cup plus ¼ cup sesame ginger salad dressing, divided**
- 4 **boneless skinless chicken breast halves (4 ounces each)**

1. Preheat broiler. In a large bowl, combine the pineapple, bok choy, red cabbage and ⅓ cup sesame ginger salad dressing; toss to coat.
2. Place the chicken in a 15x10x1-in. baking pan. Brush both sides of the chicken with remaining dressing. Broil 3-4 in. from heat 4-5 minutes on each side or until a thermometer reads 165°.
3. Divide the slaw among four bowls. Slice the chicken; arrange over slaw. Serve immediately.

PER SERVING *1 serving equals 302 cal., 13 g fat (3 g sat. fat), 63 mg chol., 433 mg sodium, 21 g carb., 2 g fiber, 24 g pro.* ***Diabetic Exchanges:*** *3 lean meat, 1½ fat, 1 starch, 1 vegetable, ½ fruit.*

FAST FIX ▶
Strawberry Mandarin Chicken Salad

This refreshing dish was a tasty success when I fixed it for a food class. Round out your menu with garlic bread and iced tea for a delicious lunch or dinner.

—**BETTY HENAGIN** MEDFORD, OR

START TO FINISH: 30 MIN.
MAKES: 6 SERVINGS

- 8 **bacon strips, chopped**
- 4 **boneless skinless chicken thighs (about 1 pound)**
- 4 **cups torn iceberg lettuce**
- 4 **cups torn red leaf lettuce**
- 2 **cans (11 ounces each) mandarin oranges, drained**
- 2 **medium tomatoes, chopped**
- 2 **cups quartered fresh strawberries**
- 2 **medium ripe avocados, peeled and sliced**
- 1 **cup salad croutons**
- 4 **green onions, chopped**
- ½ **cup shredded Colby-Monterey Jack cheese**
  Poppy seed salad dressing

1. In a large skillet, cook bacon over medium heat until crisp. Remove to paper towels to drain. Cook chicken in drippings 6-8 minutes on each side or until a thermometer reads 170°; cut into bite-size pieces.

2. Place lettuces on a large serving platter. Arrange chicken, oranges, tomatoes, berries, avocados, croutons, green onions, cheese and bacon over lettuce. Serve with salad dressing.

FREEZE IT
Patio Pintos

My mom often made her popular beans when she had a big group over for supper.

—**JOAN HALLFORD**

NORTH RICHLAND HILLS, TX

PREP: 25 MIN. • **BAKE:** 1 HOUR
MAKES: 10 SERVINGS

- ½ **pound bacon strips, chopped**
- 1 **large onion, chopped**
- 2 **garlic cloves, minced**
- 6 **cans (15 ounces each) pinto beans, rinsed and drained**
- 4 **cans (8 ounces each) tomato sauce**
- 2 **cans (4 ounces each) chopped green chilies**
- ⅓ **cup packed brown sugar**
- 1 **teaspoon chili powder**
- ¾ **teaspoon salt**
- ½ **teaspoon dried oregano**
- ¼ **teaspoon pepper**

1. Preheat oven to 350°. In a Dutch oven, cook the bacon over medium heat until crisp, stirring occasionally. Remove with a slotted spoon; drain on paper towels. Discard drippings, reserving 2 tablespoons in pan.

2. Add onion to drippings; cook and stir over medium heat 6-8 minutes or until tender. Add garlic; cook 1 minute longer. Stir in the beans, tomato sauce, chilies, brown sugar and seasonings. Sprinkle top with bacon. Bake, covered, 60-70 minutes or until heated through.

FREEZE OPTION *Freeze the cooled bean mixture in freezer containers. To use, partially thaw in refrigerator overnight. Heat through in a saucepan, stirring occasionally and adding a little water if necessary.*

STRAWBERRY MANDARIN
CHICKEN SALAD

TURKEY RAMEN
NOODLE SALAD

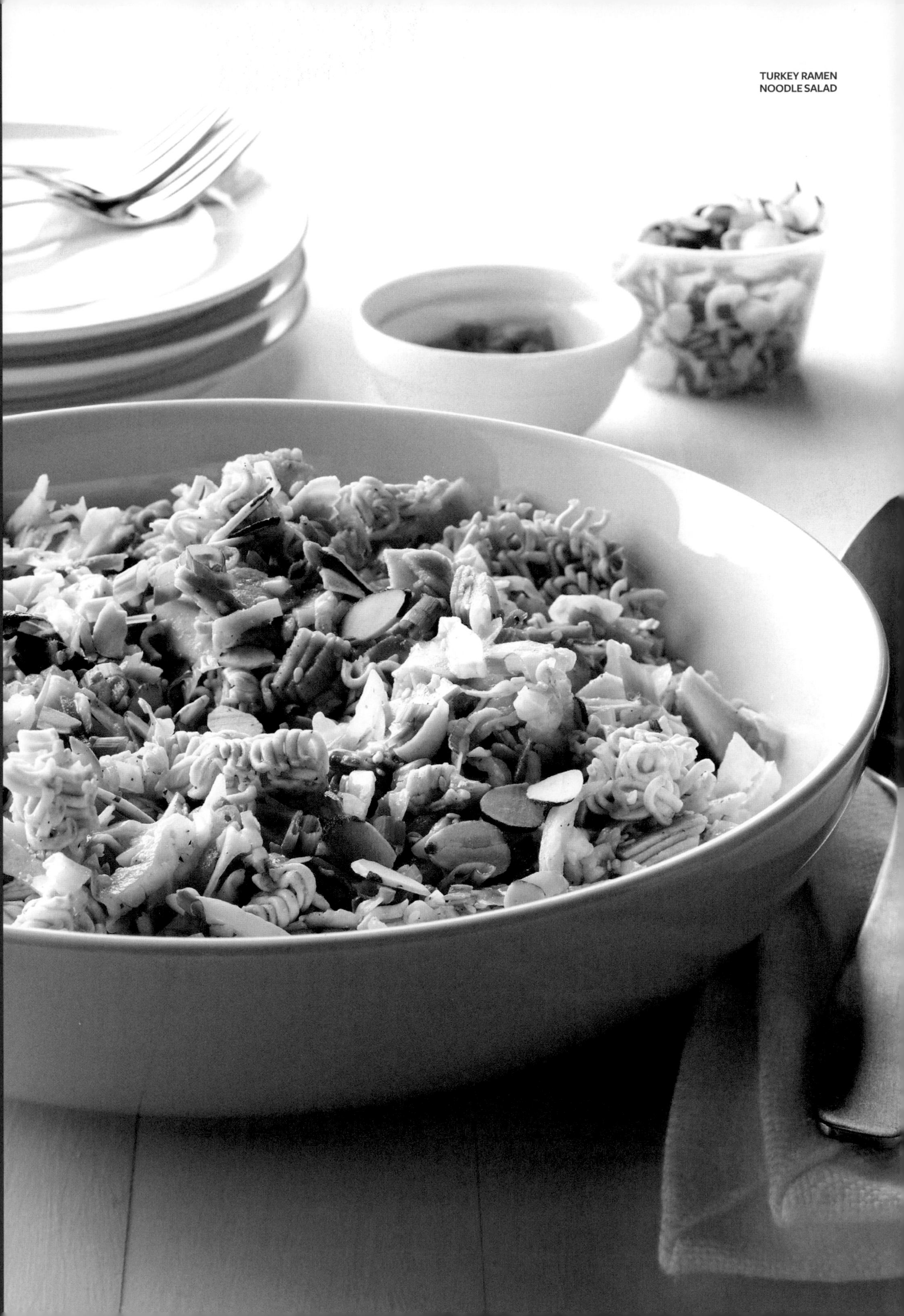

FAST FIX
Turkey Ramen Noodle Salad

My husband and I team up to fix a tasty turkey dish—he does the chopping. When we bring it to potlucks, we pack the ramen and nuts separately and toss them in at the last minute so they stay crunchy.

—**KRISTEN PALLANT** BIG ARM, MT

START TO FINISH: 20 MIN.
MAKES: 6 SERVINGS

- ⅓ cup white wine vinegar
- ¼ cup canola oil
- 3 tablespoons sugar
- ½ teaspoon pepper
- 2 packages (3 ounces each) Oriental ramen noodles
- 1 package (14 ounces) coleslaw mix
- 1 pound sliced deli turkey, chopped
- ½ cup sliced almonds, toasted
- ¼ cup sesame seeds
- Thinly sliced green onions, optional

1. In a small bowl, whisk the white wine vinegar, oil, sugar, pepper and contents of ramen noodle seasoning packets until blended.
2. Break the ramen noodles into small pieces; transfer to a large bowl. Add coleslaw mix and deli turkey. Drizzle with the salad dressing; toss to coat. Sprinkle with the almonds and sesame seeds. If desired, top with green onions. Serve immediately.
NOTE *To toast nuts, bake in a shallow pan in a 350° oven for 5-10 minutes or cook in a skillet over low heat until lightly browned, stirring occasionally.*

EAT SMART FAST FIX
Thai-Style Cobb Salad

This Asian veggie medley is like a mix of a Cobb salad and my favorite summer rolls. You can also substitute leftover cooked chicken for the rotisserie bird.

—**ELISABETH LARSEN** PLEASANT GROVE, UT

START TO FINISH: 15 MIN.
MAKES: 6 SERVINGS (¾ CUP DRESSING)

- 1 bunch romaine, torn
- 2 cups shredded rotisserie chicken
- 3 large hard-cooked eggs, finely chopped
- 1 medium ripe avocado, peeled and thinly sliced
- 1 medium carrot, shredded
- 1 medium sweet red pepper, julienned
- 1 cup fresh snow peas, halved
- ½ cup unsalted peanuts
- ¼ cup fresh cilantro leaves
- ¾ cup Asian toasted sesame salad dressing
- 2 tablespoons creamy peanut butter

1. Place the romaine on a large serving platter. Arrange shredded rotisserie chicken, hard-cooked eggs, avocado, vegetables and peanuts over romaine; sprinkle with cilantro.
2. In a small bowl, whisk the Asian toasted sesame salad dressing and creamy peanut butter until smooth. Serve with salad.
PER SERVING *1 serving equals 382 cal., 25 g fat (5 g sat. fat), 135 mg chol., 472 mg sodium, 18 g carb., 5 g fiber, 23 g pro.*

SPRING CHICKEN AND PEA SALAD

EAT SMART FAST FIX
Spring Chicken and Pea Salad

Here's a refreshing, satisfying choice for a springtime luncheon or light dinner.

—**ROXANNE CHAN** ALBANY, CA

START TO FINISH: 20 MIN.
MAKES: 4 SERVINGS

- 1 cup fresh peas
- 2 cups torn curly or Belgian endive
- 2 cups torn radicchio
- 2 cups chopped rotisserie chicken
- ½ cup sliced radishes
- 2 tablespoons chopped red onion
- 2 tablespoons fresh mint leaves, torn

DRESSING
- 2 tablespoons olive oil
- ¼ teaspoon grated lemon peel
- 1 tablespoon lemon juice
- 1 tablespoon mint jelly
- 1 garlic clove, minced
- ¼ teaspoon salt
- ¼ teaspoon pepper
- Toasted pine nuts, optional

1. In a large saucepan, bring ½ in. of water to a boil. Add the peas; cover and cook 5-8 minutes or until tender.
2. Drain peas; place in a large bowl. Add the endive, radicchio, chicken, radishes, onion and mint. In a small saucepan, combine oil, lemon peel, juice, mint jelly, garlic, salt and pepper; cook and stir over medium-low heat 4-6 minutes or until jelly is melted. Drizzle over the salad; toss to coat. If desired, sprinkle with pine nuts.
NOTE *Frozen peas may be substituted for fresh peas; thaw before using.*
PER SERVING *1½ cups equals 250 cal., 12 g fat (2 g sat. fat), 62 mg chol., 225 mg sodium, 12 g carb., 3 g fiber, 23 g pro. Diabetic Exchanges: 3 lean meat, 1½ fat, 1 vegetable, ½ starch.*

Vegetable Ribbons

Have garden veggies? Using a vegetable peeler, cut 3 medium carrots and 2 medium zucchini lengthwise into very thin strips. Melt 2 tablespoons butter in a large skillet over medium heat and add ¾ cup chicken broth. Bring it to a boil; cook until the liquid is reduced to ⅓ cup. Add the vegetable strips and 1 tablespoon parsley; cook and stir for 2 minutes or just until crisp-tender. Sprinkle with the remaining parsley. Serve with a slotted spoon. *Makes 4 servings.*

—**PATTY SINGSTOCK** RACINE, WI

VIBRANT BLACK-EYED
PEA SALAD

Summer Splash Chicken Salad

When the weather's perfect for eating on the patio, I frequently pull out this recipe. The juicy watermelon and mango give it that "splash" of summer.

—**BARBARA SPITZER** LODI, CA

START TO FINISH: 20 MIN.
MAKES: 4 SERVINGS

- ½ cup plain yogurt
- 4½ teaspoons brown sugar
- ½ teaspoon grated lime peel
- 1 tablespoon lime juice
- ¼ teaspoon salt
- 2 cups cubed cooked chicken breast
- 1 cup green grapes, halved
- 1 cup chopped peeled mango
- 1 cup chopped seedless watermelon
- 4 cups torn Bibb or Boston lettuce
- ¼ cup chopped pistachios, toasted

1. In a bowl, mix the first five ingredients until blended. Add the chicken, green grapes, mango and watermelon; toss gently to combine.
2. Divide lettuce among four plates; top with chicken mixture. Sprinkle with pistachios.
NOTE *To toast nuts, bake in a shallow pan in a 350° oven for 5-10 minutes or cook in a skillet over low heat until lightly browned, stirring occasionally.*
PER SERVING *1 cup chicken mixture with 1 cup lettuce and 1 tablespoon pistachios equals 262 cal., 7 g fat (2 g sat. fat), 58 mg chol., 249 mg sodium, 27 g carb., 3 g fiber, 24 g pro.* **Diabetic Exchanges:** *3 lean meat, 1 vegetable, 1 fruit, 1 fat, ½ starch.*

Vibrant Black-Eyed Pea Salad

My black-eyed pea salad always reminds me of a Southern cooking class I took with my husband while visiting Georgia.

—**DANIELLE ULAM** HOOKSTOWN, PA

PREP: 25 MIN. + CHILLING
MAKES: 10 SERVINGS

- 2 cans (15½ ounces each) black-eyed peas, rinsed and drained
- 2 cups grape tomatoes, halved
- 1 each small green, yellow and red pepper, finely chopped
- 1 small red onion, chopped
- 1 celery rib, chopped
- 2 tablespoons minced fresh basil

DRESSING
- ¼ cup red wine vinegar or balsamic vinegar
- 1 tablespoon stone-ground mustard
- 1 teaspoon minced fresh oregano or ¼ teaspoon dried oregano
- ¾ teaspoon salt
- ½ teaspoon freshly ground pepper
- ¼ cup olive oil

1. In a large bowl, combine peas, grape tomatoes, peppers, onion, celery and basil. In a small bowl, whisk vinegar, mustard, oregano, salt and pepper. Gradually whisk in oil until blended.
2. Drizzle dressing over salad; toss to coat. Refrigerate, covered, at least 3 hours before serving.
PER SERVING *¾ cup equals 130 cal., 6 g fat (1 g sat. fat), 0 chol., 319 mg sodium, 15 g carb., 3 g fiber, 5 g pro.* *Diabetic Exchanges: 1 starch, 1 fat.*

Gourmet Garden Tomato Salad

Who knew gourmet could be so easy? Cut 1½ pounds red, yellow and orange tomatoes into ¼-in. slices; arrange them on a serving platter. In a small bowl, whisk ⅓ cup olive oil, ⅓ cup balsamic vinegar, 1 tablespoon sugar, ¼ teaspoon salt and ¼ teaspoon pepper. Drizzle over the tomatoes. Sprinkle with ½ cup crumbled feta cheese and ⅓ cup thinly sliced fresh basil leaves. *Makes 6 servings.*

—**STACY KIBLER** CENTERVILLE, OH

SALMON AND SPUD SALAD

Potato-Bean Salad with Herb Dressing

The veggies in my garden inspired me to fix a creamy combo of beans, spuds and fresh herbs. The ranch-style dressing gets its zip from Creole mustard.

—**CHRIS CUMMER** BAYONNE, NJ

PREP: 15 MIN. • **COOK:** 20 MIN. + CHILLING
MAKES: 6 SERVINGS

- 1 pound potatoes (about 2 medium), peeled and cubed
- ½ pound fresh green beans, trimmed and cut into 2-inch pieces

DRESSING
- ⅓ cup buttermilk
- 2 tablespoons mayonnaise
- 2 tablespoons sour cream
- 1 tablespoon Creole mustard
- 1 tablespoon minced chives
- 1 tablespoon minced fresh parsley or 1 teaspoon dried parsley flakes
- 1½ teaspoons snipped fresh dill or ½ teaspoon dill weed
- 1½ teaspoons cider vinegar
- 1 garlic clove, minced
- ½ teaspoon salt
- ⅛ teaspoon celery seed
- ⅛ teaspoon pepper

1. Place potatoes in a large saucepan; add water to cover. Bring to a boil. Reduce the heat; cook, uncovered, 10-15 minutes or until tender, adding green beans during the last 4 minutes of cooking. Drain; cool completely.
2. In a small bowl, mix the dressing ingredients. Pour dressing over potato mixture; toss to coat. Refrigerate, covered, until cold.
PER SERVING ⅔ *cup equals 109 cal., 5 g fat (1 g sat. fat), 6 mg chol., 305 mg sodium, 14 g carb., 2 g fiber, 2 g pro.* **Diabetic Exchanges:** *1 starch, 1 fat.*

TOP TIP

When my husband and I want to use up extra ingredients or leftovers, we toss them into a salad for a quick, satisfying meal. Keeping lettuce in the fridge ensures we can make a salad any time we have leftovers!

—**KIM LUCAS** GOSHEN, IN

Salmon and Spud Salad

I decided to move toward a healthier lifestyle—and started in the kitchen. My grilled salmon and potato dinner has everything I need to feel satisfied.

—**MATTHEW TEIXEIRA** MILTON, ON

START TO FINISH: 30 MIN.
MAKES: 4 SERVINGS

- 1 pound fingerling potatoes
- ½ pound fresh green beans
- ½ pound fresh asparagus
- 4 salmon fillets (6 ounces each)
- 1 tablespoon plus ⅓ cup red wine vinaigrette, divided
- ¼ teaspoon salt
- ¼ teaspoon pepper
- 4 cups fresh arugula or baby spinach
- 2 cups cherry tomatoes, halved
- 1 tablespoon minced fresh chives

1. Cut potatoes lengthwise in half. Trim and cut the green beans and asparagus into 2-in. pieces. Place the potatoes in a 6-qt. stockpot; add water to cover. Bring to a boil. Reduce heat; cook, uncovered, 10-15 minutes or until tender, adding green beans and asparagus during the last 4 minutes of cooking. Drain.
2. Meanwhile, brush salmon with 1 tablespoon red wine vinaigrette; sprinkle with salt and pepper. Moisten a paper towel with cooking oil; using long-handled tongs, rub on grill rack to coat lightly. Place fish on grill rack, skin side down. Grill, covered, over medium-high heat or broil 4 in. from heat 6-8 minutes or until the fish just begins to flake easily with a fork.
3. In a large bowl, combine the potato mixture, arugula, cherry tomatoes and chives. Drizzle with the remaining red wine vinaigrette; toss to coat. Serve with salmon.
PER SERVING *1 salmon fillet with 2 cups salad equals 480 cal., 23 g fat (4 g sat. fat), 85 mg chol., 642 mg sodium, 33 g carb., 6 g fiber, 34 g pro.* **Diabetic Exchanges:** *5 lean meat, 2 vegetable, 1½ starch, 1½ fat.*

SWEET POTATO FRIES
WITH BLUE CHEESE

RED CABBAGE
WITH BACON

EAT SMART ⑤INGREDIENTS FAST FIX

Sweet Potato Fries with Blue Cheese

As a child, I couldn't stand sweet potatoes. After I got married, I learned about their nutritional benefits and began trying them again with my husband. We discovered they make awesome fries with apricot preserves and blue cheese.

—KATRINA KRUMM APPLE VALLEY, MN

START TO FINISH: 25 MIN.
MAKES: 2 SERVINGS

- 1 **tablespoon olive oil**
- 2 **medium sweet potatoes (about 1¼ pounds), peeled and cut into ½-in.-thick strips**
- 1 **tablespoon apricot preserves**
- ¼ **teaspoon salt**
- 3 **tablespoons crumbled blue cheese**

In a large skillet, heat oil over medium heat. Add the sweet potatoes; cook 12-15 minutes or until tender and lightly browned, turning occasionally.

Add the apricot preserves, stirring to coat; sprinkle with salt. Top with the crumbled blue cheese.

PER SERVING *1 serving equals 246 cal., 11 g fat (3 g sat. fat), 9 mg chol., 487 mg sodium, 34 g carb., 3 g fiber, 5 g pro.*

FAST FIX

Red Cabbage with Bacon

Like cabbage but looking for a different preparation method? Shred and steam it, then add bacon and a tangy sauce as a side dish for a pork or poultry entree.

—SHERRI MELOTIK OAK CREEK, WI

START TO FINISH: 25 MIN.
MAKES: 6 SERVINGS

- 1 **medium head red cabbage (about 2 pounds), shredded**
- 8 **bacon strips, chopped**
- 1 **small onion, quartered and thinly sliced**
- 2 **tablespoons all-purpose flour**
- ¼ **cup packed brown sugar**
- ½ **cup water**
- ¼ **cup cider vinegar**
- 1 **teaspoon salt**
- ⅛ **teaspoon pepper**

1. In a large saucepan, place steamer basket over 1 in. of water. Place the cabbage in basket. Bring the water to a boil. Reduce heat to maintain a simmer; steam, covered, 6-8 minutes or just until tender.

2. Meanwhile, in a large skillet, cook bacon over medium heat until crisp, stirring occasionally. Remove with a slotted spoon; drain on paper towels. Discard bacon drippings, reserving 2 tablespoons in pan.

3. Add the onion to bacon drippings; cook and stir over medium-high heat 4-6 minutes or until tender. Stir in flour and brown sugar until blended. Gradually stir in water and vinegar. Bring to a boil, stirring constantly; cook and stir 1-2 minutes or until thickened. Stir in the cabbage, bacon, salt and pepper.

In our house, easy Herbed Butternut Squash is a wintertime staple. It requires just a handful of ingredients.

—JENNIFER TIDWELL FAIR OAKS, CA

HERBED BUTTERNUT SQUASH

EAT SMART ⑤ **INGREDIENTS FAST FIX**

Herbed Butternut Squash

START TO FINISH: 25 MIN.
MAKES: 6 SERVINGS

- 1 medium butternut squash (about 3 pounds)
- 1 tablespoon olive oil
- 1½ teaspoons dried oregano
- 1 teaspoon dried thyme
- ½ teaspoon salt
- ¼ teaspoon pepper

Peel and cut the squash crosswise into ½-in.-thick slices; remove and discard seeds. In a large bowl, toss the squash with the remaining ingredients. Grill, covered, over medium heat or broil 4 in. from heat 6-8 minutes on each side or until tender.

PER SERVING *1 serving equals 108 cal., 2 g fat (trace sat. fat), 0 chol., 205 mg sodium, 23 g carb., 7 g fiber, 2 g pro. Diabetic Exchanges: 1½ starch, ½ fat.*

EAT SMART FAST FIX

Mediterranean Orzo Chicken Salad

On hot days, I turn to this cool supper that has a refreshing lemony dressing. The recipe calls for convenient rotisserie chicken, but if you have leftover grilled meat from the night before, use that instead for some smoky flavor.

—SUSAN KIEBOAM STREETSBORO, OH

START TO FINISH: 25 MIN.
MAKES: 6 SERVINGS

- 2 cups uncooked whole wheat orzo pasta
- 2 cups shredded rotisserie chicken
- 10 cherry tomatoes, halved
- ½ cup crumbled tomato and basil feta cheese
- 1 can (2¼ ounces) sliced ripe olives, drained
- ¼ cup chopped sweet onion
- ¼ cup olive oil
- 2 tablespoons lemon juice
- ½ teaspoon salt
- ¼ teaspoon dried oregano

1. Cook the whole wheat orzo pasta according to the package directions. Drain the pasta; rinse with cold water and drain well.

2. In a large bowl, combine the pasta, shredded rotisserie chicken, cherry tomatoes, feta cheese, ripe olives and sweet onion. In a small bowl, whisk the remaining ingredients until blended. Drizzle over salad; toss to coat.

PER SERVING *1 cup equals 397 cal., 16 g fat (3 g sat. fat), 47 mg chol., 407 mg sodium, 40 g carb., 10 g fiber, 22 g pro. Diabetic Exchanges: 3 lean meat, 2½ starch, 2 fat.*

MEDITERRANEAN ORZO
CHICKEN SALAD

QUINOA TABBOULEH SALAD

EAT SMART

Quinoa Tabbouleh Salad

Tabbouleh salad is super simple and filling. Try red quinoa for a slightly earthier flavor.
—**LOGAN LEVANT** LOS ANGELES, CA

PREP: 15 MIN. • **COOK:** 15 MIN. + COOLING
MAKES: 6 SERVINGS

- 2 cups water
- 1 cup quinoa, rinsed
- ¾ cup packed fresh parsley sprigs, stems removed
- ⅓ cup fresh mint leaves
- ¼ cup coarsely chopped red onion
- 1 garlic clove, minced
- 1 cup grape tomatoes
- ½ English cucumber, cut into 1-inch pieces
- 2 tablespoons lemon juice
- 2 tablespoons olive oil
- 1 teaspoon salt
- ½ teaspoon pepper
- ¼ teaspoon ground allspice

1. In a large saucepan, bring water to a boil. Add quinoa. Reduce heat; simmer, covered, 12-15 minutes or until liquid is absorbed. Remove from the heat; fluff with a fork. Transfer to a large bowl; cool completely.
2. Place the parsley, mint, onion and garlic in a food processor; pulse until finely chopped. Add tomatoes and cucumber; pulse until coarsely chopped. Add mixture to quinoa.
3. In a small bowl, whisk the lemon juice, oil and seasonings until blended; drizzle over quinoa mixture and toss to coat. Serve at room temperature or refrigerate until serving.
NOTE *Look for quinoa in the cereal, rice or organic food aisle.*
PER SERVING *⅔ cup equals 163 cal., 6 g fat (1 g sat. fat), 0 chol., 403 mg sodium, 22 g carb., 3 g fiber, 5 g pro.*
Diabetic Exchanges: 1½ starch, 1 fat.

EAT SMART FAST FIX

Orange Chicken Spinach Salad

Refreshing yet hearty, this lightly dressed main dish with chunks of chicken is always a hit with family and friends. Pair it with a fresh-baked batch of your favorite rolls or breadsticks for a dinner you'll want to enjoy again and again.
—**JEAN MURAWSKI** GROSSE POINTE PARK, MI

START TO FINISH: 20 MIN.
MAKES: 4 SERVINGS

- 6 ounces fresh baby spinach (about 8 cups)
- 3 cups cubed cooked chicken breast
- 1 can (15 ounces) mandarin oranges, drained
- 1 medium sweet red pepper, chopped
- ½ cup chopped red onion
- 2 tablespoons orange juice
- 2 tablespoons cider vinegar
- 1 tablespoon olive oil
- ½ teaspoon Italian seasoning
- 1 garlic clove, minced
- ⅛ teaspoon salt
- 2 tablespoons crumbled goat cheese

In a large bowl, combine the first five ingredients. In a small bowl, whisk the orange juice, cider vinegar, olive oil, Italian seasoning, garlic and salt until blended. Drizzle the dressing over the salad and toss to coat. Top with the crumbled goat cheese.
PER SERVING *2½ cups equals 293 cal., 9 g fat (3 g sat. fat), 86 mg chol., 211 mg sodium, 18 g carb., 2 g fiber, 34 g pro.*
Diabetic Exchanges: 4 lean meat, 1 vegetable, 1 fruit, 1 fat.

FAST FIX

White Bean Arugula Salad

The Italian flag inspired my red, white and green medley topped with Parmesan.
—**MALIA ESTES** ALLSTON, MA

START TO FINISH: 30 MIN.
MAKES: 4 SERVINGS

- 4 slices pancetta, chopped
- 2 tablespoons olive oil
- ¼ cup chopped sweet onion
- ⅔ cup cherry tomatoes, halved
- 1 teaspoon minced fresh rosemary or ¼ teaspoon dried rosemary, crushed
- ¼ teaspoon salt
- ¼ teaspoon pepper
- 2 cans (15 ounces each) white kidney or cannellini beans, rinsed and drained
- 3 tablespoons red wine vinegar
- 4 fresh basil leaves, thinly sliced
- 2 cups torn fresh arugula or baby spinach
- ¼ cup shaved Parmesan cheese

1. In a small skillet, cook the pancetta over medium heat until crisp, stirring occasionally. Remove with a slotted spoon; drain on paper towels.
2. In same pan, heat oil and drippings over medium heat. Add onion; cook and stir 1-2 minutes or until tender. Add the tomatoes, rosemary, salt and pepper; cook 2-3 minutes longer or until the tomatoes are softened. Cool slightly.
3. In a large bowl, combine the beans, tomato mixture, pancetta, red wine vinegar and basil. Add arugula and cheese; toss to coat.

Oh-So-Good Creamy Mashed Potatoes

Short on time? Go with a proven winner. Start by simmering 8 peeled and quartered large Yukon Gold potatoes in salted water for 20-25 minutes or until tender. In a large saucepan, heat 2½ cups 2% milk, ½ cup butter, 3 teaspoons garlic salt and 1 teaspoon pepper. Drain the potatoes, then mash them with the milk mixture and ¼ cup sour cream. Sprinkle with parsley. *Makes 18 servings.*
—**BRITTANY JACKSON** SEYMOUR, WI

WHITE BEAN
ARUGULA SALAD

CHICKEN
TOSTADA SALAD

Cheddar & Spinach Twice-Baked Potatoes

My husband is a rancher who really loves hearty potato dishes. Consider these spuds cowboy-approved!
—JODY AUGUSTYN LOUP CITY, NE

PREP: 1¼ HOURS • **BAKE:** 20 MIN.
MAKES: 12 SERVINGS

- 6 large baking potatoes (about 12 ounces each)
- ½ cup 2% milk
- 6 tablespoons butter, softened
- 1 package (10 ounces) frozen chopped spinach, thawed and squeezed dry
- ¾ cup shredded Monterey Jack cheese
- ¾ cup shredded cheddar cheese, divided
- ¼ cup finely chopped red onion
- 1 teaspoon salt
- ¼ teaspoon pepper

1. Preheat oven to 375°. Scrub the potatoes; pierce several times with a fork. Place in a foil-lined 15x10x1-in. baking pan; bake 60-70 minutes or until tender.
2. When cool enough to handle, cut each potato lengthwise in half. Scoop out pulp, leaving ¼-in.-thick shells. In a large bowl, mash pulp with milk and butter, adding spinach, Monterey Jack cheese, ¼ cup cheddar cheese, onion, salt and pepper.
3. Spoon into potato shells; return to pan. Sprinkle with remaining cheddar cheese. Bake 20-25 minutes or until heated through and cheese is melted.

CHEDDAR & SPINACH
TWICE-BAKED POTATOES

FAST FIX
Chicken Tostada Salad

When I want to prepare this recipe but am out of tostada shells, I simply substitute taco shells. I break them in half, lay them flat and pile on the delicious toppings. It's a great Southwestern meal.
—**EDIE DESPAIN** LOGAN, UT

START TO FINISH: 10 MIN.
MAKES: 4 SERVINGS

- 1 package (8 ounces) shredded lettuce
- 1 medium tomato, cut into wedges
- ½ cup reduced-fat ranch salad dressing
- ¼ cup sliced ripe olives
- 2 tablespoons taco sauce
- 4 tostada shells
- 2 packages (6 ounces each) ready-to-use Southwestern chicken strips
- ½ cup shredded Mexican cheese blend

In a large bowl, combine the first five ingredients. Arrange lettuce mixture over the tostada shells. Top with the chicken and cheese.

FAST FIX
Smoked Turkey Salad with Raspberries

Here's a zingy salad that features smoked deli turkey, raspberries, cheese and basil. The key is the pepper jelly dressing.
—**DEBRA KEIL** OWASSO, OK

START TO FINISH: 15 MIN.
MAKES: 4 SERVINGS

- 2 tablespoons red wine vinegar
- 1 tablespoon jalapeno pepper jelly
- 2 teaspoons Dijon mustard
- ⅓ cup olive oil
- 6 cups fresh baby spinach (about 6 ounces)
- 8 ounces thinly sliced deli smoked turkey, cut into strips
- 1 cup crumbled goat or feta cheese
- 1 cup fresh raspberries
- ¼ cup loosely packed basil leaves, thinly sliced

1. In a small bowl, whisk the vinegar, pepper jelly and mustard until blended. Gradually whisk in oil until blended.
2. Divide spinach among four plates; top with remaining ingredients. Serve with dressing.

1. In a large skillet, heat the butter over medium-high heat. Add beans; cook and stir 3-4 minutes or until crisp-tender.

2. Add the radishes; cook 2-3 minutes longer or until vegetables are tender, stirring occasionally. Stir in sugar and salt; sprinkle with nuts.

NOTE *To toast nuts, bake in a shallow pan in a 350° oven for 5-10 minutes or cook in a skillet over low heat until lightly browned, stirring occasionally.*

PER SERVING *1/2 cup equals 75 cal., 6 g fat (2 g sat. fat), 8 mg chol., 177 mg sodium, 5 g carb., 2 g fiber, 2 g pro.*

Diabetic Exchanges: *1 vegetable, 1 fat.*

SPINACH & BACON SALAD WITH PEACHES

FAST FIX >
Spinach & Bacon Salad with Peaches

Peaches and bacon? Absolutely! I fixed this colorful combo for a summer party, and guests couldn't get enough.

—**MEGAN RIOFSKI** FRANKFORT, IL

START TO FINISH: 25 MIN.
MAKES: 8 SERVINGS (1½ CUPS DRESSING)

- 1 cup olive oil
- ⅓ cup cider vinegar
- ¼ cup sugar
- 1 teaspoon celery seed
- 1 teaspoon ground mustard
- ½ teaspoon salt

SALAD
- 6 cups fresh baby spinach (about 6 ounces)
- 2 medium peaches, sliced
- 1¾ cups sliced fresh mushrooms
- 3 large hard-cooked eggs, halved and sliced
- ½ pound bacon strips, cooked and crumbled
- 1 small red onion, halved and thinly sliced
- ¼ cup sliced almonds, toasted
  Grated Parmesan cheese

Place the first six ingredients in a blender; cover and process until blended. In a large bowl, combine the baby spinach, peaches, mushrooms, hard-cooked eggs, bacon, red onion and almonds. Serve with the dressing and Parmesan cheese.

NOTE *To toast nuts, bake in a shallow pan in a 350° oven for 5-10 minutes or cook in a skillet over low heat until lightly browned, stirring occasionally.*

EAT SMART FAST FIX >
Sauteed Radishes with Green Beans

Cook your garden-grown radishes for a deliciously different side. Green beans and wax beans are perfect complements.

—**PAMELA JANE KAISER** MANSFIELD, MO

START TO FINISH: 20 MIN.
MAKES: 4 SERVINGS

- 1 tablespoon butter
- ½ pound fresh green or wax beans, trimmed
- 1 cup thinly sliced radishes
- ½ teaspoon sugar
- ¼ teaspoon salt
- 2 tablespoons pine nuts, toasted

EAT SMART FAST FIX >
Fiesta Coleslaw

Creamy coleslaw with a touch of jalapeno heat makes a zippy accompaniment for barbecue chicken or pork. I like to scoop some on fish tacos and po'boys, too.

—**FAY MORELAND** WICHITA FALLS, TX

START TO FINISH: 20 MIN.
MAKES: 10 SERVINGS

- 1 package (14 ounces) coleslaw mix
- 1 cup chopped peeled jicama
- 6 radishes, halved and sliced
- 4 jalapeno peppers, seeded and finely chopped
- 1 medium onion, chopped
- ⅓ cup minced fresh cilantro
- ½ cup mayonnaise
- ¼ cup cider vinegar
- 2 tablespoons sugar
- ½ teaspoon salt
- ½ teaspoon celery salt
- ¼ teaspoon coarsely ground pepper
  Lime wedges, optional

1. In a large bowl, combine the first six ingredients. In a small bowl, whisk the mayonnaise, cider vinegar, sugar and seasonings. Pour over the coleslaw mixture; toss to coat.

2. Refrigerate coleslaw, covered, until serving. If desired, serve coleslaw with lime wedges.

NOTE *Wear disposable gloves when cutting hot peppers; the oils can burn skin. Avoid touching your face.*

PER SERVING *3/4 cup equals 114 cal., 9 g fat (1 g sat. fat), 4 mg chol., 242 mg sodium, 8 g carb., 2 g fiber, 1 g pro.*

Diabetic Exchanges: *2 fat, 1 vegetable.*

EAT SMART FAST FIX
Arugula & Brown Rice Salad

When we have company, an arugula salad with brown rice is usually on the menu. I've shared the recipe countless times.

—**MINDY OSWALT** WINNETKA, CA

START TO FINISH: 25 MIN.
MAKES: 4 SERVINGS

- 1 package (8.8 ounces) ready-to-serve brown rice
- 7 cups fresh arugula or baby spinach (about 5 ounces)
- 1 can (15 ounces) garbanzo beans or chickpeas, rinsed and drained
- 1 cup (4 ounces) crumbled feta cheese
- ¾ cup loosely packed basil leaves, torn
- ½ cup dried cherries or cranberries

DRESSING
- ¼ cup olive oil
- ¼ teaspoon grated lemon peel
- 2 tablespoons lemon juice
- ¼ teaspoon salt
- ⅛ teaspoon pepper

1. Heat the brown rice according to package directions. Transfer to a large bowl; cool slightly.

2. Stir the arugula, garbanzo beans, feta cheese, basil and dried cherries into the brown rice. In a small bowl, whisk the dressing ingredients. Drizzle dressing over the salad; toss to coat. Serve immediately.

PER SERVING *2 cups equals 473 cal., 22 g fat (5 g sat. fat), 15 mg chol., 574 mg sodium, 53 g carb., 7 g fiber, 13 g pro.*

ARUGULA & BROWN RICE SALAD

ASIAN BARBECUE CHICKEN SLAW

FAST FIX
Asian Barbecue Chicken Slaw

Springtime in the South means cabbage is plentiful, and we love using it for this slaw.

—**PAULA TODORA** FORT WORTH, TX

START TO FINISH: 25 MIN.
MAKES: 4 SERVINGS

- ¼ cup reduced-sodium soy sauce
- ¼ cup honey
- 3 tablespoons canola oil
- 2 tablespoons rice vinegar
- ½ cup barbecue sauce
- 1 pound boneless skinless chicken breasts, cut into strips
- ¼ teaspoon pepper
- ¼ cup honey mustard salad dressing
- 1 package (14 ounces) coleslaw mix
- 3 green onions, chopped
- 4 tablespoons sliced almonds, toasted, divided
- 3 teaspoons sesame seeds, toasted, divided

1. In a large bowl, whisk soy sauce, honey, canola oil and rice vinegar until blended. Pour half of the honey mixture into a small bowl; stir in the barbecue sauce.

2. Sprinkle the chicken with pepper. Place a large nonstick skillet coated with cooking spray over medium-high heat. Add the chicken; cook and stir 4-6 minutes or until no longer pink. Add the barbecue sauce mixture and heat through.

3. Meanwhile, whisk honey mustard salad dressing into remaining honey mixture until blended. Add coleslaw mix, green onions, 3 tablespoons almonds and 2 teaspoons sesame seeds; toss to coat. Serve with chicken. Sprinkle servings with remaining almonds and sesame seeds.

NOTE *To toast nuts, bake in a shallow pan in a 350° oven for 5-10 minutes or cook in a skillet over low heat until lightly browned, stirring occasionally.*

Garlic Roasted Brussels Sprouts

START TO FINISH: 30 MIN.
MAKES: 12 SERVINGS (½ CUP EACH)

- 2 pounds fresh Brussels sprouts, trimmed and halved
- 2 medium red onions, cut into 1-inch pieces
- 3 tablespoons olive oil
- 7 garlic cloves, finely chopped
- 1 teaspoon salt
- ½ teaspoon pepper

1. Preheat oven to 425°. Divide the Brussels sprouts and onions between two foil-lined 15x10x1-in. baking pans.
2. In a small bowl, mix the olive oil, garlic, salt and pepper; drizzle half of the mixture over each pan and toss to coat. Roast 20-25 minutes or until tender, stirring occasionally and switching position of pans halfway.

PER SERVING *½ cup equals 69 cal., 4 g fat (1 g sat. fat), 0 chol., 215 mg sodium, 8 g carb., 3 g fiber, 3 g pro.* **Diabetic Exchanges:** *1 vegetable, ½ fat.*

Honey & Ginger Glazed Carrots

For both weeknights and special events, we make sweet-tangy carrots flavored with ginger, lemon and honey. Swap out the almonds for pecans if you prefer.
—**LAURA MIMS** LITTLE ELM, TX

START TO FINISH: 25 MIN.
MAKES: 6 SERVINGS

- 1½ pounds fresh carrots, sliced
- ½ cup golden raisins
- 3 tablespoons honey
- 2 tablespoons butter
- 2 tablespoons lemon juice
- 1½ teaspoons ground ginger
- ½ teaspoon salt
- ½ cup slivered almonds, toasted

1. Place carrots in a large saucepan; add water to cover. Bring to a boil. Cook, covered, 6-8 minutes or until crisp-tender. Drain and return to pan.
2. Stir in the golden raisins, honey, butter, lemon juice, ginger and salt; cook and stir 4-5 minutes longer or until the carrots are tender. Just before serving, sprinkle with the slivered almonds.

NOTE *To toast nuts, bake in a shallow pan in a 350° oven for 5-10 minutes or cook in a skillet over low heat until lightly browned, stirring occasionally.*
PER SERVING *⅔ cup equals 204 cal., 9 g fat (3 g sat. fat), 10 mg chol., 307 mg sodium, 32 g carb., 5 g fiber, 4 g pro.* **Diabetic Exchanges:** *2 vegetable, 1½ fat, 1 starch.*

My roommate and I used to fix Garlic Roasted Brussels Sprouts at least twice a week. Now I prepare this wholesome side for all sorts of occasions.
—**KATHERINE MOORE-COLASURD** CINCINNATI, OH

GARLIC ROASTED BRUSSELS SPROUTS

Michelle Babbie's
Potato, Sausage &
Kale Soup PAGE 39

½ teaspoon garlic powder
½ teaspoon pepper
2 medium red potatoes, cut into ½-inch cubes
2 cups sliced fresh kale
3 cups 2% milk
1 cup heavy whipping cream
1 tablespoon cornstarch
¼ cup cold water

1. In a large saucepan, cook the sausage and onion over medium heat 4-6 minutes or until the sausage is no longer pink and the onion is tender, breaking up the sausage into crumbles; drain.
2. Stir in seasonings. Add potatoes, kale, milk and heavy whipping cream; bring to a boil. Reduce heat; simmer, covered, 10-15 minutes or until the potatoes are tender.
3. In a small bowl, mix the cornstarch and cold water until smooth; stir into the soup. Return to a boil, stirring constantly; cook and stir 1-2 minutes or until thickened.

PEPPERED PORK PITAS

FAST FIX
Cilantro-Avocado Tuna Salad Sandwiches
Lime juice and cilantro in tuna salad—who would have thought? The unusual combo adds pizzazz to a lunchtime staple.
—**HEATHER WALDORF** BLACK MOUNTAIN, NC

START TO FINISH: 15 MIN.
MAKES: 4 SERVINGS

2 pouches (5 ounces each) albacore white tuna in water
⅓ cup mayonnaise
3 tablespoons minced fresh cilantro
2 tablespoons lime juice
2 garlic cloves, minced
¼ teaspoon salt
⅛ teaspoon pepper
8 slices whole wheat bread, toasted if desired
4 slices Muenster or provolone cheese
1 medium ripe avocado, peeled and sliced

In a small bowl, mix the first seven ingredients. Spread the tuna mixture over four slices of bread; top with the cheese, avocado and remaining bread. Serve immediately.

EAT SMART ⑤**INGREDIENTS** **FAST FIX**
Peppered Pork Pitas
Here's a terrific meal for weeknights or anytime. Cracked black pepper and garlic give the strips of pork a nice pop. I load the meat mixture, lettuce and mayo onto fun-to-eat pita breads.
—**KATHERINE WHITE** CLEMMONS, NC

START TO FINISH: 20 MIN.
MAKES: 4 SERVINGS

1 pound boneless pork loin chops, cut into thin strips
1 tablespoon olive oil
2 teaspoons coarsely ground pepper
2 garlic cloves, minced
1 jar (12 ounces) roasted sweet red peppers, drained and julienned
4 whole pita breads, warmed
Garlic mayonnaise and torn leaf lettuce, optional

In a small bowl, combine the pork, olive oil, pepper and garlic; toss to coat. Place a large skillet over medium-high heat. Add the pork mixture; cook and stir until no longer pink. Stir in the roasted red peppers; heat through. Serve on pita breads with mayonnaise and lettuce if desired.
PER SERVING 1 sandwich equals 380 cal., 11 g fat (3 g sat. fat), 55 mg chol., 665 mg sodium, 37 g carb., 2 g fiber, 27 g pro. **Diabetic Exchanges:** 3 lean meat, 2 starch, 1 fat.

FAST FIX
Potato, Sausage & Kale Soup
When I let my young son pick out seed packets, he chose kale, which grew like crazy. This satisfying soup helped make good use of our harvest and rivals a restaurant version we love.
—**MICHELLE BABBIE** MALONE, NY

START TO FINISH: 30 MIN.
MAKES: 4 SERVINGS

½ pound bulk pork sausage
1 medium onion, finely chopped
2 teaspoons chicken bouillon granules

FAST FIX
Bacon Brie Grilled Cheese

It's fun to put a new twist on old-school grilled cheese. My creation stacks spinach, apple and Brie on pumpernickel. If you'd prefer a more compact sandwich, press a heavy pan on it while toasting.

—GEORGE WILKINS MAYS LANDING, NJ

START TO FINISH: 30 MIN.
MAKES: 4 SERVINGS

- 4 **tablespoons olive oil, divided**
- 2 **teaspoons lemon juice**
- 2 **teaspoons honey**
- ⅛ **teaspoon salt**
- ⅛ **teaspoon pepper**
- 1 **cup fresh baby spinach**
- 1 **round (8 ounces) Brie cheese, cut into ⅛-inch slices**
- 8 **slices pumpernickel bread**
- 8 **cooked bacon strips**
- 1 **medium apple, thinly sliced**

1. In a small bowl, whisk 2 tablespoons olive oil, lemon juice, honey, salt and pepper until blended. Add the spinach; toss to coat.

2. Place half of the Brie cheese on four bread slices. Layer with bacon, spinach mixture, apple and remaining cheese. Top with the remaining bread; brush the outsides of sandwiches with the remaining oil.

3. In a large skillet or grill pan, toast the sandwiches over medium heat 3-4 minutes on each side or until golden brown and cheese is melted.

TACO STEW

BACON BRIE GRILLED CHEESE

FREEZE IT | FAST FIX
Taco Stew

The ingredients in this recipe may be simple, but together they make a truly awesome stew. I like to sprinkle on some crushed tortilla chips for crunch.

—SUZANNE FRANCIS MARYSVILLE, WA

START TO FINISH: 30 MIN.
MAKES: 6 SERVINGS

- 1 **pound ground beef**
- 2 **cans (15 ounces each) black beans, rinsed and drained**
- 2 **cans (10 ounces each) diced tomatoes and green chilies**
- 1 **can (15 ounces) tomato sauce**
- 1½ **cups frozen corn (about 7 ounces)**
- 2 **teaspoons chili powder**
- ½ **teaspoon ground cumin**
  Crushed tortilla chips, optional

1. In a large saucepan, cook the beef over medium heat 6-8 minutes or until no longer pink, breaking the beef into crumbles; drain.

2. Stir in the black beans, tomatoes, tomato sauce, corn, chili powder and cumin. Bring to a boil. Reduce heat; simmer 5-10 minutes to allow flavors to blend. If desired, top each serving with tortilla chips.

FREEZE OPTION *Freeze cooled stew in freezer containers. To use, partially thaw in the refrigerator overnight. Heat through in a saucepan, stirring occasionally and adding a little water if necessary.*

DID YOU KNOW?

What's the difference between soup and stew? Soup is a combination of veggies, meat or fish cooked in liquid, while traditional stew is prepared by stewing—that is, the food is barely covered with liquid and simmered for a long time in a covered pot. Taco Stew (recipe at left) is a speedier option.

Beef Stroganoff Sandwiches

Here's an American version of traditional Russian comfort food. We layer a beef Stroganoff mixture and cheese on bread and broil for an open-faced favorite.

—ALISON GARCIA BEATRICE, NE

START TO FINISH: 25 MIN.
MAKES: 6 SERVINGS

- 1 **pound ground beef**
- 1 **cup sliced fresh mushrooms**
- 1 **small green pepper, finely chopped**
- 1 **small onion, finely chopped**
- 1 **envelope ranch dip mix**
- ¾ **cup sour cream**
- 1 **loaf (about 8 ounces) French bread**
- 2 **cups (8 ounces) shredded part-skim mozzarella cheese**

1. Preheat broiler. In a large skillet, cook beef, mushrooms, green pepper and onion over medium-high heat 8-10 minutes or until beef is no longer pink, breaking up beef into crumbles; drain. Stir in dip mix and sour cream.

2. Cut the French bread horizontally in half; place halves on a baking sheet, cut side up. Broil 3-4 in. from the heat 1-2 minutes or until lightly toasted. Remove from broiler.

3. Spoon beef mixture over the bread. Sprinkle with mozzarella cheese. Broil 1-2 minutes longer or until the cheese is lightly browned. To serve, cut each bread half into three pieces.

Satisfying Tomato Soup

When a craving hit and I just had to have tomato soup, I headed for the kitchen and came up with my own. My sister Joan likes it chunky-style, so she skips the last step of pureeing it in a blender.

—MARIAN BROWN MISSISSAUGA, ON

START TO FINISH: 30 MIN.
MAKES: 4 SERVINGS

- 2 **teaspoons canola oil**
- ¼ **cup finely chopped onion**
- ¼ **cup finely chopped celery**
- 2 **cans (14½ ounces each) diced tomatoes, undrained**
- 1½ **cups water**
- 2 **teaspoons brown sugar**
- ½ **teaspoon salt**
- ½ **teaspoon dried basil**
- ¼ **teaspoon dried oregano**
- ¼ **teaspoon coarsely ground pepper**

1. In a large saucepan, heat oil over medium-high heat. Add onion and celery; cook and stir 2-4 minutes until tender. Add the remaining ingredients. Bring to a boil. Reduce heat; simmer, uncovered, 10 minutes to allow flavors to blend.

2. Puree the soup using an immersion blender. Or, cool the soup slightly and puree in batches in a blender; return to pan and heat through.

FREEZE OPTION *Freeze cooled soup in freezer containers. To use, partially thaw in the refrigerator overnight. Heat through in a saucepan, stirring occasionally and adding a little water if necessary.*

PER SERVING *1¼ cups equals 76 cal., 2 g fat (trace sat. fat), 0 chol., 627 mg sodium, 13 g carb., 4 g fiber, 2 g pro.* ***Diabetic Exchanges:*** *2 vegetable, ½ fat.*

BEEF STROGANOFF SANDWICHES

MINI CHICKEN &
BISCUIT SANDWICHES

⑤ INGREDIENTS **FAST FIX**
Mini Chicken & Biscuit Sandwiches

My 11-year-old son invented these tasty sliders during dinner one night when he plunked his chicken on a biscuit. The rest of us tried it his way, and now we have these mini sandwiches all the time.

—JODIE KOLSAN PALM COAST, FL

START TO FINISH: 30 MIN.
MAKES: 5 SERVINGS

- 1 tube (12 ounces) refrigerated buttermilk biscuits
- 5 boneless skinless chicken breasts (4 ounces each)
- ½ teaspoon salt
- ½ teaspoon dried thyme
- ¼ teaspoon pepper
- 1 tablespoon canola oil
- 1 tablespoon butter
   Optional toppings: cranberry chutney, lettuce leaves, sliced tomato and red onion

1. Bake the buttermilk biscuits according to the package directions. Meanwhile, cut the chicken crosswise in half. Pound with a meat mallet to ¼-in. thickness. Sprinkle with salt, thyme and pepper.

2. In a large skillet, heat oil and butter over medium-high heat. Add chicken in batches; cook 2-3 minutes on each side or until no longer pink. Split biscuits in half; top with chicken and toppings as desired. Replace tops.

EAT SMART **FAST FIX**
Chickpea 'n' Red Onion Burgers

When the weather turns chilly and we retire the grill to the garage, I bake my chickpea veggie burgers. I've found that even diehard meat-eaters enjoy them.

—LILY JULOW LAWRENCEVILLE, GA

START TO FINISH: 30 MIN.
MAKES: 6 SERVINGS

- 1 large red onion, thinly sliced
- ¼ cup fat-free red wine vinaigrette
- 2 cans (15 ounces each) chickpeas or garbanzo beans, rinsed and drained
- ⅓ cup chopped walnuts
- ¼ cup toasted wheat germ or dry bread crumbs
- ¼ cup packed fresh parsley sprigs
- 2 large eggs
- 1 teaspoon curry powder
- ½ teaspoon pepper
- ⅓ cup fat-free mayonnaise
- 2 teaspoons Dijon mustard
- 6 sesame seed hamburger buns, split
- 6 lettuce leaves
- 3 tablespoons thinly sliced fresh basil leaves

1. Preheat oven to 375°. In a small bowl, mix the onion and vinaigrette. Place chickpeas, walnuts, wheat germ and parsley in a food processor; pulse until blended. Add eggs, curry and pepper; process until smooth.

2. Shape into six patties. Place on a baking sheet coated with cooking spray. Bake 10-15 minutes or until a thermometer reads 160°.

3. In a small bowl, mix mayonnaise and Dijon mustard; spread over the cut sides of hamburger buns. Serve the patties on buns with lettuce, basil and onion mixture.

PER SERVING *1 burger equals 386 cal., 12 g fat (2 g sat. fat), 72 mg chol., 732 mg sodium, 54 g carb., 9 g fiber, 16 g pro.*

FREEZE IT **FAST FIX**
Meatball & Pasta Soup

Thanks to this flavorful soup full of beef and orzo pasta, kids eat their spinach and actually like it. Add a basket of rolls or a loaf of French bread for a hearty meal that pleases the whole family.

—LAURA GREENBERG LAKE BALBOA, CA

START TO FINISH: 30 MIN.
MAKES: 8 SERVINGS (3 QUARTS)

- 8 cups vegetable stock
- 1 garlic clove, minced
- 1 teaspoon salt, divided
- 1 large egg
- ½ cup dry bread crumbs
- ¼ cup 2% milk
- 2 tablespoons ketchup
- 2 teaspoons Worcestershire sauce
- 1 teaspoon onion powder
- ½ teaspoon pepper
- 1 pound lean ground beef (90% lean)
- 4 medium carrots, chopped
- 1 cup uncooked orzo pasta
- 1 package (6 ounces) fresh baby spinach

1. In a 6-qt. stockpot, bring vegetable stock, garlic and ¾ teaspoon salt to a boil. Meanwhile, in a large bowl, mix the egg, bread crumbs, milk, ketchup, Worcestershire sauce, onion powder, pepper and remaining salt. Add beef; mix lightly but thoroughly. Shape into 1-in. meatballs.

2. Add carrots, pasta and meatballs to boiling stock. Reduce heat; simmer, uncovered, 10-12 minutes or until meatballs are cooked through and pasta is tender, stirring occasionally. Stir in spinach until wilted.

FREEZE OPTION *Freeze cooled soup in freezer containers. To use, partially thaw in the refrigerator overnight. Heat through in a saucepan, stirring occasionally and adding a little water if necessary.*

Waldorf Turkey Pitas

Try stuffing creamy Waldorf salad in a pita for a satisfying lunch anytime. In a large bowl, combine 2 cups cubed cooked turkey breast, 2 finely chopped celery ribs, 1 diced tart apple, 1 cup halved seedless red grapes, ½ cup fat-free mayonnaise and 2 ounces diced fresh mozzarella cheese. Line 8 whole wheat pita pocket halves with 2 cups fresh baby spinach; fill with the turkey mixture. *Makes 4 servings.*

—KEVIN SOBOTKA STATEN ISLAND, NY

PRESTO
PIZZA PATTIES

EAT SMART   FREEZE IT   FAST FIX

Presto Pizza Patties

Here's my secret weapon on busy days: Pizza burgers, with the patties made ahead of time. I keep them in the freezer and pull out some whenever I need to.

—**BARBARA SCHINDLER** NAPOLEON, OH

START TO FINISH: 30 MIN.
MAKES: 6 SERVINGS

- 1   **can (8 ounces) pizza sauce, divided**
- ½   **cup seasoned bread crumbs**
- ½   **cup finely chopped green pepper**
- ¼   **cup finely chopped onion**
- 2   **large egg whites**
- 1   **garlic clove, minced**
- 1   **pound lean ground beef (90% lean)**
- 6   **slices Italian bread (½ inch thick)**
- 2   **teaspoons olive oil**
- 1½ **teaspoons Italian seasoning**
- ½   **cup shredded part-skim mozzarella cheese**

1. In a large bowl, combine ⅓ cup pizza sauce, seasoned bread crumbs, green pepper, onion, egg whites and garlic. Add the beef; mix lightly but thoroughly. Shape the mixture into six oval patties.

2. In a large nonstick skillet, cook the patties over medium heat 4-5 minutes on each side or until a thermometer reads 160°.

3. Meanwhile, place the bread on an ungreased baking sheet. Brush tops with olive oil; sprinkle with Italian seasoning. Broil 3-4 in. from heat 1-2 minutes or until golden brown.

4. Place remaining pizza sauce in a microwave-safe bowl. Microwave, covered, on high for 10-20 seconds or until heated through. Place patties on toast; top with sauce and cheese.

FREEZE OPTION *Place the patties on a plastic wrap-lined baking sheet; wrap and freeze until firm. Remove from the pan and transfer to a large resealable plastic bag; return to freezer. Freeze remaining pizza sauce in an airtight container. To use, cook frozen patties and pizza sauce as directed, increasing time as necessary for a thermometer to read 160° for patties and for sauce to be heated through.*

PER SERVING *1 serving equals 299 cal., 11 g fat (4 g sat. fat), 53 mg chol., 527 mg sodium, 26 g carb., 2 g fiber, 23 g pro.* **Diabetic Exchanges:** *3 lean meat, 1½ starch.*

EAT SMART   FREEZE IT   FAST FIX ▶

Greek Sloppy Joes

A little feta cheese puts a delicious spin on sloppy joes. If you have leftover meat filling, try stuffing it into pitas.

—**SONYA LABBE** WEST HOLLYWOOD, CA

START TO FINISH: 25 MIN.
MAKES: 6 SERVINGS

- 1   **pound lean ground beef (90% lean)**
- 1   **small red onion, chopped**
- 2   **garlic cloves, minced**
- 1   **can (15 ounces) tomato sauce**
- 1   **teaspoon dried oregano**
- 2   **cups chopped romaine**
- 6   **kaiser rolls, split and toasted**
- ½   **cup crumbled feta cheese**

1. In a large skillet, cook the beef, onion and garlic over medium heat 6-8 minutes or until beef is no longer pink, breaking up beef into crumbles; drain. Stir in the tomato sauce and oregano. Bring to a boil. Reduce heat; simmer, uncovered, 8-10 minutes or until sauce is slightly thickened, stirring occasionally.

2. Place romaine on roll bottoms; top with meat mixture. Sprinkle with feta cheese; replace tops.

FREEZE OPTION *Freeze the cooled meat mixture in freezer containers. To use, partially thaw in refrigerator overnight. Heat through in a saucepan, stirring occasionally and adding a little water if necessary.*

PER SERVING *1 sandwich equals 337 cal., 10 g fat (4 g sat. fat), 52 mg chol., 767 mg sodium, 36 g carb., 3 g fiber, 24 g pro.* **Diabetic Exchanges:** *3 lean meat, 2 starch, 1 vegetable.*

GREEK SLOPPY JOES

QUICK CHICKEN &
WILD RICE SOUP

FAST FIX ▶
Quick Chicken & Wild Rice Soup

My mother-in-law always raves about the chicken and rice soup we serve at our house. I adjusted the ingredients several times until the combination was just right.
—TERESA JACOBSON ST. JOHNS, FL

START TO FINISH: 30 MIN.
MAKES: 4 SERVINGS

- 1 package (6.2 ounces) fast-cooking long grain and wild rice mix
- 2 tablespoons butter
- 1 small onion, finely chopped
- 1 celery rib, finely chopped
- 1 medium carrot, finely chopped
- 1 garlic clove, minced
- 2 tablespoons all-purpose flour
- 3 cups 2% milk
- 1½ cups chicken broth
- 2 cups cubed cooked chicken

1. Cook the rice mix according to the package directions.
2. Meanwhile, in a large saucepan, heat butter over medium-high heat. Add onion, celery and carrot; cook and stir 6-8 minutes or until tender. Add garlic; cook 1 minute longer. Stir in flour until blended; gradually whisk in milk and broth. Bring to a boil, stirring constantly; cook and stir 1-2 minutes or until slightly thickened.
3. Stir in chicken and rice mixture; heat through.

Falafel Chicken Burgers with Lemon Sauce

This is the first recipe I created myself, and I still prepare it all the time. I top each patty with lemon sauce, arugula and an onion ring. Use extra falafel mix in meatballs or to coat fish, poultry or veggies.
—NICOLE MEDEROS HOBOKEN, NJ

PREP: 35 MIN. • **COOK:** 10 MIN.
MAKES: 4 SERVINGS

- 4 frozen onion rings, optional

SAUCE
- 1 carton (5.3 ounces) fat-free lemon Greek yogurt
- ¼ teaspoon ground cumin
- ¼ teaspoon dill weed
- ⅛ teaspoon salt
- ⅛ teaspoon paprika

BURGERS
- ¼ cup minced fresh parsley
- 3 tablespoons crumbled cooked bacon
- 3 garlic cloves, minced
- ¾ teaspoon salt
- ¾ teaspoon curry powder
- ½ teaspoon pepper
- ¼ teaspoon ground cumin
- 1 pound ground chicken
- 1 package (6 ounces) falafel mix
- 4 teaspoons canola oil
- 4 sesame seed hamburger buns, split
- 1 cup fresh arugula or baby spinach

1. If desired, prepare the onion rings according to package directions.
2. Meanwhile, in a small bowl, mix the sauce ingredients. In a large bowl, mix the first seven burger ingredients. Add chicken; mix lightly but thoroughly. Shape into four ½-in.-thick patties. Place ½ cup falafel mix in a shallow bowl (save the remaining falafel mix for another use). Press chicken patties into falafel mix, patting to help the coating adhere.
3. In a large nonstick skillet, heat the oil over medium-high heat. Add the chicken patties; cook 4-5 minutes on each side or until a thermometer reads 165°. Serve the patties on buns with the sauce, arugula and, if desired, onion ring.

FAST FIX ▶
Chipotle Turkey Club Sandwich

A nearby roadside stand sells gorgeous tomatoes every summer, and we take full advantage to satisfy our craving for BLTs. We enhance the sandwiches with smoked turkey, Swiss and chipotle mayo.
—PAMELA SHANK PARKERSBURG, WV

START TO FINISH: 15 MIN.
MAKES: 4 SERVINGS

- ¼ cup reduced-fat chipotle mayonnaise
- 8 slices whole wheat bread, toasted
- 8 lettuce leaves
- ½ pound thinly sliced deli smoked turkey
- 16 cooked center-cut bacon strips
- 4 slices reduced-fat Swiss cheese
- 8 slices tomato

Spread the chipotle mayonnaise over four slices of toast. Layer with lettuce, deli turkey, bacon, cheese and tomato; top with remaining toast.

Tex-Mex Cheesesteak Sandwiches reflect our family's passion for all things Southwestern. If you crave even more firepower, add chopped jalapenos.

—**JOAN HALLFORD** NORTH RICHLAND HILLS, TX

TEX-MEX CHEESESTEAK SANDWICHES

FAST FIX
Tex-Mex Cheesesteak Sandwiches

START TO FINISH: 25 MIN.
MAKES: 4 SERVINGS

- 1 **package (15 ounces) refrigerated beef tips with gravy**
- 1 **tablespoon canola oil**
- 1 **medium onion, halved and thinly sliced**
- 1 **banana pepper, cut into strips**
- ⅛ **teaspoon salt**
- ⅛ **teaspoon pepper**
- 4 **whole wheat hoagie buns, split**
- ¼ **cup mayonnaise**
- ⅛ **teaspoon chili powder, optional**
- 8 **slices pepper jack cheese**

1. Preheat broiler. Heat beef tips with gravy according to package directions. Meanwhile, in a small skillet, heat oil over medium-high heat. Add onion and pepper; cook and stir 4-6 minutes or until tender. Stir in salt and pepper.

2. Place the hoagie buns on a baking sheet, cut side up. Mix mayonnaise and, if desired, chili powder; spread on the bottoms of buns. Layer with beef tips, onion mixture and pepper jack cheese. Broil 3-4 in. from the heat 1-2 minutes or until cheese is melted and buns are toasted.

FREEZE IT **FAST FIX**
Spicy Sausage Soup with Tortellini

Both of my daughters requested the recipe for this favorite soup when they moved out on their own. I usually cook the tortellini separately, but you can let it plump up in the broth, too.

—**CYNTHIA KRAKOWIAK** LANGHORNE, PA

START TO FINISH: 30 MIN.
MAKES: 8 SERVINGS (3 QUARTS)

- 2 **cartons (32 ounces each) chicken broth**
- 1 **pound bulk hot or mild Italian sausage**
- 1 **package (9 ounces) refrigerated cheese tortellini**
- 1 **can (14½ ounces) fire-roasted or Italian diced tomatoes**
- 1 **teaspoon Italian seasoning**
- 3 **cups fresh spinach, thinly sliced**

1. In a 6-qt. stockpot, bring the chicken broth to a boil. Carefully drop the Italian sausage by heaping teaspoonfuls into the boiling chicken broth. Add the cheese tortellini, fire-roasted tomatoes and Italian seasoning; return to a boil.

2. Reduce heat; simmer, uncovered, 8-10 minutes or until the sausage is cooked through and the cheese tortellini is tender. Stir in the spinach until wilted.

FREEZE OPTION *Freeze cooled soup in freezer containers. To use, partially thaw in the refrigerator overnight. Heat through in a saucepan, stirring occasionally and adding a little broth if necessary.*

Chicken & Caramelized Onion Grilled Cheese

My grilled cheese combines chicken with caramelized sweet onions, red peppers, Swiss cheese and sourdough bread. Yum!

—KADIJA BRIDGEWATER BOCA RATON, FL

PREP: 40 MIN. • **GRILL:** 15 MIN.
MAKES: 4 SERVINGS

- 2 tablespoons olive oil
- 2 large sweet onions, thinly sliced
- ¾ teaspoon salt, divided
- 1 teaspoon minced fresh rosemary or ¼ teaspoon dried rosemary, crushed
- 2 boneless skinless chicken breast halves (6 ounces each)
- 2 tablespoons lemon juice
- ¼ teaspoon pepper
- ¼ cup mayonnaise
- ⅓ cup finely chopped roasted sweet red peppers
- 8 slices sourdough bread
- 12 slices Swiss cheese
- 2 tablespoons butter, softened

1. In a large skillet, heat oil over medium heat. Add the sweet onions and ¼ teaspoon salt; cook and stir 6-8 minutes or until softened. Reduce the heat to medium-low; cook for 30-40 minutes or until deep golden brown, stirring occasionally. Stir in the rosemary.

2. Meanwhile, pound chicken with a meat mallet to ½-in. thickness. Drizzle with lemon juice; sprinkle with pepper and remaining salt. Grill, covered, over medium heat or broil 4 in. from heat 5-7 minutes on each side or until no longer pink. Cut into strips.

3. In a small bowl, mix mayonnaise and red peppers. Spread half of the mayonnaise mixture over four slices of bread. Layer with one slice of Swiss cheese, chicken, onions and two slices of Swiss cheese. Spread the remaining mayonnaise mixture over remaining bread; place over top. Spread outsides of sandwiches with butter.

4. Grill sandwiches, covered, over medium heat or broil 4 in. from heat 2-3 minutes on each side or until golden brown and cheese is melted.

FAST FIX

Tuscan Cauliflower Soup

A traditional Tuscan soup has lots of potatoes, but I make mine the low-carb way by using cauliflower instead. I think it has an even heartier flavor.

—HEATHER BEWLEY BEMIDJI, MN

START TO FINISH: 30 MIN.
MAKES: 8 SERVINGS (2½ QUARTS)

- 4 cups fresh cauliflowerets (about 14 ounces)
- 2 cans (14½ ounces each) reduced-sodium chicken broth
- 2 cups water
- 2 garlic cloves, minced
- 1 pound bulk Italian sausage
- 1 cup sliced fresh mushrooms
- 1 cup heavy whipping cream
- ¼ teaspoon pepper
- ½ pound bacon strips, cooked and crumbled

1. In a large saucepan, combine the cauliflower, broth, water and garlic; bring to a boil. Simmer, uncovered, 12-15 minutes or until the cauliflower is tender.

2. Meanwhile, in a large skillet, cook sausage and mushrooms over medium heat 6-8 minutes or until sausage is no longer pink, breaking up sausage into crumbles. Remove with a slotted spoon; drain on paper towels.

3. Add sausage and mushrooms to cauliflower mixture; return to a boil. Reduce the heat; simmer, uncovered, 5 minutes. Stir in cream and pepper; heat through. Serve with bacon.

TUSCAN CAULIFLOWER SOUP

REUBEN CALZONES

Chili Rellenos Sandwiches

Since my earliest days of cooking, I've tried and experimented with many new recipes. But one thing hasn't changed—I still love to prepare these zippy grilled sandwiches stuffed with green chilies and Monterey Jack cheese. They're simple, quick and satisfying every time.
—**GLADYS HILL** QULIN, MO

START TO FINISH: 25 MIN.
MAKES: 3 SERVINGS

- 1 **can (4 ounces) chopped green chilies, drained**
- 6 **slices white bread**
- 3 **slices Monterey Jack cheese**
- 2 **large eggs**
- 1 **cup 2% milk**
- 3 **tablespoons butter**
  Salsa, optional

1. Mash the chopped green chilies with a fork; spread over three slices of bread. Top with the Monterey Jack cheese and remaining bread. In a shallow bowl, whisk eggs and milk until blended.
2. In a large skillet, heat 1 tablespoon butter over medium heat. Dip both sides of sandwich in the egg mixture. Place in the skillet; toast 2-3 minutes on each side or until golden brown and the cheese is melted.
3. Repeat with the remaining butter and sandwiches. If desired, serve sandwiches with salsa.

⑤ INGREDIENTS FAST FIX ▶
Reuben Calzones

I'm a fan of classic Reubens. On a whim, I decided to put the ingredients in a pizza pocket instead of on rye bread. My family gave the calzones a thumbs-up.
—**NICKIE FRYE** EVANSVILLE, IN

START TO FINISH: 30 MIN.
MAKES: 4 SERVINGS

- 1 **tube (13.8 ounces) refrigerated pizza crust**
- 4 **slices Swiss cheese**
- 1 **cup sauerkraut, rinsed and well drained**
- ½ **pound sliced cooked corned beef**
  Thousand Island salad dressing

1. Preheat oven to 400°. On a lightly floured surface, unroll the pizza crust dough and pat into a 12-in. square. Cut into four squares.
2. Layer a fourth of the Swiss cheese, sauerkraut and corned beef diagonally over half of each square to within ½ in. of the edges. Fold one corner of the square over the filling to the opposite corner, forming a triangle; press edges with a fork to seal. Place on greased baking sheets.
3. Bake 15-18 minutes or until golden brown. Serve calzones with Thousand Island salad dressing.

Tomato-Basil Grilled Cheese

Just you for lunch? Indulge in a dressed-up favorite that's great anytime. Layer a slice of sourdough bread with 2 ounces sliced fresh mozzarella cheese, 1 tablespoon minced fresh basil and two tomato slices. Sprinkle on salt and pepper to taste and top the sandwich with another slice of bread. Spread the outside with 1½ teaspoons softened butter. Cook the sandwich in a preheated panini maker or indoor electric grill until the bread is browned and the cheese is melted. *Makes 1 serving.*
—**KATHRYN HUDSON** BETHEL PARK, PA

Asian Turkey Burger with Apple Slaw

When I wanted to make turkey burgers a little more exciting, I thought of adding hoisin sauce, gingerroot and garlic. Now we eat them about once a week.
—**ASHLEY GAYLE** ELLICOTT CITY, MD

START TO FINISH: 30 MIN.
MAKES: 4 SERVINGS

- 3 green onions, finely chopped
- 2 tablespoons hoisin sauce
- 1 tablespoon minced fresh gingerroot
- 2 garlic cloves, minced
- ½ teaspoon salt
- ¼ teaspoon pepper
- 1¼ pounds ground turkey
- 1 tablespoon olive oil

SLAW
- 3 tablespoons olive oil
- 1 tablespoon cider vinegar
- 1 teaspoon Dijon mustard
- ¼ teaspoon salt
- ⅛ teaspoon pepper
- 2 medium apples, julienned
- 2 green onions, finely chopped

ASSEMBLY
- 4 hamburger buns, split and toasted
- 2 tablespoons hoisin sauce

1. In a large bowl, mix green onions, hoisin sauce, ginger, garlic, salt and pepper. Add the ground turkey; mix lightly but thoroughly. Shape into four ¾-in.-thick patties.
2. In a large nonstick skillet, heat the oil over medium heat. Cook burgers 7-9 minutes on each side or until a thermometer reads 165°.
3. Meanwhile, for the slaw, in a large bowl, whisk the olive oil, cider vinegar, mustard, salt and pepper. Add apples and green onions; toss to coat.
4. To assemble, spread the bottoms of buns with hoisin sauce. Top with the burgers; replace tops of buns. Serve with apple slaw.

FREEZE OPTION *Place patties on a plastic wrap-lined baking sheet; wrap and freeze until firm. Remove from pan and transfer to a resealable plastic freezer bag; return to freezer. To use, cook the frozen patties as directed, increasing time as necessary for a thermometer to read 165°.*

I came up with Tortillini Primavera Soup by tweaking an idea I found in a magazine years ago. Even two of the biggest meat lovers I know, my husband and son, will happily dig into a big bowlful. If I'm really pressed for time, I just skip adding the fresh basil.
—**KARI GEORGE** ELLICOTT CITY, MD

Tortellini Primavera Soup

START TO FINISH: 25 MIN.
MAKES: 4 SERVINGS

- 2 cartons (32 ounces each) chicken broth
- 1 package (10 ounces) julienned carrots
- 1 package (9 ounces) refrigerated cheese tortellini
- 1 cup frozen peas (about 4 ounces)
- ¼ teaspoon pepper
  Thinly sliced fresh basil leaves

In a large saucepan, bring the broth to a boil. Add carrots, tortellini, peas and pepper; return to a boil. Cook, uncovered, 7-9 minutes or until pasta is tender. Top servings with basil.

FREEZE OPTION *Freeze cooled soup in freezer containers. To use, partially thaw in the refrigerator overnight. Heat through in a saucepan, stirring occasionally.*

TORTELLINI
PRIMAVERA SOUP

SOUTHWEST TURKEY
LETTUCE WRAPS

One-Pot Spinach Beef Soup

Here's my idea of a winning weeknight meal. I cook the ground beef in a stockpot, then toss in everything else. A little grated Parmesan adds a nice garnish.

—JULIE DAVIS JACKSONVILLE, FL

START TO FINISH: 30 MIN.
MAKES: 8 SERVINGS

- 1 pound ground beef
- 3 garlic cloves, minced
- 2 cartons (32 ounces each) reduced-sodium beef broth
- 2 cans (14½ ounces each) diced tomatoes with green pepper, celery and onion, undrained
- 1 teaspoon dried basil
- ½ teaspoon pepper
- ½ teaspoon dried oregano
- ¼ teaspoon salt
- 3 cups uncooked bow tie pasta
- 4 cups fresh spinach, coarsely chopped
  Grated Parmesan cheese

1. In a 6-qt. stockpot, cook beef and garlic over medium heat 6-8 minutes or until beef is no longer pink, breaking up beef into crumbles; drain. Stir in broth, tomatoes and seasonings; bring to a boil. Stir in pasta; return to a boil. Cook, uncovered, 7-9 minutes or until pasta is tender.

2. Stir in the spinach until wilted. Sprinkle servings with cheese.

ONE-POT SPINACH BEEF SOUP

EAT SMART **FREEZE IT** **FAST FIX**

Southwest Turkey Lettuce Wraps

Bored with the same old taco routine? Give these south-of-the-border lettuce wraps a try. I tweaked a friend's recipe to suit my family's tastes, and we've been enjoying it regularly ever since.

—ALLY BILLHORN WILTON, IA

START TO FINISH: 25 MIN.
MAKES: 6 SERVINGS

- 2 pounds extra-lean ground turkey
- 1 small onion, finely chopped
- 1 can (15 ounces) tomato sauce
- 2 tablespoons chili powder
- ½ teaspoon salt
- ¾ teaspoon ground cumin
- ½ teaspoon pepper
- 18 Bibb or iceberg lettuce leaves
- ¾ cup shredded cheddar cheese
  Optional toppings: sour cream, salsa and guacamole

1. In a large skillet, cook the turkey and onion over medium-high heat 8-10 minutes or until the turkey is no longer pink and the onion is tender, breaking up turkey into crumbles.

2. Stir in the tomato sauce and seasonings. Bring to a boil. Reduce heat; simmer, covered, 10-12 minutes to allow the flavors to blend. Serve in lettuce leaves with cheese and toppings as desired.

FREEZE OPTION *Freeze the cooled meat mixture in freezer containers. To use, partially thaw in refrigerator overnight. Heat through in a saucepan, stirring occasionally and adding a little water if necessary.*

PER SERVING *3 filled lettuce wraps (calculated without optional toppings) equals 251 cal., 7 g fat (3 g sat. fat), 75 mg chol., 806 mg sodium, 7 g carb., 2 g fiber, 43 g pro.* **Diabetic Exchanges:** *5 lean meat, 1 vegetable.*

FAST FIX ▶

Grilled Pesto Ham and Provolone Sandwiches

Why settle for an ordinary grilled cheese? Pesto, fresh basil and pickled peppers add zesty flavor. We serve the sandwiches with minestrone or a crisp salad.

—**PRISCILLA YEE** CONCORD, CA

START TO FINISH: 20 MIN.
MAKES: 4 SERVINGS

- 2 tablespoons mayonnaise
- 4 teaspoons prepared pesto
- 8 slices sourdough bread
- 8 ounces thinly sliced deli ham
- ½ cup loosely packed basil leaves
- 4 pickled sweet cherry peppers, chopped
- 1 plum tomato, thinly sliced
- ¾ cup shredded provolone cheese
- 2 tablespoons butter, softened

1. In a small bowl, mix mayonnaise and pesto; spread over four slices of bread. Layer with the deli ham, basil, peppers, plum tomato and provolone cheese. Top with the remaining bread. Spread the outsides of sandwiches with butter.
2. On a griddle, toast the sandwiches over medium heat 2-3 minutes on each side or until golden brown and the cheese is melted.

EAT SMART   FREEZE IT   FAST FIX ▶

Family-Pleasing Sloppy Joes

My grandmother shared this recipe with me long ago. Through the years, I've made a few changes here and there to give the saucy filling even more pizzazz.

—**JILL ZOSEL** SEATTLE, WA

START TO FINISH: 30 MIN.
MAKES: 6 SERVINGS

- 1 pound lean ground turkey
- 1 small onion, chopped
- 2 garlic cloves, minced
- 1 tablespoon sugar
- 1 tablespoon all-purpose flour
- ¼ teaspoon pepper
- 1 cup ketchup
- 1 tablespoon Worcestershire sauce
- 1 tablespoon prepared mustard
- 1 tablespoon barbecue sauce
- 6 hamburger buns, split

1. In a large skillet, cook the ground turkey and onion over medium heat 6-8 minutes or until the turkey is no longer pink, breaking up turkey into crumbles; drain if necessary. Add the garlic; cook 1 minute longer. Stir in the sugar, flour and pepper until blended.
2. Stir in ketchup, Worcestershire sauce, mustard and barbecue sauce. Bring to a boil. Reduce heat; simmer, covered, 10 minutes to allow flavors to blend. Spoon meat mixture onto bun bottoms; replace tops.
FREEZE OPTION *Freeze the cooled meat mixture in freezer containers. To use, partially thaw in refrigerator*

FAMILY-PLEASING SLOPPY JOES

overnight. Heat through in a saucepan, stirring occasionally and adding a little water if necessary.
PER SERVING *1 sandwich equals 297 cal., 8 g fat (2 g sat. fat), 52 mg chol., 846 mg sodium, 38 g carb., 1 g fiber, 19 g pro.* ***Diabetic Exchanges:*** *2½ starch, 2 lean meat.*

FAST FIX ▶

Chicken, Asparagus & Corn Chowder

Creamy homemade chowder tastes like a special treat. Keep this one in mind when you have leftover or rotisserie chicken.

—**JENNIFER VO** IRVINE, CA

START TO FINISH: 30 MIN.
MAKES: 4 SERVINGS

- 2 tablespoons olive oil
- ¾ cup cut fresh asparagus (1-inch pieces)
- 1 small onion, finely chopped
- 2 tablespoons all-purpose flour
- ½ teaspoon salt
- ¼ teaspoon garlic powder
- ⅛ to ¼ teaspoon pepper
- 1 can (14½ ounces) chicken broth
- ½ cup fat-free half-and-half
- 1½ cups cubed cooked chicken breast
- ¾ cup frozen corn

1. In a large saucepan, heat the olive oil over medium heat. Add asparagus and onion; cook and stir 3-4 minutes or until tender.
2. Stir in flour, salt, garlic powder and pepper until blended; gradually stir in the chicken broth and half-and-half. Bring to a boil, stirring constantly; cook and stir 3-5 minutes or until slightly thickened. Add the chicken and corn; heat through.

Tangy Beef Chili

Like chili but don't want a long simmering time? Here's a speedy but delicious choice. Just cook 1 pound 90% lean ground beef with 1 chopped green pepper and onion, breaking beef into crumbles; drain. Stir in 29 ounces undrained no-salt-added diced tomatoes, 15 ounces Ranch Style beans, 4 teaspoons chili powder, 1¼ teaspoon ground cumin and ½ teaspoon pepper. Simmer for 15 minutes. Top each bowl with a wedge of The Laughing Cow light blue cheese. *Makes 6 servings.*

—**LUANN MANER** TAYLOR, AZ

**Cindy Worth's
Sun-Dried Tomato & Chicken
Spinach Salad** *PAGE 61*

30-Minute Menus

Dinnertime has never been easier! Every main dish in this chapter includes a complementary side, beverage or dessert. What's more, you can fix each meal from start to finish in 30 minutes—or less!

**Melissa Halonen's
Thai Chicken Tacos**
PAGE 59

**Lorraine Caland's
Maple-Thyme Chicken Thighs**
PAGE 68

**Jean Komlos'
Fire-Roasted Ziti
with Sausage** *PAGE 66*

TURKEY SCALLOPINI
WITH MARSALA SAUCE

(5) INGREDIENTS FAST FIX

Apple, White Cheddar & Arugula Tarts

These tarts remind me of fall in Michigan, where I grew up. Enjoy them as a meatless meal or add meat for heartier fare.
—**MARIA DAVIS** HERMOSA BEACH, CA

START TO FINISH: 30 MIN.
MAKES: 4 SERVINGS

- 1 sheet frozen puff pastry, thawed
- 1 cup (4 ounces) shredded white cheddar cheese
- 2 medium apples, thinly sliced
- 2 tablespoons olive oil
- 1 tablespoon lemon juice
- 3 cups fresh arugula or baby spinach

1. Preheat oven to 400°. On a lightly floured surface, unfold the puff pastry; roll into a 12-in. square. Cut pastry into four squares; place on a parchment paper-lined baking sheet.
2. Sprinkle half of each square with cheese to within ¼ in. of edges; top with apples. Fold pastry over filling. Press edges with a fork to seal. Bake 16-18 minutes or until golden brown.
3. In a bowl, whisk oil and lemon juice until blended; add arugula and toss to coat. Serve with tarts.

(5) INGREDIENTS FAST FIX

Turkey Scallopini with Marsala Sauce

My family requests scallopini for dinner at least once a month, and I'm happy to oblige. The slightly sweet Marsala wine sauce really brings together the turkey slices and linguine. I sprinkle on a little shredded Parmesan cheese at the end for the finishing touch.
—**BRIANA KNIGHT** FERNDALE, WA

START TO FINISH: 30 MIN.
MAKES: 4 SERVINGS

- ½ cup all-purpose flour
- ½ teaspoon salt
- ½ teaspoon pepper
- 1 package (17.6 ounces) turkey breast cutlets
- 2 tablespoons olive oil
- 1½ cups Marsala wine
- 3 tablespoons butter
- 3 tablespoons shredded Parmesan cheese
  Hot cooked linguine, optional

1. In a large resealable plastic bag, mix flour, salt and pepper. Add cutlets, one at a time; close bag and shake to coat.
2. In a large skillet; heat the oil over medium heat. Add the turkey cutlets; cook 3-4 minutes on each side or until the meat is no longer pink.
3. Remove the turkey from the pan. Stir in Marsala wine. Bring to a boil; cook 8-10 minutes or until liquid is reduced to about ½ cup. Stir in butter until melted. Return turkey to pan; heat through. Serve with cheese and, if desired, linguine.

ON THE SIDE
Fresh Mozzarella Tomato Salad

Slice 2 medium tomatoes and 6 ounces fresh mozzarella cheese; arrange on a serving platter. Drizzle with 3 tablespoons olive oil; sprinkle with 4 teaspoons minced fresh basil, and salt and pepper to taste. *Makes 4 servings.*
—**REGINA WOOD** MACKENZIE, BC

ON THE SIDE
Grilled Pear Sundaes

Peel, halve and core 4 pears; cut each into 6 wedges. Sprinkle with 1 tablespoon sugar, ¼ teaspoon cinnamon and a dash of pepper. Grill, covered, on a greased grill rack over indirect medium heat 2-3 minutes on each side or until tender. Serve with vanilla ice cream and honey. *Makes 4 servings.*
—**TASTE OF HOME** TEST KITCHEN

APPLE, WHITE CHEDDAR & ARUGULA TARTS

TOMATO STEAK SANDWICHES

My Thai Chicken Tacos were inspired by a Vietnamese banh mi sandwich. If you have the opportunity, let the carrot and cucumber strips marinate in some rice vinegar before you serve up supper.

—MELISSA HALONEN SPOKANE, WA

(5) INGREDIENTS FAST FIX

Tomato Steak Sandwiches

One evening when we didn't have much in the refrigerator, my husband and I used what we had on hand and came up with open-faced steak sandwiches. They were a hit! We've put them on our menus many times since—and have even doubled the recipe when company dropped by.

—TESSA EDWARDS PROVO, UT

START TO FINISH: 15 MIN.
MAKES: 6 SERVINGS

- 2 teaspoons canola oil
- 1 beef top sirloin steak (1 pound), cut into thin strips
- ⅛ teaspoon salt
  Dash pepper
- 3 plain bagels, split
- ⅓ cup cream cheese, softened
- 6 thick slices tomato
- 6 slices part-skim mozzarella cheese

1. Preheat broiler. In a large skillet, heat the oil over medium heat. Add the steak strips; cook and stir 3-5 minutes or until browned; drain. Stir in the salt and pepper.
2. Spread the cut sides of bagels with cream cheese. Transfer bagels to an ungreased baking sheet; spoon the beef over bagels. Top with tomato and mozzarella cheese. Broil 4-6 in. from the heat 3-5 minutes or until cheese is melted and lightly browned.

ON THE SIDE
Watermelon Grape Salad

Mix 3 cups cubed, seeded watermelon and 3 cups seedless red grapes. Whisk ⅓ cup white grape juice, 1½ teaspoons finely chopped fresh tarragon and 1½ teaspoons honey. Pour over fruit and toss to coat. Serve immediately. *Makes 6 servings.*

—SUE GRONHOLZ BEAVER DAM, WI

FAST FIX
Thai Chicken Tacos

START TO FINISH: 25 MIN.
MAKES: 6 SERVINGS

- 12 taco shells
- 1 rotisserie chicken, skin removed, shredded
- 1 bottle (11½ ounces) Thai peanut sauce, divided
- 1 medium cucumber, julienned
- 1 medium carrot, julienned
- ⅓ cup minced fresh cilantro

1. Heat the taco shells according to package directions. Meanwhile, in a large skillet, combine the chicken and ½ cup peanut sauce; heat through.
2. In a small bowl, mix the cucumber, carrot and cilantro. Serve the chicken in taco shells with cucumber mixture and remaining peanut sauce.

ON THE SIDE
Sesame Slaw

In a large bowl, combine 4 cups coleslaw mix, ½ cup chopped green pepper and 2 tablespoons chopped onion. Whisk ⅓ cup cider vinegar, ¼ cup sugar, 2 tablespoons toasted sesame seeds and ¼ teaspoon salt. Pour over cabbage mixture; toss to coat. Cover; refrigerate until serving. *Makes 4 servings.*

—JESSIE LEE STROBBE SMITHS CREEK, MI

(5) INGREDIENTS | FAST FIX ▶

Pierogi Quesadillas

When I had hungry children in the house but only leftovers in the fridge, I invented Pierogi Quesadillas. Now I always make them to use up extra potatoes and meat.

—ANDREA DIBBLE SOLON, IA

START TO FINISH: 15 MIN.
MAKES: 4 SERVINGS

- 1 package (24 ounces) refrigerated sour cream and chive mashed potatoes
  Butter-flavored cooking spray
- 8 flour tortillas (8 inches)
- 1 cup chopped fully cooked ham
- ½ cup shredded cheddar cheese

1. Heat mashed potatoes according to package directions.
2. Spritz cooking spray over one side of each tortilla. Place half of tortillas on a griddle, greased side down. Spread with mashed potatoes; top with the ham, cheese and remaining tortillas, greased side up. Cook over medium heat 2-3 minutes on each side or until golden brown and cheese is melted.

ON THE SIDE
Sweet Pepper Skillet

Thinly slice 2 medium green peppers, 1 medium sweet yellow pepper, 1 medium sweet red pepper and 1 medium onion. Saute peppers and onion in 2 teaspoons olive oil for 5-7 minutes or until peppers are crisp-tender. Stir in 1 minced garlic clove, ¼ teaspoon salt and ¼ teaspoon pepper; cook and stir 1-2 minutes longer. *Makes 4 servings.*

—SUNDRA HAUCK BOGALUSA, LA

PIEROGI QUESADILLAS

PEACHY PORK WITH RICE

EAT SMART FAST FIX ▶
Peachy Pork with Rice

Peach preserves sweeten the spicy salsa in this entree. Adjust the heat level to taste by using mild or hot salsa and seasoning.

—MELISSA MOLAISON HAWKINSVILLE, GA

START TO FINISH: 30 MIN.
MAKES: 4 SERVINGS

- 1½ cups uncooked instant brown rice
- 1 pork tenderloin (1 pound), cut into 1-inch cubes
- 2 tablespoons olive oil
- 2 tablespoons reduced-sodium taco seasoning
- 1 cup salsa
- 3 tablespoons peach preserves

1. Cook the rice according to package directions. Meanwhile, place pork in a large bowl; drizzle with oil. Sprinkle with taco seasoning; toss to coat.
2. Place a large nonstick skillet coated with cooking spray over medium heat. Add pork; cook and stir 8-10 minutes or until no longer pink. Stir in salsa and preserves; heat through. Serve with rice.

PER SERVING *1 cup pork mixture with ½ cup rice equals 387 cal., 12 g fat (2 g sat. fat), 63 mg chol., 540 mg sodium, 42 g carb., 2 g fiber, 25 g pro.* ***Diabetic Exchanges:*** *3 lean meat, 2½ starch, 1½ fat.*

ON THE SIDE
Seasoned Green Beans

Place 3½ cups trimmed fresh green beans in a steamer basket; place in a saucepan over 1 in. of water. Bring to a boil; cover and steam for 7-8 minutes or until beans are crisp-tender. Combine 2 tablespoons melted butter, ½ teaspoon seasoned salt, ¼ teaspoon chili powder, ⅛ teaspoon garlic powder and ⅛ teaspoon onion powder. Drain beans; add butter mixture and toss to coat. *Makes 4 servings.*

—KATHERINE FIRTH ORO BALLAY, AZ

FAST FIX ▶
Pizza in a Bowl

On hectic days, it's reassuring to know that my family can sit down for dinner only minutes after we walk in the door. This recipe makes it possible! Prepare a double batch to wow the crowd at your next potluck or other event.

—**VIRGINIA KRITES** CRIDERSVILLE, OH

START TO FINISH: 25 MIN.
MAKES: 6 SERVINGS

- 8 **ounces uncooked rigatoni (about 3 cups)**
- ¾ **pound ground beef**
- ½ **cup chopped onion**
- 1 **can (15 ounces) pizza sauce**
- ⅔ **cup condensed cream of mushroom soup, undiluted**
- 2 **cups (8 ounces) shredded part-skim mozzarella cheese**
- 1 **package (3½ ounces) sliced pepperoni**

1. Cook rigatoni according to package directions; drain. Meanwhile, in a large skillet, cook the beef and onion over medium heat 6-8 minutes or until beef is no longer pink, breaking up beef into crumbles; drain. Add pizza sauce, soup and cheese; cook and stir over low heat until cheese is melted.

2. Stir the rigatoni and pepperoni into beef mixture. Heat through.

ON THE SIDE
Italian Torte

Combine 1 cup ricotta cheese, ¼ cup miniature semisweet chocolate chips and 3 tablespoons sugar. Split 1 loaf (10¾ ounces) frozen pound cake (thawed) into three horizontal layers. Place bottom layer on a serving plate; top with half of the cheese mixture. Repeat layers. Top with remaining cake. *Makes 6 servings.*

—**THERESA STEWART** NEW OXFORD, PA

MUSHROOM PASTRAMI HOAGIES

Mushroom Pastrami Hoagies

My husband is a firefighter, so I make easy meals like this that I can deliver to him.

—DEANNA EADS KINGMAN, AZ

START TO FINISH: 25 MIN.
MAKES: 6 SERVINGS

3	tablespoons butter
1	pound sliced fresh mushrooms
1	large onion, halved and sliced
2	medium sweet red peppers, julienned
2	garlic cloves, minced
¼	teaspoon salt
¼	teaspoon pepper
6	hoagie buns, split
1½	pounds sliced deli pastrami
12	slices provolone cheese

1. Preheat broiler. In a 6-qt. stockpot, heat the butter over medium heat. Add the mushrooms, onion and red peppers; cook and stir 5-7 minutes or until tender. Add garlic; cook 1 minute longer. Drain vegetable mixture; stir in salt and pepper.
2. Arrange the hoagie buns on a baking sheet. Layer the bottoms of hoagie buns with the deli pastrami and vegetable mixture; top with the provolone cheese. Broil 4-5 in. from heat 1-2 minutes or until the provolone cheese is melted and the tops of buns are toasted.

ON THE SIDE
Pretzel Mustard Dip

Combine ¼ cup mayonnaise, ¼ cup yellow or Dijon mustard, 2 tablespoons finely chopped onion, 2 tablespoons ranch salad dressing mix and 2¼ teaspoons prepared horseradish. Cover; refrigerate for at least 30 minutes. Serve with pretzels or fresh vegetables. *Makes about ½ cup.*

—BONNIE CAPPER-ECKSTEIN

MAPLE GROVE, MN

Applesauce-Glazed Pork Chops

I glaze my baked pork chops with a sweet, smoky, apple-flavored sauce. They're on the table in just half an hour—perfect for time-crunched weeknights.

—BRENDA CAMPBELL OLYMPIA, WA

START TO FINISH: 30 MIN.
MAKES: 4 SERVINGS

4	bone-in pork loin chops (½ inch thick and 7 ounces each)
1	cup unsweetened applesauce
¼	cup packed brown sugar
1	tablespoon barbecue sauce
1	tablespoon Worcestershire sauce
1	garlic clove, minced
½	teaspoon salt
½	teaspoon pepper

1. Preheat oven to 350°. Place the pork chops in a 13x9-in. baking dish coated with cooking spray. In a small bowl, mix the remaining ingredients; spoon over chops.
2. Bake, uncovered, 20-25 minutes or until a thermometer reads 145°. Let stand 5 minutes before serving.
PER SERVING *1 pork chop with ⅓ cup sauce equals 291 cal., 9 g fat (3 g sat. fat), 86 mg chol., 442 mg sodium, 22 g carb., 1 g fiber, 30 g pro.* **Diabetic Exchanges:** *4 lean meat, 1 starch, ½ fruit.*

ON THE SIDE
Pronto Potato Pancakes

Place 2 eggs and 1 halved small onion in a blender; process until blended. Add 2 cubed, peeled medium potatoes; process until finely chopped. Transfer to a bowl. Add 2-4 tablespoons all-purpose flour, ½ teaspoon salt and ⅛ teaspoon cayenne. Heat 2 tablespoons canola oil in a large nonstick skillet over medium heat. Drop batter by ¼ cupfuls into oil. Fry in batches until golden brown on both sides, using additional oil as needed. Drain on paper towels. *Makes 4 servings.*

—DARLENE BRENDEN SALEM, OR

MEDITERRANEAN TILAPIA

Mediterranean Tilapia tops mild-flavored fish fillets with tomatoes, artichokes, ripe olives and feta cheese. For variety, try the variations at the end of the recipe.
—**ROBIN BRENNEMAN** HILLIARD, OH

EAT SMART ⑤INGREDIENTS FAST FIX

Mediterranean Tilapia

START TO FINISH: 20 MIN.
MAKES: 6 SERVINGS

- 6 **tilapia fillets (6 ounces each)**
- 1 **cup canned Italian diced tomatoes**
- ½ **cup water-packed artichoke hearts, chopped**
- ½ **cup sliced ripe olives**
- ½ **cup crumbled feta cheese**

Preheat oven to 400°. Place tilapia fillets in a 15x10x1-in. baking pan coated with cooking spray. Top with the tomatoes, artichoke hearts, ripe olives and cheese. Bake, uncovered, 15-20 minutes or until the fish flakes easily with a fork.
PER SERVING *1 fillet equals 197 cal., 4 g fat (2 g sat. fat), 88 mg chol., 446 mg sodium, 5 g carb., 1 g fiber, 34 g pro. Diabetic Exchanges: 5 lean meat, ½ fat.*
ITALIAN TILAPIA *Follow method as directed but top the fillets with 1 cup diced tomatoes with roasted garlic, ½ cup each julienned roasted sweet red pepper, sliced fresh mushrooms and diced fresh mozzarella cheese, and ½ teaspoon dried basil.*
SOUTHWEST TILAPIA *Follow method as directed but top the fillets with 1 cup diced tomatoes with mild green chilies, ½ cup each cubed avocado, frozen corn (thawed) and cubed cheddar cheese, and ½ teaspoon dried cilantro.*

ON THE SIDE
Lemony Couscous with Toasted Nuts

In a large saucepan, combine 1¾ cup chicken stock, 3 tablespoons lemon juice, 2 tablespoons butter, ¼ teaspoon salt and ⅛ teaspoon pepper; bring to a boil. Stir in 1 package (10 ounces) couscous. Remove from heat; let stand, covered, 5-10 minutes or until liquid is absorbed. Stir in ¼ cup toasted pine nuts and ¼ cup toasted sliced almonds. *Makes 6 servings.*
—**MARIE MCCONNELL** SHELBYVILLE, IL

FAST FIX ▶
Ham with Pineapple Salsa

A dear friend shared this with me when she moved from Hawaii to Colorado.
—**DAWN WILSON** BUENA VISTA, CO

START TO FINISH: 25 MIN.
MAKES: 4 SERVINGS

- 1 **can (8 ounces) crushed pineapple, drained**
- 2 **tablespoons orange marmalade**
- 1 **tablespoon minced fresh cilantro**
- 2 **teaspoons finely chopped seeded jalapeno pepper**
- 2 **teaspoons lime juice**
- ¼ **teaspoon salt**
- 1 **bone-in fully cooked ham steak (1½ pounds)**

1. Preheat broiler. In a small bowl, mix the first six ingredients.
2. Place ham on an ungreased baking sheet. Broil 3 in. from heat 3-4 minutes on each side or until a thermometer reads 140°. Cut ham into serving-size pieces. Serve with pineapple salsa.
NOTE *Wear disposable gloves when cutting hot peppers; the oils can burn skin. Avoid touching your face.*

ON THE SIDE
Cardamom Carrots

In a saucepan, bring 1 in. of water, 1 pound julienned carrots and ½ teaspoon salt to a boil; reduce the heat. Cover and simmer 6-8 minutes or until crisp-tender; drain. In a large skillet, combine 2 tablespoons butter, 2 tablespoons brown sugar, ½ teaspoon ground cardamom and ½ teaspoon grated orange peel. Cook and stir over medium heat for 1-2 minutes or until thickened. Add the carrots; toss to coat. *Makes 4 servings.*
—**JOAN HALLFORD** NORTH RICHLAND HILLS, TX

HAM WITH PINEAPPLE SALSA

FAST FIX ▶

Fire-Roasted Ziti with Sausage

Want a break from the mealtime routine? Slices of smoked sausage and fire-roasted spaghetti sauce bring zesty flavor to this pasta dish. With a simple green salad on the side, you'll have an Italian feast.

—**JEAN KOMLOS** PLYMOUTH, MI

START TO FINISH: 30 MIN.
MAKES: 8 SERVINGS

- 8 **ounces uncooked ziti or rigatoni (about 3 cups)**
- 1 **can (28 ounces) Italian diced tomatoes, drained**
- 1 **jar (24 ounces) fire-roasted tomato and garlic pasta sauce**
- 1 **package (16 ounces) smoked sausage, sliced**
- 2 **cups (8 ounces) shredded part-skim mozzarella cheese, divided**
- 1 **cup (8 ounces) 4% cottage cheese**

1. In a Dutch oven, cook ziti according to package directions for al dente. Drain; return to pot.
2. Add the tomatoes, pasta sauce and sausage to the ziti; heat through over medium heat, stirring occasionally. Stir in 1 cup mozzarella cheese and cottage cheese. Sprinkle with the remaining mozzarella. Cook, covered, 2-5 minutes or until cheese is melted.

ON THE SIDE
Salad with Basil Vinaigrette

In a small bowl, whisk ⅓ cup white wine vinegar, 3 tablespoons minced fresh basil, 3 tablespoons olive oil, 1 tablespoon honey, ½ teaspoon salt and ¼ teaspoon pepper until blended. Combine 12 cups torn mixed salad greens and 2 cups halved cherry tomatoes. Drizzle with vinaigrette; toss to coat. Sprinkle with ¼ cup shredded Parmesan cheese. *Makes 8 servings.*

—**KRISTIN RIMKUS** SNOHOMISH, WA

FIRE-ROASTED ZITI WITH SAUSAGE

MUSHROOM PEAR MELTS

⑤INGREDIENTS FAST FIX ▶

Mushroom Pear Melts

I love the pairing of mushrooms and cheese. Put that combination on toast with fresh pear slices, then broil for a scrumptious open-faced sandwich.

—**MARLA HYATT** ST. PAUL, MN

START TO FINISH: 25 MIN.
MAKES: 4 SERVINGS

- 2 **tablespoons butter**
- 4 **cups sliced fresh shiitake or baby portobello mushrooms (about 10 ounces)**
- ½ **teaspoon salt**
- ¼ **teaspoon pepper**
- 8 **slices whole wheat bread, toasted**
- 2 **large ripe Bosc pears, thinly sliced**
- 8 **slices provolone cheese**

1. Preheat broiler. In a large skillet, heat the butter over medium-high heat. Add mushrooms; cook and stir 5-7 minutes or until tender. Stir in salt and pepper.
2. Place toasts on a rack of a broiler pan. Top with mushrooms; layer with pears and cheese. Broil 3-4 in. from heat 2-3 minutes or until the cheese is lightly browned.

ON THE SIDE
Oh-So-Easy Tomato Cream Soup

Place 2 cups 2% milk, 1 can (14½ ounces) undrained diced tomatoes, 1 package (8 ounces) softened cream cheese, ¼ cup coarsely chopped fresh basil, ½ teaspoon salt and ⅛ teaspoon pepper in a blender; cover and process until smooth. Transfer soup to a large saucepan; heat through. *Makes 4 servings.*

—**EILEEN KORECKO** HOT SPRINGS VILLAGE, AR

One of Mom's favorite recipes inspired Crispy Sage Chicken Tenders. Hers were smothered with gravy, but we like them coated with panko bread crumbs.
—**DEB PERRY** TRAVERSE CITY, MI

CRISPY SAGE
CHICKEN TENDERS

Turkey & Vegetable Barley Soup

With ingredients I had on hand, I stirred up this soup packed with turkey, barley and veggies. If you happen to have corn, beans or celery, toss those in, too!
—**LISA WIGER** ST. MICHAEL, MN

START TO FINISH: 30 MIN.
MAKES: 6 SERVINGS

- 1 **tablespoon canola oil**
- 5 **medium carrots, chopped**
- 1 **medium onion, chopped**
- ⅔ **cup quick-cooking barley**
- 6 **cups reduced-sodium chicken broth**
- 2 **cups cubed cooked turkey breast**
- 2 **cups fresh baby spinach**
- ½ **teaspoon pepper**

1. In a large saucepan, heat oil over medium-high heat. Add carrots and onion; cook and stir 4-5 minutes or until carrots are crisp-tender.
2. Stir in the barley and chicken broth; bring to a boil. Reduce heat; simmer, covered, 10-15 minutes or until the carrots and barley are tender. Stir in the turkey, baby spinach and pepper; heat through.
PER SERVING 1⅓ cups equals 208 cal., 4 g fat (1 g sat. fat), 37 mg chol., 662 mg sodium, 23 g carb., 6 g fiber, 21 g pro. **Diabetic Exchanges:** 2 lean meat, 1 starch, 1 vegetable, ½ fat.

ON THE SIDE
Spinach Flatbreads

In a small skillet, saute ⅔ cup sliced onion in 2 teaspoons olive oil until tender; set aside. Place 4 whole pita breads on an ungreased baking sheet; brush with 2 teaspoons olive oil. Layer with 2 cups fresh baby spinach, onion and 1½ cups shredded part-skim mozzarella cheese. Sprinkle with ¼ teaspoon pepper. Bake at 425° for 6-8 minutes or until the cheese is melted. Makes 4 servings.
—**KRISTEN WESTBROOK** PITTSBURGH, PA

Crispy Sage Chicken Tenders

START TO FINISH: 30 MIN.
MAKES: 4 SERVINGS

- ½ **cup buttermilk**
- ¾ **teaspoon salt**
- ¼ **teaspoon hot pepper sauce**
- ⅛ **teaspoon pepper**
- 1 **pound chicken tenderloins**
- 1 **cup panko (Japanese) bread crumbs**
- 2 **to 3 tablespoons fresh minced sage**
  Oil for frying
  Salt to taste
  Ranch salad dressing, optional

1. In a bowl, whisk the buttermilk, salt, hot pepper sauce and pepper until blended. Add the chicken tenderloins, turning to coat; let stand 15 minutes. In a shallow bowl, toss the panko bread crumbs with sage.

2. In a deep skillet, heat 1 in. of oil to 365°. Dip tenderloins in crumb mixture to coat both sides, patting to help the coating adhere. Fry chicken 2-3 minutes on each side or until deep golden brown. Drain on paper towels. Sprinkle with additional salt to taste. If desired, serve with ranch dressing.
PER SERVING 1 serving (calculated without dressing) equals 227 cal., 11 g fat (1 g sat. fat), 67 mg chol., 320 mg sodium, 6 g carb., trace fiber, 27 g pro.

ON THE SIDE
Oven Fries

Preheat oven to 400°. Cut 4 medium potatoes into 12 wedges each. Combine 1 tablespoon olive oil, 2½ teaspoons paprika, ¾ teaspoon salt and ¾ teaspoon garlic powder. Add potatoes; toss to coat. Transfer to a greased 15x10x1-in. baking pan. Bake 40-45 minutes or until tender, turning once. Makes 4 servings.
—**HEATHER BYERS** PITTSBURGH, PA

EAT SMART ⑤INGREDIENTS FAST FIX

Maple-Thyme Chicken Thighs

We eat a lot of chicken at our house. To keep things interesting, I try to figure out different ways to serve it—but that can be challenging. Luckily my family went crazy for the maple, mustard and thyme flavors in this grilled recipe. Now I share it at potlucks, too.

—**LORRAINE CALAND** SHUNIAH, ON

START TO FINISH: 15 MIN.
MAKES: 6 SERVINGS

- 2 tablespoons stone-ground mustard
- 2 tablespoons maple syrup
- 1 teaspoon minced fresh thyme or ½ teaspoon dried thyme
- ½ teaspoon salt
- ½ teaspoon pepper
- 6 boneless skinless chicken thighs (about 1½ pounds)

1. In a small bowl, mix the first five ingredients. Moisten a paper towel with cooking oil; using long-handled tongs, rub on the grill rack to coat lightly.

2. Grill the chicken, covered, over medium heat 4-5 minutes on each side or until a thermometer reads 170°. Brush frequently with the mustard mixture during the last 4 minutes of cooking.

PER SERVING *1 chicken thigh equals 188 cal., 9 g fat (2 g sat. fat), 76 mg chol., 363 mg sodium, 5 g carb., trace fiber, 21 g pro.* **Diabetic Exchange:** *3 lean meat.*

ON THE SIDE
Ginger-Orange Squash

Puncture 1 butternut squash (about 3 pounds) several times with a fork; place on a microwave-safe plate. Microwave on high 5 minutes. Cut into quarters; remove seeds. Return the butternut squash to the plate; microwave, covered with waxed paper, 12-14 minutes or until soft, turning the pieces over halfway. Scoop out the squash into a bowl; stir in 3 tablespoons thawed orange juice concentrate, 3 tablespoons brown sugar, 4 teaspoons butter and ¼ teaspoon ground ginger. *Makes 6 servings.*

—**VONNA WENDT** EPHRATA, WA

BACON-TURKEY SUBS

FAST FIX

Bacon-Turkey Subs

On balmy fall days, this sweet and smoky sandwich is a real treat. In colder weather, we switch to pita bread and pull out our countertop grill to make melts.

—**RACHEL BINDULSKI** COROLLA, NC

START TO FINISH: 20 MIN.
MAKES: 8 SERVINGS

- ¼ cup mayonnaise
- 2 tablespoons minced fresh basil or 2 teaspoons dried basil
- 1 loaf (about 1 pound) French bread
- ¾ pound sliced deli smoked turkey
- 12 slices cheddar cheese
- 1 large apple, sliced
- 12 cooked bacon strips

1. In a small bowl, mix mayonnaise and basil. Cut the bread horizontally in half; spread the cut surfaces with the mayonnaise mixture.

2. Layer the bottom half of the bread with the deli turkey, cheese, apple and bacon; replace top of bread. Cut into eight slices.

ON THE SIDE
Caramel Fruit Dip

In a small bowl, beat 8 ounces softened cream cheese until smooth. Beat in ½ cup caramel ice cream topping, ¼ cup honey and ¼ teaspoon cinnamon. Serve with fresh fruit. Store in the refrigerator. *Makes 2 cups.*

—**POLLY LYNAM-BLOOM** MEQUON, WI

Sesame Cilantro Shrimp

When I don't feel like spending much time in the kitchen, I usually reach for shrimp because it cooks quickly. With just a few other ingredients—cilantro, salad dressing, lime juice and rice—I can have a hot meal on the table in 10 minutes.
—TAMI PENUNURI LEAGUE CITY, TX

START TO FINISH: 10 MIN.
MAKES: 4 SERVINGS

- 1 tablespoon plus ½ cup reduced-fat Asian toasted sesame salad dressing, divided
- 1 pound uncooked shrimp (31-40 per pound), peeled and deveined
  Lime wedges
- ¼ cup chopped fresh cilantro
- 3 cups cooked brown rice, optional

1. In a large nonstick skillet, heat 1 tablespoon sesame salad dressing over medium heat. Add the shrimp; cook and stir 1 minute.

2. Stir in remaining dressing; cook, uncovered, 1-2 minutes longer or until shrimp turn pink. To serve, squeeze lime juice over top; sprinkle with cilantro. If desired, serve with rice.
PER SERVING ½ cup shrimp mixture (calculated without rice) equals 153 cal., 4 g fat (trace sat. fat), 138 mg chol., 461 mg sodium, 9 g carb., trace fiber, 20 g pro. **Diabetic Exchanges:** 3 lean meat, ½ starch, ½ fat.

ON THE SIDE
Chocolate-Almond Banana Splits

In a microwave, melt 4 chopped milk chocolate candy bars (1.45 ounces each) with 6 tablespoons heavy whipping cream. Stir until blended; keep warm. Halve 4 medium bananas lengthwise; arrange in four dessert dishes. Add ½ cup chocolate ice cream to each; top with the warm chocolate sauce and toasted chopped almonds. Makes 4 servings.
—CANDACE MCMENAMIN LEXINGTON, SC

PITAWURST

Pitawurst

Every August, our town hosts a bratwurst festival. To celebrate, we fix these pockets stuffed with sausage and sauerkraut.
—BROOKE YOUNG BUCYRUS, OH

START TO FINISH: 30 MIN.
MAKES: 4 SERVINGS

- 1 package (19 ounces) uncooked bratwurst links, casings removed
- 1 medium onion, chopped
- 1 small green pepper, chopped
- 1 can (14 ounces) sauerkraut, rinsed and well drained
- ½ cup sour cream
- 2 tablespoons stone-ground mustard
- 8 pita pocket halves, warmed

1. In a large skillet, cook bratwurst, onion and pepper over medium heat 8-10 minutes or until bratwurst is no longer pink and vegetables are tender, breaking up bratwurst into crumbles; drain. Stir in sauerkraut; heat through.
2. For the sauce, in a small bowl, mix the sour cream and mustard. Fill the pita halves with bratwurst mixture; serve with sauce.

ON THE SIDE
Peanut Butter Shakes

In a blender, combine 1½ cups vanilla ice cream, 12 miniature peanut butter cups, ¼ cup 2% milk and 3 tablespoons creamy peanut butter; cover and process for 1-2 minutes or until blended. Pour into chilled glasses; serve shakes immediately. Makes 2 servings.
—JODY KEYSOR CADYVILLE, NY

SESAME CILANTRO SHRIMP

**Amy Tong's
Tropical Beef Wrap**
PAGE 84

Give Me 5 or Fewer

The family favorites in this chapter require just a handful of ingredients. (Recipes may also call for salt, pepper, canola or olive oil, or water.) So go ahead—enjoy something simple but sensational tonight!

Jana Rippee's Thai Shrimp Pasta PAGE 72

Evelyn Cleare's Skillet Chicken with Barbecue Onion PAGE 81

Rebecca Nisewonder's Jalapeno Popper Quesadillas PAGE 86

SMOKED PORK CHOPS
& PIEROGIES DINNER

Thai Shrimp Pasta

I came up with this dish for my son when he was home from the Navy. He's a huge fan of Thai food, and I wanted to serve something that was special but not too complicated or time-consuming to fix. This entree was perfect—and there wasn't a noodle left in the bowl!

—JANA RIPPEE CASA GRANDE, AZ

START TO FINISH: 30 MIN.
MAKES: 4 SERVINGS

- 8 **ounces thin flat rice noodles**
- 1 **tablespoon curry powder**
- 1 **pound uncooked shrimp (31-40 per pound), peeled and deveined**
- 1 **can (13.66 ounces) light coconut milk**
- ¼ **teaspoon salt**
- ¼ **teaspoon pepper**
- ½ **cup minced fresh cilantro**
  Lime wedges, optional

1. Soak the rice noodles according to the package directions. Meanwhile, in a large dry skillet over medium heat, toast the curry powder until aromatic, about 1-2 minutes. Stir in the shrimp, coconut milk, salt and pepper. Bring to a boil. Reduce the heat; simmer, uncovered, 5-6 minutes or until the shrimp turn pink.
2. Drain the rice noodles. Add the rice noodles and minced cilantro to the pan; heat through. If desired, serve with lime wedges.
PER SERVING *1 cup equals 361 cal., 9 g fat (5 g sat. fat), 138 mg chol., 284 mg sodium, 44 g carb., 2 g fiber, 22 g pro. Diabetic Exchanges: 3 lean meat, 2½ starch, 1 fat.*

Smoked Pork Chops & Pierogies Dinner

My husband often lobbies to have smoked chops with pierogies for dinner. Balsamic vinegar lends a sweet-and-sour touch.

—BARBARA PEABODY GREEN VALLEY, AZ

START TO FINISH: 30 MIN.
MAKES: 4 SERVINGS

- 1 **pound fresh green beans, trimmed**
- ¼ **teaspoon salt**
- ¼ **teaspoon pepper**
- 1 **teaspoon olive oil**
- 4 **smoked boneless pork chops**
- 2 **tablespoons butter**
- 1 **package (1 pound) frozen pierogies (flavor of your choice)**
- ⅓ **cup balsamic vinegar**

1. In a large saucepan, bring 7 cups water to a boil. Add the green beans; cook, uncovered, 4-6 minutes or until crisp-tender. Drain; sprinkle with salt and pepper.
2. Meanwhile, in a large skillet, heat olive oil over medium heat. Add the pork chops; cook 2-3 minutes on each side or until heated through. Remove from the pan; keep warm. Add the butter to the same pan. Add the frozen pierogies; cook 6-8 minutes or until golden brown and heated through, turning occasionally. Remove from pan; keep warm.
3. In same skillet, bring balsamic vinegar to a boil. Reduce the heat to medium-low; cook 1-2 minutes or until slightly thickened. Serve pork chops with pierogies and green beans; drizzle with balsamic syrup.

Noodle Rice Pilaf

Here's a side that always pleases. Heat ¼ cup butter (cubed) over medium-high heat in a large saucepan. Add 1 cup uncooked long grain rice and ½ cup uncooked fine egg noodles; cook for 3 minutes or until browned. Stir in 2¾ cups chicken broth; cover and simmer for 20-25 minutes or until rice is tender. Stir in 2 tablespoons minced fresh parsley. *Makes 4 servings.*

—KATHY SCHRECENGOST OSWEGO, NY

CRISPY SMASHED
HERBED POTATOES

Ginger Salmon with Brown Rice

Bottled salad dressing makes it easy to glaze salmon and boost the flavor of rice.

—**NAYLET LAROCHELLE** MIAMI, FL

START TO FINISH: 25 MIN.
MAKES: 4 SERVINGS

- 4 **salmon fillets (6 ounces each)**
- 5 **tablespoons reduced-fat sesame ginger salad dressing, divided**

RICE
- ⅓ **cup shredded carrot**
- 4 **green onions, chopped, divided**
- 1½ **cups instant brown rice**
- 1½ **cups water**
- ⅓ **cup reduced-fat sesame ginger salad dressing**

1. Preheat oven to 400°. Place fillets on a foil-lined baking sheet; brush with 3 tablespoons dressing. Bake, uncovered, 10-12 minutes or until fish just begins to flake easily with a fork. Brush with remaining dressing.
2. Meanwhile, place a large saucepan coated with cooking spray over medium heat. Add carrot and half of the onion; cook and stir 2-3 minutes or until crisp-tender. Add rice and water; bring to a boil. Reduce heat; simmer, covered, 5 minutes.
3. Remove from heat; stir in dressing. Let stand, covered, 5 minutes or until liquid is absorbed and rice is tender. Fluff with a fork; serve with salmon. Sprinkle with remaining green onions.
PER SERVING *1 fillet with ½ cup rice mixture equals 446 cal., 19 g fat (3 g sat. fat), 85 mg chol., 605 mg sodium, 34 g carb., 2 g fiber, 32 g pro.* ***Diabetic Exchanges:*** *5 lean meat, 2 starch, 2 fat.*

GINGER SALMON
WITH BROWN RICE

⑤INGREDIENTS

Crispy Smashed Herbed Potatoes

While reading a local newspaper, I found a recipe with an intriguing title. As described, the red potatoes are crispy, herbed and smashed. They're also delicious!

—**ALTHEA DYE** HOWARD, OH

PREP: 25 MIN. • **BAKE:** 20 MIN.
MAKES: 4 SERVINGS

- 12 **small red potatoes (about 1½ pounds)**
- 3 **tablespoons olive oil**
- ¼ **cup butter, melted**
- ¾ **teaspoon salt**
- ¼ **teaspoon pepper**
- 3 **tablespoons minced fresh chives**
- 1 **tablespoon minced fresh parsley**

1. Preheat oven to 450°. Place the red potatoes in a large saucepan; add water to cover. Bring to a boil. Reduce heat; cook, uncovered, 15-20 minutes or until tender. Drain.
2. Drizzle the oil over the bottom of a 15x10x1-in. baking pan; arrange the potatoes over the oil. Using a potato masher, flatten the potatoes to ½-in. thickness. Brush potatoes with butter; sprinkle with salt and pepper.
3. Roast 20-25 minutes or until golden brown. Sprinkle with chives and parsley.

⑤INGREDIENTS FAST FIX

Pecan-Coconut Crusted Tilapia

When I have dinner guests who are on special diets, I rely on my fish fillets coated in crunchy pecans and coconut.

—**CAITLIN ROTH** CHICAGO, IL

START TO FINISH: 25 MIN.
MAKES: 4 SERVINGS

- 2 **large eggs**
- ½ **cup finely shredded unsweetened coconut**
- ½ **cup finely chopped pecans**
- ½ **teaspoon salt**
- ¼ **teaspoon crushed red pepper flakes**
- 4 **tilapia fillets (6 ounces each)**
- 2 **tablespoons canola oil**

1. In a shallow bowl, whisk the eggs. In a separate shallow bowl, combine the coconut, pecans, salt and pepper flakes. Dip the tilapia fillets in the eggs, then in the coconut mixture, patting to help coating adhere.

2. In a large skillet, heat the oil over medium heat. In batches, add the tilapia fillets and cook 2-3 minutes on each side or until lightly browned and the tilapia just begins to flake easily with a fork.

NOTE *Look for unsweetened coconut in the baking or health food section.*

PECAN-COCONUT
CRUSTED TILAPIA

EASY BEEF PIES

FREEZE IT ⑤INGREDIENTS FAST FIX

Easy Beef Pies

We eat a lot of French dip sandwiches and often have extra meat. Here's how I put it to good use! Buy a package of refrigerated beef roast from the store to enjoy these savory pies anytime. They're awesome drenched in cheese dip.

—**JENNIE WEBER** PALMER, AK

START TO FINISH: 30 MIN.
MAKES: 4 SERVINGS

- 1 **package (15 ounces) refrigerated beef roast au jus**
- 1 **tablespoon canola oil**
- ¼ **cup each finely chopped onion and green pepper**
- 1 **garlic clove, minced**
- 1 **package (14.1 ounces) refrigerated pie pastry**
- 1 **cup (4 ounces) shredded Mexican cheese blend**
- **Salsa con queso dip, optional**

1. Preheat oven to 425°. Drain beef, reserving ¼ cup juices; shred meat with two forks. In a large skillet, heat oil over medium-high heat. Add onion and pepper; cook and stir 1-2 minutes or until tender. Add the garlic; cook 30 seconds longer. Remove from heat; stir in beef and reserved juices.

2. Unroll one pastry sheet; cut in half. Layer ¼ cup shredded cheese and about ⅓ cup beef mixture over half of each pastry to within ½ in. of edge. Fold pastry over filling; press edges with a fork to seal. Place on a greased baking sheet. Repeat with remaining pastry and filling.

3. Bake 15-18 minutes or until golden brown. If desired, serve with dip.

FREEZE OPTION *Freeze the cooled pastries in a resealable plastic freezer bag. To use, reheat the pastries on a greased baking sheet in a preheated 350° oven until heated through.*

Orange Soda Sherbet

PREP: 5 MIN. + CHILLING
PROCESS: 30 MIN. + FREEZING
MAKES: 2 QUARTS

- 3 cans (12 ounces each) orange soda
- 1 can (14 ounces) sweetened condensed milk
- 1 can (8 ounces) crushed pineapple, undrained

1. Refrigerate unopened cans of soda, milk and pineapple until completely cold. In a large bowl, combine soda, milk and pineapple; mix until blended.
2. Fill the cylinder of ice cream maker no more than two-thirds full; freeze according to manufacturer's directions. (Refrigerate any remaining mixture until ready to freeze.)
3. Transfer the orange sherbet to freezer containers, allowing headspace for expansion. Freeze 2-4 hours or until firm.

(5) INGREDIENTS | FAST FIX
Caesar Chicken with Feta

This 10-minute skillet chicken is a lifesaver on our craziest days. We can still have a home-cooked meal and skip the takeout!
—**DENISE CHELPKA** PHOENIX, AZ

START TO FINISH: 10 MIN.
MAKES: 4 SERVINGS

- 4 boneless skinless chicken breast halves (4 ounces each)
- ½ teaspoon salt
- ¼ teaspoon pepper
- 2 teaspoons olive oil
- 1 medium tomato, chopped
- ¼ cup creamy Caesar salad dressing
- ½ cup crumbled feta cheese

Sprinkle chicken with salt and pepper. In a large skillet, heat the olive oil over medium-high heat. Brown chicken on one side. Turn chicken; add the tomato and Caesar salad dressing to skillet. Cook, covered, 6-8 minutes or until a thermometer inserted in chicken reads 165°. Sprinkle with cheese.

DID YOU KNOW?

Feta is a white, salty, semi-firm cheese. Although feta is associated mostly with Greek cooking, *feta* comes from the Italian word *fette*, meaning slice of food.

For birthday celebrations, we set up our old-fashioned ice cream maker and crank out Orange Soda Sherbet. It's a hit with children and adults alike.
—**HEATHER CRAFT** PADUCAH, KY

ORANGE SODA SHERBET

CHEESY CHICKEN
& BROCCOLI ORZO

⑤ INGREDIENTS FAST FIX
Cheesy Chicken & Broccoli Orzo

Broccoli-and-rice casserole is at the top of our list of comfort foods. But when we need something on the table in just half an hour, this dinner loaded with chicken and orzo never disappoints.
—**MARY SHIVERS** ADA, OK

START TO FINISH: 30 MIN.
MAKES: 6 SERVINGS

- 1¼ **cups uncooked orzo pasta**
- 2 **packages (10 ounces each) frozen broccoli with cheese sauce**
- 2 **tablespoons butter**
- 1½ **pounds boneless skinless chicken breasts, cut into ½-inch cubes**
- 1 **medium onion, chopped**
- ¾ **teaspoon salt**
- ½ **teaspoon pepper**

1. Cook orzo according to package directions. Meanwhile, heat broccoli with cheese sauce according to package directions.

2. In a large skillet, heat butter over medium heat. Add chicken, onion, salt and pepper; cook and stir 6-8 minutes or until chicken is no longer pink and onion is tender. Drain orzo. Stir orzo and broccoli with cheese sauce into skillet; heat through.

⑤ INGREDIENTS FAST FIX
Balsamic-Glazed Pork Tenderloin

Pull out your ovenproof skillet for a juicy pork tenderloin that goes from stovetop to oven. Balsamic vinegar and brown sugar create a sweet-tangy glaze.
—**LISA MORIARTY** WILTON, NH

START TO FINISH: 30 MIN.
MAKES: 4 SERVINGS

- 1 **pork tenderloin (1 pound)**
- ¼ **teaspoon salt**
- ¼ **teaspoon pepper**
- 1 **tablespoon canola oil**
- ½ **cup balsamic vinegar**
- ½ **cup packed brown sugar**

1. Preheat oven to 425°. Sprinkle the pork tenderloin with salt and pepper. In a large ovenproof skillet, heat the oil over medium-high heat. Brown pork tenderloin on all sides. Remove pork from the pan.

2. Remove pan from heat; add vinegar, stirring to loosen browned bits from pan. Stir in brown sugar. Return pork to pan, turning to coat.

3. Bake 8-10 minutes or until a thermometer reads 145°, turning occasionally. Remove the pork to a serving platter; tent with foil. Let stand 5 minutes before slicing. Pour the glaze over pork before serving.

Strawberry Mousse Parfaits

With a dessert this simple, it's hard to resist! Place two thawed 10-ounce packages frozen sweetened sliced strawberries in a food processor; process until pureed. Cook and stir puree and 1 tablespoon plus 2 teaspoons cornstarch until thickened; chill. Set aside 1 cup mixture. Stir in one 14-ounce can sweetened condensed milk, 2 tablepoons orange juice and ⅛ teaspoon red food coloring (if desired) to remaining mixture; fold in 2 cups heavy cream, whipped. Spoon half of cream mixture into 12 parfait dishes. Layer each with berry mixture and remaining cream mixture. Refrigerate until serving. *Makes 12 parfaits.*
—**MARY LOU TIMPSON** COLORADO CITY, AZ

SKILLET CHICKEN
WITH OLIVES

EAT SMART (**5**)**INGREDIENTS** **FAST FIX**
Skillet Chicken with Olives

While I was visiting my cousin in Italy, she prepared a wonderful chicken dish with olives for lunch. Now it's become a family favorite stateside, too.
—**JOSEPH PISANO** REVERE, MA

START TO FINISH: 20 MIN.
MAKES: 4 SERVINGS

- 4 **boneless skinless chicken thighs (about 1 pound)**
- 1 **teaspoon dried rosemary, crushed**
- ½ **teaspoon pepper**
- ¼ **teaspoon salt**
- 1 **tablespoon olive oil**
- ½ **cup pimiento-stuffed olives, coarsely chopped**
- ¼ **cup white wine or chicken broth**
- 1 **tablespoon drained capers, optional**

1. Sprinkle chicken with rosemary, pepper and salt. In a large skillet, heat oil over medium-high heat. Brown chicken on both sides.

2. Add the olives, wine and, if desired, capers. Reduce heat; simmer, covered, 2-3 minutes or until a thermometer inserted in chicken reads 170°.
PER SERVING *1 serving (calculated without capers) equals 237 cal., 15 g fat (3 g sat. fat), 76 mg chol., 571 mg sodium, 2 g carb., trace fiber, 21 g pro.* **Diabetic Exchanges:** *3 lean meat, 2 fat.*

(**5**)**INGREDIENTS** **FAST FIX**
Pineapple-Dijon Pork Chops

Dress up pork with Dijon, chardonnay and tangy fruit flavor. If you like, replace the pineapple preserves with apricot or peach.
—**JANE WHITTAKER** PENSACOLA, FL

START TO FINISH: 25 MIN.
MAKES: 4 SERVINGS

- 4 **boneless pork loin chops (6 ounces each)**
- ½ **teaspoon seasoned salt**
- 1 **tablespoon canola oil**
- ¾ **cup pineapple preserves**
- ¼ **cup chardonnay or chicken broth**
- 3 **tablespoons Dijon mustard**

1. Sprinkle pork chops with seasoned salt. In a large skillet, heat the oil over medium-high heat. Brown pork chops on both sides.

2. In a small bowl, mix the pineapple preserves, chardonnay and Dijon mustard; add to the pan. Reduce the heat; simmer, covered, 5-7 minutes or until a thermometer inserted in the pork reads 145°. Let stand 5 minutes before serving.

EAT SMART (**5**)**INGREDIENTS** **FAST FIX**
White Bean & Chicken Chili

To create this quick and easy white chili, I combined parts of three different recipes. It's mild enough for everyone to dig in.
—**JULIE WHITE** YACOLT, WA

START TO FINISH: 20 MIN.
MAKES: 6 SERVINGS

- 3 **cans (15 ounces each) white kidney or cannellini beans, undrained**
- 1 **can (4 ounces) chopped green chilies**
- 3 **teaspoons chicken bouillon granules**
- 3 **teaspoons ground cumin**
- 2 **cups water**
- 3 **cups cubed cooked chicken or turkey**
  Minced fresh cilantro, optional

1. In a large saucepan, combine the first five ingredients; bring to a boil. Reduce the heat; simmer, uncovered, 2-3 minutes to allow flavors to blend, stirring occasionally.

2. Stir in the chicken; heat through. If desired, sprinkle with cilantro.
FREEZE OPTION *Freeze cooled chili in freezer containers. To use, partially thaw in the refrigerator overnight. Heat through in a saucepan, stirring occasionally and adding a little water if necessary.*
PER SERVING *304 cal., 6 g fat (1 g sat. fat), 63 mg chol., 747 mg sodium, 30 g carb., 9 g fiber, 29 g pro.* **Diabetic Exchanges:** *3 lean meat, 2 starch.*

WEEKNIGHT CHICKEN
CORDON BLEU

(5) INGREDIENTS **FAST FIX**

Weeknight Chicken Cordon Bleu

Have you ever clipped a recipe from a magazine—and discovered too late that you missed part of it? I figured out this one, and my son says it's his favorite.

—MARY ANN TURK JOPLIN, MO

START TO FINISH: 30 MIN.
MAKES: 4 SERVINGS

- 4 **boneless skinless chicken breast halves (6 ounces each)**
- ½ **teaspoon salt**
- ¼ **teaspoon pepper**
- 1 **tablespoon plus 2 teaspoons canola oil, divided**
- 3 **cups cut fresh green beans (2-inch)**
- 1 **cup sliced fresh mushrooms**
- 4 **thin slices deli ham**
- 4 **slices part-skim mozzarella cheese**

1. Sprinkle chicken breast halves with salt and pepper. In a large skillet, heat 1 tablespoon oil over medium heat.

Add the chicken; cook 4-6 minutes on each side or until a thermometer reads 165°. Remove from pan.

2. Heat the remaining oil in same pan. Add beans and mushrooms; cook and stir 3-4 minutes or until the beans are crisp-tender. Return chicken to pan; top each breast with a slice of ham and cheese. Cook, covered, 1-2 minutes or just until cheese melts.

(5) INGREDIENTS **FAST FIX**

Cheese Ravioli with Veggies

When ravioli is on the menu, my family gets to the table fast. Sometimes I throw in peas, corn, broccoli or zucchini instead of the frozen veggie medley.

—AMY BURNS CHARLESTON, IL

START TO FINISH: 25 MIN.
MAKES: 6 SERVINGS

- 1 **package (25 ounces) frozen cheese ravioli**
- 1 **package (16 ounces) frozen California-blend vegetables**
- ¼ **cup butter, melted**
- ¼ **teaspoon salt-free seasoning blend**
- ¼ **cup shredded Parmesan cheese**

1. Fill a 6-qt. stockpot two-thirds full with water; bring to a boil. Add cheese ravioli and vegetables; return to a boil. Cook 6-8 minutes or until ravioli and vegetables are tender; drain.

2. Gently stir in butter. Sprinkle with the seasoning blend and shredded Parmesan cheese.

TOP TIP

For an easy dinner when I have extra homemade spaghetti sauce, I layer the sauce with frozen cheese ravioli, then top it all off with some shredded cheese and pop it in the oven. Put a little of the sauce in the bottom of the baking dish first to keep the ravioli from sticking.

—LAURA BARNES O'FALLON, IL

Chicken with Cherry Wine Sauce

⑤ INGREDIENTS FAST FIX

My dad is a chef and taught me to cook at an early age. This entree was the first recipe I made by myself. A sauce made with sweet cherries, butter, sugar and red wine adds a little elegance to plain chicken.
—**BEN DIAZ** AZUSA, CA

START TO FINISH: 30 MIN.
MAKES: 4 SERVINGS

- 4 **boneless skinless chicken breast halves (8 ounces each)**
- ¼ **teaspoon salt**
- ¼ **teaspoon pepper**
- 7 **tablespoons butter, divided**
- ⅔ **cup dry red wine**
- 1 **tablespoon sugar**
- ½ **cup fresh or frozen pitted dark sweet cherries, thawed**

1. Preheat oven to 350°. Sprinkle the chicken with the salt and pepper. In a large skillet, heat 2 tablespoons butter over medium-high heat. Brown the chicken on both sides. Transfer to a greased 15x10x1-in. baking pan. Bake 12-15 minutes or until a thermometer reads 165°.
2. Meanwhile, in a small saucepan, combine the dry red wine and sugar. Bring to a boil; cook, uncovered, 4-5 minutes or until liquid is reduced by half. Reduce the heat to low; whisk in the remaining butter, 1 tablespoon at a time, until blended. Stir in the cherries; serve with chicken.

Brussels Sprouts with Bacon & Garlic

⑤ INGREDIENTS FAST FIX

Whenever we're expecting dinner guests, I put these Brussels sprouts on the menu. They pair well with many main courses, and everyone who samples the garlicky dish thinks it looks and tastes delicious. For an extra-special touch, use pancetta in place of the bacon.
—**MANDY RIVERS** LEXINGTON, SC

START TO FINISH: 30 MIN.
MAKES: 12 SERVINGS (¾ CUP EACH)

- 2 **pounds fresh Brussels sprouts (about 10 cups)**
- 8 **bacon strips, coarsely chopped**
- 3 **garlic cloves, minced**
- ¾ **cup chicken broth**
- ½ **teaspoon salt**
- ¼ **teaspoon pepper**

1. Trim the Brussels sprouts. Cut Brussels sprouts lengthwise in half; cut crosswise into thin slices. In a 6-qt. stockpot, cook the bacon over medium heat until crisp, stirring occasionally. Add the garlic; cook 30 seconds longer. Remove with a slotted spoon; drain on paper towels.
2. Add the sliced Brussels sprouts to the bacon drippings; cook and stir 4-6 minutes or until Brussels sprouts begin to brown lightly. Stir in the chicken broth, salt and pepper; cook, covered, 4-6 minutes longer or until Brussels sprouts are tender. Stir in the bacon mixture.

SOUTHWEST
KIELBASA BOWLS

Southwest Kielbasa Bowls

⑤ INGREDIENTS FAST FIX

Here's our at-home take on restaurant burrito bowls. We start with rice, kielbasa and black beans, then top 'em with salsa, red onion and cilantro. Substitute a spicier sausage if you want to crank up the heat!
—**ABBY WILLIAMSON** DUNEDIN, FL

START TO FINISH: 20 MIN.
MAKES: 4 SERVINGS

- 2 **cups uncooked instant brown rice**
- 2 **tablespoons olive oil**
- 1 **package (14 ounces) smoked turkey kielbasa, cut into ¼-inch slices**
- 1 **can (15 ounces) black beans, rinsed and drained**
- 1½ **cups fresh salsa**
- ¼ **cup finely chopped red onion**
  Fresh cilantro leaves, optional

1. Cook the brown rice according to the package directions.
2. Meanwhile, in a large skillet, heat the olive oil over medium-high heat. Add the turkey kielbasa; cook and stir 4-6 minutes or until browned. Stir in the black beans and salsa. Divide the brown rice among four bowls. Top with the kielbasa mixture, red onion and, if desired, cilantro.

Spinach-Basil Pesto

Homemade pesto may sound complicated and time-consuming to prepare, but this spinach version proves it's easy enough to whip up in your own kitchen to toss with pasta or spread on appetizer toasts. Place 6 halved garlic cloves in a food processor; pulse until finely chopped. Add 3 cups fresh baby spinach, 1½ cups loosely packed basil leaves and ¾ cup toasted shelled walnuts or pine nuts. Pulse until chopped. Add 1 cup grated Parmesan cheese, ½ teaspoon salt and a dash of pepper. Continue processing while gradually adding ¾ cup olive oil. *Makes 1¾ cups.*
—**JAYE BEELER** GRAND RAPIDS, MI

I first served Chicken & Waffles as an appetizer, but everyone loves it as a main course, too. With just four ingredients, the dish couldn't be easier to prepare.

—**LISA RENSHAW** KANSAS CITY, MO

CHICKEN & WAFFLES

⑤ INGREDIENTS FAST FIX
Chicken & Waffles

START TO FINISH: 25 MIN.
MAKES: 4 SERVINGS

- 12 frozen crispy chicken strips (about 18 ounces)
- ½ cup honey
- 2 teaspoons hot pepper sauce
- 8 frozen waffles, toasted

1. Bake the chicken strips according to the package directions. Meanwhile, in a small bowl, mix the honey and pepper sauce.
2. Cut chicken into bite-size pieces; serve on toasted waffles. Drizzle with the honey mixture.

⑤ INGREDIENTS FAST FIX
Tropical Beef Wrap

For my finicky little ones, I roll up these fast and fruity sandwich wraps. The kids are always happy, and it's a terrific way to use leftover roast beef.

—**AMY TONG** ANAHEIM, CA

START TO FINISH: 15 MIN.
MAKES: 4 SERVINGS

- 1 carton (8 ounces) spreadable pineapple cream cheese
- 4 flour tortillas (10 inches)
- 4 cups fresh baby spinach (about 4 ounces)
- ¾ pound thinly sliced deli roast beef
- 1 medium mango, peeled and sliced

Spread the cream cheese over tortillas to within 1 in. of the edges. Layer with the spinach, roast beef and mango. Roll up tightly and serve.

⑤ INGREDIENTS FAST FIX
Ravioli with Apple Chicken Sausage

Transform butternut squash ravioli into a hearty dinner. The simple sauce features apple chicken sausage, creamed spinach, syrup and pumpkin pie spice.

—**MARY BRODEUR** MILLBURY, MA

START TO FINISH: 30 MIN.
MAKES: 4 SERVINGS

- 1 package (18 ounces) frozen butternut squash ravioli
- 2 packages (10 ounces each) frozen creamed spinach
- 1 tablespoon olive oil
- 1 package (12 ounces) fully cooked apple chicken sausage links or flavor of your choice, cut into ½-inch slices
- 1 teaspoon maple syrup
- ¼ teaspoon pumpkin pie spice

1. Cook the butternut squash ravioli according to the package directions. Prepare creamed spinach according to the package directions. Meanwhile, in a large skillet, heat the olive oil over medium heat. Add sausage; cook and stir 2-4 minutes or until browned.
2. Drain ravioli. Add ravioli, spinach, maple syrup and pie spice to sausage; heat through.

RAVIOLI WITH APPLE CHICKEN SAUSAGE

PORK CHOPS WITH
TOMATO-BACON TOPPING

1. Sprinkle tilapia fillets with salt and pepper. In a large nonstick skillet, heat oil over medium heat. Add fillets; cook 2-3 minutes on each side or until fish just begins to flake easily with a fork. Remove and keep warm.

2. Add butter, wine and lemon juice to same pan; cook and stir until butter is melted. Serve with the fish; sprinkle with almonds.

⑤ INGREDIENTS FAST FIX
Quick Sausage-Stuffed Squash

With a dark green skin and bright orange interior, acorn squash makes a colorful bowl for this meaty filling. To change it up a bit, substitute maple-flavored sausage.

—**MARY MAGNER** CEDAR RAPIDS, IA

START TO FINISH: 20 MIN.
MAKES: 4 SERVINGS

- 2 **medium acorn squash**
- 1 **pound bulk pork sausage**
- 1 **small onion, finely chopped**
- 1 **celery rib, finely chopped**
- ⅓ **cup sour cream**
  Freshly ground pepper

1. Cut the acorn squash lengthwise in half; remove and discard the seeds. Using a sharp knife, cut a thin slice from the bottom of both squash halves to allow them to sit flat. Place squash in a microwave-safe dish, cut side down. Microwave, covered, on high 10-12 minutes or until tender.

2. Meanwhile, in a large skillet, cook the sausage, onion and celery over medium heat 6-8 minutes or until the sausage is no longer pink and the vegetables are tender, breaking up sausage into crumbles. Remove pan from heat; drain. Stir in sour cream.

3. Turn the acorn squash cut side up. Spoon the sausage mixture into the centers of squash halves. Microwave, covered, 1-2 minutes or until heated through. Sprinkle with pepper.
NOTE *This recipe was tested in a 1,100-watt microwave.*

⑤ INGREDIENTS FAST FIX
Pork Chops with Tomato-Bacon Topping

My husband and I teamed up to create pork chops topped with bacon, sun-dried tomatoes, brown sugar and rosemary. The entree is quick enough for weekdays but nice enough for guests.

—**TRISHA KLEMPEL** SIDNEY, MT

START TO FINISH: 30 MIN.
MAKES: 4 SERVINGS

- 4 **thick-sliced bacon strips, chopped**
- 4 **boneless pork loin chops (6 ounces each)**
- ½ **teaspoon salt**
- ¼ **teaspoon pepper**
- ¼ **cup julienned oil-packed sun-dried tomatoes**
- 2 **tablespoons brown sugar**
- 2 **teaspoons minced fresh rosemary or ½ teaspoon dried rosemary, crushed**

1. Preheat broiler. In a large ovenproof skillet, cook the bacon over medium heat until crisp, stirring occasionally. Remove with a slotted spoon; drain on paper towels.

2. Sprinkle pork chops with salt and pepper. Add chops to drippings; cook 3-4 minutes on each side or until a thermometer reads 145°. Meanwhile, in a small bowl, mix bacon, tomatoes, brown sugar and rosemary.

3. Spoon tomato mixture over chops. Broil 3-4 in. from heat 1-2 minutes or until brown sugar is melted.

⑤ INGREDIENTS FAST FIX
Lemon-Butter Tilapia with Almonds

Want a special meal but not a lot of prep work in the kitchen? This lemony, buttery fish tastes like an indulgence—and takes 10 minutes from start to finish!

—**RAMONA PARRIS** MARIETTA, GA

START TO FINISH: 10 MIN.
MAKES: 4 SERVINGS

- 4 **tilapia fillets (4 ounces each)**
- ½ **teaspoon salt**
- ¼ **teaspoon pepper**
- 1 **tablespoon olive oil**
- ¼ **cup butter, cubed**
- ¼ **cup white wine or chicken broth**
- 2 **tablespoons lemon juice**
- ¼ **cup sliced almonds**

(5) INGREDIENTS · FAST FIX
Breaded Pork Tenderloin

My teenage daughter is always reluctant to eat meat unless it resembles something from a restaurant. When I drizzle ranch dressing or barbecue sauce on this breaded pork tenderloin, it's a hit.
—**DONNA CARNEY** NEW LEXINGTON, OH

START TO FINISH: 30 MIN.
MAKES: 4 SERVINGS

- 1 pork tenderloin (1 pound)
- ⅓ cup all-purpose flour
- ⅓ cup corn bread/muffin mix
- ½ teaspoon salt
- ¼ teaspoon pepper
- 1 large egg, beaten
- 4 tablespoons canola oil, divided
  Ranch or barbecue sauce, optional

1. Cut the pork tenderloin crosswise into ½-in. slices. In a shallow bowl, mix flour, muffin mix, salt and pepper. Place egg in a separate shallow bowl. Dip pork in egg, then in flour mixture, patting to help coating adhere.
2. In a large skillet, heat 2 tablespoons oil over medium heat. Add half of the pork; cook 3-4 minutes on each side or until a thermometer reads 145°. Drain on paper towels. Wipe the skillet clean; repeat with remaining oil and pork. If desired, serve with sauce.

BREADED PORK TENDERLOIN

CREAMY SKILLET NOODLES WITH PEAS

(5) INGREDIENTS · FAST FIX
Creamy Skillet Noodles with Peas

I've been making this creamy noodle side for years. Both kids and adults go for it.
—**ANITA GROFF** PERKIOMENVILLE, PA

START TO FINISH: 25 MIN.
MAKES: 6 SERVINGS

- ¼ cup butter, cubed
- 2 tablespoons canola oil
- 5 cups uncooked fine egg noodles
- 2½ cups frozen peas (about 10 ounces)
- 2½ cups chicken broth
- 1 cup half-and-half cream
- ½ teaspoon salt
- ¼ teaspoon pepper

1. In a large skillet, heat the butter and oil over medium heat. Add the egg noodles; cook and stir 2-3 minutes or until lightly browned.
2. Stir in peas, broth, half-and-half cream, salt and pepper. Bring to a boil. Reduce the heat; simmer, covered, 10-12 minutes or until noodles are tender, stirring occasionally.

(5) INGREDIENTS · FAST FIX
Jalapeno Popper Quesadillas

Jalapeno poppers stuffed inside cheesy quesadillas? Yes, please! Bacon adds even more flavor to the zippy wedges.
—**REBECCA NISEWONDER** RICHMOND, IN

START TO FINISH: 25 MIN.
MAKES: 4 SERVINGS

- 8 flour tortillas (8 inches)
- 1 carton (8 ounces) spreadable cream cheese
- ½ pound bacon strips, cooked and crumbled
- 5 jalapeno peppers, seeded and finely chopped
- 2 cups (8 ounces) shredded cheddar cheese

1. Preheat oven to 400°. Place half of the tortillas on two greased baking sheets. Spread with the cream cheese; sprinkle with bacon, jalapeno peppers and cheddar cheese. Top with the remaining tortillas.
2. Bake 8-10 minutes or until golden brown and cheese is melted.

(5)INGREDIENTS FAST FIX

Scallops with Wilted Spinach

Two of my favorite foods are bacon and seafood. This entree lets me enjoy them together with white wine, shallots and baby spinach. Soak up the tasty broth with fresh-baked bread or rolls.

—**DEBORAH WILLIAMS** PEORIA, AZ

START TO FINISH: 25 MIN.
MAKES: 4 SERVINGS

- 4 **bacon strips, chopped**
- 12 **sea scallops (about 1½ pounds), side muscles removed**
- 2 **shallots, finely chopped**
- ½ **cup white wine or chicken broth**
- 8 **cups fresh baby spinach (about 8 ounces)**

1. In a large nonstick skillet, cook the bacon over medium heat until crisp, stirring occasionally. Remove with a slotted spoon; drain on paper towels. Discard the bacon drippings, reserving 2 tablespoons. Wipe the skillet clean if necessary.

2. Pat scallops dry with paper towels. In the same skillet, heat 1 tablespoon bacon drippings over medium-high heat. Add scallops; cook 2-3 minutes on each side or until golden brown and firm. Remove from pan; keep warm

3. Heat remaining bacon drippings in same pan over medium-high heat. Add shallots; cook and stir 2-3 minutes or until tender. Add the white wine; bring to a boil, stirring to loosen the browned bits from the pan. Add the spinach; cook and stir 1-2 minutes or until wilted. Stir in the bacon. Serve with the scallops.

DID YOU KNOW?

Members of the bivalve mollusk family, scallops are commonly found in two groups—the sea scallop, yielding 10-20 per pound, and the much smaller bay scallop, yielding 60-90 per pound. Scallops are usually available shucked, are sold fresh or frozen, and range in color from pale beige to creamy pink. They can be broiled, pan-fried, deep-fried or grilled, and cook in minutes.

SCALLOPS WITH
WILTED SPINACH

**Priscilla Yee's
Skillet BBQ Beef
Pot Pie** PAGE 100

Express Entrees

Look here for more than 50 main dishes and meal-in-one favorites. Each recipe goes together from start to finish in 30 minutes or less, so you'll always have time for a home-cooked dinner.

Lisa Montgomery's Sausage Broccoli Simmer PAGE 93

Shana Conradt's Sausage & Feta Stuffed Tomatoes PAGE 91

Gloria Bradley's Almond-Crusted Chops with Cider Sauce PAGE 91

ITALIAN SAUSAGE WITH
ARTICHOKES AND FETA

FAST FIX

Stovetop Turkey Tetrazzini

A very special aunt shared this fun twist on creamy turkey tetrazzini. I think her version is even better the next day.

—**TASIA COX** NICEVILLE, FL

START TO FINISH: 30 MIN.
MAKES: 6 SERVINGS

- 8 ounces uncooked spaghetti
- 2 tablespoons butter
- 1 cup sliced fresh mushrooms
- 1 celery rib, chopped
- ½ cup chopped onion
- 1 package (8 ounces) cream cheese, cubed
- 1 can (10½ ounces) condensed chicken broth, undiluted
- 2 cups chopped cooked turkey
- 1 jar (2 ounces) diced pimientos, drained
- ¼ teaspoon salt
- ¼ cup grated Parmesan cheese

1. Cook the spaghetti according to package directions; drain. Meanwhile, in a large skillet, heat the butter over medium-high heat. Add mushrooms, celery and onion; cook and stir 6-8 minutes or until the mushrooms are tender.

2. Add cream cheese and broth; cook, uncovered, over low heat 4-6 minutes or until blended, stirring occasionally. Add the turkey, pimientos, salt and spaghetti; heat through, tossing to coat. Serve with Parmesan cheese.

STOVETOP TURKEY
TETRAZZINI

FREEZE IT **FAST FIX**

Italian Sausage with Artichokes and Feta

To impress our guests, we serve Italian sausage and artichoke hearts with pasta. Everyone says it tastes like a restaurant specialty. The meat mixture is good over rice and potatoes, too.

—**AYSHA SCHURMAN** AMMON, ID

START TO FINISH: 25 MIN.
MAKES: 4 SERVINGS

- 1 pound bulk Italian sausage
- 1 small red onion, finely chopped
- 1 garlic clove, minced
- 1 jar (7½ ounces) marinated quartered artichoke hearts, drained and coarsely chopped
- ½ cup tomato sauce
- ¼ cup dry red wine or chicken broth
- ½ teaspoon Italian seasoning
- ½ cup crumbled feta cheese
  Minced fresh parsley, optional
  Hot cooked gemelli or spiral pasta

1. In a large skillet, cook the Italian sausage, red onion and garlic over medium heat 6-8 minutes or until sausage is no longer pink and onion is tender, breaking up sausage into crumbles; drain.

2. Stir in artichokes, tomato sauce, wine and seasoning; heat through. Gently stir in the cheese. If desired, sprinkle with parsley. Serve with pasta.

FREEZE OPTION *Freeze the cooled sausage mixture in freezer containers. To use, partially thaw in refrigerator overnight. Place the sausage mixture in a saucepan; heat through, stirring occasionally and adding a little broth or water if necessary.*

BLACK BEAN 'N' CORN
QUESADILLAS

Black Bean 'n' Corn Quesadillas

One of the best things about these veggie quesadillas is that they're baked, so the whole batch is ready at the same time.
—**SUSAN FRANKLIN** LITTLETON, CO

START TO FINISH: 30 MIN.
MAKES: 6 SERVINGS

- 1 can (15 ounces) black beans, rinsed and drained, divided
- 2 teaspoons olive oil
- 1 small onion, finely chopped
- 1 can (11 ounces) Mexicorn, drained
- 1 teaspoon ground cumin
- 1 teaspoon chili powder
- 6 ounces fresh baby spinach (about 8 cups)
- 8 flour tortillas (8 inches)
- ¾ cup shredded reduced-fat Colby-Monterey Jack cheese or Mexican cheese blend

1. Preheat oven to 400°. In a small bowl, mash 1 cup of black beans with a fork.
2. In a large skillet, heat the olive oil over medium-high heat. Add onion; cook and stir until tender. Stir in the corn, cumin, chili powder, mashed black beans and remaining black beans; heat through. Stir in spinach just until wilted.
3. Spread four flour tortillas with the bean mixture; sprinkle with cheese. Top with the remaining tortillas. Place on two ungreased baking sheets.
4. Bake 8-10 minutes or until cheese is melted. Cut each into six wedges.
PER SERVING *4 wedges equals 358 cal., 9 g fat (3 g sat. fat), 10 mg chol., 900 mg sodium, 56 g carb., 5 g fiber, 15 g pro.*

Almond-Crusted Chops with Cider Sauce

Finely ground almonds give pork chops a crunchy crust, and my apple cider sauce makes them tangy, creamy and sweet.
—**GLORIA BRADLEY** NAPERVILLE, IL

START TO FINISH: 20 MIN.
MAKES: 4 SERVINGS

- ½ cup panko (Japanese) bread crumbs
- ½ cup ground almonds
- ⅓ cup all-purpose flour
- ½ teaspoon salt, divided
- 2 large eggs, beaten
- 4 boneless pork loin chops (¾ inch thick and 4 ounces each)
- 3 tablespoons olive oil
- 1 cup apple cider or juice
- 4 ounces cream cheese, cubed
- 1 tablespoon honey, optional
  Minced chives

1. In a shallow bowl, mix crumbs and almonds. In another shallow bowl, mix flour and ¼ teaspoon salt. Place eggs in a separate shallow bowl. Dip chops in the flour to coat both sides; shake off excess. Dip in egg, then in crumb mixture, patting to help coating adhere.
2. In a large skillet, heat the olive oil over medium heat. Add pork chops; cook 3-4 minutes on each side or until a thermometer reads 145°. Remove; keep warm. Wipe skillet clean.
3. In same skillet over medium heat, combine apple cider, cream cheese, remaining salt and, if desired, honey. Cook and stir 2 minutes. Serve with pork chops; sprinkle with chives.

Sausage & Feta Stuffed Tomatoes

As a weight loss coach, I introduced my clients and blog followers to this tasty dish.
—**SHANA CONRADT** APPLETON, WI

START TO FINISH: 25 MIN.
MAKES: 4 SERVINGS

- 3 Italian turkey sausage links (4 ounces each), casings removed
- 1 cup (4 ounces) crumbled feta cheese, divided
- 8 plum tomatoes
- ¼ teaspoon salt
- ¼ teaspoon pepper
- 3 tablespoons balsamic vinegar
  Minced fresh parsley

1. Preheat oven to 350°. In a large skillet, cook sausage over medium heat 4-6 minutes or until no longer pink, breaking into crumbles. Transfer to a small bowl; stir in ½ cup feta cheese.
2. Cut tomatoes in half lengthwise. Scoop out pulp, leaving a ½-in. shell; discard pulp. Sprinkle the tomatoes with salt and pepper; transfer to an ungreased 13x9-in. baking dish. Spoon sausage mixture into shells; drizzle with vinegar. Sprinkle with remaining feta.
3. Bake, uncovered, 10-12 minutes or until heated through. Sprinkle with minced parsley.
PER SERVING *200 cal., 10 g fat (4 g sat. fat), 46 mg chol., 777 mg sodium, 12 g carb., 3 g fiber, 16 g pro.* **Diabetic Exchanges:** *2 medium-fat meat, 1 vegetable, ½ starch.*

EAT SMART FAST FIX
Black Bean Pasta

This vegetarian entree has fabulous flavor.
I toss in fresh rosemary whenever I have it.
—ASHLYNN AZAR BEAVERTON, OR

START TO FINISH: 25 MIN.
MAKES: 6 SERVINGS

- 9 ounces uncooked whole wheat fettuccine
- 1 tablespoon olive oil
- 1¾ cups sliced baby portobello mushrooms
- 1 garlic clove, minced
- 1 can (15 ounces) black beans, rinsed and drained
- 1 can (14½ ounces) diced tomatoes, undrained
- 1 teaspoon dried rosemary, crushed
- ½ teaspoon dried oregano
- 2 cups fresh baby spinach

1. Cook the whole wheat fettuccine according to the package directions. Meanwhile, in a large skillet, heat the oil over medium-high heat. Add the mushrooms; cook and stir 4-6 minutes or until tender. Add the garlic; cook 1 minute longer.

2. Stir in the black beans, tomatoes, rosemary and oregano; heat through. Stir in spinach until wilted. Drain fettuccine; add to bean mixture and toss to combine.

PER SERVING *⅔ cup bean mixture with ⅔ cup pasta equals 255 cal., 3 g fat (trace sat. fat), 0 chol., 230 mg sodium, 45 g carb., 9 g fiber, 12 g pro.* **Diabetic Exchanges:** *3 starch, 1 lean meat, ½ fat.*

ZUCCHINI & SAUSAGE
STOVETOP CASSEROLE

Head to your garden or the local farm stand for ingredients, then start cooking Zucchini & Sausage Stovetop Casserole. If you prefer, use zucchini that's grated instead of sliced.
—LEANN GRAY TAYLORSVILLE, UT

FAST FIX
Zucchini & Sausage Stovetop Casserole

START TO FINISH: 30 MIN.
MAKES: 6 SERVINGS

- 1 pound bulk pork sausage
- 1 tablespoon canola oil
- 3 medium zucchini, thinly sliced
- 1 medium onion, chopped
- 1 can (14½ ounces) stewed tomatoes, cut up
- 1 package (8.8 ounces) ready-to-serve long grain rice
- 1 teaspoon prepared mustard
- ½ teaspoon garlic salt
- ¼ teaspoon pepper
- 1 cup (4 ounces) shredded sharp cheddar cheese

1. In a large skillet, cook sausage over medium heat 5-7 minutes or until no longer pink, breaking into crumbles. Drain and remove sausage from pan.

2. In the same pan, heat the oil over medium heat. Add the zucchini and onion; cook and stir 5-7 minutes or until tender. Stir in sausage, tomatoes, rice, mustard, garlic salt and pepper. Bring to a boil. Reduce heat; simmer, covered, 5 minutes to allow the flavors to blend.

3. Remove from heat; sprinkle with cheese. Let stand, covered, 5 minutes or until cheese is melted.

BLACK BEAN PASTA

Apricot Cranberry Chicken

I used to try making complicated recipes. Now that I have children, I need to keep things simpler. This tangy, fruity chicken pleases the whole family.

—**BROOKE RUZEK** ELK RIVER, MN

START TO FINISH: 30 MIN.
MAKES: 4 SERVINGS

- 1½ **pounds chicken tenderloins, divided**
- ¼ **teaspoon salt**
- 2 **tablespoons olive oil, divided**
- 1 **medium onion, chopped**
- ¾ **cup chicken broth**
- ½ **cup dried cranberries**
- ½ **cup apricot preserves**
- 2 **tablespoons cider vinegar**

1. Sprinkle chicken with salt. In a large skillet, heat 1 tablespoon olive oil over medium-high heat and brown half of the chicken on both sides. Remove from the pan; repeat with remaining oil and chicken.
2. Add onion to same pan; cook and stir over medium heat 2-3 minutes or until tender. Stir in broth, cranberries, preserves and vinegar; return to a boil. Reduce the heat; simmer, uncovered, 2-3 minutes or until slightly reduced.

3. Return the chicken to pan; cook, uncovered, 4-6 minutes longer or until the chicken is no longer pink, turning chicken halfway.

Salmon with Spinach & White Beans

My husband is a true-blue Southerner who loves pork. But when I served a meal of broiled salmon with garlicky beans and spinach, it won him over.

—**MARY ELLEN HOFSTETTER**
BRENTWOOD, TN

START TO FINISH: 15 MIN.
MAKES: 4 SERVINGS

- 4 **salmon fillets (4 ounces each)**
- 2 **teaspoons plus 1 tablespoon olive oil, divided**
- 1 **teaspoon seafood seasoning**
- 1 **garlic clove, minced**
- 1 **can (15 ounces) white kidney or cannellini beans, rinsed and drained**
- ¼ **teaspoon salt**
- ¼ **teaspoon pepper**
- 1 **package (8 ounces) fresh spinach**
  Lemon wedges

1. Preheat broiler. Rub the salmon with 2 teaspoons oil; sprinkle with the seafood seasoning. Place on a greased rack of a broiler pan. Broil 5-6 in. from the heat 5-7 minutes or until the fish just begins to flake easily with a fork.
2. Meanwhile, in a large skillet, heat the remaining oil over medium heat. Add garlic; cook 15-30 seconds or until fragrant. Add beans, salt and pepper, stirring to coat beans with garlic oil. Stir in spinach until wilted. Serve the salmon with the spinach mixture and lemon wedges.

PER SERVING *1 fillet with ½ cup spinach mixture equals 317 cal., 17 g fat (3 g sat. fat), 57 mg chol., 577 mg sodium, 16 g carb., 5 g fiber, 24 g pro.* **Diabetic Exchanges:** *3 lean meat, 2 vegetable, 1 fat, ½ starch.*

Sausage Broccoli Simmer

Want to get a complete dinner from just one dish? Loaded with sausage, pasta and veggies, this is all you need.

—**LISA MONTGOMERY** ELMIRA, ON

START TO FINISH: 30 MIN.
MAKES: 4 SERVINGS

- 2 **cups uncooked spiral pasta**
- 1 **pound Italian turkey sausage links, cut into ¼-inch slices**
- 1 **medium bunch broccoli, cut into florets**
- ½ **cup sliced red onion**
- 1 **can (14½ ounces) no-salt-added diced tomatoes, undrained**
- 1 **tablespoon minced fresh basil or 1 teaspoon dried basil**
- 1 **tablespoon minced fresh parsley or 1 teaspoon dried parsley flakes**
- 1 **teaspoon sugar**

1. Cook the spiral pasta according to the package directions. Meanwhile, in a large skillet, cook and stir sausage, broccoli and onion 5-6 minutes or until broccoli is crisp-tender.
2. Add the tomatoes, basil, parsley and sugar. Bring to a boil. Reduce the heat; simmer, covered, 8-10 minutes or until the broccoli is tender. Drain the pasta; add to skillet and heat through.

PER SERVING *1 serving equals 384 cal., 12 g fat (2 g sat. fat), 68 mg chol., 760 mg sodium, 44 g carb., 8 g fiber, 28 g pro.* **Diabetic Exchanges:** *3 medium-fat meat, 2 starch, 2 vegetable.*

APRICOT CRANBERRY CHICKEN

CURRY CHICKEN AND RICE

PEPPERED SOLE

1. Preheat oven to 375°. In a small saucepan, mix 2 tablespoons brown sugar, 2 tablespoons soy sauce, ginger, garlic and pepper.

2. Place turkey in a 13x9-in. baking dish coated with cooking spray; drizzle with half of the soy sauce mixture. Bake, uncovered, 25-30 minutes or until a thermometer reads 165°.

3. Meanwhile, add cornstarch and the remaining brown sugar and soy sauce to the remaining mixture in saucepan; stir until smooth. Stir in broth. Bring to a boil; cook and stir 1-2 minutes or until thickened. Cut turkey into slices; serve with sauce.

PER SERVING *4 ounces cooked turkey equals 212 cal., 2 g fat (1 g sat. fat), 69 mg chol., 639 mg sodium, 14 g carb., trace fiber, 35 g pro.* **Diabetic Exchanges:** *4 lean meat, 1 starch.*

FAST FIX ▶

Easy Chicken Paprikash

I first prepared this Hungarian dish for my husband years ago. We still love it paired with hot buttered noodles.

—**SUSAN WILDMAN** HASLETT, MI

START TO FINISH: 25 MIN.
MAKES: 4 SERVINGS

- 4   **cups uncooked egg noodles**
- ¾   **pound boneless skinless chicken breasts, cubed**
- 2   **medium onions, finely chopped**
- ½   **teaspoon salt**
- ¼   **teaspoon pepper**
- 2   **large tomatoes, seeded and chopped**
- 3   **teaspoons paprika**
- 1   **cup (8 ounces) sour cream**
      Sliced green onions, optional

1. Cook the egg noodles according to the package directions. Meanwhile, place a large nonstick skillet coated with cooking spray over medium heat. Add chicken, onions, salt and pepper; cook and stir 4-5 minutes or until the chicken is no longer pink.

2. Add tomatoes and paprika. Cook, covered, 5-7 minutes or until tomatoes are tender, stirring occasionally. Stir in sour cream; heat through (do not allow to boil). Drain the noodles; serve with chicken mixture. If desired, sprinkle with green onions.

EAT SMART FAST FIX ▶

Peppered Sole

This is the only way my daughter will eat fish. Because the sole cooked with sliced fresh mushrooms is a healthy choice, it's a winner with me, too!

—**JEANNETTE BAYE** AGASSIZ, BC

START TO FINISH: 25 MIN.
MAKES: 4 SERVINGS

- 2   **tablespoons butter**
- 2   **cups sliced fresh mushrooms**
- 2   **garlic cloves, minced**
- 4   **sole fillets (4 ounces each)**
- ¼   **teaspoon paprika**
- ¼   **teaspoon lemon-pepper seasoning**
- ⅛   **teaspoon cayenne pepper**
- 1   **medium tomato, chopped**
- 2   **green onions, thinly sliced**

1. In a large skillet, heat butter over medium-high heat. Add mushrooms; cook and stir until tender. Add garlic; cook 1 minute longer. Place fillets over mushrooms. Sprinkle with paprika, lemon-pepper and cayenne.

2. Cook, covered, over medium heat 5-10 minutes or until fish just begins to flake easily with a fork. Sprinkle with tomato and green onions.

PER SERVING *1 serving equals 174 cal., 7 g fat (4 g sat. fat), 69 mg chol., 166 mg sodium, 4 g carb., 1 g fiber, 23 g pro.* **Diabetic Exchanges:** *3 lean meat, 1½ fat, 1 vegetable.*

EAT SMART FAST FIX ▶

Garlic-Ginger Turkey Tenderloins

Here's a recipe to consider if you like Chinese food but not the inconvenience and cost of getting takeout. The saucy tenderloins have lots of authentic flavor and also use reduced-sodium ingredients.

—*TASTE OF HOME* TEST KITCHEN

START TO FINISH: 30 MIN.
MAKES: 4 SERVINGS

- 3   **tablespoons brown sugar, divided**
- 2   **tablespoons plus 2 teaspoons reduced-sodium soy sauce, divided**
- 2   **tablespoons minced fresh gingerroot**
- 6   **garlic cloves, minced**
- ½   **teaspoon pepper**
- 1   **package (20 ounces) turkey breast tenderloins**
- 1   **tablespoon cornstarch**
- 1   **cup reduced-sodium chicken broth**

LEMON-OLIVE
CHICKEN WITH ORZO

EAT SMART **FAST FIX**
Lemon-Olive Chicken with Orzo

Is your family big on pasta? Shake things up with tiny, rice-shaped orzo. I like to use the whole wheat variety.
—**NANCY BROWN** DAHINDA, IL

START TO FINISH: 30 MIN.
MAKES: 4 SERVINGS

- 1 **tablespoon olive oil**
- 4 **boneless skinless chicken thighs (about 1 pound)**
- 1 **can (14½ ounces) reduced-sodium chicken broth**
- ⅔ **cup uncooked whole wheat orzo pasta**
- ½ **medium lemon, cut into 4 wedges**
- ½ **cup pitted Greek olives, sliced**
- 1 **tablespoon lemon juice**
- 1 **teaspoon dried oregano**
- ¼ **teaspoon pepper**

1. In a large nonstick skillet, heat the olive oil over medium heat. Brown the chicken thighs on both sides; remove from the pan.
2. Add the chicken broth to skillet; increase the heat to medium-high. Cook 1-2 minutes, stirring to loosen browned bits from the pan. Stir in the remaining ingredients; bring to a boil. Reduce the heat; simmer, uncovered, 5 minutes, stirring occasionally.
3. Return the chicken to pan. Cook, covered, 5-8 minutes or until pasta is tender and a thermometer inserted in chicken reads 170°.
PER SERVING *1 serving equals 346 cal., 17 g fat (3 g sat. fat), 76 mg chol., 784 mg sodium, 22 g carb., 5 g fiber, 26 g pro. Diabetic Exchanges: 3 lean meat, 2 fat, 1 starch.*

FREEZE IT **FAST FIX**
Shortcut Sausage Jambalaya

My shortcut version of jambalaya has a secret ingredient: instant coffee granules! They add roasty, toasty flavor. It's part of the reason this quick and easy dinner is one of my husband's top picks.
—**BETTY HENAGIN** MEDFORD, OR

START TO FINISH: 20 MIN.
MAKES: 4 SERVINGS

- 1 **package (8.8 ounces) ready-to-serve long grain rice**
- 1 **tablespoon butter**
- 1 **small onion, chopped**
- 1 **celery rib, chopped**
- 1 **small green pepper, chopped**
- 1 **package (14 ounces) smoked turkey kielbasa, sliced**
- ¼ **teaspoon salt**
- ¼ **teaspoon garlic powder**
- ¼ **teaspoon pepper**
- ⅛ **teaspoon cayenne pepper, optional**
- 1 **can (14½ ounces) no-salt-added diced tomatoes, undrained**
- 1 **cup salsa**
  Dash instant coffee granules

1. Heat rice according to package directions. Meanwhile, in a large skillet, heat butter over medium-high heat. Add the onion, celery and green pepper; cook and stir 4-6 minutes or until tender. Stir in the kielbasa, salt, garlic powder, pepper and, if desired, cayenne; cook and stir 2-3 minutes or until kielbasa is browned.
2. Add tomatoes, salsa and coffee granules; heat through. Stir in rice.
FREEZE OPTION *Do not heat or add rice. Freeze cooled meat mixture in a freezer container. To use, partially thaw in refrigerator overnight. Heat rice according to package directions. Place meat mixture in a large skillet; heat through, stirring occasionally and adding a little water if necessary. Proceed as directed.*

EAT SMART **FAST FIX** ▶
Skewerless Stovetop Kabobs

When I fix this dinner, we never have leftovers. It's great on the grill, too.

—JENNIFER MITCHELL ALTOONA, PA

START TO FINISH: 30 MIN.
MAKES: 4 SERVINGS

- 1 pork tenderloin (1 pound), cut into ¾-inch cubes
- ¾ cup fat-free Italian salad dressing, divided
- 2 large green peppers, cut into ¾-inch pieces
- 2 small zucchini, cut into ½-inch slices
- 1 large sweet onion, cut into wedges
- ½ pound medium fresh mushrooms, halved
- 1 cup cherry tomatoes
- ¼ teaspoon pepper
- ⅛ teaspoon seasoned salt

1. In a large nonstick skillet, cook pork over medium-high heat in ¼ cup salad dressing until no longer pink. Remove from pan.

2. In same pan, cook peppers, zucchini, onion, mushrooms, tomatoes, pepper and seasoned salt in remaining salad dressing until vegetables are tender. Return pork to skillet; heat through.

PER SERVING *2 cups equals 236 cal., 5 g fat (2 g sat. fat), 65 mg chol., 757 mg sodium, 22 g carb., 4 g fiber, 27 g pro. Diabetic Exchanges: 3 lean meat, 2 starch.*

EAT SMART **FAST FIX** ▶
Black Beans with Bell Peppers & Rice

Here's a vegetarian supper my children gobble up every time I make it. For them, the more cheese, the better!

—STEPHANIE LAMBERT MOSELEY, VA

START TO FINISH: 30 MIN.
MAKES: 6 SERVINGS

- 1 tablespoon olive oil
- 1 each medium sweet yellow, orange and red pepper, chopped
- 1 large onion, chopped
- 2 garlic cloves, minced
- 2 cans (15 ounces each) black beans, rinsed and drained
- 1 package (8.8 ounces) ready-to-serve brown rice
- 1½ teaspoons ground cumin
- ½ teaspoon dried oregano
- 1½ cups (6 ounces) shredded Mexican cheese blend, divided
- 3 tablespoons minced fresh cilantro

1. In a large skillet, heat the olive oil over medium-high heat. Add the peppers, onion and garlic; cook and stir 6-8 minutes or until tender. Add black beans, rice, cumin and oregano; heat through.

2. Stir in 1 cup cheese; sprinkle with the remaining cheese. Remove from the heat. Let stand, covered, 5 minutes or until the cheese is melted. Sprinkle with cilantro.

PER SERVING *1 cup equals 347 cal., 12 g fat (6 g sat. fat), 25 mg chol., 477 mg sodium, 40 g carb., 8 g fiber, 15 g pro. Diabetic Exchanges: 2½ starch, 2 lean meat, 1 fat.*

EAT SMART **FAST FIX** ▶
Raspberry Pork Medallions

With a berry glaze, this pork is nice enough for company. We round out the meal with wild rice pilaf and steamed veggies.

—TRISHA KRUSE EAGLE, ID

START TO FINISH: 25 MIN.
MAKES: 4 SERVINGS

- 1 pork tenderloin (1 pound)
- 1 tablespoon canola oil
- 2 tablespoons reduced-sodium soy sauce
- 1 garlic clove, minced
- ½ teaspoon ground ginger
- 1 cup fresh raspberries
- 2 tablespoons seedless raspberry spreadable fruit
- 2 teaspoons minced fresh basil
- ½ teaspoon minced fresh mint, optional

1. Cut tenderloin crosswise into eight slices; pound each with a meat mallet to ½-in. thickness. In a large skillet, heat oil over medium-high heat. Add pork; cook 3-4 minutes on each side or until a thermometer reads 145°. Remove from pan; keep warm.

2. Reduce the heat to medium-low; add soy sauce, garlic and ginger to pan, stirring to loosen browned bits from pan. Add the raspberries, spreadable fruit, basil and, if desired, mint; cook and stir 2-3 minutes or until slightly thickened. Serve with pork.

PER SERVING *3 ounces cooked pork with 3 tablespoons sauce equals 206 cal., 8 g fat (2 g sat. fat), 64 mg chol., 333 mg sodium, 10 g carb., 2 g fiber, 24 g pro. Diabetic Exchanges: 3 lean meat, ½ starch, ½ fat.*

SKEWERLESS STOVETOP KABOBS

EASY ASIAN GLAZED
MEATBALLS

After going
to different
Mexican
restaurants
and trying
chiles rellenos, I wanted
to prepare them at home.
My husband and I teamed
up to create Chili-Stuffed
Poblano Peppers.

—LORRIE GRABCZYNSKI
COMMERCE TOWNSHIP, MI

FAST FIX
Easy Asian Glazed Meatballs

As a writer and busy mom of three hungry boys, I need to get family-pleasing food on the dinner table without delay. These Asian-style glazed meatballs make a great meal served over hot rice.

—**AMY DONG** WOODBURY, MN

START TO FINISH: 20 MIN.
MAKES: 4 SERVINGS

- ½ cup hoisin sauce
- 2 tablespoons rice vinegar
- 4 teaspoons brown sugar
- 1 teaspoon garlic powder
- 1 teaspoon Sriracha Asian hot chili sauce
- ½ teaspoon ground ginger
- 1 package (12 ounces) frozen fully cooked homestyle or Italian meatballs
  Thinly sliced green onions and toasted sesame seeds, optional
  Hot cooked rice

1. In a large saucepan, mix the first six ingredients until blended. Add the frozen meatballs, stirring to coat; cook, covered, over medium-low heat 12-15 minutes or until heated through, stirring occasionally.
2. If desired, sprinkle with green onions and toasted sesame seeds. Serve with rice.

FAST FIX
Skillet BBQ Beef Pot Pie

Pot pie is classic comfort food but can be time-consuming to fix. My version is speedier and uses leftover stuffing.

—**PRISCILLA YEE** CONCORD, CA

START TO FINISH: 25 MIN.
MAKES: 4 SERVINGS

- 1 pound lean ground beef (90% lean)
- ⅓ cup thinly sliced green onions, divided
- 2 cups frozen mixed vegetables, thawed
- ½ cup salsa
- ½ cup barbecue sauce
- 3 cups cooked cornbread stuffing
- ½ cup shredded cheddar cheese
- ¼ cup chopped sweet red pepper

1. In a large skillet, cook the beef and ¼ cup green onions over medium heat 6-8 minutes or until beef is no longer pink, breaking into crumbles; drain. Stir in the mixed vegetables, salsa and barbecue sauce; cook, covered, over medium-low heat 4-5 minutes or until heated through.
2. Layer the cornbread stuffing over the beef; sprinkle with the shredded cheese, pepper and remaining green onion. Cook, covered, 3-5 minutes longer or until heated through and cheese is melted.

FAST FIX
Chili-Stuffed Poblano Peppers

START TO FINISH: 30 MIN.
MAKES: 4 SERVINGS

- 1 pound lean ground turkey
- 1 can (15 ounces) chili without beans
- ¼ teaspoon salt
- 1½ cups (6 ounces) shredded Mexican cheese blend, divided
- 1 medium tomato, finely chopped
- 4 green onions, chopped
- 4 large poblano peppers
- 1 tablespoon olive oil

1. Preheat broiler. In a large skillet, cook the turkey over medium heat 5-7 minutes or until no longer pink, breaking into crumbles; drain. Add chili and salt; heat through. Stir in ½ cup cheese, tomato and onions.
2. Meanwhile, cut poblano peppers lengthwise in half; remove the seeds. Place on a foil-lined 15x10x1-in. baking pan, cut side down; brush with the oil. Broil 4 in. from heat until skins blister, about 5 minutes.
3. With tongs, turn poblano peppers. Fill with turkey mixture; sprinkle with remaining cheese. Broil 1-2 minutes longer or until cheese is melted.
NOTE *Wear disposable gloves when cutting hot peppers; the oils can burn skin. Avoid touching your face.*

CHILI-STUFFED
POBLANO PEPPERS

GARLIC-PORK
TORTILLA ROLLS

EAT SMART FAST FIX
Saucy Beef with Broccoli

When I'm looking for a fast entree, I toss together a beef and broccoli stir-fry that's ready in just 30 minutes.
—ROSA EVANS ODESSA, MO

START TO FINISH: 30 MIN.
MAKES: 2 SERVINGS

- 1 tablespoon cornstarch
- ½ cup reduced-sodium beef broth
- ¼ cup sherry or additional beef broth
- 2 tablespoons reduced-sodium soy sauce
- 1 tablespoon brown sugar
- 1 garlic clove, minced
- 1 teaspoon minced fresh gingerroot
- 2 teaspoons canola oil, divided
- ½ pound beef top sirloin steak, cut into ¼-inch strips
- 2 cups fresh broccoli florets
- 8 green onions, cut into 1-inch pieces

1. In a small bowl, mix the first seven ingredients. In a large nonstick skillet, heat 1 teaspoon oil over medium-high heat. Add the beef; stir-fry 1-2 minutes or until no longer pink. Remove from the pan.
2. Stir-fry broccoli in the remaining oil 4-5 minutes or until crisp-tender. Add green onions; cook 1-2 minutes longer or just until tender.
3. Stir cornstarch mixture and add to pan. Bring to a boil; cook and stir for 2-3 minutes or until thickened. Return beef to pan; heat through.
PER SERVING *1¼ cups equals 313 cal., 11 g fat (3 g sat. fat), 68 mg chol., 816 mg sodium, 20 g carb., 4 g fiber, 29 g pro.*

SAUCY BEEF WITH BROCCOLI

FAST FIX
Garlic-Pork Tortilla Rolls

To make our own Asian-style tortilla rolls, we use teriyaki-flavored pork, mandarin oranges, lettuce and French-fried onions. They're super simple but oh so good!
—JODI NOBILE SCOTIA, NY

START TO FINISH: 25 MIN.
MAKES: 4 SERVINGS

- 1 tablespoon canola oil
- 1 pound thin boneless pork loin chops (½ inch thick), cut into strips
- ½ cup reduced-sodium teriyaki sauce
- 3 garlic cloves, minced
- 1 teaspoon onion powder
- 4 flour tortillas (8 inches)
- 2 cups shredded romaine
- 1 can (11 ounces) mandarin oranges, drained
- ½ cup French-fried onions

1. In a large skillet, heat olive oil over medium heat. Add pork; cook and stir 4-5 minutes or until no longer pink. Add teriyaki sauce, garlic and onion powder; cook 3 minutes longer, stirring occasionally.
2. Using tongs, place about ⅔ cup pork mixture down center of each tortilla. Top with romaine, oranges and onions. Fold bottom of tortilla over filling; fold both sides to close. Serve immediately. If desired, serve with remaining pan sauce.

TOP TIP

Stored in a heavy-duty resealable plastic bag, unpeeled gingerroot may be frozen for up to 1 year. When needed, just peel and grate or mince.

LEMON & ROSEMARY CHICKEN

Lemon & Rosemary Chicken

This baked chicken featuring a tangy sauce is a family favorite. My sister even requests it for dinner on her birthday.

—**LAUREL DALZELL** MANTECA, CA

START TO FINISH: 30 MIN.
MAKES: 4 SERVINGS

- 4 **boneless skinless chicken breast halves (4 ounces each)**
- ¼ **teaspoon salt**
- ¼ **teaspoon pepper**
- 2 **teaspoons canola oil**
- 1 **shallot, finely chopped**
- 1 **tablespoon minced fresh rosemary or 1 teaspoon dried rosemary, crushed**
- ½ **cup reduced-sodium chicken broth**
- 2 **teaspoons grated lemon peel**
- 4½ **teaspoons lemon juice**
- ¼ **cup cold butter**

1. Preheat oven to 400°. Sprinkle the chicken with salt and pepper. In a large skillet, heat the oil over medium heat; brown chicken on both sides. Transfer to a 15x10x1-in. baking pan; reserve drippings. Bake chicken, uncovered, 8-10 minutes or until a thermometer reads 165°.
2. Meanwhile, in same skillet, cook and stir the shallot and rosemary in drippings until tender. Stir in broth. Bring to a boil; cook until the liquid is reduced by half. Reduce heat to low; stir in the lemon peel and lemon juice. Whisk in butter, 1 tablespoon at a time, until creamy. Serve with chicken.

FAST FIX

Creamy Sausage-Mushroom Rigatoni

While vacationing in Rome, we ate at an amazing restaurant near the Pantheon. Our meal lasted 3 hours! Enjoying my sausage rigatoni brings back many wonderful memories of that trip.

—**BARBARA ROOZROKH** BROOKFIELD, WI

START TO FINISH: 30 MIN.
MAKES: 6 SERVINGS

- 1 **package (16 ounces) rigatoni**
- 1 **pound bulk Italian sausage**
- 2 **teaspoons butter**
- 1 **pound sliced fresh mushrooms**
- 2 **garlic cloves, minced**
- ½ **teaspoon salt**
- ¼ **teaspoon pepper**
- 2 **cups heavy whipping cream**
  Minced fresh parsley, optional

1. Cook the rigatoni according to the package directions.
2. Meanwhile, in a large skillet, cook the Italian sausage over medium heat 4-6 minutes or until no longer pink, breaking into crumbles; drain and remove sausage from pan.
3. In the same skillet, heat the butter over medium heat. Add mushrooms, garlic, salt and pepper; cook, covered, 4 minutes, stirring occasionally. Uncover; cook and stir 2-3 minutes or until mushrooms are tender and liquid is evaporated.
4. Stir in the heavy whipping cream; bring to a boil. Reduce the heat; cook, uncovered, 8-10 minutes or until slightly thickened. Return sausage to skillet; heat through. Drain pasta; serve with sauce. If desired, sprinkle with parsley.

EAT SMART **FAST FIX**

Cod with Bacon & Balsamic Tomatoes

Let's face it—everything really is better with bacon! I fry it up, add cod fillets to the pan and finish with grape tomatoes.

—**MAUREEN MCCLANAHAN** ST. LOUIS, MO

START TO FINISH: 30 MIN.
MAKES: 4 SERVINGS

- 4 **center-cut bacon strips, chopped**
- 4 **cod fillets (5 ounces each)**
- ½ **teaspoon salt**
- ¼ **teaspoon pepper**
- 2 **cups grape tomatoes, halved**
- 2 **tablespoons balsamic vinegar**

1. In a large skillet, cook bacon over medium heat until crisp, stirring occasionally. Remove with a slotted spoon; drain on paper towels.
2. Sprinkle fillets with salt and pepper. Add fillets to bacon drippings; cook over medium-high heat 4-6 minutes on each side or until fish just begins to flake easily with a fork. Remove and keep warm.
3. Add the grape tomatoes to skillet; cook and stir 2-4 minutes or until the tomatoes are softened. Stir in balsamic vinegar; reduce heat to medium-low. Cook 1-2 minutes longer or until sauce is thickened. Serve cod with tomato mixture and bacon.
PER SERVING *1 fillet with ¼ cup tomato mixture and 1 tablespoon bacon equals 178 cal., 6 g fat (2 g sat. fat), 64 mg chol., 485 mg sodium, 5 g carb., 1 g fiber, 26 g pro.* **Diabetic Exchanges:** *4 lean meat, 1 vegetable.*

CHEESE TORTELLINI WITH
TOMATOES AND CORN

EAT SMART **FAST FIX**
Cheese Tortellini with Tomatoes and Corn

Fresh corn, tomatoes and basil bring the taste of summer to tortellini. This recipe is nice for picnics and easy to double, too.

—**SALLY MALONEY** DALLAS, GA

START TO FINISH: 25 MIN.
MAKES: 4 SERVINGS

- 1 package (9 ounces) refrigerated cheese tortellini
- 3⅓ cups fresh or frozen corn (about 16 ounces)
- 2 cups cherry tomatoes, quartered
- 2 green onions, thinly sliced
- ¼ cup minced fresh basil
- 2 tablespoons grated Parmesan cheese
- 4 teaspoons olive oil
- ¼ teaspoon garlic powder
- ⅛ teaspoon pepper

In a 6-qt. stockpot, cook the cheese tortellini according to the package directions, adding corn during the last 5 minutes of cooking. Drain; transfer to a large bowl. Add the remaining ingredients; toss to coat.
PER SERVING *1¾ cups equals 366 cal., 12 g fat (4 g sat. fat), 30 mg chol., 286 mg sodium, 57 g carb., 5 g fiber, 14 g pro.*

FAST FIX
Chicken Verde Quesadillas

I used packaged grilled chicken and the veggies I had in the fridge to fix quesadillas. Just add sour cream and pico de gallo if you want, and you're good to go.

—**JULIE MERRIMAN** SEATTLE, WA

START TO FINISH: 30 MIN.
MAKES: 4 SERVINGS

- 2 tablespoons olive oil, divided
- 1 large sweet onion, halved and thinly sliced
- 1½ cups frozen corn
- 1 small zucchini, chopped
- 1 poblano pepper, thinly sliced
- 2 cups frozen grilled chicken breast strips, thawed and chopped
- ¾ cup green enchilada sauce
- ¼ cup minced fresh cilantro
- ¼ teaspoon salt
- ⅛ teaspoon pepper
- 8 flour tortillas (10 inches)
- 4 cups (16 ounces) shredded Monterey Jack cheese
  Pico de gallo and sour cream, optional

1. Preheat oven to 400°. In a large skillet, heat 1 tablespoon oil over medium-high heat. Add the sweet onion, corn, zucchini and poblano pepper; cook and stir 8-10 minutes or until tender. Add chicken strips, enchilada sauce, cilantro, salt and pepper; heat through.
2. Brush the remaining oil over one side of each flour tortilla. Place half of the tortillas on two baking sheets, oiled side down. Sprinkle each with ½ cup shredded cheese. Top with 1 cup chicken mixture, remaining cheese and tortillas, oiled side up.
3. Bake 7-9 minutes or until golden brown and the cheese is melted. If desired, serve with pico de gallo and sour cream.

Chicken & Garlic with Fresh Herbs

The secret to this savory skillet chicken is the combination of garlic, rosemary and thyme. With mashed potatoes or thick slices of crusty bread on the side, it's an amazing 30-minute meal.

—JAN VALDEZ LOMBARD, IL

START TO FINISH: 30 MIN.
MAKES: 6 SERVINGS

- 6 boneless skinless chicken thighs (about 1½ pounds)
- ½ teaspoon salt
- ¼ teaspoon pepper
- 1 tablespoon olive oil
- 10 garlic cloves, peeled and halved
- 2 tablespoons brandy or chicken stock
- 1 cup chicken stock
- 1 teaspoon minced fresh rosemary or ¼ teaspoon dried rosemary, crushed
- ½ teaspoon minced fresh thyme or ⅛ teaspoon dried thyme
- 1 tablespoon minced fresh chives

1. Sprinkle chicken with salt and pepper. In a large skillet, heat oil over medium-high heat. Brown chicken on both sides. Remove from pan.
2. Remove skillet from heat; add halved garlic cloves and brandy. Return to heat; cook and stir over medium heat 1-2 minutes or until liquid is almost evaporated.
3. Stir in stock, rosemary and thyme; return the chicken to pan. Bring to a boil. Reduce heat; simmer, uncovered, 6-8 minutes or until a thermometer reads 170°. Sprinkle with chives.
PER SERVING *1 chicken thigh with 2 tablespoons cooking juices equals 203 cal., 11 g fat (3 g sat. fat), 76 mg chol., 346 mg sodium, 2 g carb., trace fiber, 22 g pro.* **Diabetic Exchanges:** *3 lean meat, ½ fat.*

SIMPLE SAUSAGE PASTA TOSS

Simple Sausage Pasta Toss

When you're eating lighter but want bold flavor, Italian turkey sausage is a terrific option. Try it on your next spaghetti night.

—*TASTE OF HOME* TEST KITCHEN

START TO FINISH: 25 MIN.
MAKES: 5 SERVINGS

- 8 ounces uncooked multigrain spaghetti
- ¼ cup seasoned bread crumbs
- 1 teaspoon olive oil
- ¾ pound Italian turkey sausage links, cut into ½-inch slices
- 1 garlic clove, minced
- 2 cans (14½ ounces each) no-salt-added diced tomatoes, undrained
- 1 can (2¼ ounces) sliced ripe olives, drained

1. Cook the spaghetti according to the package directions; drain. Meanwhile, in a large skillet, toss the bread crumbs with oil; cook and stir over medium heat until toasted. Remove from pan.
2. Add sausage to same pan; cook and stir over medium heat until no longer pink. Add garlic; cook 30-60 seconds longer. Stir in the tomatoes and olives; heat through. Add spaghetti and toss to combine. Sprinkle with the toasted bread crumbs before serving.
PER SERVING *1⅔ cups equals 340 cal., 10 g fat (2 g sat. fat), 41 mg chol., 689 mg sodium, 44 g carb., 6 g fiber, 21 g pro.* **Diabetic Exchanges:** *3 lean meat, 2 starch, 1 vegetable, ½ fat.*

CHICKEN & GARLIC WITH FRESH HERBS

EAT SMART FAST FIX ▶

Pizzaiola Chops

My cousin gave me her pork chop recipe, and I made a few adjustments from there. Taste as you go—and try the Italian trick of sprinkling on more oregano to give it that little extra "something."

—**LORRAINE CALAND** SHUNIAH, ON

START TO FINISH: 30 MIN.
MAKES: 4 SERVINGS

- 2 tablespoons olive oil, divided
- 4 boneless pork loin chops (6 ounces each)
- 1 teaspoon salt, divided
- ¼ teaspoon pepper, divided
- 1½ cups sliced baby portobello mushrooms
- 1 medium sweet yellow pepper, coarsely chopped
- 1 medium sweet red pepper, coarsely chopped
- 2 large tomatoes, chopped
- ½ cup white wine or chicken broth
- 1 tablespoon minced fresh oregano or ½ teaspoon dried oregano
- 2 garlic cloves, minced
  Hot cooked rice, optional

1. In a large skillet, heat 1 tablespoon oil over medium-high heat. Season the pork chops with ½ teaspoon salt and ⅛ teaspoon pepper. Brown the pork chops on both sides. Remove chops from the pan.

2. In the same pan, heat the remaining oil over medium-high heat. Add the baby portobello mushrooms, yellow pepper and red pepper; cook and stir 3-4 minutes or until the portobello mushrooms are tender. Add tomatoes, white wine, oregano, garlic and the remaining salt and pepper. Bring to a boil. Reduce the heat; simmer, uncovered, 2 minutes.

3. Return the pork chops to the pan. Cook, covered, 5-7 minutes or until a thermometer inserted in pork reads 145°. Let stand 5 minutes; if desired, serve with rice.

PER SERVING *1 pork chop and 1 cup vegetable mixture (calculated without rice) equals 351 cal., 17 g fat (5 g sat. fat), 82 mg chol., 647 mg sodium, 10 g carb., 2 g fiber, 35 g pro.* **Diabetic Exchanges:** *5 lean meat, 1½ fat, 1 vegetable.*

CHICKEN VEGGIE SKILLET

EAT SMART FAST FIX ▶

Chicken Veggie Skillet

I thought of this as a way to use up leftover vegetables. My husband took one bite and said I should write it down!

—**REBEKAH BEYER** SABETHA, KS

START TO FINISH: 30 MIN.
MAKES: 6 SERVINGS

- 1½ pounds boneless skinless chicken breasts, cut into ½-inch strips
- ½ teaspoon salt
- ¼ teaspoon pepper
- 6 teaspoons olive oil, divided
- ½ pound sliced fresh mushrooms
- 1 small onion, halved and sliced
- 2 garlic cloves, minced
- 1 pound fresh asparagus, trimmed and cut into 1-inch pieces
- ½ cup sherry or chicken stock
- 2 tablespoons cold butter, cubed

1. Sprinkle the chicken strips with salt and pepper. In a large skillet, heat 1 teaspoon oil over medium-high heat. Add half of the chicken; cook and stir 3-4 minutes or until no longer pink. Remove from the pan. Repeat with 1 teaspoon oil and remaining chicken.

2. In same pan, heat 2 teaspoons oil. Add the mushrooms and onion; cook and stir 2-3 minutes or until tender. Add the garlic; cook 1 minute longer. Add to chicken.

3. Heat the remaining oil in the pan. Add asparagus; cook 2-3 minutes or until crisp-tender. Add to chicken and mushrooms.

4. Add the sherry to skillet, stirring to loosen browned bits from pan. Bring to a boil; cook 1-2 minutes or until the liquid is reduced to 2 tablespoons. Return chicken and vegetables to pan; heat through. Remove from the heat; stir in butter, 1 tablespoon at a time.

PER SERVING *1 cup equals 228 cal., 11 g fat (4 g sat. fat), 73 mg chol., 384 mg sodium, 6 g carb., 1 g fiber, 25 g pro.* **Diabetic Exchanges:** *3 lean meat, 2 fat, 1 vegetable.*

Stir-Fried Steak & Veggies

Why get Chinese takeout? Here's a stir-fry you'll have ready in less than half an hour.

—**VICKY PRIESTLEY** ALUM CREEK, WV

START TO FINISH: 25 MIN.
MAKES: 6 SERVINGS

- 1½ **cups uncooked instant brown rice**
- 1 **tablespoon cornstarch**
- ½ **cup cold water**
- ¼ **cup reduced-sodium soy sauce**
- 1 **tablespoon brown sugar**
- ¾ **teaspoon ground ginger**
- ½ **teaspoon chili powder**
- ¼ **teaspoon garlic powder**
- ¼ **teaspoon pepper**
- 2 **tablespoons canola oil, divided**
- 1 **pound beef top sirloin steak, cut into ½-inch cubes**
- 1 **package (16 ounces) frozen stir-fry vegetable blend, thawed**

1. Cook the brown rice according to the package directions. Meanwhile, in a small bowl, mix the cornstarch, water, soy sauce, brown sugar and seasonings until smooth.

2. In a large nonstick skillet coated with cooking spray, heat 1 tablespoon oil over medium-high heat. Add the steak; stir-fry until no longer pink. Remove from the pan. Stir-fry the vegetables in the remaining oil until crisp-tender.

3. Stir the cornstarch mixture and add to the pan. Bring to a boil; cook and stir 1-2 minutes or until sauce is thickened. Return the steak to pan; heat through. Serve with rice.

PER SERVING *¾ cup stir-fry with ½ cup rice equals 304 cal., 8 g fat (2 g sat. fat), 42 mg chol., 470 mg sodium, 37 g carb., 3 g fiber, 19 g pro.* **Diabetic Exchanges:** *2 lean meat, 2 vegetable, 1½ starch, 1 fat.*

STIR-FRIED STEAK & VEGGIES

Thai Chicken Linguine

When I'm serving dinner for a big group, I prepare a double batch of this simple, Thai-inspired chicken with linguine. People of all ages enjoy it.

—**TERI RUMBLE** JENSEN BEACH, FL

START TO FINISH: 30 MIN.
MAKES: 6 SERVINGS

- 8 **ounces uncooked whole wheat linguine**
- ⅓ **cup reduced-sodium soy sauce**
- ¼ **cup lime juice**
- 3 **tablespoons brown sugar**
- 2 **tablespoons rice vinegar**
- 1 **tablespoon Thai chili sauce**
- 2 **tablespoons peanut oil, divided**
- 1 **pound boneless skinless chicken breasts, cubed**
- 1 **cup fresh snow peas**
- 1 **medium sweet red pepper, julienned**
- 4 **garlic cloves, minced**
- 2 **large eggs, beaten**
- ⅓ **cup chopped unsalted peanuts**

1. Cook linguine according to package directions. Meanwhile, in a small bowl, mix soy sauce, lime juice, brown sugar, vinegar and chili sauce until blended.

2. In a large nonstick skillet, heat 1 tablespoon oil over medium-high heat. Add chicken; stir-fry 5-7 minutes or until no longer pink. Remove from the pan. Stir-fry snow peas and pepper in remaining oil until the vegetables are crisp-tender. Add the garlic; cook 1 minute longer. Add eggs; cook and stir until set.

3. Drain linguine; add to the vegetable mixture. Stir the soy sauce mixture and add to the pan. Bring to a boil. Add the chicken; heat through. Sprinkle with peanuts.

PER SERVING *1⅓ cups equals 377 cal., 13 g fat (2 g sat. fat), 104 mg chol., 697 mg sodium, 44 g carb., 5 g fiber, 25 g pro.* **Diabetic Exchanges:** *3 starch, 3 lean meat, 2 fat.*

PORK & VEGETABLE
SPRING ROLLS

Shrimp Orzo with Feta

In this seafood entree, lemon and cilantro add freshness while feta lends richness.
—**SARAH HUMMEL** MOON TOWNSHIP, PA

START TO FINISH: 25 MIN.
MAKES: 4 SERVINGS

- 1¼ cups uncooked whole wheat orzo pasta
- 2 tablespoons olive oil
- 2 garlic cloves, minced
- 2 medium tomatoes, chopped
- 2 tablespoons lemon juice
- 1¼ pounds uncooked shrimp (26-30 per pound), peeled and deveined
- 2 tablespoons minced fresh cilantro
- ¼ teaspoon pepper
- ½ cup crumbled feta cheese

1. Cook orzo according to package directions. Meanwhile, in a large skillet, heat the oil over medium heat. Add the garlic; cook and stir 1 minute. Add tomatoes and lemon juice. Bring to a boil. Stir in shrimp. Reduce heat; simmer, uncovered, 4-5 minutes or until shrimp turn pink.

2. Drain orzo. Add orzo, cilantro and pepper to the shrimp mixture; heat through. Sprinkle with feta cheese.

PER SERVING *1 cup equals 406 cal., 12 g fat (3 g sat. fat), 180 mg chol., 307 mg sodium, 40 g carb., 9 g fiber, 33 g pro.* **Diabetic Exchanges:** *4 lean meat, 2 starch, 1 fat.*

SHRIMP ORZO
WITH FETA

Pork & Vegetable Spring Rolls

Rice paper wrappers are a quick, fun way to serve salad ingredients as a hand-held snack or meal. Try it and see!
—**MARLA STRADER** OZARK, MO

START TO FINISH: 30 MIN.
MAKES: 4 SERVINGS

- 2 cups thinly sliced romaine
- 1½ cups cubed cooked pork
- 1 cup thinly sliced fresh spinach
- ¾ cup julienned carrot
- ⅓ cup thinly sliced celery
- ⅓ cup dried cherries, coarsely chopped
- 1 tablespoon sesame oil
- 12 round rice paper wrappers (8 inches)
- ¼ cup sliced almonds
- ¼ cup wasabi-coated green peas
  Sesame ginger salad dressing

1. In a large bowl, combine the first six ingredients. Drizzle with sesame oil; toss to coat.

2. Fill a large shallow dish partway with water. Dip a rice paper wrapper into the water just until pliable, about 45 seconds (do not soften completely); allow excess water to drip off.

3. Place the rice paper wrapper on a flat surface. Layer the salad mixture, almonds and peas across the bottom third of wrapper. Fold in both ends of wrapper; fold bottom side over filling, then roll up tightly. Place on a serving plate, seam side down. Repeat with remaining ingredients. Serve with salad dressing.

PER SERVING *3 spring rolls (calculated without salad dressing) equals 255 cal., 12 g fat (3 g sat. fat), 48 mg chol., 91 mg sodium, 19 g carb., 3 g fiber, 18 g pro.* **Diabetic Exchanges:** *3 lean meat, 1 starch, 1 vegetable, 1 fat.*

My recipe for Spicy Lasagna Skillet Dinner bails me out when I'm running out of time on weeknights. A leafy salad and buttery garlic toast are easy sides.
—**DONNA BOOTH** TOMAHAWK, KY

SPICY LASAGNA
SKILLET DINNER

Pork Medallions in Mustard Sauce

I like to pair apricot preserves with pork medallions and wondered how else I could dress them up. Some experimenting in the kitchen led to a mustard sauce flavored with apple juice and garlic.
—**TAHNIA FOX** TRENTON, MI

START TO FINISH: 30 MIN.
MAKES: 4 SERVINGS

- ½ cup reduced-sodium chicken broth
- 2 tablespoons thawed apple juice concentrate
- 4½ teaspoons stone-ground mustard
- 1 pork tenderloin (1 pound), cut into ½-inch slices
- ¼ teaspoon salt
- ¼ teaspoon pepper
- 1 tablespoon olive oil
- 2 garlic cloves, minced
- 1 teaspoon cornstarch
- 2 tablespoons cold water
- 1 tablespoon minced fresh parsley

1. In a small bowl, mix chicken broth, apple juice concentrate and mustard. Sprinkle the pork with salt and pepper. In a large nonstick skillet, heat oil over medium-high heat. Brown pork on both sides; remove from pan.
2. Add the garlic to same pan; cook and stir 1 minute. Add broth mixture, stirring to loosen browned bits from pan. Bring to a boil. Reduce the heat; simmer, uncovered, 6-8 minutes or until liquid is reduced to about ⅓ cup.
3. Return pork to pan; cook, covered, over low heat 3-4 minutes or until a thermometer inserted in pork reads 145°. Mix cornstarch and cold water until smooth; stir into pan. Bring to a boil; cook and stir 2 minutes or until thickened. Sprinkle with parsley.
PER SERVING *3 ounces cooked pork equals 193 cal., 7 g fat (2 g sat. fat), 63 mg chol., 356 mg sodium, 6 g carb., 1 g fiber, 23 g pro.* **Diabetic Exchanges:** *3 lean meat, ½ starch, ½ fat.*

Spicy Lasagna Skillet Dinner

START TO FINISH: 30 MIN.
MAKES: 6 SERVINGS

- 1 package (6.4 ounces) lasagna dinner mix
- 1 pound lean ground beef (90% lean)
- 1 large onion, chopped
- 1 medium green pepper, chopped
- 1 garlic clove, minced
- 1 jar (14 ounces) meatless spaghetti sauce
- ½ cup chunky salsa
- 1 teaspoon garlic powder
- 1 teaspoon Italian seasoning
- ½ teaspoon dried thyme
- ½ teaspoon ground cumin
- ¼ teaspoon salt
- ¼ teaspoon crushed red pepper flakes
- 1 cup (4 ounces) shredded mozzarella and provolone cheese blend

1. Fill a large saucepan three-fourths full with water; bring to a boil. Add the pasta from the lasagna dinner mix; cook, uncovered, 10-12 minutes or until tender.
2. Meanwhile, in a large skillet, cook the beef, onion, green pepper and garlic over medium heat 6-8 minutes or until the beef is no longer pink and the vegetables are tender, breaking up the beef into crumbles; drain.
3. Stir in the meatless spaghetti sauce, chunky salsa, seasonings and contents of the seasoning packet from lasagna dinner. Bring to a boil. Reduce the heat; simmer, uncovered, 5 minutes. Remove from heat.
4. Drain the pasta. Add to the tomato mixture; toss to coat. Sprinkle with the shredded cheese; let stand, covered, until cheese is melted.
FREEZE OPTION *Freeze the cooled pasta mixture and cheese in separate freezer containers. To use, partially thaw in the refrigerator overnight. Heat through in a skillet, stirring occasionally and adding a little water if necessary. Remove from the heat. Sprinkle with the cheese; let stand, covered, until cheese is melted.*

FREEZE IT EAT SMART FAST FIX

Tomato & Garlic Butter Bean Dinner

When I get home late and want nothing more than a hot meal, I turn to this dish. The noodles can cook at the same time.
—**JESSICA MEYERS** AUSTIN, TX

START TO FINISH: 15 MIN.
MAKES: 4 SERVINGS

- 1 tablespoon olive oil
- 2 garlic cloves, minced
- 2 cans (14½ ounces) no-salt-added petite diced tomatoes, undrained
- 1 can (16 ounces) butter beans, rinsed and drained
- 6 cups fresh baby spinach (about 6 ounces)
- ½ teaspoon Italian seasoning
- ¼ teaspoon pepper
  Hot cooked pasta and grated Parmesan cheese, optional

In a large skillet, heat olive oil over medium-high heat. Add garlic; cook and stir 30-45 seconds or until tender. Add tomatoes, beans, spinach, Italian seasoning and pepper; cook until the spinach is wilted, stirring occasionally. If desired, serve with pasta and cheese.

FREEZE OPTION *Freeze the cooled bean mixture in freezer containers. To use, partially thaw in refrigerator overnight. Heat through in a saucepan, stirring occasionally and adding a little water if necessary.*

PER SERVING *1¼ cups (calculated without pasta and cheese) equals 147 cal., 4 g fat (1 g sat. fat), 0 chol., 353 mg sodium, 28 g carb., 9 g fiber, 8 g pro.* **Diabetic Exchanges:** *2 starch, ½ fat.*

TOMATO & GARLIC BUTTER BEAN DINNER

MAPLE SAUSAGE SKILLET

FAST FIX

Maple Sausage Skillet

Maple syrup brings a wonderful touch of sweetness to savory kielbasa and fresh vegetables. For even more green in the skillet, I sometimes add a little broccoli.
—**DOTTIE TARLTON** MALVERN, AR

START TO FINISH: 25 MIN.
MAKES: 2 SERVINGS

- 1 teaspoon canola oil
- ½ pound fully cooked kielbasa or Polish sausage, sliced
- 1½ cups sliced fresh mushrooms
- 1 medium green pepper, thinly sliced
- 1 small onion, halved and sliced
- 1 celery rib, sliced
- 2 tablespoons maple syrup
- ¼ teaspoon pepper
  Hot cooked rice

In a large skillet, heat the oil over medium-high heat. Add sausage; cook and stir 3-4 minutes or until lightly browned. Add vegetables; cook and stir 3-4 minutes longer or until vegetables are crisp-tender. Stir in the syrup and pepper; heat through. Serve with rice.

TOP TIP

Consider cooking extra rice to freeze. Packaged in freezer containers or heavy-duty resealable plastic bags, cooked rice will keep in the freezer for up to 6 months. To reheat, just add 2 tablespoons of liquid for each cup of rice; microwave it or cook it in a saucepan until heated through.

Santa Fe Chicken and Rice

This cheesy chicken over Southwest-style rice makes an almost effortless dinner.

—**DEBRA COOK** PAMPA, TX

START TO FINISH: 30 MIN.
MAKES: 2 SERVINGS

- 2 teaspoons butter
- ½ cup chopped onion
- ⅔ cup chicken broth
- ½ cup salsa
- ⅛ teaspoon garlic powder
- ½ cup uncooked long grain rice
- 2 boneless skinless chicken breast halves (5 ounces each)
- ⅓ cup shredded cheddar cheese
  Chopped fresh cilantro, optional

1. In a small skillet, heat butter over medium-high heat. Add onion; cook and stir until tender.
2. Add the chicken broth, salsa and garlic powder; bring to a boil. Stir in rice; return to a boil. Place the chicken over rice. Reduce the heat; simmer, covered, 20-25 minutes or until rice is tender and a thermometer inserted in the chicken reads 165°, turning chicken halfway.
3. Remove from heat. Sprinkle with the cheese; cover and let stand until cheese is melted. If desired, sprinkle with cilantro.

Speedy Salmon Stir-Fry

A staple where I live, salmon is delicious in a stir-fry. For a twist, use the juice and peel of a lime instead of an orange.

—**JONI HILTON** ROCKLIN, CA

START TO FINISH: 30 MIN.
MAKES: 4 SERVINGS

- ¼ cup reduced-fat honey mustard salad dressing
- 2 tablespoons orange juice
- 1 tablespoon minced fresh gingerroot
- 1 tablespoon reduced-sodium soy sauce
- 1 tablespoon molasses
- 1 teaspoon grated orange peel
- 4 teaspoons canola oil, divided
- 1 pound salmon fillets, skin removed and cut into 1-inch pieces
- 1 package (16 ounces) frozen stir-fry vegetable blend
- 2⅔ cups hot cooked brown rice
- 1 tablespoon sesame seeds, toasted

1. In a small bowl, whisk the first six ingredients. In a large skillet, heat 2 teaspoons oil over medium-high heat. Add the salmon fillets; cook and gently stir 3-4 minutes or until the fish just begins to flake easily with a fork. Remove from pan.
2. In same pan, heat remaining oil. Add the vegetable blend; stir-fry until crisp-tender. Add the salad dressing mixture. Return the salmon to skillet. Gently combine; heat through. Serve with rice; sprinkle with sesame seeds.
PER SERVING *1 cup stir-fry with ⅔ cup rice equals 498 cal., 19 g fat (3 g sat. fat), 57 mg chol., 394 mg sodium, 54 g carb., 5 g fiber, 26 g pro.*

Sausage Orecchiette Pasta

I tried coming up with a lighter version of my favorite pasta served at an Italian restaurant. Here's the result—and I think it tastes even better!

—**MELANIE TRITTEN** CHARLOTTE, NC

START TO FINISH: 25 MIN.
MAKES: 6 SERVINGS

- 4 cups uncooked orecchiette or small tube pasta
- 1 package (19½ ounces) Italian turkey sausage links, casings removed
- 3 garlic cloves, minced
- 1 cup white wine or chicken broth
- 4 cups small fresh broccoli florets
- 1 can (14½ ounces) diced tomatoes, drained
- ⅓ cup grated Parmesan cheese

1. Cook pasta according to package directions. Meanwhile, in a large skillet, cook sausage over medium heat 6-8 minutes or until no longer pink, breaking into crumbles. Add garlic; cook 1 minute longer. Add white wine, stirring to loosen browned bits from pan. Bring to a boil; cook 1-2 minutes or until liquid is reduced by half.
2. Stir in the broccoli and tomatoes. Reduce the heat; simmer, covered, 4-6 minutes or until the broccoli is crisp-tender. Drain the pasta; add to the skillet and toss to coat. Serve with Parmesan cheese.
PER SERVING *1⅔ cups equals 363 cal., 8 g fat (2 g sat. fat), 38 mg chol., 571 mg sodium, 48 g carb., 5 g fiber, 20 g pro.* **Diabetic Exchanges:** *3 lean meat, 2½ starch, 1 vegetable.*

SANTA FE CHICKEN AND RICE

SOUTHWEST
SKILLET CHOPS

Southwest Skillet Chops

These easy chops get zip from a relish of jalapeno, onion, corn and olives.
—**LINDA CIFUENTES** MAHOMET, IL

START TO FINISH: 25 MIN.
MAKES: 4 SERVINGS

- 4 **boneless pork loin chops (6 ounces each)**
- ¾ **teaspoon salt**
- ¼ **teaspoon pepper**
- 2 **tablespoons butter, divided**
- 1 **tablespoon olive oil**
- ½ **small red onion, sliced**
- 1 **jalapeno pepper, seeded and finely chopped**
- ½ **cup frozen corn, thawed**
- 3 **tablespoons lime juice**
- ¼ **cup sliced ripe olives or green olives with pimientos, optional**

1. Sprinkle the pork chops with salt and pepper. In a large skillet, heat 1 tablespoon butter and olive oil over medium-high heat. Brown pork chops on both sides. Remove from pan.
2. In same skillet, heat remaining butter. Add onion and jalapeno; cook and stir 2-3 minutes or until tender. Return chops to skillet. Add corn, juice and, if desired, olives; cook, covered, 4-6 minutes or until a thermometer inserted in pork reads 145°. Let stand 5 minutes before serving.
NOTE *Wear disposable gloves when cutting hot peppers; the oils can burn skin. Avoid touching your face.*

Turkey a la King with Rice

Put leftover turkey to great use! If you like, substitute noodles or biscuits for the rice.
—**PAT LEMKE** BRANDON, WI

START TO FINISH: 30 MIN.
MAKES: 4 SERVINGS

- 2 **tablespoons butter**
- 1¾ **cups sliced fresh mushrooms**
- 1 **celery rib, chopped**
- ¼ **cup chopped onion**
- ¼ **cup chopped green pepper**
- ¼ **cup all-purpose flour**
- 1 **cup reduced-sodium chicken broth**
- 1 **cup fat-free milk**
- 2 **cups cubed cooked turkey breast**
- 1 **cup frozen peas**
- ½ **teaspoon salt**
- 2 **cups hot cooked rice**

1. In a large nonstick skillet, heat the butter over medium-high heat. Add mushrooms, celery, onion and pepper; cook and stir until tender.
2. In a small bowl, mix flour and broth until smooth; stir into the vegetable mixture. Stir in the milk. Bring to a boil; cook and stir 1-2 minutes or until thickened. Add turkey, peas and salt; heat through. Serve with rice.
PER SERVING *1¼ cups turkey mixture with ½ cup rice equals 350 cal., 7 g fat (4 g sat. fat), 76 mg chol., 594 mg sodium, 40 g carb., 3 g fiber, 30 g pro.*
Diabetic Exchanges: *3 lean meat, 2 starch, 1½ fat, 1 vegetable.*

Weeknight Cabbage Kielbasa Skillet

I like the challenge of cooking wholesome meals that have big flavor. This home-style dinner recipe, which came from a dear friend, is especially popular with my son. He rated it a 10 out of 10!
—**BEVERLY BATTY** FOREST LAKE, MN

START TO FINISH: 30 MIN.
MAKES: 4 SERVINGS

- 1½ **teaspoons cornstarch**
- ¼ **cup cider vinegar**
- 1 **tablespoon honey**
- 1 **teaspoon Dijon mustard**
- ¼ **teaspoon salt**
- ¼ **teaspoon pepper**
- 1 **tablespoon canola oil**
- 1 **package (14 ounces) smoked turkey kielbasa, cut into ¼-inch slices**
- 2 **medium red potatoes (about 8 ounces), cut into ½-inch cubes**
- ½ **cup sliced sweet onion**
- ½ **cup chopped sweet red pepper**
- 4 **bacon strips, cooked and crumbled**
- ½ **cup water**
- 1 **teaspoon beef bouillon granules**
- 1 **package (14 ounces) coleslaw mix**

1. In a small bowl, whisk the first six ingredients until smooth. In a large skillet, heat the oil over medium-high heat. Add turkey kielbasa, potatoes, onion, red pepper and bacon; cook and stir 3-5 minutes or until the kielbasa is lightly browned.
2. Add the water and beef bouillon; bring to a boil. Reduce heat; simmer, covered, 6-8 minutes or until potatoes are almost tender. Add coleslaw; cook, covered, 4-6 minutes longer or until tender, stirring occasionally.
3. Stir the cornstarch mixture and add to the pan. Bring to a boil; cook and stir 1-2 minutes or until sauce is thickened.

Asian Vegetable Pasta

Satisfy your craving for pasta! Bring 4 quarts water to a boil. Add 8 ounces angel hair pasta and 1 pound fresh asparagus (cut into 1-in. pieces); cook for 3 minutes. Stir in ¾ cup julienned carrots; cook for 1 minute or until pasta is tender; drain. In a saucepan, combine ⅓ cup reduced-fat creamy peanut butter, 3 tablespoons each reduced-sodium soy sauce and rice vinegar, 2 tablespoons brown sugar and ½ teaspoon crushed red pepper flakes. Bring to a boil, stirring constantly. Toss with pasta. Sprinkle with ¼ cup chopped unsalted peanuts. *Makes 5 servings.*

—**MITZI SENTIFF** ANNAPOLIS, MD

Bess Blanco's
Easy Asian Chicken
Slaw PAGE 118

Finished in 15

Have only 15 minutes to spare? That's all the time you need to serve your family delicious, satisfying home-cooked food. Just try any of the main dishes, sides, desserts and snacks in this chapter.

Robert Bishop's Stuffed Sole with Shrimp *PAGE 121*

Milford Herman's Microwaved Parmesan Chicken *PAGE 118*

Gaylene Anderson's Camping Haystacks *PAGE 125*

JALAPENO
HUMMUS

FAST FIX

Pesto Vermicelli with Bay Scallops

Indulge in a seafood entree that tastes like a restaurant specialty but is so easy to make. Thanks to convenient prepared pesto, this is it! I get the vermicelli going and cook everything else together in one skillet. Include a quick tossed green salad on the side for a dinner you and your family will want again and again.

—MARILYN LUSTGARTEN WENTZVILLE, MO

START TO FINISH: 15 MIN.
MAKES: 4 SERVINGS

8 ounces uncooked vermicelli
¼ cup butter, cubed
1 teaspoon garlic powder
¼ teaspoon dried oregano
⅛ teaspoon pepper
1 pound bay scallops
¼ cup white wine or chicken broth
⅓ cup prepared pesto

1. Cook the vermicelli according to the package directions. Meanwhile, in a large skillet, heat the butter, garlic powder, oregano and pepper over medium heat. Add the bay scallops and white wine; cook and stir for 5-6 minutes or until the scallops are firm and opaque.
2. Reduce the heat to low. Stir in the prepared pesto; heat through. Drain the vermicelli; add to the skillet. Toss to combine.

FAST FIX

Jalapeno Hummus

Chopped jalapeno peppers give hummus a kick. I pair it with vegetables, but it's good with crackers and tortilla chips, too.

—LISA ARMSTRONG MURRAY, KY

START TO FINISH: 15 MIN.
MAKES: 4 CUPS

2 cans (15 ounces each) garbanzo beans or chickpeas, rinsed and drained
⅔ cup roasted tahini
½ cup water
⅓ cup lemon juice
¼ cup olive oil
2 tablespoons minced garlic
2 tablespoons pickled jalapeno slices, chopped
1 tablespoon juice from pickled jalapeno slices
½ to 1 teaspoon crushed red pepper flakes
½ teaspoon salt
½ teaspoon pepper
⅛ teaspoon paprika
Assorted fresh vegetables

Place the first 11 ingredients in a food processor; cover and process until well blended. Garnish with paprika. Serve with assorted fresh vegetables.

Banana Smoothie

Like all the nutrition in a banana but bored with eating plain fruit? Blend together a fun and refreshing smoothie for a fast breakfast or snack. Combine 2 cups milk, 2 medium ripe bananas, ¼ cup honey and ½ teaspoon vanilla extract in a blender until smooth. Stir if necessary. Pour into chilled glasses; serve immediately. *Makes 3 servings.*

—RO ANN COX LENOIR, NC

Peaches & Cream

I love spending quality time in the kitchen with my daughter. We came up with a simple dessert that celebrates summer by featuring lots of fresh fruit.

—DORIT RITTER-HADDAD LIVINGSTON, NJ

START TO FINISH: 15 MIN.
MAKES: 4 SERVINGS

- 1 **cup heavy whipping cream**
- ½ **teaspoon vanilla extract**
- 4 **medium peaches, halved and pitted**
- 1 **cup sliced fresh strawberries**
- 1 **large banana, peeled and sliced**
- ¼ **cup packed brown sugar**

In a small bowl, beat the cream until it begins to thicken. Add the vanilla; beat until soft peaks form. Arrange the fruit on a platter; top with the whipped cream. Sprinkle with brown sugar.

TOP TIP

Choose peaches that give slightly to palm pressure and have an intense fragrance. Avoid those that are hard or have soft spots. To remove the pit, cut the peach from stem to stem all the way around, twist it in opposite directions and lift out the pit.

GINGERSNAP PEAR TRIFLES

⑤INGREDIENTS FAST FIX ▶

Gingersnap Pear Trifles

Crystallized ginger adds both sweetness and spice to these elegant personal-size treats. With layer after layer of mellow pears, crushed gingersnaps and lemony whipped cream, the five-ingredient trifles are fuss-free and especially nice to serve during fall and winter.

—*TASTE OF HOME* TEST KITCHEN

START TO FINISH: 10 MIN.
MAKES: 2 SERVINGS

- ½ **cup heavy whipping cream**
- ¼ **cup lemon curd**
- ½ **cup crushed gingersnap cookies**
- 1 **cup chopped canned pears**
- 2 **tablespoons chopped crystallized ginger**

1. In a small bowl, beat the heavy whipping cream until soft peaks form. Fold in the lemon curd.
2. Layer half of the crushed gingersnap cookies, pears and whipped cream in two dessert dishes. Repeat the layers. Sprinkle with chopped crystallized ginger. Serve immediately.

PEACHES & CREAM

CREAMY WASABI SPREAD

⑤ INGREDIENTS | **FAST FIX**

Creamy Wasabi Spread

Impressive appetizers don't get much simpler than this! Guests will flock around the Asian-style spread that requires only cream cheese, toasted sesame seeds, prepared wasabi and soy sauce. Set out crackers and wait for the compliments.

—**TAMMIE BALON** BOYCE, VA

START TO FINISH: 10 MIN.
MAKES: 8 SERVINGS

- 1 package (8 ounces) cream cheese
- ¼ cup prepared wasabi
- 2 tablespoons sesame seeds, toasted
- 2 tablespoons soy sauce
  Rice crackers

1. Place the cream cheese on a cutting board; split into two layers. Spread the prepared wasabi over the bottom half; replace top layer.
2. Press both sides into sesame seeds. Place on a shallow serving plate; pour soy sauce around the cheese. Serve with rice crackers.

⑤ INGREDIENTS | **FAST FIX**

Easy Asian Chicken Slaw

Using convenient rotisserie chicken is a great time-saver for busy cooks. The first time I served this main-dish slaw, the bowl went back to the kitchen scraped clean.

—**BESS BLANCO** VAIL, AZ

START TO FINISH: 15 MIN.
MAKES: 8 SERVINGS

- 1 package (3 ounces) ramen noodles
- 1 rotisserie chicken, skin removed, shredded
- 1 package (16 ounces) coleslaw mix
- 6 green onions, finely chopped
- 1 cup reduced-fat Asian toasted sesame salad dressing

Discard the seasoning packet from the ramen noodles or save for another use. Break the ramen noodles into small pieces; place in a large bowl. Add the shredded chicken, coleslaw mix and green onions. Drizzle with the salad dressing; toss to coat.

⑤ INGREDIENTS | **FAST FIX**

Microwaved Parmesan Chicken

A wholesome, home-cooked dinner from the microwave? Yes! A friend gave me her 10-minute recipe, and it's been a mainstay on our menus ever since.

—**MILFORD HERMAN** GARDEN, MI

START TO FINISH: 10 MIN.
MAKES: 2 SERVINGS

- 2 boneless skinless chicken breast halves (4 ounces each)
- 4 teaspoons reduced-sodium soy sauce
- ¼ teaspoon garlic powder
- ⅛ teaspoon pepper
- ¼ cup grated Parmesan cheese
- 1 teaspoon butter

Place the chicken in a microwave-safe dish. Top with soy sauce, garlic powder and pepper. Sprinkle with Parmesan cheese and dot with butter. Cover and cook on high for 4-5 minutes or until a thermometer reads 170°.

EASY ASIAN CHICKEN SLAW

HERB HAPPY
GARLIC BREAD

Herb Happy Garlic Bread

Fresh herbs and two cheeses make this garlic bread a standout. Pair it with pizza, lasagna or spaghetti for an Italian feast.

—*TASTE OF HOME* TEST KITCHEN

START TO FINISH: 15 MIN.
MAKES: 12 SERVINGS

- ½ cup butter, softened
- ¼ cup grated Romano cheese
- 2 tablespoons minced fresh basil or 2 teaspoons dried basil
- 1 tablespoon minced fresh parsley
- 3 garlic cloves, minced
- 1 French bread baguette
- 4 ounces crumbled goat cheese

1. In a small bowl, mix the first five ingredients until blended. Cut the French bread baguette crosswise in half; cut each piece lengthwise in half. Spread the cut sides of baguette with butter mixture. Place on an ungreased baking sheet.

2. Bake, uncovered, at 425° for 7-9 minutes or until lightly toasted. Sprinkle with the goat cheese; bake 1-2 minutes longer or until the cheese is softened. Cut into slices.

⑤ INGREDIENTS   FAST FIX ▶
Caprese Salad Kabobs

Why not trade in the usual vegetable party platter for kabobs? They're fun to eat and easy enough for kids to assemble.

—**CHRISTINE MITCHELL** GLENDORA, CA

START TO FINISH: 10 MIN.
MAKES: 12 KABOBS

- 24 grape tomatoes
- 12 cherry-size fresh mozzarella cheese balls
- 24 fresh basil leaves
- 2 tablespoons olive oil
- 2 teaspoons balsamic vinegar

On each of 12 wooden appetizer skewers, alternately thread two tomatoes, one cheese ball and two basil leaves; place on a serving plate. In a small bowl, whisk the olive oil and balsamic vinegar; drizzle over the kabobs just before serving.

TOP TIP

Want another fast idea for appetizer kabobs? Thread hard salami chunks, pitted ripe or pimiento-stuffed olives, cherry tomatoes and fresh mozzarella cheese pearls on skewers, then drizzle on zesty Italian salad dressing.

CHERRY CREAM
CHEESE DESSERT

FAST FIX ▶
Cherry Cream Cheese Dessert

Layer cherries, graham cracker crumbs and a cream cheese filling for tempting parfaits. It's easy to change them up if the mood strikes by substituting a different kind of pie filling. For example, use apple and a little cinnamon for a taste of fall.

—**MELODY MELLINGER** MYERSTOWN, PA

START TO FINISH: 15 MIN.
MAKES: 8 SERVINGS

- ¾ cup graham cracker crumbs (about 12 squares)
- 2 tablespoons sugar
- 2 tablespoons butter, melted

FILLING
- 1 package (8 ounces) cream cheese, softened
- 1 can (14 ounces) sweetened condensed milk
- ⅓ cup lemon juice
- 1 teaspoon vanilla extract
- 1 can (21 ounces) cherry pie filling

1. In a small bowl, combine the graham cracker crumbs, sugar and butter. Divide among eight dessert dishes, about 4 rounded teaspoonfuls in each.

2. In a small bowl, beat the cream cheese until smooth. Gradually add the sweetened condensed milk until blended. Beat in the lemon juice and vanilla. Spoon ¼ cup into each dish. Top with the cherry pie filling, about ¼ cup in each.

FAST FIX ▶
Stuffed Sole with Shrimp

If you like seafood but are usually short on time, try this simple entree. It's a snap to assemble and cooks in just minutes in the microwave. The recipe even works with chicken instead of sole.

—**ROBERT BISHOP** LEXINGTON, KY

START TO FINISH: 15 MIN.
MAKES: 2 SERVINGS

- 2 sole fillets (6 ounces each), halved lengthwise
- 1½ teaspoons lemon juice
  Dash onion powder
- 1 can (4 ounces) small shrimp, rinsed and drained
- 3 tablespoons 2% milk
- 2 tablespoons finely chopped celery
- 2 tablespoons butter, melted, divided
- 1 teaspoon minced fresh parsley
- ½ cup cubed bread, toasted
  Dash paprika

1. Drizzle the sole fillets with the lemon juice; sprinkle with the onion powder. Set aside.

2. In a microwave-safe dish, combine the shrimp, milk, celery, 1 tablespoon butter and parsley. Cover; microwave on high for 1-1½ minutes or until the celery is tender. Stir in toasted bread cubes. Spoon shrimp mixture down the center of each sole fillet. Starting with a short side, roll up and secure with toothpicks.

3. Place in a shallow microwave-safe dish coated with cooking spray. Brush with the remaining butter; sprinkle with paprika. Cover and microwave on high for 3-5 minutes or until the fish flakes easily with a fork. Let stand for 5 minutes before serving. Discard the toothpicks.

NOTE *This recipe was tested in a 1,100-watt microwave.*

FAST FIX ▶
French Dip Subs with Beer au Jus

Sub sandwiches piled with tender roast beef are great with a beer dipping sauce. Banana peppers make a fun garnish.

—**SUSAN SIMONS** EATONVILLE, WA

START TO FINISH: 15 MIN.
MAKES: 6 SERVINGS

- 2 garlic cloves, minced
- 1 tablespoon butter
- 1 pound thinly sliced deli roast beef
- 2 tablespoons spicy ketchup
- 4 teaspoons Worcestershire sauce
- ½ teaspoon dried basil
- ½ teaspoon dried oregano
- ¼ teaspoon pepper
- 1 bottle (12 ounces) dark beer or nonalcoholic beer
- 6 hoagie buns, split

In a large skillet, saute the garlic in the butter for 1 minute. Add beef, ketchup, Worcestershire sauce, basil, oregano and pepper. Stir in beer. Bring to a boil. Reduce heat; simmer, uncovered, for 2 minutes, stirring frequently. Using a slotted spoon, place beef on buns. Serve with cooking juices.

FRENCH DIP SUBS WITH BEER AU JUS

SOUTHWEST
TORTILLA
SCRAMBLE

(5) INGREDIENTS FAST FIX ▸

Southwest Tortilla Scramble

Here's my version of a deconstructed breakfast burrito. It's quick but has the Southwestern ingredients and flavors our family craves. I always use hefty corn tortillas instead of the flour variety, which can get lost in the scramble.

—**CHRISTINE SCHENHER** EXETER, CA

START TO FINISH: 15 MIN.
MAKES: 2 SERVINGS

- 4 **large egg whites**
- 2 **large eggs**
- ¼ **teaspoon pepper**
- 2 **corn tortillas (6 inches), halved and cut into strips**
- ¼ **cup chopped fresh spinach**
- 2 **tablespoons shredded reduced-fat cheddar cheese**
- ¼ **cup salsa**

1. In a large bowl, whisk egg whites, eggs and pepper. Stir in the tortillas, spinach and cheese.
2. Heat a large skillet coated with cooking spray over medium heat. Pour in the egg mixture; cook and stir until the eggs are thickened and no liquid egg remains. Top with salsa.

FAST FIX ▸

Grilled Salmon with Garlic Mayo

This terrific recipe has become a standby because it makes a special weekday dinner with a minimum of fuss. If the weather's not right for grilling, pop the fillets under the broiler. While they cook, I whip up the tasty garlic mayonnaise.

—**DONNA NOEL** GRAY, ME

START TO FINISH: 15 MIN.
MAKES: 4 SERVINGS

- 3 **tablespoons plus 1 teaspoon olive oil, divided**
- ½ **teaspoon dried rosemary, crushed**
- 4 **salmon fillets (6 ounces each)**
- 8 **garlic cloves, peeled**
- 1 **tablespoon lemon juice**
- ¾ **cup mayonnaise**
- 2 **tablespoons plain yogurt**
- 1 **tablespoon Dijon mustard**

1. Combine 3 tablespoons olive oil and the rosemary; drizzle over the salmon fillets. Using long-handled tongs, moisten a paper towel with cooking oil and lightly coat the grill rack. Grill, covered, over medium heat or broil 4 in. from the heat for 10-12 minutes or until the fish flakes easily with a fork.
2. Meanwhile, in a small microwave-safe bowl, combine the garlic cloves and remaining olive oil. Microwave, uncovered, on high for 20-30 seconds or until softened; transfer to a blender. Add the remaining ingredients. Cover and process until blended. Serve with the salmon.

Indian Cucumber Salad

This side is so refreshing! In a large bowl, combine ½ cup plain yogurt, ½ cup sour cream and ¼ teaspoon salt. Add 1½ cups chopped cucumbers, 1 chopped medium onion, 1 medium seeded chopped tomato and 1 tablespoon chopped seeded jalapeno pepper; stir until blended. Garnish with fresh cilantro leaves if desired. *Makes 6 servings.*

—**JEMIMA MADHAVAN** LINCOLN, NE

AVOCADO BEAN DIP

Raspberry Cheesecake Floats

I've yet to meet a cheesecake I didn't like! Rich cream cheese and tangy raspberries make a decadent combination in these ice cream floats. They're so yummy, I indulge even in the chill of winter.

—DEIRDRE COX KANSAS CITY, MO

START TO FINISH: 15 MIN.
MAKES: 6 SERVINGS

- 2 cans (12 ounces each) cream soda, divided
- ¼ teaspoon almond extract
- 3 ounces cream cheese, softened
- 1 package (12 ounces) frozen unsweetened raspberries
- 4 cups vanilla ice cream, softened if necessary, divided

TOPPINGS
- Whipped cream
- Fresh blackberries and blueberries

1. Place ½ cup soda, almond extract, cream cheese, raspberries and 2 cups vanilla ice cream in a blender; cover and process until smooth.
2. Divide among six tall glasses. Top with remaining vanilla ice cream and soda. Garnish with whipped cream and berries. Serve immediately.

RASPBERRY CHEESECAKE FLOATS

Guacamole is such a good, wholesome snack. With a consistency that's similar to hummus, Avocado Bean Dip packs in extra fiber and is perfect for dipping baked chips.

—RAQUEL HAGGARD EDMOND, OK

Avocado Bean Dip

START TO FINISH: 15 MIN.
MAKES: 2 CUPS

- 1 can (15 ounces) white kidney or cannellini beans, rinsed and drained
- 1 medium ripe avocado, peeled and cubed
- ½ cup fresh cilantro leaves
- 3 tablespoons lime juice
- ½ teaspoon onion powder
- ½ teaspoon garlic powder
- ½ teaspoon chipotle hot pepper sauce
- ¼ teaspoon salt
- ¼ teaspoon ground cumin
  Baked tortilla chips

In a food processor, combine the first nine ingredients; cover and process until smooth. Serve with chips.
PER SERVING ¼ cup (calculated without chips) equals 80 cal., 4 g fat (trace sat. fat), 0 chol., 143 mg sodium, 10 g carb., 4 g fiber, 3 g pro. **Diabetic Exchanges:** ½ starch, ½ fat.

BROILED CHICKEN
& ARTICHOKES

FAST FIX
Fruit Salad with Raspberry Vinaigrette

A homemade vinaigrette gives my salad a tangy finishing touch. Toss in mandarin oranges, strawberries, blueberries or whatever fruit is in season.

—MARK TRINKLEIN RACINE, WI

START TO FINISH: 10 MIN.
MAKES: 1¼ CUPS

- 1 package (10 ounces) frozen sweetened raspberries, thawed and drained
- ⅓ cup seedless raspberry jam
- 2 tablespoons cider vinegar
- 2 tablespoons lemon juice
- ½ cup olive oil
- ⅛ teaspoon salt
  Dash pepper
  Dash ground nutmeg
  Assorted fresh fruit

In a blender, process raspberries until pureed. Strain to remove the seeds. Return the puree to blender. Add jam, cider vinegar and lemon juice; cover and process until smooth. Add oil, salt, pepper and nutmeg; cover and process until blended. Serve with fruit.

FRUIT SALAD WITH
RASPBERRY VINAIGRETTE

(5) INGREDIENTS FAST FIX
Broiled Chicken & Artichokes

My wife and I first sampled this entree as newlyweds, and we've been hooked ever since. Parmesan, parsley, olive oil and seasonings are all it takes to dress up the chicken thighs and artichokes.

—CHRIS KOON MIDLOTHIAN, VA

START TO FINISH: 15 MIN.
MAKES: 8 SERVINGS

- 8 boneless skinless chicken thighs (about 2 pounds)
- 2 jars (7½ ounces each) marinated quartered artichoke hearts, drained
- 2 tablespoons olive oil
- 1 teaspoon salt
- ½ teaspoon pepper
- ¼ cup shredded Parmesan cheese
- 2 tablespoons minced fresh parsley

1. Preheat boiler. In a large bowl, toss chicken and artichokes with oil, salt and pepper. Transfer to a broiler pan.
2. Broil 3 in. from heat 8-10 minutes or until a thermometer inserted in chicken reads 170°, turning chicken and artichokes halfway through cooking. Sprinkle with cheese. Broil 1-2 minutes longer or until cheese is melted. Sprinkle with parsley.

(5) INGREDIENTS FAST FIX
Cheddar Mashed Cauliflower

Want an alternative to mashed potatoes? Try cheesy cauliflower. Even people who aren't watching their carbs like it.

—CHRYSTAL BAKER STUDIO CITY, CA

START TO FINISH: 15 MIN.
MAKES: 6 SERVINGS

- 2 medium heads cauliflower, broken into florets
- ⅓ cup 2% milk
- 1 tablespoon minced fresh rosemary
- ½ teaspoon salt
- 1 cup (4 ounces) shredded sharp cheddar cheese

In a Dutch oven, bring 1 in. of water to a boil. Add cauliflower; cover and cook for 5-10 minutes or until tender. Drain; return to pan. Mash cauliflower with the milk, rosemary and salt. Stir in the cheddar cheese until melted.

Camping Haystacks

START TO FINISH: 15 MIN.
MAKES: 2 SERVINGS

- 1 **can (15 ounces) chili with beans**
- 2 **packages (1 ounce each) corn chips**
- ½ **cup shredded cheddar cheese**
- 1½ **cups chopped lettuce**
- 1 **small tomato, chopped**
- ½ **cup salsa**
- 2 **tablespoons sliced ripe olives**
- 2 **tablespoons sour cream**

In a small saucepan, heat the chili. Divide corn chips between two plates; top with chili. Layer with the cheese, lettuce, tomato, salsa, ripe olives and sour cream. Serve immediately.

Open-Faced Ham and Apple Melts

Boring sandwiches need not apply! These flavorful melts stack sweet-tangy apple slices, savory deli ham and Swiss cheese onto whole wheat English muffins spread with Dijon mustard. They make a terrific snack or light lunch anytime.

—**SALLY MALONEY** DALLAS, GA

START TO FINISH: 15 MIN.
MAKES: 4 SERVINGS

- 2 **whole wheat English muffins, split**
- 2 **teaspoons Dijon mustard**
- 4 **slices deli ham**
- ½ **medium apple, thinly sliced**
- 2 **slices reduced-fat Swiss cheese, halved**

1. Place the English muffin halves cut side up on a baking sheet. Broil 4-6 in. from the heat for 2-3 minutes or until golden brown.
2. Spread with the Dijon mustard. Top with the deli ham, apple slices and Swiss cheese. Broil 3-4 minutes longer or until cheese is melted.
PER SERVING *1 English muffin half equals 130 cal., 3 g fat (1 g sat. fat), 14 mg chol., 429 mg sodium, 17 g carb., 3 g fiber, 10 g pro.*

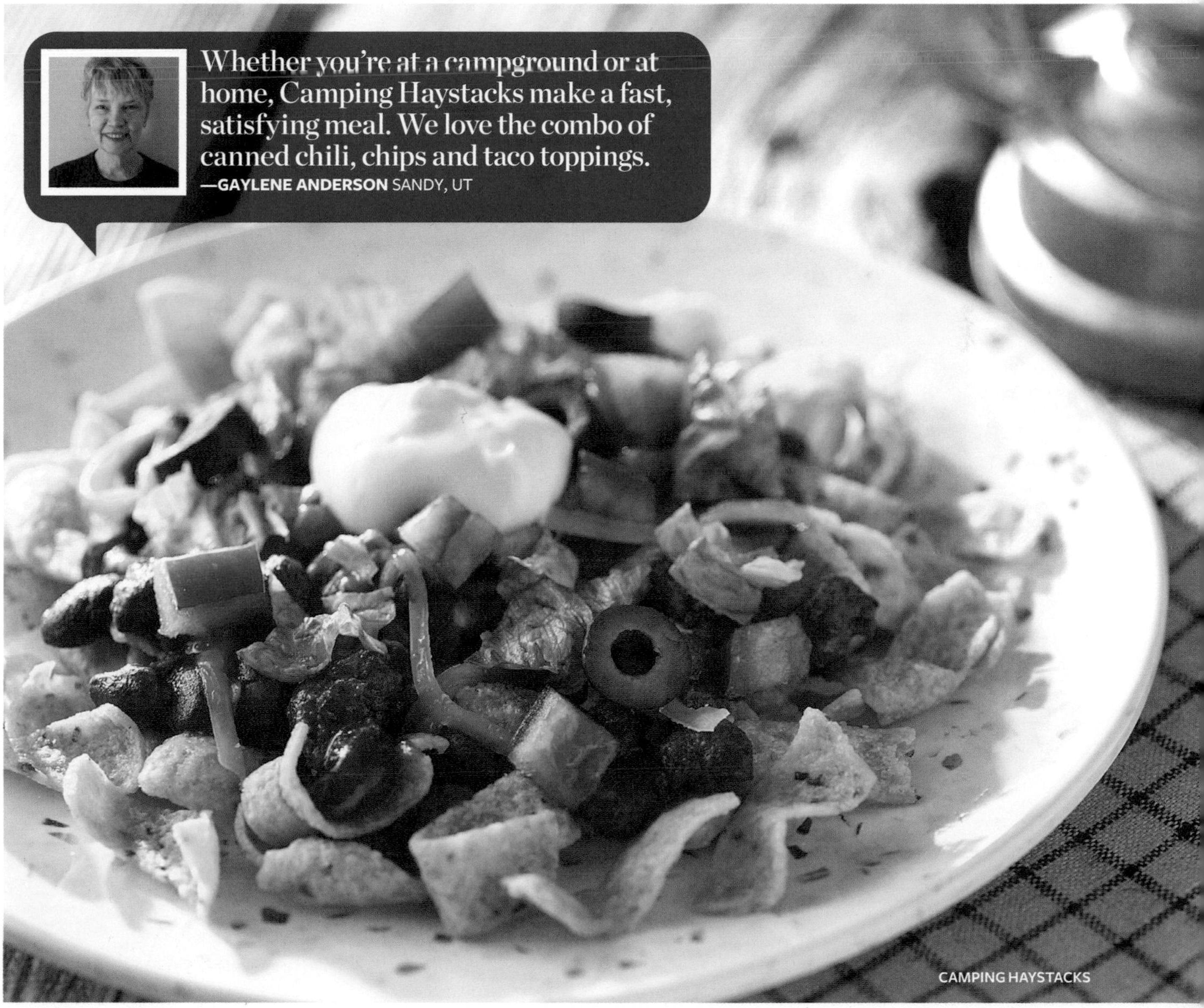

Whether you're at a campground or at home, Camping Haystacks make a fast, satisfying meal. We love the combo of canned chili, chips and taco toppings.
—**GAYLENE ANDERSON** SANDY, UT

CAMPING HAYSTACKS

Susan Lavery's
**Beef & Noodle
Casserole** PAGE 138

Casseroles & Oven Dishes

Craving something freshly baked, piping hot and delicious?
Thanks to the simple yet family-pleasing recipes here,
you'll be pulling out a pan of pure comfort in no time.

**Joni Hilton's
Jamaican Salmon with
Coconut Cream Sauce**
PAGE 128

**Jennifer Bender's
Broiled Cheese Stuffed
Portobellos** *PAGE 133*

**Danielle Woodward's
Shrimp & Crab Pizza**
PAGE 141

BREAKFAST
EGG CASSEROLE

Jamaican Salmon with Coconut Cream Sauce

We try to eat salmon on a regular basis because of its health benefits. This entree is so delicious, it's my go-to when guests are joining us for dinner.

—**JONI HILTON** ROCKLIN, CA

START TO FINISH: 30 MIN.
MAKES: 4 SERVINGS

- 4 **salmon fillets (6 ounces each)**
- 3 **tablespoons mayonnaise**
- 4 **teaspoons Caribbean jerk seasoning**
- ⅓ **cup sour cream**
- ¼ **cup cream of coconut**
- 1 **teaspoon grated lime peel**
- ¼ **cup lime juice**
- ½ **cup flaked coconut, toasted**

1. Preheat oven to 350°. Place salmon fillets in a greased 13x9-in. baking dish. Spread the mayonnaise over fillets; sprinkle with jerk seasoning.
2. Bake 18-22 minutes or until fish just begins to flake easily with a fork. Meanwhile, for the sauce, in a small saucepan, combine sour cream, cream of coconut, lime peel and lime juice; cook and stir over medium-low heat until blended.
3. Drizzle the fillets with the sauce; sprinkle with coconut.
NOTE *To toast the coconut, bake in a shallow pan in a 350° oven for 5-10 minutes or cook in a skillet over low heat until golden brown, stirring occasionally.*

Breakfast Egg Casserole

My husband and I raise ducks, and we're always interested in recipes that put the eggs to good use. Here's a favorite.

—**NANCY ZIMMERMAN**
CAPE MAY COURT HOUSE, NJ

PREP: 15 MIN. • **BAKE:** 30 MIN.
MAKES: 12 SERVINGS

- 1 **tablespoon olive oil**
- 1 **small red onion, chopped**
- 1 **medium sweet red pepper, chopped**
- 1 **medium green pepper, chopped**
- 1 **cup sliced fresh mushrooms**
- 12 **large eggs, lightly beaten**
- 1 **can (12 ounces) evaporated milk**
- ½ **cup all-purpose flour**
- 1 **teaspoon baking powder**
- 1½ **teaspoons salt-free seasoning blend**
- ¾ **teaspoon salt**
- ¼ **teaspoon pepper**
- 4 **cups (16 ounces) shredded cheddar or Monterey Jack cheese**

1. Preheat oven to 350°. In a large skillet, heat the oil over medium heat. Add onion and red and green peppers; cook and stir 4-5 minutes or until crisp-tender. Add mushrooms; cook 2-3 minutes or until tender. Remove from heat.
2. In a large bowl, whisk the eggs, milk, flour, baking powder, seasoning blend, salt and pepper until blended. Stir in cheese and vegetable mixture. Transfer to a greased 13x9-in. baking dish. Bake, uncovered, 30-35 minutes or until set.

Italian Mushroom Meat Loaf

Shake up meat loaf night! Combine 1 large lightly beaten egg, ¼ pound chopped fresh mushrooms, ½ cup each old-fashioned oats and chopped red onion, ¼ cup ground flaxseed and ½ teaspoon pepper. Mix in 19½ ounces Italian turkey sausage links (casings removed) and 1 pound 90% lean ground beef. Shape into a 10x4-in. loaf in a greased 13x9-in. baking dish. Bake, uncovered, at 350° for 50 minutes; drain. Top with 1 cup marinara sauce. Bake 10-15 minutes longer or until a thermometer reads 165°. *Makes 8 servings.*

—**KIM SUMRALL** APTOS, CA

SPICY VEGGIE PASTA BAKE

FAST FIX
Spicy Veggie Pasta Bake

Dad liked to cook with a cast-iron skillet. Now when I do, I remember his amazing culinary skills. I keep the tradition going with my vegetable pasta.

—SONYA GOERGEN MOORHEAD, MN

START TO FINISH: 30 MIN.
MAKES: 6 SERVINGS

- 3 cups uncooked spiral pasta
- 1 medium yellow summer squash
- 1 small zucchini
- 1 medium sweet red pepper
- 1 medium green pepper
- 1 tablespoon olive oil
- 1 small red onion, halved and sliced
- 1 cup sliced fresh mushrooms
- ½ teaspoon salt
- ¼ teaspoon pepper
- ¼ teaspoon crushed red pepper flakes
- 1 jar (24 ounces) spicy marinara sauce
- 8 ounces fresh mozzarella cheese pearls
  Grated Parmesan cheese and julienned fresh basil, optional

1. Preheat oven to 375°. Cook pasta according to package directions for al dente; drain.
2. Cut yellow squash, zucchini and peppers into ¼-in. julienne strips. In a 12-in. cast-iron skillet, heat oil over medium-high heat. Add onion, mushrooms and julienned vegetables; cook and stir 5-7 minutes or until crisp-tender. Stir in the seasonings. Add marinara sauce and pasta; toss to combine. Top with cheese pearls.
3. Transfer to oven; bake, uncovered, 10-15 minutes or until cheese is melted. If desired, sprinkle with Parmesan cheese and basil before serving.

EAT SMART
Mexicali Casserole

Kids gobble up this Mexican-style supper. The flavor is mild enough for children yet spiced to please adults, too.

—GERTRUDIS MILLER EVANSVILLE, IN

PREP: 15 MIN. • **BAKE:** 55 MIN.
MAKES: 6 SERVINGS

- 1 pound lean ground turkey
- 2 medium onions, chopped
- 1 small green pepper, chopped
- 1 garlic clove, minced
- 1 can (16 ounces) kidney beans, rinsed and drained
- 1 can (14½ ounces) diced tomatoes, undrained
- 1 cup water
- ⅔ cup uncooked long grain rice
- ⅓ cup sliced ripe olives
- 1 teaspoon chili powder
- ½ teaspoon salt
- ½ cup shredded reduced-fat cheddar cheese

1. Preheat oven to 375°. In a large skillet coated with cooking spray, cook the turkey, onions and green pepper over medium heat 6-8 minutes or until meat is no longer pink and vegetables are tender, breaking up the meat into crumbles. Add garlic; cook 1 minute longer. Drain.
2. Stir in the kidney beans, tomatoes, water, rice, ripe olives, chili powder and salt. Transfer to an 11x7-in. baking dish coated with cooking spray. Bake, covered, 50-55 minutes or until the rice is tender.
3. Sprinkle with the cheddar cheese. Bake, uncovered, 5 minutes longer or until cheese is melted.

PER SERVING *1 serving equals 348 cal., 10 g fat (3 g sat. fat), 66 mg chol., 508 mg sodium, 41 g carb., 9 g fiber, 24 g pro. Diabetic Exchanges: 3 lean meat, 2 starch, 2 vegetable.*

⑤INGREDIENTS FAST FIX
Cheesy Chili Fries

Our family is all about chili fries, but the ones served at restaurants aren't usually the healthiest choices. This better-for-you version with olive oil and meatless chili satisfies our cravings. Use reduced-fat cheese to cut even more calories.

—BEVERLY NOWLING BRISTOL, FL

START TO FINISH: 30 MIN.
MAKES: 4 SERVINGS

- 5 cups frozen seasoned curly fries
- 1 tablespoon olive oil
- 1 can (15 ounces) vegetarian chili with beans
- 1 cup (4 ounces) shredded cheddar cheese
  Optional toppings: sour cream, thinly sliced green onions and cubed avocado

1. Preheat oven to 450°. Place fries on an ungreased 15x10x1-in. baking pan; drizzle with oil and toss to coat. Bake according to package directions.
2. Divide the fries among four 2-cup baking dishes; top each with chili and cheddar cheese. Bake 5-7 minutes or until the cheese is melted. Serve with toppings as desired.

NOTE *You may use an 8-in. square baking dish instead of four 2-cup baking dishes. Bake as directed.*

Frito Pie

Frito pies are famous in the Southwest. They're spicy, salty, cheesy—just fabulous!
—**JAN MOON** ALAMOGORDO, NM

START TO FINISH: 30 MIN.
MAKES: 6 SERVINGS

- 1 **pound ground beef**
- 1 **medium onion, chopped**
- 2 **cans (15 ounces each) Ranch Style beans (pinto beans in seasoned tomato sauce)**
- 1 **package (9¾ ounces) Fritos corn chips**
- 2 **cans (10 ounces each) enchilada sauce**
- 2 **cups (8 ounces) shredded cheddar cheese**
  Thinly sliced green onions, optional

1. Preheat oven to 350°. In a large skillet, cook the beef and onion over medium heat 6-8 minutes or until beef is no longer pink and onion is tender, breaking up beef into crumbles; drain. Stir in beans; heat through.

2. Reserve 1 cup chips for the topping. Place the remaining chips in a greased 13x9-in. baking dish. Layer with meat mixture, enchilada sauce and cheese; top with reserved chips.

3. Bake, uncovered, 15-20 minutes or until cheese is melted. If desired, sprinkle with green onions.

HASH BROWN MAPLE SAUSAGE CASSEROLE

FRITO PIE

Hash Brown Maple Sausage Casserole

This sensational casserole has a lot going for it, but I think the best part is the surprise layer of gooey Gruyere.
—**ANUJA ARGADE** FOSTER CITY, CA

PREP: 15 MIN. • **BAKE:** 45 MIN. + STANDING
MAKES: 8 SERVINGS

- 1 **pound maple pork sausage**
- ½ **cup cubed peeled sweet potato**
- 2 **tablespoons olive oil**
- 1 **package (30 ounces) frozen shredded hash brown potatoes, thawed**
- 1½ **cups (6 ounces) shredded Gruyere or cheddar cheese**
- 2 **cups coarsely chopped fresh kale (tough stems removed)**
- ¾ **cup fresh or frozen corn**
- 5 **large eggs, lightly beaten**
- 2 **cups half-and-half cream**
- 1 **teaspoon salt**
- ½ **teaspoon pepper**
  Maple syrup, optional

1. Preheat oven to 375°. In a large skillet, cook sausage and sweet potato over medium-high heat 5-7 minutes or until the sausage is no longer pink, breaking up the sausage into crumbles. Remove with a slotted spoon; drain on paper towels.

2. Meanwhile, coat the bottom of a 12-in. ovenproof skillet with olive oil. Reserve ½ cup hash browns for the topping; add remaining potatoes to skillet, pressing firmly with a spatula to form an even layer.

3. Layer with cheese, kale and corn; top with sausage mixture and reserved hash browns. In a bowl, whisk the eggs, cream, salt and pepper until blended; pour over top.

4. Bake, uncovered, 45-55 minutes or until the edges are golden brown and the egg portion is set. Cover loosely with foil during the last 10 minutes if needed to prevent overbrowning. Let stand 20 minutes before serving. If desired, serve with syrup.

½ teaspoon salt
¼ teaspoon onion powder
¼ teaspoon pepper
½ cup panko (Japanese) bread
    crumbs
    Cooking spray
2 tablespoons minced fresh cilantro
    or parsley

Crunchy Oven-Baked Tilapia

This fish is perfectly crunchy. Dipping it in the lime mayo takes it over the top!
—**LESLIE PALMER** SWAMPSCOTT, MA

START TO FINISH: 25 MIN.
MAKES: 4 SERVINGS

4 tilapia fillets (6 ounces each)
¼ teaspoon grated lime peel
1 tablespoon lime juice
1 tablespoon reduced-fat
    mayonnaise

1. Preheat oven to 425°. Place tilapia fillets on a baking sheet coated with cooking spray. In a small bowl, mix the lime peel, lime juice, mayonnaise, salt, onion powder and pepper. Spread the mayonnaise mixture over fish fillets. Sprinkle with bread crumbs; spritz with cooking spray.
2. Bake 15-20 minutes or until fish just begins to flake easily with a fork. Sprinkle with cilantro.

PER SERVING *1 fillet equals 186 cal., 3 g fat (1 g sat. fat), 84 mg chol., 401 mg sodium, 6 g carb., trace fiber, 33 g pro.* **Diabetic Exchanges:** *5 lean meat, ½ starch.*

ADED TATER TOT BAKE

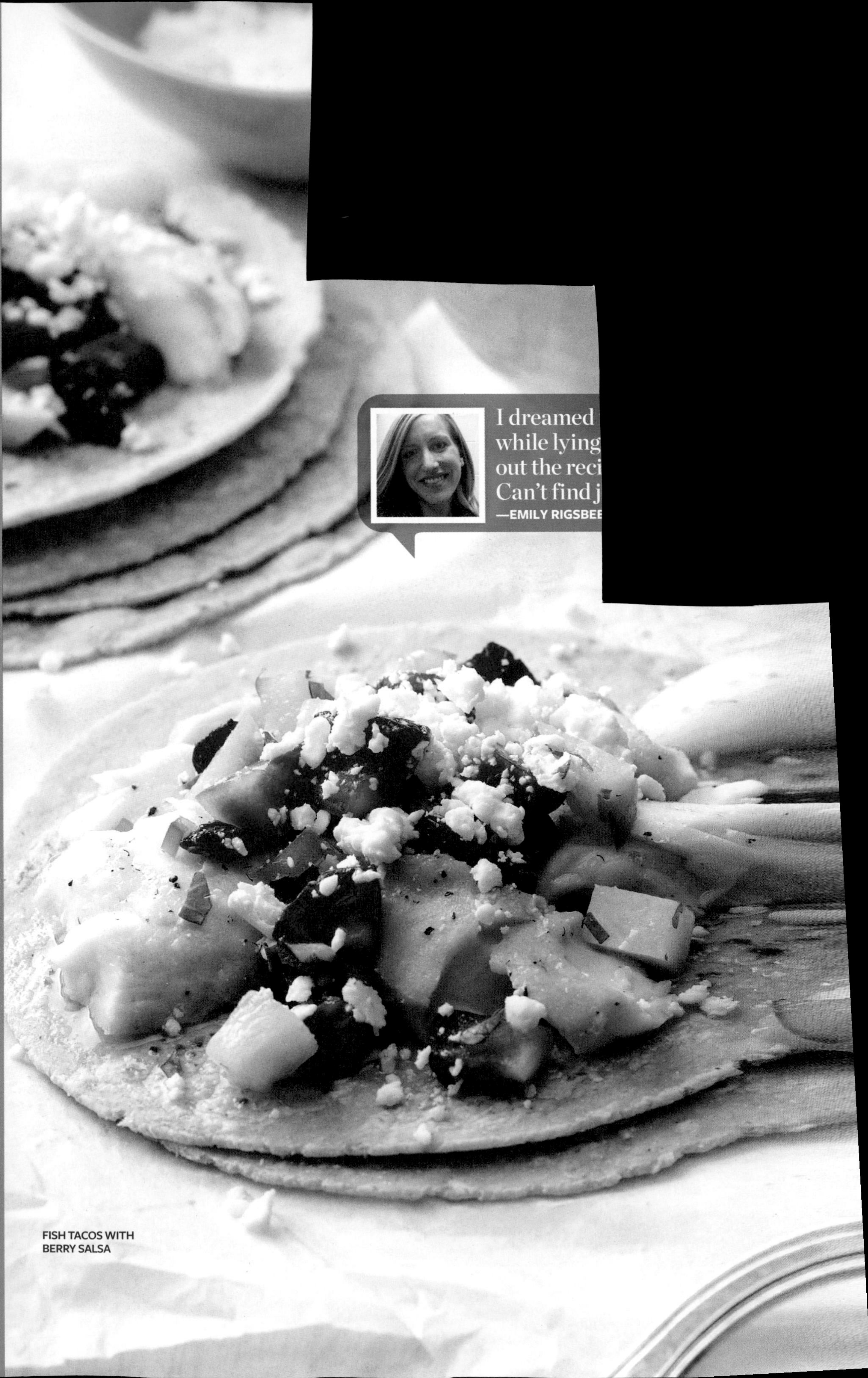

I dreamed
while lying
out the reci
Can't find j
—EMILY RIGSBEE

**FISH TACOS WITH
BERRY SALSA**

NEW ENGLAND BEAN &
BOG CASSOULET

Moving to a state in the Northeast introduced me to many wonderful regional dishes. New England Bean & Bog Cassoulet pays tribute to a French classic and is one of my favorite discoveries.
—**DEVON DELANEY** WESTPORT, CT

New England Bean & Bog Cassoulet

PREP: 15 MIN. • **COOK:** 35 MIN.
MAKES: 8 SERVINGS (3½ QUARTS)

- 5 **tablespoons olive oil, divided**
- 8 **boneless skinless chicken thighs (about 2 pounds)**
- 1 **package (12 ounces) fully cooked Italian chicken sausage links, cut into ½-in. slices**
- 4 **shallots, finely chopped**
- 2 **teaspoons minced fresh rosemary or ½ teaspoon dried rosemary, crushed**
- 2 **teaspoons minced fresh thyme or ½ teaspoon dried thyme**
- 1 **can (28 ounces) fire-roasted diced tomatoes, undrained**
- 1 **can (16 ounces) baked beans**
- 1 **cup chicken broth**
- ½ **cup fresh or frozen cranberries**
- 3 **day-old croissants, cubed (about 6 cups)**
- ½ **teaspoon lemon-pepper seasoning**
- 2 **tablespoons minced fresh parsley**

1. Preheat oven to 400°. In a Dutch oven, heat 2 tablespoons oil over medium heat. In batches, brown the chicken thighs on both sides; remove from the pan, reserving the drippings. Add sausage; cook and stir until lightly browned. Remove from pan.

2. In the same pan, heat 1 tablespoon oil over medium heat. Add shallots, rosemary and thyme; cook and stir 1-2 minutes or until the shallots are tender. Stir in fire-roasted tomatoes, baked beans, chicken broth and cranberries. Return chicken thighs and sausage to the pan; bring to a boil. Bake, covered, 20-25 minutes or until chicken is tender.

3. Toss croissants with remaining oil; sprinkle with lemon-pepper seasoning. Arrange over chicken mixture. Bake, uncovered, 12-15 minutes or until the croissants are golden brown. Sprinkle with parsley.

BAKED BEEF TACOS

Baked Beef Tacos

Take a fresh approach to tacos—bake 'em! The shell bottoms get soft while the tops stay crisp and crunchy.

—PATRICIA STAGICH ELIZABETH, NJ

PREP: 15 MIN. • **BAKE:** 20 MIN.
MAKES: 12 SERVINGS

- 1½ **pounds ground beef**
- 1 **envelope taco seasoning**
- 2 **cans (10 ounces each) diced tomatoes and green chilies, divided**
- 1 **can (16 ounces) refried beans**
- 2 **cups (8 ounces) shredded Mexican cheese blend, divided**
- ¼ **cup chopped fresh cilantro**
- 1 **teaspoon hot pepper sauce, optional**
- 12 **taco shells**
  Chopped green onions

1. Preheat oven to 425°. In a large skillet, cook beef over medium heat 6-8 minutes or until no longer pink, breaking into crumbles; drain. Stir in taco seasoning and 1 can of undrained tomatoes; heat through.

2. Meanwhile, in a bowl, mix beans, ½ cup cheese, cilantro, remaining can of undrained tomatoes and, if desired, pepper sauce. Spread onto the bottom of a greased 13x9-in. baking dish.

3. Stand taco shells upright over bean mixture. Fill each with 1 tablespoon cheese and about ⅓ cup beef mixture. Bake, covered, 15 minutes.

4. Uncover; sprinkle with remaining cheese. Bake, uncovered, 5-7 minutes or until the cheese is melted and the shells are lightly browned. Sprinkle with green onions.

Ham & Swiss Baked Penne

As a child, I loved the hot ham and Swiss sandwiches served at a local fast-food restaurant. I think of them whenever I take a bite of this melty, gooey pasta.

—ALLY BILLHORN WILTON, IA

START TO FINISH: 30 MIN.
MAKES: 6 SERVINGS

- 2⅓ cups uncooked penne pasta
- 3 tablespoons butter
- 3 tablespoons all-purpose flour
- 2 cups 2% milk
- 1 cup half-and-half cream
- 1½ cups (6 ounces) shredded Swiss cheese
- ½ cup shredded Colby cheese
- 2 cups cubed fully cooked ham

TOPPING

- ¼ cup seasoned bread crumbs
- ¼ cup grated Parmesan cheese
- 2 tablespoons butter, melted

1. Preheat oven to 375°. Cook penne pasta according to package directions for al dente; drain.
2. Meanwhile, in a large saucepan, melt 3 tablespoons butter over medium heat. Stir in the flour until smooth; gradually whisk in the milk and cream. Bring to a boil, stirring constantly; cook and stir 1-2 minutes or until thickened. Gradually stir in the Swiss and Colby cheeses until melted. Add the ham and pasta; toss to coat.
3. Transfer to a greased 11x7-in. baking dish. In a small bowl, mix the topping ingredients; sprinkle over the pasta. Bake, uncovered, 15-20 minutes or until bubbly.

Pepperoni Pizza Casserole

Feeding a crowd? Here's a great option. Loaded with popular pizza ingredients, the hearty casserole is a winner with all ages and makes a complete meal with a salad and garlic bread. If you prefer, replace the ground turkey with beef.

—DEBBIE STALEY MOUNT VERNON, IL

PREP: 25 MIN. • **BAKE:** 30 MIN.
MAKES: 2 CASSEROLES (6 SERVINGS EACH)

- 1 package (16 ounces) egg noodles
- 2 pounds ground turkey
- ⅓ cup chopped onion
- 1 jar (24 ounces) meatless spaghetti sauce
- 1 can (10 ounces) diced tomatoes and green chilies
- 1 can (8 ounces) mushroom stems and pieces, drained
- 2 cups (8 ounces) shredded part-skim mozzarella cheese
- 2 cups (8 ounces) shredded cheddar cheese
- 1 cup (4 ounces) shredded Parmesan cheese
- 3 ounces sliced turkey pepperoni

1. In a Dutch oven, cook egg noodles according to package directions; drain.
2. Meanwhile, in a large skillet, cook the turkey and onion over medium heat until the meat is no longer pink, breaking meat into crumbles; drain. Stir in spaghetti sauce and tomatoes. Bring to a boil. Reduce heat; simmer, uncovered, for 5 minutes. Stir in the egg noodles.
3. Transfer to two greased 13x9-in. baking dishes. Sprinkle each with mushrooms, cheeses and pepperoni.
4. Bake, uncovered, at 350° for 30-35 minutes or until heated through and the cheeses have melted. Let stand for 5 minutes before serving.

Crab-Topped Tomato Slices

When camping, my wife and I top large tomato slices with spicy chunks of crab, then heat them over the fire. They're just as good popped into the oven at home.

—THOMAS FAGLON SOMERSET, NJ

START TO FINISH: 30 MIN.
MAKES: 4 SERVINGS

- 1 carton (8 ounces) mascarpone cheese
- 2 tablespoons finely chopped sweet red pepper
- 1½ teaspoons grated lemon peel
- 2 tablespoons lemon juice
- 1 teaspoon seafood seasoning
- 1 teaspoon hot pepper sauce
- ½ teaspoon salt
- ¼ teaspoon freshly ground pepper
- 2 cans (6 ounces each) lump crabmeat, drained
- 8 slices tomato (½ inch thick)
  Minced chives

1. Preheat oven to 375°. In a large bowl, combine the first eight ingredients; gently stir in crab.
2. Place tomato slices on a foil-lined baking sheet; top with crab mixture. Bake 12-15 minutes or until heated through. Sprinkle with chives.

HAM & SWISS BAKED PENNE

CURRY-ROASTED
TURKEY AND POTATOES

Beef & Noodle Casserole

Here's our top choice for comfort food.
It's cheesy, creamy, bubbly—delicious!
—SUSAN LAVERY MCKINNEY, TX

PREP: 15 MIN. • **BAKE:** 15 MIN. + STANDING
MAKES: 6 SERVINGS

- 2 **cups uncooked elbow macaroni**
- 1 **pound ground beef**
- 1 **can (14½ ounces) diced tomatoes, drained**
- 1 **can (8 ounces) tomato sauce**
- 1 **tablespoon sugar**
- ½ **teaspoon salt**
- ¼ **teaspoon garlic salt**
- ¼ **teaspoon pepper**
- 1 **cup (8 ounces) sour cream**
- 3 **ounces cream cheese, softened**
- 3 **green onions, chopped**
- 1 **cup (4 ounces) shredded cheddar cheese**

1. Preheat oven to 350°. In a 6-qt. stockpot, cook macaroni according to package directions for al dente; drain and return to pot.
2. Meanwhile, in a large skillet, cook beef over medium heat 6-8 minutes or until no longer pink, breaking into crumbles; drain. Stir in the tomatoes, sauce, sugar and seasonings. Transfer to a greased 11x7-in. baking dish.
3. Stir sour cream, cream cheese and green onions into macaroni. Spoon over beef mixture, spreading evenly. Sprinkle with cheese.
4. Bake, covered, 15-20 minutes or until bubbly. Let stand 10 minutes before serving.

EAT SMART **FAST FIX**
Curry-Roasted Turkey and Potatoes

Honey and mustard go together so well.
They add that little extra something to
my roasted turkey and potatoes.
—CAROL WITCZAK TINLEY PARK, IL

START TO FINISH: 30 MIN.
MAKES: 4 SERVINGS

- 1 **pound Yukon Gold potatoes (about 3 medium), cut into ½-inch cubes**
- 2 **medium leeks (white portion only), thinly sliced**
- 2 **tablespoons canola oil, divided**
- ½ **teaspoon pepper, divided**
- ¼ **teaspoon salt, divided**
- 3 **tablespoons Dijon mustard**
- 3 **tablespoons honey**
- ¾ **teaspoon curry powder**
- 1 **package (17.6 ounces) turkey breast cutlets**
   Minced fresh cilantro or thinly sliced green onions, optional

1. Preheat oven to 450°. Place the potatoes and leeks in a 15x10x1-in. baking pan coated with cooking spray. Drizzle with 1 tablespoon canola oil; sprinkle with ¼ teaspoon pepper and ⅛ teaspoon salt. Stir to coat. Roast 15 minutes, stirring once.
2. Meanwhile, in a small bowl, combine mustard, honey, curry powder and remaining oil. Sprinkle turkey with remaining salt and pepper.
3. Drizzle 2 tablespoons mustard mixture over potatoes; stir to coat. Place turkey over potato mixture; drizzle with remaining mustard mixture. Roast 6-8 minutes longer or until the turkey is no longer pink and the potatoes are tender. If desired, sprinkle with cilantro.
PER SERVING *3 ounces cooked turkey with ¾ cup potato mixture equals 393 cal., 9 g fat (1 g sat. fat), 71 mg chol., 582 mg sodium, 44 g carb., 3 g fiber, 33 g pro.* **Diabetic Exchanges:** *4 lean meat, 3 starch, 1½ fat.*

Asian Citrus Salmon

We love this! Marinate four 6-ounce salmon fillets in ½ cup each orange juice and reduced-sodium soy sauce, ¼ cup sliced red onion, ¼ cup olive oil, 2 minced garlic cloves, 2 teaspoons minced fresh gingerroot and ½ teaspoon grated orange peel for 30 minutes. Drain and discard marinade. Broil 4-6 in. from the heat for 10-12 minutes or until fish flakes easily with a fork. Sprinkle with ¼ teaspoon salt and ⅛ teaspoon pepper; top with ½ cup toasted slivered almonds. *Makes 4 servings.*
—RANDI AMADOR DINUBA, CA

Breads in a Jiffy

Yes, you do have time to bake! Thanks to convenient shortcuts and quick ideas, surprising your family with something tender, golden and scrumptious from the oven is as easy as can be.

Judy Van Heek's Peanut Butter & Jam Muffins *PAGE 147*

Tressa Nicholls' Raspberry Breakfast Braid *PAGE 151*

Jay Davis' Apple-Bacon Mini Loaves *PAGE 146*

FRUIT & NUT BREAD

EAT SMART
Garlic Knotted Rolls

It's so easy to bake a pan of cute, yummy knots using store-bought frozen dough.
—**KATHY HARDING** RICHMOND, MO

PREP: 15 MIN. + RISING • **BAKE:** 15 MIN.
MAKES: 10 ROLLS

- 1 loaf (1 pound) frozen bread dough, thawed
- 1½ teaspoons dried minced onion
- 3 tablespoons butter
- 4 garlic cloves, minced
- ⅛ teaspoon salt
- 1 large egg, beaten
- 1 teaspoon poppy seeds

1. Pat out dough on a work surface; sprinkle with minced onion and knead until combined. Divide dough in half. Shape each piece into five balls. Roll each ball into a 10-in. rope; tie into a knot. Tuck ends under. Place the rolls 2 in. apart on a greased baking sheet.
2. In a small skillet over medium heat, melt butter. Add garlic and salt; cook and stir 1-2 minutes. Brush over rolls. Cover and let rise until doubled, about 30 minutes.
3. Preheat oven to 375°. Brush the tops with egg; sprinkle with the poppy seeds. Bake 15-20 minutes or until golden brown.
PER SERVING *1 roll equals 168 cal., 6 g fat (2 g sat. fat), 30 mg chol., 315 mg sodium, 22 g carb., 2 g fiber, 5 g pro.* ***Diabetic Exchanges:*** *1½ starch, 1 fat.*

EAT SMART
Fruit & Nut Bread

Dotted with walnuts and lots of dried fruit, this pretty round loaf makes the perfect hostess gift during the holiday season.
—**PRISCILLA GILBERT**
INDIAN HARBOUR BEACH, FL

PREP: 15 MIN. + RISING
BAKE: 20 MIN. + COOLING
MAKES: 1 LOAF (12 WEDGES)

- 1 loaf (1 pound) frozen bread dough, thawed
- ⅓ cup chopped walnuts
- ¼ cup golden raisins
- ¼ cup raisins
- ¼ cup dried cranberries
- ¼ cup chopped dates
- 1 large egg white
- 1 tablespoon honey

1. Turn bread dough onto a floured surface; roll out to 1-in. thickness. Sprinkle walnuts, raisins, cranberries and dates over the dough; fold over and knead well until the fruit and nuts are evenly mixed into dough.
2. Shape into a round loaf; place in a greased 9-in. round baking pan. Cover; let rise until doubled, about 30 minutes.
3. Beat the egg white and honey; brush over loaf. With a sharp knife, make 2 shallow crosses across the top of loaf. Bake at 350° for 20-25 minutes or until golden brown. Transfer to a wire rack.
PER SERVING *1 slice equals 170 cal., 4 g fat (trace sat. fat), 0 chol., 217 mg sodium, 30 g carb., 2 g fiber, 5 g pro.* ***Diabetic Exchange:*** *2 starch.*

Cranberry Quick Bread

Keep this in mind for Christmas or any occasion that calls for a special treat. In a large bowl, combine 1½ cups all-purpose flour, ¾ cup sugar, 1 teaspoon baking powder, ¼ teaspoon each salt and baking soda. Whisk 1 large egg, ½ cup orange juice, 2 tablespoons melted butter and 1 tablespoon water. Stir into the dry ingredients just until moistened. Fold in 1½ cups coarsely chopped fresh or frozen cranberries. Transfer the batter to a greased and floured 8x4-in. loaf pan. Bake at 350° for 45-50 minutes or until a toothpick comes out clean. Cool for 10 minutes before removing from the pan to a wire rack. *Makes 12 servings.*
—**KAREN CZECHOWICZ** OCALA, FL

EAT SMART

Peanut Butter & Jam Muffins

Selling youngsters on wholesome bran muffins is a breeze. Just say PB&J!

—JUDY VAN HEEK CROFTON, NE

PREP: 20 MIN. • **BAKE:** 15 MIN.
MAKES: 1 DOZEN

- 1 **cup all-purpose flour**
- 1 **cup oat bran**
- ½ **cup packed brown sugar**
- 2 **teaspoons baking powder**
- ½ **teaspoon salt**
- ¼ **teaspoon baking soda**
- 1 **cup 2% milk**
- ½ **cup unsweetened applesauce**
- ⅓ **cup peanut butter**
- 1 **large egg white**
- 2 **tablespoons honey**
- ¼ **cup seedless strawberry jam**

1. In a large bowl, combine the flour, oat bran, brown sugar, baking powder, salt and baking soda. In a small bowl, beat milk, applesauce, peanut butter, egg white and honey on low speed until smooth; stir into dry ingredients just until moistened.
2. Fill greased or foil-lined muffin cups half full. Drop 1 teaspoon seedless strawberry jam into the center of each muffin; cover with the remaining muffin batter.
3. Bake at 400° for 15-20 minutes or until a toothpick inserted in muffin comes out clean. Cool for 5 minutes before removing from pan to a wire rack. Serve warm.
PER SERVING *1 muffin equals 161 cal., 5 g fat (1 g sat. fat), 2 mg chol., 244 mg sodium, 29 g carb., 2 g fiber, 5 g pro.* **Diabetic Exchanges:** *2 starch, ½ fat.*

Jalapeno Hush Puppies

These Southern-style favorites have a crunchy exterior that contrasts perfectly with the moist corn bread. Hot sauce and jalapenos kick up the heat.

—*TASTE OF HOME* TEST KITCHEN

PREP: 15 MIN. • **COOK:** 5 MIN./BATCH
MAKES: 2½ DOZEN

- 1½ **cups yellow cornmeal**
- ½ **cup all-purpose flour**
- 1 **teaspoon baking powder**
- 1 **teaspoon salt**
- 2 **large eggs, lightly beaten**
- ¾ **cup 2% milk**
- 2 **jalapeno peppers, seeded and minced**
- ¼ **cup finely chopped onion**
- 1 **teaspoon Louisiana-style hot sauce**
  Oil for deep-fat frying

1. In a large bowl, combine the cornmeal, flour, baking powder and salt. In another bowl, beat the eggs, milk, jalapenos, onion and hot sauce. Stir into the dry ingredients just until combined.
2. In an electric skillet or deep fryer, heat oil to 375°. Drop tablespoonfuls of batter, a few at a time, into hot oil. Fry until golden brown on both sides. Drain on paper towels. Serve warm.
NOTE *Wear disposable gloves when cutting hot peppers; the oils can burn skin. Avoid touching your face.*

DID YOU KNOW?

Cornmeal can be white, yellow or blue depending on which strain of corn is used. Traditionally, white cornmeal is more popular in the South, while yellow is the preferred variety in the North. Blue cornmeal is available in many specialty stores. All three types of cornmeal may be used interchangeably in recipes.

PEANUT BUTTER & JAM MUFFINS

APPLE-RHUBARB BREAD

RASPBERRY
BREAKFAST BRAID

Honey Lemon Muffins

Honey's subtle sweetness comes through in every bite of these moist little goodies. It's the ideal counterpoint to the tangy lemon juice and grated peel in both the batter and the icing. Nibble with a cup of your favorite tea—sheer bliss!

—**RACHEL HART** WILDOMAR, CA

START TO FINISH: 30 MIN.
MAKES: 10 MUFFINS

- 1 **cup all-purpose flour**
- ½ **cup whole wheat flour**
- 1 **teaspoon baking powder**
- ¼ **teaspoon baking soda**
- ¼ **teaspoon salt**
- 1 **large egg**
- ½ **cup honey**
- ¼ **cup lemon juice**
- ¼ **cup butter, melted**
- ½ **teaspoon grated lemon peel**

DRIZZLE

- ¼ **cup confectioners' sugar**
- 1 **teaspoon lemon juice**
  Additional grated lemon peel

1. In a large bowl, combine the flours, baking powder, baking soda and salt. In another bowl, combine the egg, honey, lemon juice, butter and lemon peel. Stir into the dry ingredients just until moistened.

2. Coat muffin cups with cooking spray or use paper liners; fill one-half full with batter.

3. Bake at 375° for 15-18 minutes or until a toothpick inserted near the center comes out clean. Cool for 5 minutes before removing from the pan to a wire rack.

4. In a small bowl, combine the confectioners' sugar and lemon juice; drizzle over warm muffins. Sprinkle with additional lemon peel.

PER SERVING *1 muffin equals 178 cal., 5 g fat (3 g sat. fat), 33 mg chol., 171 mg sodium, 31 g carb., 1 g fiber, 3 g pro. **Diabetic Exchanges:** 2 starch, 1 fat.*

Raspberry Breakfast Braid

My drizzled breakfast braid recipe calls for raspberries, but I've also used a mix of different berries. Have fun experimenting!

—**TRESSA NICHOLLS** SANDY, OR

PREP: 20 MIN. • **BAKE:** 15 MIN.
MAKES: 12 SERVINGS

- 2 **cups biscuit/baking mix**
- 1 **package (3 ounces) cream cheese, cubed**
- ¼ **cup cold butter, cubed**
- ⅓ **cup 2% milk**
- 1¼ **cups fresh raspberries**
- 3 **tablespoons sugar**
- ¼ **cup vanilla frosting**

1. Preheat oven to 425°. Place the biscuit mix in a large bowl. Cut in the cream cheese and butter until mixture resembles coarse crumbs. Stir in the milk just until moistened. Turn onto a lightly floured surface; knead gently 8-10 times.

2. On a greased baking sheet, roll the dough into an 18x12-in. rectangle. Spoon raspberries down center third of dough; sprinkle with sugar.

3. On each long side, cut 1-in.-wide strips about 2½ in. into the center. Starting at one end, fold alternating strips at an angle across raspberries; seal the ends.

4. Bake 15-20 minutes or until golden brown. Remove to a wire rack to cool slightly. In a microwave-safe dish, microwave vanilla frosting on high 5-10 seconds or until of the desired consistency; drizzle over pastry.

Ever since I tried Flaky Whole Wheat Biscuits, the kind made with white flour just don't seem as good! Top these with whipped cream and berries as a dessert.

—**TRISHA KRUSE** EAGLE, ID

FLAKY WHOLE
WHEAT BISCUITS

EAT SMART **FAST FIX**

Flaky Whole Wheat Biscuits

START TO FINISH: 25 MIN.
MAKES: 10 BISCUITS

- 1 cup all-purpose flour
- 1 cup whole wheat flour
- 3 teaspoons baking powder
- 1 tablespoon brown sugar
- 1 teaspoon baking soda
- ½ teaspoon salt
- ¼ cup cold butter
- 1 cup 2% milk

1. In a large bowl, combine the first six ingredients. Cut in butter until mixture resembles coarse crumbs. Stir in milk just until moistened. Turn onto a lightly floured surface; knead 8-10 times.

2. Pat or roll out the biscuit dough to ½-in. thickness; cut with a floured 2½-in. biscuit cutter. Place 2 in. apart on an ungreased baking sheet. Bake at 425° for 8-10 minutes or until golden brown.

PER SERVING *1 biscuit equals 144 cal., 6 g fat (3 g sat. fat), 14 mg chol., 417 mg sodium, 21 g carb., 2 g fiber, 4 g pro. Diabetic Exchanges: 1½ starch, 1 fat.*

Drizzled Butternut Bread

My two young children love this drizzled bread. Mashed butternut squash creates a soft texture and blends well with the cinnamon. The vanilla icing is a bonus!

—MISTY THOMPSON GAYLESVILLE, AL

PREP: 15 MIN. • **BAKE:** 55 MIN. + COOLING
MAKES: 2 LOAVES (12 SLICES EACH)

- 1 cup butter, softened
- 1 package (8 ounces) cream cheese, softened
- 2 cups sugar
- 3 large eggs
- 2 cups mashed cooked butternut squash
- 1 teaspoon vanilla extract
- 3 cups all-purpose flour
- 1 teaspoon baking powder
- 1 teaspoon ground cinnamon
- ½ teaspoon salt
- ½ teaspoon baking soda
- 1 cup chopped walnuts

ICING
- 1 cup confectioners' sugar
- ½ teaspoon vanilla extract
- 6 to 8 tablespoons sweetened condensed milk

1. In a large bowl, cream the butter, cream cheese and sugar until light and fluffy. Add eggs, one at a time, beating well after each addition. Beat in squash and vanilla. Combine the flour, baking powder, cinnamon, salt and baking soda; gradually beat into the creamed mixture. Fold in walnuts.

2. Transfer to two greased 8x4-in. loaf pans. Bake at 350° for 55-65 minutes or until a toothpick inserted near the center comes out clean. Cool loaves for 10 minutes before removing from pans to wire racks to cool completely.

3. For icing, in a small bowl, combine the confectioners' sugar, vanilla and enough milk to achieve a drizzling consistency. Drizzle over loaves.

NUTTY CRANBERRY STICKY BUNS

DRIZZLED BUTTERNUT BREAD

FAST FIX
Nutty Cranberry Sticky Buns

Tangy dried cranberries and crunchy pecans give these finger-licking sticky buns the taste of Christmas. But they're so yummy, you'll want to prepare them year-round. Even the busiest cooks will have time, thanks to the convenience of refrigerated crescent roll dough.

—MARY SHIVERS ADA, OK

START TO FINISH: 30 MIN.
MAKES: 9 BUNS

- 1 tube (8 ounces) refrigerated crescent rolls
- ½ cup dried cranberries
- ¼ cup packed brown sugar, divided
- 2 tablespoons butter, melted
- 2 tablespoons maple syrup
- ⅔ cup chopped pecans

1. Unroll the crescent roll dough into one long rectangle; seal the seams and perforations. Sprinkle with the dried cranberries and 2 tablespoons brown sugar. Roll up jelly-roll style, starting with a short side; pinch seam to seal. Cut into nine slices.

2. In a small bowl, combine butter, maple syrup and remaining brown sugar; spread onto the bottom of a greased 8-in. square baking dish. Sprinkle with the pecans. Place rolls, cut sides down, over pecans.

3. Bake at 375° for 18-22 minutes or until golden brown. Immediately invert rolls onto a serving platter. Serve warm.

Christy Scott Campbell's Sausage & Sweet Potato Hash PAGE 163

Breakfast & Brunch

Wake up with a sunny selection of egg casseroles, chocolaty pancakes, cool smoothies and more. You'll find recipes that are easy enough to fix on even the busiest mornings. What a way to start the day!

Fay Moreland's Cheesy Ham & Egg Sandwiches PAGE 161

Karen Sikora's Pumpkin Smoothies PAGE 162

Jeanette Kass' Michigan Fruit Baked Oatmeal PAGE 164

SUMMER BREAKFAST SKILLET

FAST FIX ▶
Sausage, Egg and Cheddar Farmer's Breakfast

When we're camping, we end up eating breakfast late—and everyone comes to the table hungry! This meaty favorite has sausage, hash browns and cheese for a satisfying meal every time. It really gets us going for outdoor activities.

—**BONNIE ROBERTS** NEWAYGO, MI

START TO FINISH: 30 MIN.
MAKES: 4 SERVINGS

- 6 **large eggs**
- ⅓ **cup 2% milk**
- ½ **teaspoon dried parsley flakes**
- ¼ **teaspoon salt**
- 6 **ounces bulk pork sausage**
- 1½ **cups frozen cubed hash brown potatoes, thawed**
- ¼ **cup chopped onion**
- 1 **cup (4 ounces) shredded cheddar cheese**

1. Whisk the eggs, milk, parsley and salt; set aside. In a large skillet, cook sausage over medium heat until no longer pink; remove and drain. In the same skillet, cook potatoes and onion for 5-7 minutes or until tender. Return sausage to the pan.
2. Add the egg mixture; cook and stir until almost set. Sprinkle with cheddar cheese. Cover and cook for 1-2 minutes or until cheese is melted.

Summer Breakfast Skillet

I sizzle up spicy chorizo with colorful veggies, eggs and cheddar for a zippy Southwestern skillet. Spoon it into taco shells or tortillas for a fun variation.

—**ANDREA RIVERA** WESTBURY, NY

PREP: 20 MIN. • **COOK:** 15 MIN.
MAKES: 4 SERVINGS

- ½ **pound fresh chorizo or bulk spicy pork sausage**
- 1 **medium sweet yellow pepper, chopped**
- 1 **medium sweet red pepper, chopped**
- 1 **medium onion, chopped**
- 3 **medium tomatoes, chopped**
- 2 **small zucchini, chopped**
- 2 **garlic cloves, minced**
- 1 **teaspoon paprika**
- 4 **large eggs**
- ¼ **teaspoon salt**
- ¼ **teaspoon pepper**
- ½ **cup shredded cheddar cheese**

1. In a large skillet, cook the chorizo, peppers and onion over medium heat 4-6 minutes or until the chorizo is cooked through, breaking the chorizo into crumbles; drain. Stir in tomatoes, zucchini, garlic and paprika; cook, covered, 5-7 minutes longer or until vegetables are tender.
2. With the back of a spoon, make four wells in the vegetable mixture; break an egg into each well. Sprinkle the eggs with salt and pepper. Cook, covered, 4-6 minutes or until the egg whites are completely set and the yolks begin to thicken but are not hard.
3. Remove from heat; sprinkle with cheese. Let stand, covered, 5 minutes or until cheese is melted.

Strawberry Banana Blast

Jump-start mornings with nutritious fruit as a beverage. In a blender, combine 1 cup orange juice, 2 cups frozen unsweetened strawberries, 1 sliced frozen medium banana and ¾ cup strawberry-banana yogurt; cover and process until blended. Pour into chilled glasses; serve immediately. *Makes 4 servings.*

—**COLLEEN BELBEY** WARWICK, RI

⑤ INGREDIENTS FAST FIX

Fresh Corn Omelet

I use homegrown corn and from-scratch salsa to fix a simple but sensational omelet. To customize it, sprinkle on mushrooms, onions, peppers or meat.

—**WILLIAM STONE** ROBSON, WV

START TO FINISH: 25 MIN.
MAKES: 4 SERVINGS

- 10 **large eggs**
- 2 **tablespoons water**
- ¼ **teaspoon salt**
- ¼ **teaspoon pepper**
- 2 **teaspoons plus 2 tablespoons butter, divided**
- 1 **cup fresh or frozen corn, thawed**
- ½ **cup shredded cheddar cheese**
  Fresh salsa

1. In a small bowl, whisk eggs, water, salt and pepper until blended. In a large nonstick skillet, heat 2 teaspoons butter over medium heat. Add corn; cook and stir 1-2 minutes or until tender. Remove from pan.

2. In the same pan, heat 1 tablespoon butter over medium-high heat. Pour in half of egg mixture. Mixture should set immediately at edges. As eggs set, push cooked portions toward the center, letting uncooked eggs flow underneath. When eggs are thickened and no liquid egg remains, spoon half of the corn on one side; sprinkle with ¼ cup cheese. Fold omelet in half. Cut in half; slide each half onto a plate.

3. Repeat with remaining butter, egg mixture and filling. Serve with salsa.

EAT SMART FAST FIX

Cocoa Pancakes

We love these chocolaty whole wheat pancakes! They taste like a special treat.

—**LISA DEMARSH** MT. SOLON, VA

START TO FINISH: 25 MIN.
MAKES: 8 PANCAKES

- ¾ **cup whole wheat flour**
- ¼ **cup sugar**
- 2 **tablespoons baking cocoa**
- 1 **teaspoon baking powder**
- ⅛ **teaspoon salt**
- ⅛ **teaspoon ground nutmeg**
- ¾ **cup fat-free milk**
- ¼ **cup egg substitute**
- 1 **tablespoon reduced-fat butter, melted**
- 1 **cup fresh raspberries**
- ½ **cup fat-free vanilla yogurt**

1. In a small bowl, combine the first six ingredients. Combine the milk, egg substitute and butter; add to the dry ingredients just until moistened.

2. Pour batter by scant ¼ cupfuls onto a hot griddle coated with cooking spray; turn when bubbles form on top. Cook until second side is lightly browned. Serve with berries and yogurt.

NOTE *This recipe was tested with Land O'Lakes light stick butter.*

PER SERVING *2 pancakes with ¼ cup raspberries and 2 tablespoons yogurt equals 201 cal., 2 g fat (1 g sat. fat), 6 mg chol., 249 mg sodium, 40 g carb., 5 g fiber, 8 g pro.* **Diabetic Exchanges:** *2 starch, ½ fruit.*

FRESH CORN OMELET

EGG BASKETS BENEDICT

Egg Baskets Benedict

Indulge in the taste of traditional eggs Benedict using just four ingredients and a muffin pan. The squares of puff pastry create little cups that hold the eggs and chopped Canadian bacon. A packaged hollandaise sauce finishes each basket in a quick but decadent way.

—SALLY JACKSON FORT WORTH, TX

START TO FINISH: 30 MIN.
MAKES: 1 DOZEN (1 CUP SAUCE)

- 1 sheet frozen puff pastry, thawed
- 12 large eggs
- 6 slices Canadian bacon, finely chopped
- 1 envelope hollandaise sauce mix

1. Preheat oven to 400°. On a lightly floured surface, unfold the puff pastry. Roll into a 16x12-in. rectangle; cut into twelve 4-in. squares. Place in greased muffin cups, pressing gently onto the bottoms and up the sides, allowing the corners to point up.
2. Break and slip an egg into the center of each pastry cup; sprinkle with the chopped Canadian bacon. Bake 10-12 minutes or until the pastry is golden brown, the egg whites are completely set and the yolks begin to thicken but are not hard. Meanwhile, prepare hollandaise sauce according to package directions.
3. Remove the pastry cups to wire racks. Serve warm with prepared hollandaise sauce.

Hazelnut Mocha Coffee

I often serve this frosty coffee drink on special occasions. It's a convenient choice for parties because you can prepare the chocolate mixture a few days in advance. When guests are ready for a cup, simply brew the coffee, beat the refrigerated blend and dollop with whipped cream.

—MARY LEVERETTE COLUMBIA, SC

PREP: 5 MIN. • **COOK:** 10 MIN. + CHILLING
MAKES: 6 SERVINGS

- 4 ounces semisweet chocolate, chopped
- 1 cup heavy whipping cream
- ⅓ cup sugar
- ½ teaspoon ground cinnamon
- 2 tablespoons hazelnut liqueur
- 4½ cups hot brewed coffee
  Sweetened whipped cream, optional

1. Place the semisweet chocolate in a small bowl. In a small saucepan, bring the heavy whipping cream just to a boil. Add the sugar and cinnamon; cook and stir until sugar is dissolved. Pour over the chocolate; stir with a whisk until smooth. Stir in the hazelnut liqueur.
2. Cool to room temperature, stirring occasionally. Refrigerate, covered, until cold. Beat just until soft peaks form, about 15 seconds (do not overbeat). For each serving, spoon ¼ cup into mugs. Top with ¾ cup hot coffee; stir to dissolve. Top with sweetened whipped cream if desired.

Cheesy Ham & Egg Sandwiches

Ham, cheddar cheese and oven-fresh biscuits make breakfast sandwiches that are hearty enough for dinner. We pile on toppings like salsa, tomato, avocado, onion—even mayo and ketchup.

—FAY MORELAND WICHITA FALLS, TX

START TO FINISH: 30 MIN.
MAKES: 10 SERVINGS

- 4 cups biscuit/baking mix
- 1 cup (4 ounces) shredded cheddar cheese
- 1 cup finely chopped fully cooked ham
- 1 teaspoon coarsely ground pepper, divided
- 1 cup 2% milk
- 3 tablespoons butter, melted

EGGS

- 8 large eggs
- ½ cup 2% milk
- ¼ teaspoon coarsely ground pepper
- ⅛ teaspoon salt
- 2 tablespoons butter
- 1 cup (4 ounces) shredded cheddar cheese
  Optional toppings: salsa, sliced tomato, red onion and avocado

1. Preheat oven to 425°. In a large bowl, combine biscuit mix, cheddar cheese, ham and ½ teaspoon pepper. Add milk; mix just until moistened.
2. Turn the biscuit dough onto a lightly floured surface; knead gently 8-10 times. Pat or roll biscuit dough to 1-in. thickness; cut with a floured 2½-in. biscuit cutter. Place 2 in. apart on an ungreased baking sheet. Brush with melted butter; sprinkle with the remaining pepper. Bake 12-14 minutes or until golden brown.
3. Meanwhile, for the eggs, in a bowl, whisk the eggs, milk, pepper and salt. In a large nonstick skillet, heat the butter over medium heat. Pour in the egg mixture; cook and stir until the eggs are thickened and no liquid egg remains. Stir in the cheddar cheese; remove from heat.
4. Split warm biscuits in half. Layer the bottoms of biscuits with the egg mixture and toppings as desired. Replace tops of biscuits.

Breakfast Spuds

The whole family will dig in to this morning scramble. Bake one 20-ounce package frozen sweet potato puffs according to package directions. Whisk 8 large eggs, ⅓ cup 2% milk, ¼ teaspoon salt and ⅛ teaspoon pepper. Stir in 1 cup cubed fully cooked ham. In a large nonstick skillet, heat 1 tablespoon butter over medium heat. Add egg mixture; cook and stir until eggs are thickened and no liquid egg remains. Serve with puffs; sprinkle with shredded cheddar cheese and sliced green onions. *Makes 6 servings.*

—ANNIE RUNDLE MUSKEGO, WI

CALICO PEPPER FRITTATA

EAT SMART **FAST FIX**
Calico Pepper Frittata

This veggie frittata cooks on the stovetop, so there's no need to heat up the oven. A jalapeno pepper adds a nice kick to the lightened-up, meatless dish.

—**LORETTA KELCINSKI** KUNKLETOWN, PA

START TO FINISH: 30 MIN.
MAKES: 4 SERVINGS

- 5 **large eggs**
- 1¼ **cups egg substitute**
- 1 **tablespoon grated Romano cheese**
- ½ **teaspoon salt**
- ⅛ **teaspoon pepper**
- 1 **tablespoon olive oil**
- 1 **medium sweet red pepper, chopped**
- 1 **medium green pepper, chopped**
- 1 **jalapeno pepper, seeded and chopped**
- 1 **medium onion, chopped**
- 1 **garlic clove, minced**

1. In a large bowl, whisk the first five ingredients until blended.
2. In a large nonstick skillet, heat the oil over medium-high heat. Add the peppers and onion; cook and stir until tender. Add the garlic; cook 1 minute longer. Pour in egg mixture. Mixture should set immediately at the edges. Cook, uncovered, 8-10 minutes or until eggs are completely set, pushing the cooked portions toward the center and letting the uncooked eggs flow underneath. Cut into wedges.
NOTE *Wear disposable gloves when cutting hot peppers; the oils can burn skin. Avoid touching your face.*
PER SERVING *1 wedge equals 201 cal., 10 g fat (3 g sat. fat), 268 mg chol., 559 mg sodium, 10 g carb., 2 g fiber, 17 g pro.* **Diabetic Exchanges:** *2 lean meat, 2 vegetable, 1 fat.*

FAST FIX
Pumpkin Smoothies

Savor the flavors of fall with smoothies that blend in canned pumpkin and spices.
—**KAREN SIKORA** DAYTON, NV

START TO FINISH: 10 MIN.
MAKES: 4 SERVINGS

- 1 **can (15 ounces) solid-pack pumpkin**
- 2 **cans (5½ ounces each) evaporated milk**
- 1 **cup orange juice**
- 1 **small banana**
- ⅓ **cup packed brown sugar**
- ½ **teaspoon pumpkin pie spice**
- ¼ **teaspoon ground cinnamon**

Place all ingredients in a blender; cover and process for 30 seconds or until smooth. Pour into chilled glasses; serve immediately.

TOP TIP

Rarely use pumpkin pie spice in your cooking? Consider making your own instead of buying it. For 1 teaspoon, blend ½ teaspoon ground cinnamon, ¼ teaspoon ground ginger, ⅛ teaspoon ground nutmeg and ⅛ teaspoon ground cloves or allspice. Or, double or triple the amounts and store some in an airtight container for later. Substitute this mix for store-bought pumpkin pie spice in any recipe.

LANCE'S OWN
FRENCH TOAST

FREEZE IT ⑤INGREDIENTS FAST FIX

Lance's Own French Toast

My son Lance has loved this toast since he was a toddler. At age 2, he'd help me make it and practically knew the recipe by heart.
—**JANNA STEELE** MAGEE, MS

START TO FINISH: 25 MIN.
MAKES: 6 SERVINGS

- 4 **large eggs**
- 1 **cup 2% milk**
- 1 **tablespoon honey**
- ½ **teaspoon ground cinnamon**
- ⅛ **teaspoon pepper**
- 12 **slices whole wheat bread**
  Cinnamon sugar, optional

1. In a shallow bowl, whisk the eggs, milk, honey, cinnamon and pepper. Dip both sides of the bread in the egg mixture. Cook on a greased hot griddle 3-4 minutes on each side or until golden brown.

2. Cut into shapes. If desired, sprinkle with cinnamon sugar.

FREEZE OPTION *Cool the French toast on wire racks. Freeze between layers of waxed paper in a resealable plastic freezer bag. To use, reheat the French toast in a toaster oven on medium setting. Or, microwave each piece of toast on high for 30-60 seconds or until heated through.*

SAUSAGE & SWEET
POTATO HASH

MUSHROOM-AVOCADO
EGGS ON TOAST

Mushroom-Avocado Eggs on Toast

These open-faced breakfast sandwiches are fancy enough to serve guests.

—CAROL MCLAUGHLIN PAPILLION, NE

PREP: 25 MIN. • **BAKE:** 10 MIN.
MAKES: 6 SERVINGS

- 8 **large eggs**
- 2 **tablespoons 2% milk**
- 1 **teaspoon lemon-pepper seasoning**
- ½ **teaspoon dried basil**
- 2 **tablespoons butter, divided**
- 1 **tablespoon minced fresh chives**
- 1 **tablespoon olive oil**
- ½ **pound sliced fresh mushrooms**
- 6 **slices French bread (1 inch thick), toasted**
- 3 **ounces Brie cheese, cut into 6 slices**
- 1 **medium ripe avocado, peeled and thinly sliced**

1. Preheat oven to 350°. In a large bowl, whisk eggs, milk, lemon pepper and basil until blended. In a large nonstick skillet, heat 1 tablespoon butter over medium heat. Pour in egg mixture; cook and stir until eggs are thickened and no liquid egg remains. Gently stir in chives.

2. Meanwhile, in another skillet, heat the olive oil and remaining butter over medium-high heat. Add mushrooms; cook and stir 6-8 minutes or until tender.

3. Place toast slices on an ungreased baking sheet; top with mushrooms, eggs and cheese. Bake 8-10 minutes or until cheese is melted. Just before serving, top with avocado.

1. In a large bowl, combine the oats, dried cranberries, brown sugar, milk, chunky applesauce and almond extract. Transfer to a 3-cup baking dish coated with cooking spray; sprinkle with the sliced almonds.

2. Bake oatmeal, uncovered, at 350° for 45-50 minutes or until set. Serve with toppings if desired.

PER SERVING *1 cup (calculated without optional toppings) equals 259 cal., 4 g fat (1 g sat. fat), 3 mg chol., 73 mg sodium, 48 g carb., 4 g fiber, 10 g pro.*

"What's in the Fridge" Frittata

I use on-hand ingredients for this tasty frittata, which is so easy to fix that I make it on a regular basis. Whisk 6 large eggs. In an 8-in. ovenproof skillet, saute ⅓ cup each chopped onion, sweet red pepper and mushrooms in 1 tablespoon olive oil until tender. Reduce heat; sprinkle with 6 ounces lump crabmeat. Top with eggs. Cover and cook for 5-7 minutes or until nearly set. Sprinkle with ¼ cup shredded Swiss cheese. Broil 3-4 in. from the heat for 2-3 minutes or until eggs are completely set. Let stand for 5 minutes. *Makes 4 servings.*

—DEBORAH POSEY VIRGINIA BEACH, VA

Slow-Cooked Sensations

Want dinner fast? Take things slow! Spend just a little time in the kitchen filling your slow cooker, then go about the rest of your day—and come home to an amazing meal your family is sure to love.

Tamra Parker's Chipotle Pulled Chicken *PAGE 171*

Stephanie Loaiza's Chunky Chicken Cacciatore *PAGE 173*

Blair Lonergan's Slow Cooker Turkey Pesto Lasagna *PAGE 178*

PINEAPPLE-DIJON HAM SANDWICHES

1. In a greased 5-qt. slow cooker, combine the first seven ingredients. Cook, covered, on low 8-10 hours or until apples are tender.

2. Whisk in peanut butter until apple mixture is smooth. Cool to room temperature. Store in an airtight container in the refrigerator.

⑤ INGREDIENTS   SLOW COOKER 🍲

Root Beer Pulled Pork Sandwiches

My sister passed along her incredibly easy idea for pulled pork sandwiches splashed with root beer. They're ideal for potlucks, parties...just about any get-together at all.
—**CAROLYN PALM** WALTON, NY

PREP: 20 MIN. • **COOK:** 8½ HOURS
MAKES: 12 SERVINGS

- 1 boneless pork shoulder butt roast (3 to 4 pounds)
- 1 can (12 ounces) root beer or cola
- 1 bottle (18 ounces) barbecue sauce
- 12 kaiser rolls, split

1. Place pork roast in a 4- or 5-qt. slow cooker. Add root beer; cook, covered, on low 8-10 hours or until the meat is tender.

2. Remove the roast; cool slightly. Discard the cooking juices. Shred the pork with two forks; return to the slow cooker. Stir in barbecue sauce. Cook, covered, until heated through, about 30 minutes. Serve on rolls.

FREEZE OPTION *Freeze the cooled meat mixture in freezer containers. To use, partially thaw in refrigerator overnight. Heat through in a saucepan, stirring occasionally and adding a little water if necessary.*

SLOW COOKER 🍲

Pineapple-Dijon Ham Sandwiches

Ham is big in our family. I like to slow-cook the cubed meat with pineapple, mustard, brown sugar and veggies. We enjoy the tangy juices as a dipping sauce.
—**CAMILLE BECKSTRAND** LAYTON, UT

PREP: 20 MIN. • **COOK:** 3 HOURS
MAKES: 10 SERVINGS

- 2 pounds fully cooked ham, cut into ½-inch cubes
- 1 can (20 ounces) crushed pineapple, undrained
- 1 medium green pepper, finely chopped
- ¾ cup packed brown sugar
- ¼ cup finely chopped onion
- ¼ cup Dijon mustard
- 1 tablespoon dried minced onion
- 10 hamburger buns, split
- 10 slices Swiss cheese
  Additional Dijon mustard, optional

1. In a greased 4-qt. slow cooker, combine the first seven ingredients. Cook, covered, on low 3-4 hours or until heated through.

2. Preheat broiler. Place bun bottoms and tops on baking sheets, cut side up. Using a slotted spoon, place the ham mixture on bottoms; top with cheese. Broil 3-4 in. from the heat 1-2 minutes or until cheese is melted and tops are toasted. Replace tops. If desired, serve with additional mustard.

SLOW COOKER 🍲

Nutty Apple Butter

A native of New England, I love heading out to the orchard for fresh-picked fruit in fall. Gather some apples and peanut butter to make a creamy spread for graham crackers, bread and more.
—**BRANDIE CRANSHAW** RAPID CITY, SD

PREP: 20 MIN. • **COOK:** 8 HOURS
MAKES: 5 CUPS

- 4 pounds apples (about 8 large), peeled and chopped
- ¾ to 1 cup sugar
- ¼ cup water
- 3 teaspoons ground cinnamon
- ¼ teaspoon ground nutmeg
- ¼ teaspoon ground cloves
- ¼ teaspoon ground allspice
- ¼ cup creamy peanut butter

ROOT BEER PULLED PORK SANDWICHES

TOP-RATED
ITALIAN POT ROAST

Top-Rated
Italian Pot Roast

I'm constantly paging through magazines to collect recipes. Here's one that seemed too good not to try—and it is!

—**KAREN BURDELL** LAFAYETTE, CO

PREP: 30 MIN. • **COOK:** 6 HOURS
MAKES: 8 SERVINGS

- 1 **cinnamon stick (3 inches)**
- 6 **whole peppercorns**
- 4 **whole cloves**
- 3 **whole allspice**
- 2 **teaspoons olive oil**
- 1 **boneless beef chuck roast (2 pounds)**
- 2 **celery ribs, sliced**
- 2 **medium carrots, sliced**
- 1 **large onion, chopped**
- 4 **garlic cloves, minced**
- 1 **cup dry sherry or reduced-sodium beef broth**
- 1 **can (28 ounces) crushed tomatoes**
- ¼ **teaspoon salt**
  Hot cooked egg noodles and minced parsley, optional

1. Place the cinnamon stick, peppercorns, cloves and allspice on a double thickness of cheesecloth. Gather the corners of cloth to enclose the spices; tie securely with string.

2. In a large skillet, heat the olive oil over medium-high heat. Brown the beef roast on all sides; transfer to a 4-qt. slow cooker. Add celery, carrots and spice bag.

3. Add the onion to the same skillet; cook and stir until tender. Add garlic; cook 1 minute longer. Add the sherry, stirring to loosen browned bits from pan. Bring to a boil; cook and stir until the liquid is reduced to ⅔ cup. Stir in the tomatoes and salt; pour over roast and vegetables.

4. Cook, covered, on low 6-7 hours or until meat and vegetables are tender. Remove roast from slow cooker; keep warm. Discard the spice bag; skim fat from sauce. Serve roast and sauce with noodles and parsley, if desired.

FREEZE OPTION *Place the sliced roast in freezer containers; top with sauce. Cool and freeze. To use, partially thaw in the refrigerator overnight. Heat through in a covered saucepan, stirring gently and adding a little broth if necessary.*

PER SERVING *3 ounces cooked beef roast with ⅔ cup vegetable mixture (calculated without noodles) equals 251 cal., 12 g fat (4 g sat. fat), 74 mg chol., 271 mg sodium, 11 g carb., 3 g fiber, 24 g pro.* **Diabetic Exchanges:** *3 lean meat, 2 vegetable, ½ fat.*

Slow-Cooked Chicken Enchilada Soup

This Southwestern soup delivers a bowlful of comfort. It's even better with toppings such as avocado, cheese and sour cream.

—**HEATHER SEWELL** HARRISONVILLE, MO

PREP: 25 MIN. • **COOK:** 6 HOURS
MAKES: 8 SERVINGS (3¼ QUARTS)

- 1 **tablespoon canola oil**
- 2 **Anaheim or poblano peppers. finely chopped**
- 1 **medium onion, chopped**
- 3 **garlic cloves, minced**
- 1 **pound boneless skinless chicken breasts**
- 1 **carton (48 ounces) chicken broth**
- 1 **can (14½ ounces) Mexican diced tomatoes, undrained**
- 1 **can (10 ounces) enchilada sauce**
- 2 **tablespoons tomato paste**
- 1 **tablespoon chili powder**
- 2 **teaspoons ground cumin**
- 1 **teaspoon salt**
- ½ **teaspoon pepper**
- ½ **to 1 teaspoon chipotle hot pepper sauce, optional**
- ⅓ **cup minced fresh cilantro**
  Optional toppings: shredded cheddar cheese, cubed avocado, sour cream and crispy tortilla strips

1. In a large skillet, heat the oil over medium heat. Add the peppers and onion; cook and stir 6-8 minutes or until tender. Add the garlic; cook 1 minute longer.

2. Transfer the pepper mixture and chicken to a 5- or 6-qt. slow cooker. Stir in the broth, tomatoes, enchilada sauce, tomato paste, seasonings and, if desired, pepper sauce. Cook, covered, on low 6-8 hours or until the chicken is tender (a thermometer should read at least 165°).

3. Remove chicken from slow cooker. Shred with two forks; return to slow cooker. Stir in cilantro. Serve with toppings as desired.

FREEZE OPTION *Freeze cooled soup in freezer containers. To use, partially thaw in the refrigerator overnight. Heat through in a saucepan, stirring occasionally and adding a little water if necessary.*

My husband is a huge fan of roast beef, and I'm equally enthusiastic about slow cooking. I brought in Asian influences for my Soy-Ginger Pot Roast.
—**LISA VARNER** EL PASO, TX

SOY-GINGER POT ROAST

Soy-Ginger Pot Roast

PREP: 25 MIN. • **COOK:** 7 HOURS
MAKES: 6 SERVINGS

- 1 boneless beef chuck roast (3 to 4 pounds)
- 1 teaspoon salt
- ½ teaspoon pepper
- 1 tablespoon canola oil
- 1½ cups water
- ½ cup reduced-sodium soy sauce
- ¼ cup honey
- 3 tablespoons cider vinegar
- 3 garlic cloves, minced
- 2 teaspoons ground ginger
- 1 teaspoon ground mustard
- 1 large onion, halved and sliced
- 2 tablespoons cornstarch
- 2 tablespoons cold water

1. Sprinkle the roast with salt and pepper. In a large skillet, heat the oil over medium-high heat. Brown the roast on all sides. Transfer meat to a 5- or 6-qt. slow cooker. In a small bowl, mix water, soy sauce, honey, vinegar, garlic, ginger and mustard; pour over meat. Top with onion. Cook, covered, on low 7-9 hours or until meat is tender.
2. Remove the roast and onion to a serving platter; keep warm. Transfer the cooking juices to a large saucepan; skim fat. Bring cooking juices to a boil. In a small bowl, mix the cornstarch and cold water until smooth; stir into cooking juices. Return to a boil; cook and stir 1-2 minutes or until thickened. Serve with roast.

EAT SMART SLOW COOKER
African Peanut Sweet Potato Stew

When I was in college, my mom made an amazing African-style sweet potato stew. I shared it with friends, and now all of us enjoy it with our own families.
—**ALEXIS SCATCHELL** NILES, IL

PREP: 20 MIN. • **COOK:** 6 HOURS
MAKES: 8 SERVINGS (2½ QUARTS)

- 1 can (28 ounces) diced tomatoes, undrained
- 1 cup fresh cilantro leaves
- ½ cup chunky peanut butter
- 3 garlic cloves, halved
- 2 teaspoons ground cumin
- 1 teaspoon salt
- ½ teaspoon ground cinnamon
- ¼ teaspoon smoked paprika
- 3 pounds sweet potatoes (about 6 medium), peeled and cut into 1-inch pieces
- 1 can (15 ounces) garbanzo beans or chickpeas, rinsed and drained
- 1 cup water
- 8 cups chopped fresh kale
  Chopped peanuts and additional cilantro leaves, optional

1. Place the first eight ingredients in a food processor; process until pureed. Transfer to a 5-qt. slow cooker; stir in the sweet potatoes, beans and water.
2. Cook, covered, on low 6-8 hours or until potatoes are tender, adding kale during the last 30 minutes. If desired, top each serving with peanuts and additional cilantro.
PER SERVING *1¼ cups (calculated without chopped peanuts) equals 349 cal., 9 g fat (1 g sat. fat), 0 chol., 624 mg sodium, 60 g carb., 11 g fiber, 10 g pro*

EAT SMART SLOW COOKER
Italian Cabbage Soup

After doing yard work on chilly fall days, we come inside for a light but hearty soup like this one. Pass the bread!
—**JENNIFER STOWELL** SMITHVILLE, MO

PREP: 15 MIN. • **COOK:** 6 HOURS
MAKES: 8 SERVINGS (2 QUARTS)

- 4 cups chicken stock
- 1 can (6 ounces) tomato paste
- 1 small head cabbage (about 1½ pounds), shredded
- 1 can (15½ ounces) great northern beans, rinsed and drained
- 4 celery ribs, chopped
- 2 large carrots, chopped
- 1 small onion, chopped
- 2 fresh thyme sprigs
- 1 bay leaf
- 2 garlic cloves, minced
- ½ teaspoon salt
  Shredded Parmesan cheese, optional

1. In a 5- or 6-qt. slow cooker, whisk stock and tomato paste until blended; add the cabbage, beans, celery, carrots, onion, thyme, bay leaf, garlic and salt.

SPICED CARROTS &
BUTTERNUT SQUASH

EAT SMART SLOW COOKER 🍲
Spiced Carrots & Butternut Squash

Cumin and chili powder bring out the natural sweetness of carrots and squash.

—**COURTNEY STULTZ** COLUMBUS, KS

PREP: 15 MIN. • **COOK:** 4 HOURS
MAKES: 6 SERVINGS

- 5 large carrots, cut into ½-inch pieces (about 3 cups)
- 2 cups cubed peeled butternut squash (1-inch)
- 1 tablespoon balsamic vinegar
- 1 tablespoon olive oil
- 1 tablespoon honey
- 1 teaspoon ground cinnamon
- ½ teaspoon salt
- ½ teaspoon ground cumin
- ¼ teaspoon chili powder

Place carrots and squash in a 3-qt. slow cooker. In a small bowl, mix remaining ingredients; drizzle over the vegetables and toss to coat. Cook, covered, on low 4-5 hours or until the vegetables are tender. Gently stir before serving.
PER SERVING ⅔ cup equals 85 cal., 3 g fat (trace sat. fat), 0 chol., 245 mg sodium, 16 g carb., 3 g fiber, 1 g pro.
Diabetic Exchanges: 1 vegetable, ½ starch, ½ fat.

SLOW COOKER 🍲
Brenda's Baked Beans

When I was a child, my mother prepared her delicious baked beans all the time. Sometimes we'd transform her side dish into a meaty, kid-pleasing main course by tossing in sliced hot dogs.

—**BRENDA BROOKS** BOWIE, MD

PREP: 10 MIN. + SOAKING
COOK: 10 HOURS • **MAKES:** 6 SERVINGS

- 1 pound dried navy beans
- 1½ cups water
- ½ cup packed brown sugar
- ½ cup chopped sweet onion
- ½ cup apple juice
- 6 bacon strips, cooked and crumbled
- ¼ cup maple syrup
- ½ teaspoon ground mustard
- ¼ teaspoon ground cinnamon
- 1 teaspoon salt

1. Rinse and sort the navy beans; soak according to the package directions.
2. Drain and rinse the navy beans, discarding the liquid. Transfer beans to a 3-qt. slow cooker. Stir in the water, brown sugar, sweet onion, apple juice, bacon, maple syrup, ground mustard and cinnamon. Cook, covered, on low 10-12 hours or until beans are tender. Stir in the salt.

Slow Cooker Sausage Sandwiches

A popular family entree—pork chops and sausage served over a bed of angel hair pasta   inspired my Italian sandwiches. Now we have a new favorite to enjoy.
—**DEBRA GOFORTH** NEWPORT, TN

PREP: 20 MIN. • **COOK:** 6 HOURS
MAKES: 8 SERVINGS

- 3 **bone-in pork loin chops (7 ounces each)**
- 4 **Italian sausage links (4 ounces each)**
- 1 **can (28 ounces) whole plum tomatoes, undrained**
- 1 **can (6 ounces) tomato paste**
- 1 **teaspoon Italian seasoning**
- 3 **garlic cloves, minced**
- ¼ **teaspoon crushed red pepper flakes**
- 1 **large onion, halved and sliced**
- 1 **large sweet red pepper, cut into strips**
- 1 **large green pepper, cut into strips**
- 1 **jar (16 ounces) mild pickled pepper rings, drained**
- 8 **submarine buns, split**
- 1 **cup (4 ounces) shredded Italian cheese blend**

1. Place meats in a 5- or 6-qt. slow cooker. Place tomatoes, tomato paste, and seasonings in a food processor; pulse until chunky. Pour over meats. Cook, covered, on low 4 hours.
2. Add the onion and peppers to the slow cooker. Cook, covered, on low 2-3 hours longer or until the pork is tender, a thermometer inserted in the sausages reads 160° and vegetables are crisp-tender. Remove meat. Remove pork from bones; discard bones. Shred with two forks and cut sausages into 2-in. pieces; return to slow cooker. Serve on buns with cheese.

Chunky Chicken Cacciatore

This cacciatore is so versatile. Want to add olives or Parmesan? Go for it!
—**STEPHANIE LOAIZA** LAYTON, UT

PREP: 10 MIN. • **COOK:** 4 HOURS
MAKES: 6 SERVINGS

- 6 **boneless skinless chicken thighs (about 1½ pounds)**
- 1 **jar (24 ounces) garden-style spaghetti sauce**
- 2 **medium zucchini, cut into 1-inch slices**
- 1 **medium green pepper, cut into 1-inch pieces**
- 1 **large sweet onion, coarsely chopped**
- ½ **teaspoon dried oregano**
  Hot cooked spaghetti
  Sliced ripe olives and shredded Parmesan cheese, optional

1. Place chicken and vegetables in a 3-qt. slow cooker; sprinkle with oregano. Pour sauce over top. Cook, covered, on low 4-5 hours or until chicken is tender.
2. Remove chicken; break up slightly with two forks. Return to slow cooker. Serve with spaghetti. If desired, sprinkle with olives and cheese.
PER SERVING *1 serving (calculated without the spaghetti and optional ingredients) equals 285 cal., 11 g fat (2 g sat. fat), 76 mg chol., 507 mg sodium, 21 g carb., 3 g fiber, 24 g pro. Diabetic Exchanges: 3 lean meat, 1½ starch.*
TO MAKE AHEAD *Place the first six ingredients in a large resealable plastic freezer bag; seal bag and freeze. To use, place filled bag in refrigerator 48 hours or until the contents are completely thawed. Cook and serve as directed.*

SLOW COOKER SAUSAGE SANDWICHES

SUPER EASY COUNTRY-STYLE RIBS

SLOW COOKER 🍲
Saucy Ranch Pork and Potatoes

My sister Elyse shared a recipe for pork roast with me. After tweaking it a bit using the ingredients in my pantry, I had another delicious dinner option.

—**KENDRA ADAMSON** LAYTON, UT

PREP: 20 MIN. • **COOK:** 4 HOURS
MAKES: 6 SERVINGS

- 2 **pounds red potatoes (about 6 medium), cut into ¾-inch cubes**
- ¼ **cup water**
- 6 **boneless pork loin chops (6 ounces each)**
- 2 **cans (10¾ ounces each) condensed cream of chicken soup, undiluted**
- 1 **cup 2% milk**
- 1 **envelope ranch salad dressing mix Minced fresh parsley, optional**

1. Place the potatoes and water in a large microwave-safe dish. Microwave, covered, on high for 3-5 minutes or until potatoes are almost tender; drain.
2. Transfer potatoes and pork chops to a 4- or 5-qt. slow cooker. In a bowl, mix the condensed cream of chicken soup, milk and ranch salad dressing mix; pour over the pork chops. Cook, covered, on low 4-5 hours or until the pork chops and potatoes are tender (a thermometer inserted in the pork should read at least 145°). If desired, sprinkle with parsley.

SAUCY RANCH PORK AND POTATOES

SLOW COOKER 🍲
Super Easy Country-Style Ribs

I have fond memories of coming home to the aroma of Mom's sweet, tangy ribs.

—**STEPHANIE LOAIZA** LAYTON, UT

PREP: 10 MIN. • **COOK:** 5 HOURS
MAKES: 4 SERVINGS

- 1½ **cups ketchup**
- ½ **cup packed brown sugar**
- ½ **cup white vinegar**
- 2 **teaspoons seasoned salt**
- ½ **teaspoon liquid smoke, optional**
- 2 **pounds boneless country-style pork ribs**

In a 3-qt. slow cooker, mix first five ingredients. Add ribs; turn to coat. Cook, covered, on low 5-6 hours or until the meat is tender. Remove pork to serving plate. Skim the fat from the cooking liquid. If desired, transfer cooking liquid to a small saucepan to thicken. Bring to a boil; cook for 12-15 minutes or until the sauce is reduced to 1½ cups. Serve with ribs.
TO MAKE AHEAD *In a resealable plastic freezer bag, combine first five ingredients. Add pork; seal and freeze. To use, thaw in the refrigerator for 48 hours or until ribs are completely thawed. Cook as directed.*

SLOW COOKER 🍲
Green Chili Creamed Corn

When hosting holiday dinners or other big meals, I sometimes run out of burners on the stove. Now my slow cooker helps by simmering up a side dish of creamed corn. Green chilies, pickled jalapenos and red pepper flakes give it a nice zip.

—**PAT DAZIS** CHARLOTTE, NC

PREP: 10 MIN. • **COOK:** 3 HOURS
MAKES: 8 SERVINGS

- 6 **cups fresh or frozen corn (about 30 ounces), thawed**
- 1 **package (8 ounces) cream cheese, cubed**
- 1 **jar (4 ounces) diced pimientos, drained**
- 1 **can (4 ounces) chopped green chilies**
- ½ **cup vegetable broth**
- ¼ **cup butter, cubed**
- ¼ **cup pickled jalapeno slices, coarsely chopped**
- 1 **tablespoon sugar**
- ⅛ **teaspoon crushed red pepper flakes**

In a 3- or 4-qt. slow cooker, combine all ingredients. Cook, covered, on low 2½-3 hours or until heated through. Stir just before serving.

CHIPOTLE SHREDDED BEEF

We can't get enough of the tender meat and sensational flavor in Family-Favorite Italian Beef Sandwiches. If you like, stack 'em even higher with provolone and sauteed mushrooms.

—**LAUREN ADAMSON** LAYTON, UT

EAT SMART SLOW COOKER
Chipotle Shredded Beef

Try this rolled up in tortillas, piled in buns or served over mashed potatoes or rice. Leftovers even make great quesadillas!

—**DARCY WILLIAMS** OMAHA, NE

PREP: 25 MIN. • **COOK:** 8 HOURS
MAKES: 10 SERVINGS

- 1 teaspoon canola oil
- 1 small onion, chopped
- 1 can (28 ounces) diced tomatoes, undrained
- ¼ cup cider vinegar
- ¼ cup chopped chipotle peppers in adobo sauce plus 2 teaspoons sauce
- 6 garlic cloves, minced
- 2 tablespoons brown sugar
- 2 bay leaves
- ½ teaspoon ground cumin
- ½ teaspoon paprika
- ½ teaspoon pepper
- ¼ teaspoon ground cinnamon
- 1 boneless beef chuck roast (2½ pounds)
- 5 cups cooked brown rice
  Shredded reduced-fat cheddar cheese and reduced-fat sour cream, optional

1. In a large skillet coated with cooking spray, heat oil over medium-high heat. Add onion; cook and stir 2-3 minutes or until tender. Stir in tomatoes, vinegar, peppers with sauce, garlic, brown sugar, bay leaves and spices. Bring to a boil. Reduce the heat; simmer, uncovered, 4-6 minutes or until thickened.
2. Place roast in a 5-qt. slow cooker; add tomato mixture. Cook, covered, on low 8-10 hours or until meat is tender.
3. Discard bay leaves. Remove roast; cool slightly. Skim fat from cooking juices. Shred the beef with two forks. Return beef and juices to slow cooker; heat through. Serve with rice. If desired, top with cheese and sour cream.
FREEZE OPTION *Freeze the cooled meat mixture and juices in freezer containers. To use, partially thaw in refrigerator overnight. Heat through in a saucepan, stirring occasionally and adding a little water if necessary.*
PER SERVING *⅔ cup beef mixture with ½ cup cooked rice (calculated without optional ingredients) equals 345 cal., 13 g fat (4 g sat. fat), 74 mg chol., 194 mg sodium, 31 g carb., 3 g fiber, 26 g pro.* **Diabetic Exchanges:** *3 lean meat, 2 starch.*

FREEZE IT SLOW COOKER
Family-Favorite Italian Beef Sandwiches

PREP: 10 MIN. • **COOK:** 8 HOURS
MAKES: 12 SERVINGS

- 1 jar (16 ounces) sliced pepperoncini, undrained
- 1 can (14½ ounces) diced tomatoes, undrained
- 1 medium onion, chopped
- ½ cup water
- 2 packages Italian salad dressing mix
- 1 teaspoon dried oregano
- ½ teaspoon garlic powder
- 1 beef rump roast or bottom round roast (3 to 4 pounds)
- 12 Italian rolls, split

1. In a bowl, mix the first seven ingredients. Place roast in a 5- or 6-qt. slow cooker. Pour the pepperoncini mixture over top. Cook, covered, on low 8-10 hours or until roast is tender.
2. Remove the roast; cool slightly. Skim fat from cooking juices. Shred the meat with two forks. Return with cooking juices to slow cooker; heat through. Serve on Italian rolls.
TO MAKE AHEAD *In a large resealable plastic freezer bag, combine first seven ingredients. Add roast; seal and freeze. To use, place bag in refrigerator for 48 hours or until completely thawed. Cook and serve as directed.*
FREEZE OPTION *Freeze the cooled meat mixture and juices in freezer containers. To use, partially thaw in refrigerator overnight. Heat through in a saucepan, stirring occasionally and adding a little water if necessary.*

We attend the annual Salt Lake City Greek Festival for the awesome food. My Shredded Chicken Gyros recipe is a salute to the flavors of Greece.
—**CAMILLE BECKSTRAND** LAYTON, UT

SHREDDED CHICKEN GYROS

SLOW COOKER
Shredded Chicken Gyros

PREP: 20 MIN. • COOK: 3 HOURS
MAKES: 8 SERVINGS

- 2 medium onions, chopped
- 6 garlic cloves, minced
- 1 teaspoon lemon-pepper seasoning
- 1 teaspoon dried oregano
- ½ teaspoon ground allspice
- ½ cup water
- ½ cup lemon juice
- ¼ cup red wine vinegar
- 2 tablespoons olive oil
- 2 pounds boneless skinless chicken breasts
- 8 whole pita breads
  Toppings: tzatziki sauce, torn romaine and sliced tomato, cucumber and onion

1. In a 3-qt. slow cooker, combine the first nine ingredients; add the chicken. Cook, covered, on low 3-4 hours or until the chicken is tender (a thermometer should read at least 165°).

2. Remove the chicken from the slow cooker. Shred the chicken with two forks; return to the slow cooker.

3. Using tongs, place the chicken mixture on whole pita breads. Serve with tzatziki sauce, romaine, tomato, cucumber and onion.

EAT SMART SLOW COOKER
Hearty Busy-Day Stew

When I was still living in Missouri, a good friend of mine who was downsizing gave me her collection of family cookbooks. I was in heaven! One of them inspired my idea for an easy beef and vegetable stew. The taco seasoning may seem like an unusual ingredient, but I think it adds just the right zip.

—**KRISTEN HILLS** LAYTON, UT

PREP: 10 MIN. • COOK: 7½ HOURS
MAKES: 6 SERVINGS

- 1½ pounds beef stew meat
- 1½ pounds potatoes (about 3 medium), peeled and cut into 1-inch cubes
- 1 can (14½ ounces) diced tomatoes, undrained
- 1 can (14½ ounces) beef broth
- 2½ cups fresh baby carrots (about 12 ounces)
- 1 large tomato, chopped
- 1 medium onion, chopped
- 2 tablespoons taco seasoning
- 2 garlic cloves, minced
- ½ teaspoon salt
- 2 tablespoons cornstarch
- 2 tablespoons cold water

1. In a 5- or 6-qt. slow cooker, combine the first 10 ingredients. Cook, covered, on low 7-9 hours or until the beef stew meat and vegetables are tender.

2. In a small bowl, mix the cornstarch and cold water until smooth; gradually stir into stew. Cook, covered, on high 30-45 minutes longer or until stew is slightly thickened.

PER SERVING 1¾ cups equals 303 cal., 8 g fat (3 g sat. fat), 71 mg chol., 986 mg sodium, 32 g carb., 4 g fiber, 25 g pro.

LENTIL PUMPKIN SOUP

AUTUMN APPLE CHICKEN

FREEZE IT SLOW COOKER

Sweet & Smoky Pulled Pork Sandwiches

This roast turns out so tender, it practically shreds itself. The sandwiches are the best!
—**LAUREN ADAMSON** LAYTON, UT

PREP: 15 MIN. • **COOK:** 8 HOURS
MAKES: 10 SERVINGS

- ⅓ cup liquid smoke
- 3 tablespoons paprika
- 3 teaspoons salt
- 3 teaspoons pepper
- 1 teaspoon garlic powder
- 1 teaspoon ground mustard
- 1 boneless pork shoulder butt roast (3 to 4 pounds)
- 1 bottle (18 ounces) barbecue sauce
- 10 hamburger buns, split

1. In a small bowl, whisk the first six ingredients; rub over roast. Place roast in a 5- or 6-qt. slow cooker. Cook, covered, on low 8-10 hours or until the meat is tender.

2. Remove the roast; cool slightly. Discard cooking juices. Shred pork with two forks; return to slow cooker. Stir in barbecue sauce; heat through. Serve on buns.

FREEZE OPTION *Freeze the cooled meat mixture in freezer containers. To use, partially thaw in refrigerator overnight. Heat through in a saucepan, stirring occasionally and adding a little water if necessary.*

TO MAKE AHEAD *In a small bowl, whisk the first six ingredients; rub over roast. Place roast in a large resealable plastic freezer bag; seal and freeze. To use, thaw in refrigerator for 48 hours. Cook and serve as directed.*

SWEET & SMOKY PULLED PORK SANDWICHES

EAT SMART SLOW COOKER

Autumn Apple Chicken

I'd just been apple picking and wanted to make something new with my bounty. Slow-cooking the fruit and chicken with barbecue sauce, onion, garlic and cider filled our entire house with an absolutely mouthwatering aroma. We couldn't wait to eat—and we weren't disappointed!
—**CAITLYN HAUSER** BROOKLINE, NH

PREP: 20 MIN. • **COOK:** 3½ HOURS
MAKES: 4 SERVINGS

- 1 tablespoon canola oil
- 4 bone-in chicken thighs (about 1½ pounds), skin removed
- ¼ teaspoon salt
- ¼ teaspoon pepper
- 2 medium Fuji or Gala apples, coarsely chopped
- 1 medium onion, chopped
- 1 garlic clove, minced
- ⅓ cup barbecue sauce
- ¼ cup apple cider or juice
- 1 tablespoon honey

1. In a large skillet, heat the oil over medium heat. Brown chicken on both sides; sprinkle with salt and pepper. Transfer to a 3-qt. slow cooker; top with apples.

2. Add onion to same skillet; cook and stir over medium heat 2-3 minutes or until tender. Add garlic; cook 1 minute longer. Stir in sauce, cider and honey; increase heat to medium-high. Cook 1 minute, stirring to loosen browned bits from pan. Pour over chicken and apples. Cook, covered, on low 3½-4½ hours or until chicken is tender.

FREEZE OPTION *Freeze the cooled chicken mixture in freezer containers. To use, partially thaw in refrigerator overnight. Heat through in a covered saucepan, stirring occasionally.*

PER SERVING *1 chicken thigh with ½ cup apple mixture equals 333 cal., 13 g fat (3 g sat. fat), 87 mg chol., 456 mg sodium, 29 g carb., 3 g fiber, 25 g pro.* **Diabetic Exchanges:** *4 lean meat, 1½ starch, ½ fruit.*

SLOW COOKER
CURRY PORK

SLOW COOKER 🍲

Barbecue Chicken Cobb Salad

Give the traditional Cobb salad a tangy, saucy twist. It's how I finally convinced my family to eat more vegetables!

—**CAMILLE BECKSTRAND** LAYTON, UT

PREP: 30 MIN. • **COOK:** 3 HOURS
MAKES: 6 SERVINGS

- 1 bottle (18 ounces) barbecue sauce
- 2 tablespoons brown sugar
- ½ teaspoon garlic powder
- ¼ teaspoon paprika
- 1½ pounds boneless skinless chicken breasts
- 12 cups chopped romaine
- 3 plum tomatoes, chopped
- 2 avocados, peeled and chopped
- 2 small carrots, thinly sliced
- 1 medium sweet red or green pepper, chopped
- 3 large hard-cooked eggs, chopped
- 6 bacon strips, cooked and crumbled
- 1½ cups (6 ounces) shredded cheddar cheese
   Salad dressing of your choice

1. In a greased 3-qt. slow cooker, mix barbecue sauce, brown sugar, garlic powder and paprika. Add the chicken breasts; turn to coat. Cook, covered, on low 3-4 hours or until the chicken is tender (a thermometer should read at least 165°).

2. Remove the chicken from the slow cooker; cut into bite-size pieces. In a bowl, toss chicken with 1 cup barbecue sauce mixture. Place the romaine on a large serving platter; arrange chicken, vegetables, avocado, hard-cooked eggs, bacon and cheese over the romaine. Drizzle with salad dressing.

💬 DID YOU KNOW?

Now a world-famous dish, the Cobb salad was born at the Brown Derby restaurant in Hollywood. Legend has it that owner Bob Cobb prepared an impromptu salad for himself and Sid Grauman, who owned Grauman's Chinese Theatre. The next day, Sid returned and requested the Cobb salad, which was added to the menu.

EAT SMART SLOW COOKER 🍲

Slow Cooker Curry Pork

A busy stay-at-home mom, I'm always on the lookout for wholesome homemade food that keeps prep work to a minimum. This dinner takes only 15 minutes to put together. Then I just let it cook!

—**BEVERLY PEYCHAL** WAUKESHA, WI

PREP: 15 MIN.
COOK: 3½ HOURS + STANDING
MAKES: 10 SERVINGS

- 1½ teaspoons salt
- 1½ teaspoons hot or regular curry powder
- 1 teaspoon ground cumin
- 1 teaspoon dried oregano
- ¾ teaspoon onion powder
- ¾ teaspoon garlic powder
- ½ teaspoon pepper
- ¼ teaspoon each cayenne pepper, ground chipotle pepper and paprika
- 1½ pounds potatoes, cut into ½-inch pieces
- 4 medium carrots, thinly sliced
- 3 cups cubed peeled butternut squash (about 1 pound)
- 1 can (14½ ounces) reduced-sodium chicken broth
- 1 boneless pork loin roast (3 to 4 pounds)

1. In a small bowl, mix seasonings. In a 6-qt. slow cooker, combine the vegetables, broth and 2 teaspoons seasoning mixture. Rub remaining seasoning mixture over pork; place over vegetables. Cook, covered, on low 3½-4½ hours or until the pork and vegetables are tender (a thermometer inserted in the meat should read at least 145°).

2. Remove roast from slow cooker; tent with foil. Let stand 15 minutes before slicing. Serve with vegetables.

PER SERVING *4 ounces cooked pork with ½ cup vegetables equals 261 cal., 7 g fat (2 g sat. fat), 68 mg chol., 523 mg sodium, 21 g carb., 4 g fiber, 29 g pro. Diabetic Exchanges: 4 lean meat, 1½ starch.*

Josephine Piro's
Garlic-Herb Mini
Quiches PAGE 190

Effortless Entertaining

Wish you had more time to host guests? Now you do, thanks to the quick but party-special recipes in this chapter. Each one goes together from start to finish in just half an hour—or less!

**Sheila Parker's
Hot Quick Banana Boats**
PAGE 187

**Carol Van Sickle's
All-Occasion Punch**
PAGE 190

**Debbie Manno's
Bruschetta with Prosciutto**
PAGE 184

CHICKEN CHILI
WONTON BITES

EAT SMART FAST FIX >

Bruschetta with Prosciutto

After trying this special Italian appetizer, your guests will never believe that it takes less than half an hour to prepare.

—**DEBBIE MANNO** FORT MILL, SC

START TO FINISH: 25 MIN.
MAKES: ABOUT 6½ DOZEN

- 8 plum tomatoes, seeded and chopped
- 1 cup chopped sweet onion
- ¼ cup grated Romano cheese
- ¼ cup minced fresh basil
- 2 ounces thinly sliced prosciutto, finely chopped
- 1 shallot, finely chopped
- 3 garlic cloves, minced
- ⅓ cup olive oil
- ⅓ cup balsamic vinegar
- 1 teaspoon minced fresh rosemary
- ¼ teaspoon pepper
- ⅛ teaspoon hot pepper sauce, optional
- 1 French bread baguette (10½ ounces), cut into ¼-inch slices

1. In a large bowl, combine the first seven ingredients. In another bowl, whisk the olive oil, balsamic vinegar, rosemary, pepper and pepper sauce if desired. Pour over tomato mixture; toss to coat.

2. Place the French bread slices on an ungreased baking sheet. Broil 3-4 in. from the heat for 1-2 minutes or until golden brown. With a slotted spoon, top each bread slice with the tomato mixture.

PER SERVING *1 appetizer equals 23 cal., 1 g fat (trace sat. fat), 1 mg chol., 44 mg sodium, 3 g carb., trace fiber, 1 g pro.*

BRUSCHETTA WITH PROSCIUTTO

Everyone needs a guaranteed-to-please snack for tailgate parties or other events. Chicken Chili Wonton Bites are fun to eat, easy to grab and just plain tasty!

—**HEIDI JOBE** CARROLLTON, GA

⑤ INGREDIENTS FAST FIX

Chicken Chili Wonton Bites

START TO FINISH: 30 MIN.
MAKES: 3 DOZEN

- 36 wonton wrappers
- ½ cup buttermilk ranch salad dressing
- 1 envelope reduced-sodium chili seasoning mix
- 1½ cups shredded rotisserie chicken
- 1 cup (4 ounces) shredded sharp cheddar cheese
  Sour cream and sliced green onions, optional

1. Preheat oven to 350°. Press the wrappers into greased miniature muffin cups. Bake 4-6 minutes or until lightly browned.

2. In a small bowl, mix the buttermilk ranch salad dressing and seasoning mix; add the shredded chicken and toss to coat. Spoon 1 tablespoon filling into each wonton cup. Sprinkle with cheddar cheese.

3. Bake 8-10 minutes longer or until heated through and the wrappers are golden brown. Serve warm. If desired, top with sour cream and green onions before serving.

1. Cook pasta according to package directions. Meanwhile, in a large nonstick skillet coated with cooking spray, cook the scallops in 1 teaspoon oil over medium heat until firm and opaque; remove and keep warm.
2. In the same skillet, saute the onion in remaining oil until tender. Add the garlic; cook 1 minute longer. Stir in the vegetable broth, wine, lemon juice, salt and pepper. Bring to a boil.
3. Combine the cornstarch and cold water until smooth. Gradually stir into the pan. Bring to a boil; cook and stir for 2 minutes or until thickened. Stir in the parsley and reserved scallops; heat through.
4. Drain the pasta; serve with scallops. Sprinkle with cheese and green onions if desired.

PER SERVING *1/3 cup scallop mixture with 1 cup pasta (calculated without cheese) equals 340 cal., 4 g fat (1 g sat. fat), 28 mg chol., 527 mg sodium, 50 g carb., 2 g fiber, 22 g pro.*

HOMEMADE IRISH CREAM

FAST FIX
BBQ Ham Sliders
These snack-size ham sandwiches are sure to tide everyone over until mealtime.
—**SUSANNE ROUPE** EAST FAIRFIELD, VT

START TO FINISH: 20 MIN.
MAKES: 2 DOZEN

- 1 cup chili sauce
- ½ cup water
- 2 tablespoons sugar
- 2 tablespoons cider vinegar
- 1 tablespoon Worcestershire sauce
- 1 teaspoon onion powder
- 1 pound fully cooked ham, very thinly sliced
- 24 dinner rolls, split

1. In a large saucepan, combine the first six ingredients. Bring to a boil. Reduce the heat; simmer, uncovered, for 6-8 minutes or until slightly thickened.
2. Stir in the ham slices; heat through. Serve on rolls.

FAST FIX
Homemade Irish Cream
Coffee gets a splash of creamy goodness with this version of an Irish favorite.
—**MARCIA SEVERSON** HALLOCK, MN

START TO FINISH: 10 MIN.
MAKES: 3⅓ CUPS

- 1 can (12 ounces) evaporated milk
- 1 cup heavy whipping cream
- ½ cup 2% milk
- ¼ cup sugar
- 2 tablespoons chocolate syrup
- 1 tablespoon instant coffee granules
- 2 teaspoons vanilla extract
- ¼ teaspoon almond extract

EACH SERVING
- ½ cup brewed coffee

In a blender, combine the first eight ingredients; cover and process until smooth. Store in the refrigerator. For each serving, place coffee in a mug. Stir in ⅓ cup Irish cream. Heat mixture in a microwave if desired.
NOTE *Irish whiskey may be added to this recipe if desired.*

EAT SMART **FAST FIX**
Scallops with Angel Hair
Scallops may taste like an indulgence, but they're actually low in fat. I pair them with delicate angel hair pasta in a wine, garlic and lemon sauce. Delicious!
—**NANCY MUELLER** MENOMONEE FALLS, WI

START TO FINISH: 30 MIN.
MAKES: 4 SERVINGS

- 8 ounces uncooked angel hair pasta
- ¾ pound bay scallops
- 2 teaspoons olive oil, divided
- 1 small onion, chopped
- 2 garlic cloves, minced
- 1 cup vegetable broth
- ¼ cup dry white wine or additional vegetable broth
- 2 tablespoons lemon juice
- ¼ teaspoon salt
- ⅛ teaspoon pepper
- 2 teaspoons cornstarch
- 2 teaspoons cold water
- ¼ cup minced fresh parsley
  Shredded Parmesan cheese and thinly sliced green onions, optional

FAST FIX >

Herb Mix for Dipping Oil

Keep this flavorful herb blend on hand to quickly make an elegant dipping oil for bread whenever guests drop by. They're sure to love it!

—*TASTE OF HOME* TEST KITCHEN

START TO FINISH: 5 MIN.
MAKES: ½ CUP PER BATCH

- 1 **tablespoon dried minced garlic**
- 1 **tablespoon dried rosemary, crushed**
- 1 **tablespoon dried oregano**
- 2 **teaspoons dried basil**
- 1 **teaspoon crushed red pepper flakes**
- ½ **teaspoon salt**
- ½ **teaspoon coarsely ground pepper**

ADDITIONAL INGREDIENTS (FOR EACH BATCH)

- 1 **tablespoon water**
- ½ **cup olive oil**
- 1 **French bread baguette (10½ ounces)**

In a small bowl, combine the first seven ingredients. Store mix in an airtight container in a cool dry place for up to 6 months. Yield: 3 batches (¼ cup total).

TO PREPARE DIPPING OIL *In a small microwave-safe bowl, combine 4 teaspoons herb mix with water. Microwave, uncovered, on high for 10-15 seconds. Drain excess water. Transfer to a shallow serving plate; add oil and stir. Serve with bread.*

DIJON PORK MEDALLIONS

HERB MIX FOR DIPPING OIL

EAT SMART FAST FIX >

Dijon Pork Medallions

My husband is a big fan of Dijon mustard, so he's always happy to see these pork medallions. A dash of lemon-pepper seasoning adds an extra kick.

—**JOYCE MOYNIHAN** LAKEVILLE, MN

START TO FINISH: 20 MIN.
MAKES: 4 SERVINGS

- 1 **pork tenderloin (1 pound)**
- 1½ **teaspoons lemon-pepper seasoning**
- 2 **tablespoons butter**
- 2 **tablespoons lemon juice**
- 1 **tablespoon Worcestershire sauce**
- 1 **teaspoon Dijon mustard**
- 1 **tablespoon minced fresh parsley**

1. Cut pork into eight slices; lightly pound with a meat mallet to 1-in. thickness. Sprinkle with lemon-pepper.

2. In a large nonstick skillet, heat the butter over medium heat. Add pork; cook 3-4 minutes on each side or until a thermometer reads 145°. Remove from pan; keep warm.

3. Add lemon juice, Worcestershire sauce and Dijon mustard to skillet; cook 3-4 minutes, stirring to loosen browned bits from pan. Serve with pork; sprinkle with parsley.

PER SERVING *2 pork slices with about 2 teaspoons sauce equals 189 cal., 10 g fat (5 g sat. fat), 78 mg chol., 330 mg sodium, 2 g carb., trace fiber, 23 g pro. Diabetic Exchanges: 3 lean meat, 1 fat.*

Pineapple Rum Punch

Sip your way to a tropical island paradise! I came up with this sunny punch by stirring together my favorite Bahamian fruit juices.

—PAMELA VITTI KNOWLES
HENDERSONVILLE, NC

START TO FINISH: 10 MIN.
MAKES: 12 SERVINGS

- 3½ **cups unsweetened pineapple juice**
- 1½ **cups orange juice**
- 1 **cup coconut water**
- 1 **cup coconut rum**
- 1 **cup orange peach mango juice**
- 1 **cup dark rum**
- ¼ **cup Key lime juice**
- 3 **tablespoons Campari liqueur or grenadine syrup**

In a pitcher, combine all ingredients. Serve over ice.

Hot Quick Banana Boats

Here's a great treat for the campground or a backyard cookout. Stuffed with mini marshmallows, chocolate chips and trail mix, the bananas go on the grill in a foil bowl you can eat from.

—SHEILA PARKER RENO, NV

START TO FINISH: 20 MIN.
MAKES: 4 SERVINGS

- 4 **large unpeeled bananas**
- 8 **teaspoons semisweet chocolate chips**
- 8 **teaspoons trail mix**
- ¼ **cup miniature marshmallows**

1. Place each banana on a 12-in. square of foil; crimp and shape the foil around the bananas so they sit flat.
2. Cut each banana lengthwise about ½ in. deep, leaving ½ in. uncut at both ends of the banana. Gently pull each banana peel open, forming a pocket. Fill the pockets with the semisweet chocolate chips, trail mix and miniature marshmallows.
3. Grill the bananas, covered, over medium heat for 4-5 minutes or until the marshmallows are melted and golden brown.

TOP TIP

Look for plump bananas that are evenly yellow-colored. If they are too green, place them in a paper bag until ripe. Adding an apple to the paper bag will speed up the process. Store ripe bananas at room temperature. To prevent bruises, store them on a banana hook or hanger.

PINEAPPLE RUM PUNCH

MOCHA FONDUE

Mocha Fondue

FAST FIX

At our friends' 25th anniversary party, guests couldn't get enough of the luscious mocha-flavored fondue. Cubes of pound cake, strawberries, bananas and pineapple chunks make yummy dippers. Or try plain cookies, large marshmallows or pretzels.

—**KAREN BOEHNER** GLEN ELDER, KS

START TO FINISH: 20 MIN.
MAKES: 10 SERVINGS

- 2 cups (12 ounces) semisweet chocolate chips
- ¼ cup butter, cubed
- 1 cup heavy whipping cream
- 3 tablespoons strong brewed coffee
- ⅛ teaspoon salt
- 2 large egg yolks, lightly beaten
  Cubed pound cake, sliced bananas and fresh strawberries and pineapple chunks

1. In a heavy saucepan, combine the first five ingredients; cook and stir over medium heat until chips are melted. Remove from heat. In a small bowl, whisk a small amount of hot mixture into egg yolks; return all to pan, whisking constantly. Cook and stir until a thermometer reads 160°.
2. Transfer to a fondue pot and keep warm. Serve with cake and fruit.

Instant Chocolate Pastries

⑤ INGREDIENTS **FAST FIX**

While traveling in Europe, my sister and I discovered Nutella. Now we're always thinking of ways to incorporate it into our cooking. This favorite recipe came about after baking puff pastries filled with apples. We thought, "Why not use chocolate?" The results were absolutely scrumptious! We finish off the treats with a sprinkling of confectioners' sugar.

—**DEE WOLF** SYRACUSE, UT

START TO FINISH: 20 MIN.
MAKES: 6 SERVINGS

- 1 sheet frozen puff pastry, thawed
- 6 tablespoons Nutella
- 1 egg, beaten
  Confectioners' sugar, optional

1. Unfold the puff pastry; cut into six rectangles. Place on a greased baking sheet. Spread 1 tablespoon Nutella over half of a puff pastry rectangle; fold the puff pastry over the Nutella filling. Press the edges of pastry with a fork to seal. Repeat for the remaining pastries. Brush with beaten egg; prick the tops with a fork.
2. Bake at 400° for 10-14 minutes or until puffy and golden brown. Sprinkle with confectioners' sugar if desired. Serve warm.
NOTE *Look for Nutella in the peanut butter section.*

POUND CAKE WITH BRANDIED PEACH SAUCE

Pound Cake with Brandied Peach Sauce

FAST FIX

This spiked peach sauce is simply elegant. For a change, serve it over shortcake, ice cream...even pancakes or waffles.

—**SUZY HORVATH** MILWAUKIE, OR

START TO FINISH: 30 MIN.
MAKES: 6 SERVINGS

- 1 cup water
- 3 tablespoons brandy or apricot nectar
- 2 tablespoons sugar
- 2 tablespoons peach preserves
  Dash salt
- 3 cups sliced peeled peaches (about 5 medium) or frozen unsweetened sliced peaches
- 1 cup heavy whipping cream
- 4½ teaspoons confectioners' sugar
- 2¼ teaspoons vanilla extract, divided
- 6 slices pound cake

1. In a large saucepan, combine the water, brandy, sugar, peach preserves and salt. Bring to a boil; reduce heat. Add the peaches; cook and stir for 3-4 minutes or until tender.
2. Remove the peaches to a bowl; set aside. Bring sauce mixture to a boil; cook and stir until reduced to ½ cup.
3. Meanwhile, in a small bowl, beat heavy whipping cream until it begins to thicken. Add confectioners' sugar and ¼ teaspoon vanilla; beat until stiff peaks form.
4. Add reduced sauce and remaining vanilla to the peaches; stir gently to combine. Serve with pound cake and whipped cream.

Sparkling Pom-Berry Splash

Want to add a splash of color to cocktail hour? This bright red drink featuring just three ingredients—two fruit juices and wine—is as attractive as it is refreshing. Pour 2 ounces chilled pomegranate blueberry juice and 1 teaspoon lime juice into a champagne flute; top with ⅓ cup chilled sparkling moscato wine. If desired, garnish with fresh blueberries and lime slices threaded onto a party pick or mini skewer. *Makes 1 serving.*

—**SHIRLEY WARREN** THIENSVILLE, WI

GARLIC-HERB
MINI QUICHES

2 liters ginger ale, chilled
1 liter cherry lemon-lime soda, chilled
   Ice ring, optional

In a large punch bowl, combine the cold water and lemonade concentrate. Stir in ginger ale and lemon-lime soda. Top with an ice ring if desired. Serve immediately.

EAT SMART FAST FIX
Salmon with Balsamic Orange Sauce

Preparing this citrusy salmon is so easy, you'll want to enjoy it on busy weekdays, lazy weekends...all the time!
—*TASTE OF HOME* TEST KITCHEN

START TO FINISH: 30 MIN.
MAKES: 8 SERVINGS

8 salmon fillets (6 ounces each), skin removed
4 teaspoons grated orange peel
4 teaspoons balsamic vinegar
4 teaspoons honey
1 teaspoon salt
SAUCE
1 teaspoon cornstarch
1 cup orange juice
2 teaspoons honey
1 teaspoon balsamic vinegar
¼ teaspoon salt

1. Preheat oven to 425°. Place salmon fillets in a greased 15x10x1-in. baking pan. In a small bowl, mix the orange peel, vinegar, honey and salt; spread over fillets.
2. Roast 15-18 minutes or until fish just begins to flake easily with a fork. Meanwhile, in a small saucepan, mix cornstarch and orange juice. Bring to a boil; cook and stir 1 minute or until thickened. Stir in honey, vinegar and salt; serve with salmon.
PER SERVING *1 salmon fillet with 2 tablespoons sauce equals 299 cal., 16 g fat (3 g sat. fat), 85 mg chol., 455 mg sodium, 9 g carb., trace fiber, 29 g pro. Diabetic Exchanges: 4 lean meat, ½ starch.*

EAT SMART ⑤ INGREDIENTS FAST FIX
Garlic-Herb Mini Quiches

Looking for a wonderful little bite to dress up your brunch buffet? Phyllo tartlets with a cheesy filling are irresistible.
—**JOSEPHINE PIRO** EASTON, PA

START TO FINISH: 25 MIN.
MAKES: 45 MINI QUICHES

1 package (6½ ounces) reduced-fat garlic-herb spreadable cheese
¼ cup fat-free milk
2 large eggs
3 packages (1.9 ounces each) frozen miniature phyllo tart shells
2 tablespoons minced fresh parsley
   Minced chives, optional

1. In a small bowl, beat the spreadable cheese, milk and eggs. Place the mini phyllo tart shells on an ungreased baking sheet; fill each with 2 teaspoons mixture. Sprinkle with minced parsley.

2. Bake at 350° for 10-12 minutes or until the filling is set and the mini phyllo tart shells are lightly browned. Sprinkle with minced chives if desired. Serve warm.
PER SERVING *1 mini quiche equals 31 cal., 2 g fat (trace sat. fat), 12 mg chol., 32 mg sodium, 2 g carb., trace fiber, 1 g pro.*

⑤ INGREDIENTS FAST FIX
All-Occasion Punch

The tangy fruit flavor of this drink always brings guests back for another glassful. To keep the punch cold during the party, I add an ice ring made of cherry soda.
—**CAROL VAN SICKLE** VERSAILLES, KY

START TO FINISH: 15 MIN.
MAKES: 22 SERVINGS (1 CUP EACH)

8 cups cold water
1 can (12 ounces) frozen lemonade concentrate, thawed, plus ¾ cup thawed lemonade concentrate

30-MINUTE CHILI

1. Spoon the cherry pie filling down the center of each tortilla; fold sides and ends over the filling and roll up. Seal with toothpicks.

2. In an electric skillet or deep fryer, heat oil to 375°. Fry chimichangas, a few at a time, for 2 minutes on each side or until golden brown on both sides. Drain on paper towels. Dust with confectioners' sugar. Serve immediately.

(5)INGREDIENTS FAST FIX >
Sparkling White Grape Punch

To give this fruity refresher a light blush color, simply replace the white cranberry juice with the regular kind.

—JULIE STERCHI CAMPBELLSVILLE, KY

START TO FINISH: 10 MIN.
MAKES: 24 SERVINGS (¾ CUP)

- 1 bottle (64 ounces) white grape juice, chilled
- 1½ cups white cranberry juice, chilled
- 2 liters lemon-lime soda, chilled
  Seedless red or green grapes, optional

Just before serving, combine the juices in a 5-qt. punch bowl. Stir in the soda. Add grapes if desired.

SPARKLING WHITE GRAPE PUNCH

FAST FIX >
30-Minute Chili

After tasting the pot of chili I received from my neighbor, I just had to get the recipe. I think the pork sausage is the key.

—JANICE WESTMORELAND BROOKSVILLE, FL

START TO FINISH: 30 MIN.
MAKES: 12 SERVINGS (3 QUARTS)

- 1 pound bulk pork sausage
- 1 large onion, chopped
- 2 cans (16 ounces each) chili beans, undrained
- 1 can (28 ounces) crushed tomatoes
- 3 cups water
- 1 can (4 ounces) chopped green chilies
- 1 envelope chili seasoning mix
- 2 tablespoons sugar

In a Dutch oven, cook the sausage and onion over medium heat 6-8 minutes or until the sausage is no longer pink, breaking the sausage into crumbles; drain. Add the remaining ingredients; bring to a boil. Reduce heat; simmer, covered, 20 minutes, stirring often.

(5)INGREDIENTS FAST FIX >
Cherry Pie Chimis

Here in New Mexico, we love having these scrumptious deep-fried chimichangas for dessert after a spicy Southwestern meal. Because the chimis call for ordinary flour tortillas and convenient canned cherry pie filling, they're a breeze to assemble whenever we have a craving.

—TERRY ANN DOMINGUEZ SILVER CITY, NM

START TO FINISH: 25 MIN.
MAKES: 6 SERVINGS

- 2 cans (21 ounces each) cherry pie filling
- 6 flour tortillas (10 inches)
  Oil for deep-fat frying
  Confectioners' sugar

CROWD-PLEASING
TACO SALAD

FAST FIX ▶

Crowd-Pleasing Taco Salad

The name says it all—this beefy, cheesy Southwestern salad is always a winner with potluck guests. The bonus is that it goes together in just 30 minutes.

—ANN CAHOON BRADENTON, FL

START TO FINISH: 30 MIN.
MAKES: 10 SERVINGS

1 **pound ground beef**
½ **cup ketchup**
1 **teaspoon dried oregano**
1 **teaspoon chili powder**
½ **teaspoon salt**
¼ **teaspoon pepper**
1 **medium head iceberg lettuce, torn**
2 **medium tomatoes, diced**
1 **cup (4 ounces) shredded Mexican cheese blend**
1 **can (2¼ ounces) sliced ripe olives, drained**
½ **cup mayonnaise**
¼ **cup taco sauce**
1 **package (10½ ounces) corn chips**

1. In a large saucepan, cook beef over medium heat until no longer pink, breaking into crumbles; drain. Stir in the ketchup, oregano, chili powder, salt and pepper. Bring to a boil. Reduce heat; cover and simmer for 10 minutes.

2. In a large bowl, combine lettuce, tomatoes, cheese, olives and beef mixture. Combine the mayonnaise and taco sauce; pour over salad and toss to coat. Sprinkle with corn chips. Serve immediately.

Garlic-Rubbed T-Bones with Burgundy Mushrooms

Because T-bone steak is a fairly tender cut, marinating isn't necessary. Mushrooms and garlic are great ways to add flavor.

—**KEVIN BLACK** CEDAR RAPIDS, IA

START TO FINISH: 25 MIN.
MAKES: 4 SERVINGS

- 12 garlic cloves, minced or sliced
- 1 tablespoon olive oil
- 1 teaspoon salt
- 4 beef T-bone or porterhouse steaks (¾-inch thick and 12 ounces each)
- ½ cup butter, cubed
- 1 pound baby portobello mushrooms, thickly sliced
- ½ cup Burgundy wine or reduced-sodium beef broth

1. In a small bowl, combine the garlic, olive oil and salt; rub over both sides of steaks. Grill steaks, covered, over medium heat or broil 4 in. from the heat for 4-7 minutes on each side or until meat reaches desired doneness (for medium-rare, a thermometer should read 145°; medium, 160°; well-done, 170°).
2. Meanwhile, in a large skillet, melt the butter over medium-high heat. Add the mushrooms; cook and stir for 3-5 minutes or until almost tender. Stir in the wine; bring to a boil. Cook until liquid is reduced by half, stirring occasionally. Serve over steaks.

BANANAS FOSTER SUNDAES

GARLIC-RUBBED T-BONES WITH BURGUNDY MUSHROOMS

Bananas Foster Sundaes

I have wonderful memories of enjoying classic bananas Foster in New Orleans. As a dietitian, I wanted to create a lighter version, so I combined the best of two recipes and made a few tweaks.

—**LISA VARNER** EL PASO, TX

START TO FINISH: 15 MIN.
MAKES: 6 SERVINGS

- 1 tablespoon butter
- 3 tablespoons brown sugar
- 1 tablespoon orange juice
- ¼ teaspoon ground cinnamon
- ¼ teaspoon ground nutmeg
- 3 large firm bananas, sliced
- 2 tablespoons chopped pecans, toasted
- ½ teaspoon rum extract
- 3 cups reduced-fat vanilla ice cream

1. In a large nonstick skillet, melt the butter over medium-low heat. Stir in brown sugar, orange juice, cinnamon and nutmeg until blended.
2. Add the banana slices and pecans; cook, stirring gently, for 2-3 minutes or until the bananas are glazed and slightly softened. Remove from the heat; stir in rum extract. Serve with vanilla ice cream.
PER SERVING 1/3 cup banana mixture with 1/2 cup ice cream equals 233 cal., 7 g fat (3 g sat. fat), 23 mg chol., 66 mg sodium, 40 g carb., 2 g fiber, 4 g pro.

Andria Gaskins'
**Sausage Mac & Cheese
in a Pumpkin** PAGE 208

Holiday & Seasonal Pleasers

Whether you host a Halloween bash, Christmas dinner, Easter brunch or all of the above, this extra-big chapter has you covered! You'll find festive recipes guaranteed to delight family and friends.

Gina Quartermaine's Spring Strawberry Sangria *PAGE 202*

Jackie Wilson's Campfire Peach Cobbler *PAGE 204*

Florence Hasty's Double Chocolate Fudge *PAGE 222*

New Year's Eve Brunch at Midnight

The holiday **countdown has begun,** the stars have come out and the New Year's Eve party is still going strong. Make your guests' eyes light up by serving them **sparkling breakfast favorites** that are just as fabulous after dark as they are when the sun is rising.

FRENCH TOAST WAFFLES

Scrambled Egg Hash Brown Cups

These cute cups may resemble muffins, but they pack breakfast all-stars like eggs, hash browns, cheddar cheese and bacon. Just grab one and get munching!

—**TALON DIMARE** BULLHEAD CITY, AZ

PREP: 10 MIN. • **BAKE:** 25 MIN.
MAKES: 1 DOZEN

- 1 package (20 ounces) refrigerated Southwest-style shredded hash brown potatoes
- 6 large eggs
- ½ cup 2% milk
- ⅛ teaspoon salt
- 1 tablespoon butter
- 10 thick-sliced bacon strips, cooked and crumbled
- 1¼ cups (5 ounces) shredded cheddar Jack cheese, divided

1. Preheat oven to 400°. Divide the hash browns among 12 greased muffin cups; press onto bottoms and up sides to form cups. Bake 18-20 minutes or until light golden brown.
2. Meanwhile, in a small bowl, whisk eggs, milk and salt. In a large nonstick skillet, heat butter over medium heat. Pour in egg mixture; cook and stir until eggs are thickened and no liquid egg remains. Stir in the bacon and ¾ cup cheese. Spoon into cups; sprinkle with remaining ½ cup cheese.
3. Bake 3-5 minutes or until cheese is melted. Cool 5 minutes before removing from pan.

SCRAMBLED EGG HASH BROWN CUPS

FREEZE IT
French Toast Waffles

I prefer to cook from scratch but definitely appreciate shortcuts when time is tight. Using a waffle iron, I make a hybrid French toast that gives us the best of both worlds. It's fun to serve in strips on skewers.

—**LINDA MARTINDALE** ELKHORN, WI

PREP: 15 MIN. • **COOK:** 5 MIN./BATCH
MAKES: 16 WAFFLES

- 8 large eggs
- 2 cups 2% milk
- ½ cup sugar
- 1 teaspoon vanilla extract
- ½ teaspoon ground cinnamon
- ½ teaspoon ground nutmeg
- 16 slices Texas toast
  Maple syrup

In a large bowl, whisk the first six ingredients until blended. Dip both sides of the bread in the egg mixture. Place in a preheated waffle iron; bake 4-5 minutes or until golden brown. If desired, cut the waffles into thirds. Serve with syrup.
FREEZE OPTION *Cool the waffles on wire racks. Freeze between layers of waxed paper in resealable plastic freezer bags. Reheat frozen waffles in a toaster on medium setting.*

FAST FIX ▶
Croque Madame

My son and I prefer topping our grilled ham and cheese with a fried egg, but you can make this tasty sandwich without it. (That's called a croque monsieur!)

—CAROLYN TURNER RENO, NV

START TO FINISH: 30 MIN.
MAKES: 8 SERVINGS

- **1 pound thinly sliced Gruyere cheese, divided**
- **16 slices sourdough bread**
- **1½ pounds thinly sliced deli ham**
- **½ cup butter, softened**
- **4 to 6 tablespoons mayonnaise**

EGGS

- **2 tablespoons butter**
- **8 large eggs**
- **½ teaspoon salt**
- **½ teaspoon pepper**

1. Preheat oven to 400°. Place half of the Gruyere cheese on eight bread slices; top with the ham and remaining bread. Spread outsides of sandwiches with softened butter.

2. On a griddle, toast sandwiches over medium heat 2-3 minutes on each side or until golden brown. Spread tops with mayonnaise; top with the remaining Gruyere. Transfer to an ungreased baking sheet; bake 4-5 minutes or until cheese is melted.

3. Meanwhile, for the eggs, heat 1 tablespoon butter on griddle over medium-high heat. Break four eggs, one at a time, onto griddle. Reduce the heat to low. Cook until desired doneness, turning after whites are set if desired. Sprinkle with salt and pepper. Place eggs over sandwiches. Repeat with remaining ingredients.

Bubbly Champagne Punch

My sparkling golden punch takes only a few minutes to stir up before serving. Just freeze the fruity ice ring far enough in advance so that it's ready to go.

—ANITA GEOGHAGAN WOODSTOCK, GA

PREP: 10 MIN. + FREEZING
MAKES: 16 SERVINGS (¾ CUP)

- **3 orange slices, halved**
  Fresh or frozen cranberries
- **2½ cups unsweetened pineapple juice**
- **1½ cups ginger ale**
- **2 bottles (750 milliliters each) brut champagne, chilled**
- **1 bottle (375 milliliters) sweet white wine, chilled**
- **1 can (12 ounces) frozen lemonade concentrate, thawed**

1. Line the bottom of a 4½-cup ring mold with halved orange slices and cranberries. Combine the pineapple juice and ginger ale; pour over fruit. Freeze until solid.

2. Just before serving, unmold the ice ring into a punch bowl. Gently stir in the remaining ingredients.

CROQUE MADAME

Spring Fling

Aah, the **delights of springtime!** Celebrate warmer, brighter days with readers' best seasonal recipes. Whether you're hosting Easter brunch or a bridal shower, you'll find **sunny selections** that make the most of spring's bountiful produce and fresh flavors.

SMOKED SALMON DEVILED EGGS WITH DILL

Strawberry-Quinoa Spinach Salad

We eat quinoa with strawberries and spinach year-round, but I enjoy this salad most after going to the farmers market to get the season's first berries.

—SARAH JOHNSON INDIANAPOLIS, IN

START TO FINISH: 30 MIN.
MAKES: 4 SERVINGS

- 2 **cups water**
- 1 **cup quinoa, rinsed**
- 6 **cups torn fresh spinach (about 5 ounces)**
- 2 **cups sliced fresh strawberries**
- ½ **cup chopped walnuts, toasted**
- ½ **cup reduced-fat red wine vinaigrette**
- ¼ **cup shredded Dubliner or Parmesan cheese**
- ¼ **teaspoon freshly ground pepper**

1. In a small saucepan, bring the water to a boil. Add the quinoa. Reduce heat; simmer, covered, 12-15 minutes or until water is absorbed. Remove from heat; fluff with a fork. Cool slightly.

2. In a large bowl, combine spinach, strawberries, walnuts and quinoa. Drizzle with vinaigrette; toss to coat. Sprinkle with cheese and pepper.

NOTE *To toast nuts, bake in a shallow pan in a 350° oven for 5-10 minutes or cook in a skillet over low heat until lightly browned, stirring occasionally.*

PER SERVING *2 cups equals 355 cal., 18 g fat (3 g sat. fat), 4 mg chol., 444 mg sodium, 41 g carb., 7 g fiber, 12 g pro.*

Smoked Salmon Deviled Eggs with Dill

My family is of Danish heritage, and my husband makes our own smoked salmon. I like to mix the flaked fish into the filling of deviled eggs. A fresh dill sprig on top is a pretty finishing touch.

—CHARLOTTE GILTNER MESA, AZ

START TO FINISH: 25 MIN.
MAKES: 2 DOZEN

- 12 **hard-cooked large eggs**
- ½ **cup mayonnaise**
- ¼ **teaspoon salt**
- ¼ **teaspoon onion powder**
- ¼ **teaspoon pepper**
- ⅛ **teaspoon garlic powder**
- ¼ **cup flaked smoked salmon**
   Fresh dill sprigs

1. Cut eggs lengthwise in half. Remove yolks, reserving whites. In a small bowl, mash yolks. Stir in mayonnaise and seasonings; gently stir in salmon.

2. Spoon or pipe into the egg whites; top with the dill. Refrigerate, covered, until serving.

STRAWBERRY-QUINOA SPINACH SALAD

RHUBARB SCONES

Rhubarb Scones

With a tartness that's similar to that of a cranberry, rhubarb is perfect to add to golden brown sugar-sprinkled scones.
—**DANIELLE ULAM** HOOKSTOWN, PA

PREP: 30 MIN. • **BAKE:** 20 MIN.
MAKES: 16 SCONES

- 1¼ cups whole wheat pastry flour
- 1¼ cups all-purpose flour
- ½ cup sugar
- 1 tablespoon baking powder
- 1 teaspoon ground cardamom
- ½ teaspoon salt
- ½ cup unsalted butter, cubed
- 1½ cups finely chopped fresh or frozen rhubarb, thawed (3-4 stalks)
- ½ cup heavy whipping cream
- ¼ cup fat-free milk
- 1 teaspoon vanilla extract
  Coarse sugar

1. Preheat oven to 400°. In a large bowl, whisk the first six ingredients. Cut in the butter until the mixture resembles coarse crumbs. Add the rhubarb; toss to coat.
2. In another bowl, whisk the heavy whipping cream, milk and vanilla; stir into the crumb mixture just until moistened.
3. Turn dough onto a floured surface; knead gently 4-5 times. Divide dough in half; pat into two 6-in. circles. Cut each circle into eight wedges. Place wedges on parchment paper-lined baking sheets; sprinkle with coarse sugar. Bake 18-22 minutes or until golden brown. Serve warm.
NOTE *If using frozen rhubarb, measure rhubarb while still frozen, then thaw completely. Drain in a colander, but do not press liquid out.*

Crab Quiche with Hollandaise

At a diner, I sampled a quiche like this one. It was so amazing that I tried duplicating it at home, and we loved the results.
—**AMY KNIGHT** LAKE LINDEN, MI

PREP: 25 MIN. • **BAKE:** 35 MIN.
MAKES: 6 SERVINGS (⅔ CUP SAUCE)

  Pastry for single-crust pie (9 inches)
- 1 can (6 ounces) crabmeat, drained, flaked and cartilage removed
- 1 cup (4 ounces) shredded cheddar-Monterey Jack cheese
- ¾ cup frozen asparagus stir-fry vegetable blend, thawed
- ¼ cup finely chopped onion
- 3 large eggs
- 1 cup evaporated milk
- ½ teaspoon salt
- ¼ teaspoon pepper
- ¼ teaspoon seafood seasoning
- ⅛ teaspoon hot pepper sauce

SAUCE
- 3 large egg yolks
- 1 tablespoon water
- 1 tablespoon lemon juice
- ½ cup butter, melted
  Dash pepper

1. Roll out pastry to fit a 9-in. pie plate. Transfer pastry to plate. Trim pastry to ½ in. beyond the edge of the plate; flute edges. Line unpricked pastry with a double thickness of heavy-duty foil. Bake at 450° for 8 minutes. Remove the foil; bake 5 minutes longer. Place on a wire rack.
2. In a small bowl, combine the crab, cheese, vegetable blend and onion; transfer to crust. In another bowl, whisk the eggs, milk, salt, pepper, seafood seasoning and hot pepper sauce. Pour over crab mixture.
3. Bake at 375° for 35-40 minutes or until a knife inserted near center comes out clean. Cover edges with foil during the last 15 minutes to prevent overbrowning if necessary. Let stand for 5 minutes before cutting.
4. In a double boiler or metal bowl over simmering water, constantly whisk the egg yolks, water and lemon juice until the mixture reaches 160° or is thick enough to coat the back of a metal spoon. Reduce heat to low. Slowly drizzle in warm melted butter, whisking constantly. Whisk in pepper. Serve immediately with quiche.

CRAB QUICHE WITH HOLLANDAISE

HAM AND PEA
PASTA ALFREDO

⑤ INGREDIENTS
Spring Strawberry Sangria

Wine-infused strawberries make a lovely addition to this sparkling special-occasion beverage. I love serving it in springtime to celebrate the season.

—**GINA QUARTERMAINE** ALEXANDRIA, VA

PREP: 10 MIN. + CHILLING
MAKES: 10 SERVINGS (ABOUT 2 QUARTS)

- 4 **cups dry white wine, chilled**
- ½ **pound fresh strawberries, hulled and sliced**
- ¼ **cup sugar**
- 2 **cups club soda, chilled**
- 2 **cups champagne, chilled**

1. In a large pitcher, combine wine, strawberries and sugar. Refrigerate at least 1 hour.
2. Just before serving, stir in the club soda and champagne.

TOP TIP

Refrigerate unwashed strawberries as soon as possible; do not wash or hull until you are ready to use them. Use a strawberry huller or the tip of a serrated grapefruit spoon to easily remove the hull. Just insert the tip of the spoon into the berry next to the stem and cut around the stem.

FAST FIX ▶
Ham and Pea Pasta Alfredo

Even the kids enjoy ham and peas tossed with Romano cream sauce and pasta.

—**CR MONACHINO** KENMORE, NY

START TO FINISH: 25 MIN.
MAKES: 6 SERVINGS

- 1 **package (16 ounces) fettuccine**
- 2 **tablespoons butter**
- 1½ **pounds sliced fully cooked ham, cut into strips (about 5 cups)**
- 2 **cups fresh sugar snap peas**
- 2 **cups heavy whipping cream**
- ½ **cup grated Romano cheese**
- ¼ **teaspoon pepper**

1. Cook the fettuccine according to the package directions. Meanwhile, in a large skillet, heat the butter over medium heat. Add the ham and peas;

cook and stir 5 minutes. Stir in cream, cheese and pepper; bring to a boil. Reduce the heat; simmer, uncovered, 1-2 minutes or until sauce is slightly thickened and peas are crisp-tender.
2. Drain fettuccine; add to skillet and toss to coat. Serve immediately.

Umbrella Cupcakes

How cute—sweet umbrellas for a baby or wedding shower! Bake a dozen of your favorite cupcakes in cupcake liners. Frost and decorate as desired, then halve the cupcakes from top to bottom, leaving the liners on. Insert a trimmed bendable straw into the cut part of each cupcake, curving the bendable part to form the handle.
Makes 24 servings.

—**TIFFANY YANG** VANCOUVER, BC

Every year for his birthday, my friend Dave baked two Strawberry-Rhubarb Flip Cakes and brought them to work to share with co-workers. What a treat!

—**CHARLENE SCHWARTZ** MAPLE PLAIN, MN

STRAWBERRY-RHUBARB FLIP CAKE

CAMPFIRE PEACH COBBLER

PIZZA MOUNTAIN PIES

PREP: 25 MIN. • **COOK:** 30 MIN. + STANDING
MAKES: 8 SERVINGS

- 2 **cups all-purpose flour**
- 1 **cup sugar**
- 4 **teaspoons baking powder**
- ½ **teaspoon salt**
- 1 **cup 2% milk**
- ½ **cup butter, melted**

FILLING

- 2 **cans (15¼ ounces each) sliced peaches**
- ¼ **cup sugar**
- ½ **teaspoon ground cinnamon, optional**

1. Prepare campfire or grill for low heat, using 32-40 charcoal briquettes or large wood chips.

2. Line a 10-in. Dutch oven with heavy-duty foil. In a large bowl, combine flour, sugar, baking powder and salt. Stir in the milk and butter just until moistened. Transfer to prepared Dutch oven.

3. Drain the peaches, reserving 1 cup syrup. Spoon peaches over the batter; sprinkle with sugar and, if desired, cinnamon. Pour the reserved syrup over the fruit.

4. Cover the Dutch oven. When the briquettes or wood chips are covered with white ash, place the Dutch oven directly on top of 16-20 briquettes. Using long-handled tongs, place 16-20 briquettes on pan cover.

5. Cook 30-40 minutes or until set and the filling is bubbly. To check for doneness, use tongs to carefully lift cover. If necessary, cook 5 minutes longer. Let stand, uncovered, 15 minutes before serving.

5 INGREDIENTS FAST FIX

Pizza Mountain Pies

These yummy pudgy pies are so popular, I started making similar sandwiches for my daughter on our stove at home.
—**PAM WEIK** WEST LAWN, PA

START TO FINISH: 15 MIN.
MAKES: 1 SERVING

- 1 **tablespoon butter, softened**
- 2 **slices white bread**
- 1 **tablespoon pizza sauce**
- 4 **tablespoons shredded part-skim mozzarella cheese, divided**
- 4 **slices pepperoni**
- 1 **tablespoon chopped green pepper, optional**

1. Spread butter over bread slices; place one slice of bread in a greased sandwich iron, buttered side down. Spread with pizza sauce; layer with 2 tablespoons mozzarella cheese, pepperoni and, if desired, green

Breakfast rolls get a toasty treatment when you wrap Campfire Cinnamon Twists around skewers and warm them over the flames. Drizzled icing is the crowning touch!
—**LAUREN KNOELKE** MILWAUKEE, WI

SCRAMBLED EGG BREAD

CAMPFIRE CINNAMON TWISTS

Scrambled Egg Bread

We always eat ham, eggs and bread on camping trips, and we often have extras. Combine the leftovers, and you have this delicious morning meal. We came up with it while visiting Mount Shasta.
—**SHIRLEY MONDEAU** ROHNERT PARK, CA

PREP: 25 MIN. • **COOK:** 10 MIN.
MAKES: 4 SERVINGS

- 1 loaf (1 pound) unsliced French bread
- 2 tablespoons butter, softened, divided

FILLING
- 2 tablespoons butter, divided
- 1 small onion, chopped
- 1 cup cubed fully cooked ham
- 1 large tomato, chopped
- 6 large eggs
- ⅛ teaspoon pepper
- 1½ cups (6 ounces) shredded cheddar cheese, divided

1. Prepare campfire or grill for medium heat. Cut bread crosswise in half; cut each piece lengthwise in half. Hollow out two pieces, leaving ½-in. shells. Cut the removed bread into cubes; reserve 1½ cups (save remaining cubes for another use). Spread 1 tablespoon softened butter over bread shells. Spread remaining softened butter over remaining bread halves. Set aside.

2. In a small Dutch oven, heat 1 tablespoon butter over campfire. Add onion; cook and stir 3-4 minutes or until tender. Stir in the ham and tomato; remove from pan.

3. In a small bowl, whisk eggs and pepper. In same pan, heat remaining butter. Pour in the egg mixture; cook and stir until eggs are thickened and no liquid egg remains. Stir in the ham mixture, 1 cup cheese and reserved bread cubes. Spoon filling into bread shells; sprinkle with remaining cheese. Transfer to a 13x9-in. disposable foil pan; cover with foil.

4. Place the pan over the campfire. Cook 8-10 minutes or until heated through and the cheese is melted. Cook the reserved bread halves, buttered side down, 1-2 minutes or until toasted. Cut each piece of egg bread and toast in half.

⑤ INGREDIENTS FAST FIX
Campfire Cinnamon Twists

START TO FINISH: 25 MIN.
MAKES: 8 SERVINGS

- 2 tablespoons butter, melted
- ¼ cup sugar
- 2 teaspoons ground cinnamon
- 1 tube (12.4 ounces) refrigerated cinnamon rolls with icing

1. Place the butter in a shallow bowl. In another shallow bowl, mix sugar and cinnamon. Set aside the icing from the cinnamon rolls.

2. Separate the cinnamon rolls; cut each in half. Roll each half into a 6-in. rope. Tightly wrap one rope around a long metal skewer, starting ½ in. from the end; pinch the ends to seal. Repeat with the remaining cinnamon rolls.

3. Cook wrapped rolls over a hot campfire 4-6 minutes or until golden brown, turning occasionally. Brush with the butter; sprinkle with the cinnamon sugar.

4. Transfer the reserved icing to a resealable plastic bag; cut a small hole in a corner of the bag. Drizzle the icing over the rolls.

FAST FIX ▶
Pot of S'mores

Skip the sticks! My mom took ever-popular s'mores and put them into a Dutch oven. The hardest part is waiting for the gooey, chocolaty treats to cool so you can grab them and devour. Yum!

—JUNE DRESS MERIDIAN, ID

START TO FINISH: 25 MIN.
MAKES: 12 SERVINGS

- 1 package (14½ ounces) whole graham crackers, crushed
- ½ cup butter, melted
- 1 can (14 ounces) sweetened condensed milk
- 2 cups (12 ounces) semisweet chocolate chips
- 1 cup butterscotch chips
- 2 cups miniature marshmallows

1. Prepare grill or campfire for low heat, using 16-18 charcoal briquettes or large wood chips.

2. Line a Dutch oven with heavy-duty aluminum foil. Combine the graham cracker crumbs and butter; press onto the bottom of the pan. Pour sweetened condensed milk over the crust and sprinkle with the semisweet chocolate and butterscotch chips. Top with the miniature marshmallows.

3. Cover the Dutch oven. When the briquettes or wood chips are covered with white ash, place the Dutch oven directly on top of six of them. Using long-handled tongs, place remaining briquettes on pan cover.

4. Cook for 15 minutes or until chips are melted. To check for doneness, use the tongs to carefully lift the cover.

FREEZE IT
Old-Fashioned Coney Hot Dog Sauce

Get the whole family roasting hot dogs over the fire, then dish out this irresistible one-pot sauce and dig in.

—LORIANN CARGILL BUSTOS PHOENIX, AZ

PREP: 10 MIN. • **COOK:** 30 MIN.
MAKES: 2 CUPS

- 1 pound lean ground beef (90% lean)
- 1 cup beef stock
- 2 tablespoons tomato paste
- 1 tablespoon chili powder
- 1 tablespoon Worcestershire sauce
- ½ teaspoon salt
- ½ teaspoon onion powder
- ½ teaspoon garlic powder
- ½ teaspoon celery salt
- ½ teaspoon ground cumin
- ¼ teaspoon pepper

1. Prepare campfire or grill for medium-high heat. In a Dutch oven, cook beef over campfire 8-10 minutes or until no longer pink, breaking into crumbles. Stir in the remaining ingredients; bring to a boil.

2. Move Dutch oven to indirect heat. Cook, uncovered, 20-25 minutes or until thickened, stirring occasionally.

FREEZE OPTION *Freeze the cooled meat mixture in freezer containers. To use, partially thaw in refrigerator overnight. Heat through in a saucepan, stirring occasionally and adding a little water if necessary.*

⑤ INGREDIENTS
Dutch Oven Cheesy Bacon & Eggs

For campouts, my sister and I head into the woods on horseback. We make bacon and eggs the first morning, then enjoy the leftovers for the rest of the trip.

—MARY BURRIS OKEECHOBEE, FL

PREP: 40 MIN. • **COOK:** 25 MIN.
MAKES: 8 SERVINGS

- 1 pound bacon strips, chopped
- 1 package (20 ounces) refrigerated O'Brien hash brown potatoes
- 8 large eggs
- ½ cup half-and-half cream
- ½ to 1 teaspoon hot pepper sauce, optional
- 2 cups (8 ounces) shredded cheddar-Monterey Jack cheese

1. Prepare campfire or grill for medium-high heat, using 32-36 charcoal briquettes or large wood chips.

2. In a 10-in. Dutch oven, cook the chopped bacon over the campfire until crisp, stirring occasionally. Remove with a slotted spoon; drain on paper towels. Discard the bacon drippings, reserving 2 tablespoons in pan.

3. Carefully press potatoes onto the bottom and 1 in. up the sides of Dutch oven. In a small bowl, whisk the eggs, cream and, if desired, pepper sauce until blended. Pour over potatoes; sprinkle with bacon and cheese.

4. Cover the Dutch oven. When the briquettes or wood chips are covered with white ash, place the Dutch oven directly on top of 16-18 briquettes. Using long-handled tongs, place 16-18 briquettes on pan cover.

5. Cook 20-25 minutes or until the eggs are completely set and cheese is melted. To check for doneness, use tongs to carefully lift the cover. If necessary, cook 5 minutes longer.

⑤ INGREDIENTS
Cheese-Topped Potatoes in Foil

Similar to traditional scalloped potatoes, these cheesy packets are a must when we go camping. In winter when the cold keeps us home, I bake them in the oven.

—DENISE WHEELER NEWAYGO, MI

PREP: 15 MIN. • **COOK:** 30 MIN.
MAKES: 8 SERVINGS

- 2½ pounds potatoes (about 3 large), peeled and cut into ¼-inch slices
- 1 medium onion, finely chopped
- 5 bacon strips, cooked and crumbled
- ¼ cup butter, melted
- ½ teaspoon salt
- ¼ teaspoon pepper
- 6 slices process American cheese Sour cream, optional

1. Prepare campfire or grill for medium heat. In a large bowl, combine the first six ingredients. Place mixture on a piece of greased heavy-duty foil (about 36x12-in. rectangle). Fold the foil around mixture and crimp edges to seal tightly.

2. Cook, covered, 14-16 minutes on each side or until potatoes are tender. Open the foil carefully to allow steam to escape. Place the cheese over the potatoes; cook 2-4 minutes longer or until cheese is melted. If desired, serve with sour cream.

DUTCH OVEN CHEESY
BACON & EGGS

CHEESE-TOPPED
POTATOES IN FOIL

Pumpkin Time, Party Time!

From a **harvest party to a Halloween bash,** your fall events will be as tasty as can be with these autumn-inspired recipes. Treat guests of all ages to **seasonal specialties** like a dark and spooky cake, caramel apples, a pasta-stuffed pumpkin and more!

SAUSAGE MAC & CHEESE
IN A PUMPKIN

Sausage & Cheese in a Pumpkin

Whenever my family and friends eat this dressed-up mac, I hear raves. Spooning it into a pumpkin adds fall appeal.
—**ANDRIA GASKINS** MATTHEWS, NC

PREP: 1 HOUR 25 MIN. • **COOK:** 20 MIN.
MAKES: 8 SERVINGS

- 1 large pie pumpkin (5 to 6 pounds)
- 1 teaspoon salt
- ½ teaspoon pepper
- 8 ounces uncooked cavatappi or fusilli pasta (about 3 cups)
- ½ pound bulk mild or hot Italian sausage
- 1 small onion, chopped
- 3 tablespoons butter
- 3 tablespoons all-purpose flour
- 1½ cups half-and-half cream
- ½ cup chicken stock
- 6 slices process American cheese (about 4 ounces), quartered
- ¾ cup shredded Manchego cheese
- ¾ cup shredded Monterey Jack cheese
- 3 tablespoons grated Parmesan cheese
- 2 cups fresh spinach, coarsely chopped
- ⅓ cup chopped roasted sweet red pepper

1. Preheat oven to 350°. Wash the pumpkin. Cut a 5-in. circle around the stem; remove the top of pumpkin and set aside. Remove strings and seeds from pumpkin; discard seeds or save for roasting.

2. Sprinkle the inside of the pumpkin with salt and pepper; replace top. Place on a wire rack in a 15x10x1-in. baking pan. Bake 1-1¼ hours or until tender. Remove the top; let pumpkin stand on wire rack until ready to serve.

3. In a large saucepan, cook the pasta according to the package directions. Meanwhile, in a large skillet, cook the sausage and onion over medium heat 4-6 minutes or until the sausage is no longer pink, breaking up sausage into crumbles; drain.

4. Drain pasta, reserving ⅓ cup pasta water. In same saucepan, melt butter over medium heat. Stir in the flour until smooth; gradually whisk in the half-and-half cream and stock. Bring to a boil, stirring constantly; cook and stir 2-3 minutes or until thickened. Stir in cheeses until blended.

5. Add spinach, roasted pepper, pasta and sausage mixture; toss to combine, adding reserved pasta water to moisten if desired. Spoon into the pumpkin; serve immediately.

Acorn Treats

Have fun branching out! In a microwave, melt ½ cup chocolate chips; stir until smooth. Spread the flat side of each of 48 milk chocolate kisses with a small amount of melted chocolate; immediately attach each to one of 48 Nutter Butter Bites cookies. Cut a small hole in the corner of a pastry or plastic bag; insert a small round tip. Fill with remaining melted chocolate. Pipe a stem onto each acorn. Place on waxed paper-lined baking sheets; refrigerate until set. Store in an airtight container. *Makes 48 treats.*
—**JANE STASIK** GREENDALE, WI

Pumpkin Delight Magic Bars

My mom never wrote down her recipes, so I created this one as a tribute to her.
—**LISA GLASSMAN** BOYNTON BEACH, FL

PREP: 20 MIN. • **BAKE:** 45 MIN. + COOLING
MAKES: 2 DOZEN

- 1 package (11 ounces) vanilla wafers
- ½ cup butter, melted
- 3 ounces cream cheese, softened
- 1 can (14 ounces) sweetened condensed milk
- ½ teaspoon pumpkin pie spice
- 1 can (15 ounces) solid-pack pumpkin
- 1½ cups flaked coconut
- 1 cup white baking chips
- 1 cup dried cranberries
- 1 cup chopped pecans

1. Preheat oven to 350°. Place vanilla wafers in a food processor; pulse until coarse crumbs form. Drizzle with the melted butter; pulse until blended. Press into the bottom of a greased 13x9-in. baking pan.

2. In a large bowl, beat the cream cheese, sweetened condensed milk and pumpkin pie spice until smooth; beat in the canned pumpkin. Pour over the prepared vanilla wafer crust. Layer with the flaked coconut, white baking chips, dried cranberries and chopped pecans.

3. Bake 45-55 minutes or until golden brown. Cool in the pan on a wire rack 10 minutes.

4. Loosen the sides from the pan with a knife; cool completely. Cut into bars. Refrigerate leftovers.

PUMPKIN DELIGHT MAGIC BARS

NUTS AND SEEDS TRAIL MIX

FAST FIX
Nuts and Seeds Trail Mix

Need an excuse to show off your favorite autumn snack bowl? Fill it to the brim with a festive, fall-flavored trail mix.
—**KRISTIN RIMKUS** SNOHOMISH, WA

START TO FINISH: 5 MIN.
MAKES: 5 CUPS

- 1 cup salted pumpkin seeds or pepitas
- 1 cup unblanched almonds
- 1 cup unsalted sunflower kernels
- 1 cup walnut halves
- 1 cup dried apricots
- 1 cup dark chocolate chips

Place all ingredients in a large bowl; toss to combine. Store in an airtight container.

TOP TIP

It's easy to toast the seeds from your freshly cut pumpkin. Wash and dry the seeds. In a skillet, saute 1 cup seeds in 2 tablespoons vegetable oil for 5 minutes or until lightly browned. Using a slotted spoon, transfer seeds to an ungreased 15x10x1-in. baking pan. Sprinkle with salt or garlic salt; stir to coat. Spread in a single layer. Bake at 325° for 15-20 minutes or until crisp. Remove to paper towels to cool completely. Store in an airtight container for up to 3 weeks.

SO-EASY-IT'S-SPOOKY
BAT CAKE

SPICED CHOCOLATE
TRUFFLES

FREEZE IT
So-Easy-It's-Spooky Bat Cake

Surprise—this spooky but gorgeous fall dessert starts with a boxed devil's food cake mix. To really make it fly high, form a bat shape by laying on a simple stencil and sprinkling on cocoa. If you prefer, use confectioners' sugar instead.

—**CRYSTAL SCHLUETER** NORTHGLENN, CO

PREP: 25 MIN. + CHILLING
BAKE: 25 MIN. + COOLING
MAKES: 16 SERVINGS

- 1 **devil's food cake mix (regular size)**
FROSTING
- 1 **cup butter, softened**
- ⅔ **cup baking cocoa, sifted**
- 2 **teaspoons vanilla extract**
- 4 **cups confectioners' sugar**
- 6 **to 7 tablespoons 2% milk**
- 10 **peanut butter cups, finely chopped Dutch-processed cocoa or confectioners' sugar**

1. Prepare and bake the cake mix according to the package directions, using two 9-in. round baking pans. Cool as package directs.
2. For bat stencil, cut a bat shape from card stock. Wrap with foil.
3. For the frosting, in a large bowl, beat butter, baking cocoa and vanilla until blended. Gradually beat in the confectioners' sugar and enough milk to reach desired consistency.
4. Using a long serrated knife, trim the tops of the cakes if domed. Place one cake layer on a serving plate. Spread with 1 cup frosting; sprinkle with the chopped peanut butter cups. Top with the remaining cake layer, bottom side up. Frost the top and sides with the remaining frosting. Refrigerate until set, about 30 minutes.
5. Lay the stencil on top of the cake. Using a fine-mesh strainer, sift the Dutch-processed cocoa over frosting. Lift stencil carefully to remove.
FREEZE OPTION *Wrap the cooled cake layers in plastic wrap, then cover securely in foil; freeze. To use, thaw the cakes before unwrapping. Assemble as directed.*

Spiced Chocolate Truffles

I love whipping up chocolate truffles for family gatherings and gift giving. Someone once requested a pumpkin spice version, and now it's my signature recipe.
—GERRY COFTA MILWAUKEE, WI

PREP: 45 MIN. + CHILLING • **COOK:** 5 MIN.
MAKES: ABOUT 2 DOZEN

- 12 **ounces milk chocolate baking bars, divided**
- ½ **cup heavy whipping cream**
- 2 **tablespoons canned pumpkin**
- ¼ **teaspoon ground cinnamon**
- ¼ **teaspoon ground ginger**
- ¼ **teaspoon ground nutmeg**
  Dash ground cloves
  Baking cocoa
  Candy eyeballs, optional

1. Finely chop 10 ounces chocolate baking bars; place in a small bowl. In a small heavy saucepan, combine the heavy whipping cream, pumpkin, cinnamon, ginger, nutmeg and cloves; heat just to a boil. Pour over chocolate; let stand 5 minutes.
2. Stir with a whisk until smooth. Cool to room temperature. Refrigerate, covered, at least 4 hours.
3. Finely grate remaining chocolate; place in a small microwave-safe bowl. With hands dusted lightly with baking cocoa, shape chocolate mixture into 1-in. balls; roll in the grated chocolate. (Mixture will be soft and truffles may flatten slightly upon standing.)
4. If desired, melt unused grated chocolate in a microwave and use to attach eyeballs. Store in an airtight container in the refrigerator.
NOTE *This recipe was tested with Ghirardelli Milk Chocolate Baking Bars; results may vary when using a different product.*

DID YOU KNOW?

Halloween is the third biggest party day of the year in the U.S., behind New Year's Eve and Super Bowl Sunday. That spooky October day is also the second biggest commercial holiday—after Christmas!

ULTIMATE OREO CARAMEL APPLES

Ultimate Oreo Caramel Apples

My kids like to hand out the goodies to our neighborhood trick-or-treaters. These cookie-caramel apples were door prizes for a few lucky ghosts and goblins.
—JENNIFER GILBERT BRIGHTON, MI

PREP: 20 MIN. + CHILLING • **COOK:** 5 MIN.
MAKES: 12 SERVINGS

- 6 **wooden pop sticks**
- 6 **small Gala apples**
- 1 **package (14 ounces) caramels**
- 2 **tablespoons 2% milk**
- 20 **Oreo cookies, coarsely crushed**
- 1 **package (10 ounces) dark chocolate chips**
- 2 **tablespoons shortening**

1. Insert the wooden pop sticks into the tops of the apples. Place the caramels and milk in a small saucepan; heat and stir over medium-low heat 3-5 minutes or until smooth, stirring frequently. Dip the apples in caramel mixture, coating completely. Place on a waxed paper-lined baking sheet; let stand until set, about 10 minutes.
2. Place the crushed cookies in a shallow bowl. In top of a double boiler or a metal bowl over hot water, melt the chocolate chips and shortening; stir until smooth. Dip the apples in chocolate mixture, allowing excess to drip off; dip in the cookies, rolling to coat. Return to the baking sheet; refrigerate until set, about 15 minutes. Cut into wedges to serve.

Dark Chocolate Pudding

For a Halloween party, spoon the pudding into clear plastic cups and top each serving with a ghost Peep and candy pumpkin.
—LILY JULOW LAWRENCEVILLE, GA

PREP: 5 MIN. • **COOK:** 20 MIN. + CHILLING
MAKES: 6 SERVINGS

- ¼ **cup sugar**
- 3 **tablespoons cornstarch**
- ¼ **teaspoon salt**
- 2 **cups whole milk**
- 3 **large egg yolks**
- 1 **dark chocolate candy bar (6.8 ounces), melted**
- ½ **teaspoon vanilla extract**
  Ghost Peeps candy and candy pumpkins, optional

1. In a large saucepan, mix sugar, cornstarch and salt. Whisk in milk until smooth. Cook and stir over medium heat until thickened and bubbly. Reduce the heat to low; cook and stir 2 minutes longer. Remove from the heat.
2. In a small bowl, whisk a small amount of the hot mixture into egg yolks; return all to the pan, whisking constantly. Bring to a gentle boil; cook and stir 2 minutes. Remove from heat. Gradually stir in melted chocolate and vanilla until blended. Cool 15 minutes, stirring occasionally.
3. Transfer to a bowl; press the plastic wrap onto the surface of the pudding. Refrigerate until cold. If desired, top servings with candies.

Giving Thanks

Fill that Thanksgiving table with a juicy glazed bird and special sides worthy of Turkey Day. It's easier than you might think—simply rely on the family-favorite **holiday dishes** here. Make sure to save room for bubbly, golden Cherry Pear Pie for dessert!

HOT HOLIDAY CIDER

Hot Holiday Cider

SLOW COOKER

This slightly tart slow-cooked beverage is ideal for a holiday open house. The cider fills entire rooms with a spicy apple scent.
—**CINDY TOBIN** WEST BEND, WI

PREP: 10 MIN. • **COOK:** 3 HOURS
MAKES: 16 SERVINGS (ABOUT ¾ CUP EACH)

- 8 **cups apple cider or juice**
- 4 **cups cranberry juice**
- 2 **cups orange juice**
- ½ **cup sugar**
- 3 **cinnamon sticks (3 inches)**
- 1 **teaspoon whole allspice**
- 1 **teaspoon whole cloves**

1. In a 5- or 6-qt. slow cooker, combine the apple cider, cranberry juice, orange juice and sugar. Place cinnamon sticks, allspice and cloves on a double thickness of cheesecloth. Gather corners of the cloth to enclose spices; tie securely with string. Add to slow cooker.
2. Cook, covered, on low 3-4 hours or until heated through. Discard the spice bag. Serve warm.

No-Knead Casserole Bread

FREEZE IT

Here's a bread time-crunched cooks love. The cheesy loaf doesn't require kneading. And because it calls for rapid-rise yeast, you don't have to wait long to enjoy it!
—**PEGGY KEY** GRANT, AL

PREP: 15 MIN. + RISING • **BAKE:** 40 MIN.
MAKES: 1 LOAF (16 SLICES)

- 2 **tablespoons sugar**
- 2 **packages (¼ ounce each) quick-rise yeast**
- 1½ **teaspoons salt**
- ½ **teaspoon pepper**
- 5½ **cups all-purpose flour**
- 2 **cups water**
- 2 **tablespoons butter, cubed**
- ¾ **cup plus 2 tablespoons shredded cheddar cheese, divided**
- ¼ **cup finely chopped onion**

1. In a large bowl, mix sugar, yeast, salt, pepper and 2½ cups flour. In a small saucepan, heat water and butter to 120°-130°; stir into dry ingredients. Stir in ¾ cup cheddar cheese, onion and remaining flour, forming a soft dough. Cover with plastic wrap; let rest 10 minutes.
2. Shape dough into a ball; place in a greased 2-qt. round baking dish. Cover with a kitchen towel; let rise in a warm place until doubled, about 20 minutes. Preheat oven to 350°.
3. Bake 40-45 minutes or until golden brown. Sprinkle with the remaining cheese. Bake 5 minutes longer or until cheese is melted. Cool in baking dish 5 minutes before removing to a wire rack to cool.
FREEZE OPTION *Securely wrap and freeze cooled loaf in heavy-duty foil. To use, thaw at room temperature.*

TOP TIP

A cheesecloth spice bag makes it easy to remove and discard whole spices and/or herbs from your food or beverage before serving. A cloth tea sachet (available in tea shops) may be used in place of cheesecloth.

NO-KNEAD
CASSEROLE BREAD

APPLE CRANBERRY
CASHEW SALAD

3. Add 1½ cups broth to bottom of roasting pan. Roast turkey, uncovered, 30 minutes. Cover loosely with foil; roast 1½ hours longer.

4. Remove the turkey from oven. Warm the reserved butter mixture until the butter is melted; brush over the turkey. Continue roasting turkey, loosely covered, 1-1¾ hours or until a thermometer inserted in thickest part of thigh reads 170°-175°.

5. Remove turkey to a serving platter. Let stand 20 minutes before carving.

6. For the gravy, pour drippings and loosened browned bits from bottom of roasting pan into a large measuring cup. Skim the fat, reserving ¼ cup. Add enough broth to the drippings to measure 3 cups.

7. In a saucepan, mix reserved fat and flour until smooth; gradually whisk in broth mixture. Bring to a boil, stirring constantly; cook and stir 1-2 minutes or until thickened. Season with salt and pepper to taste. Serve with turkey.

FAST FIX

Apple Cranberry Cashew Salad

Dress up greens with crunchy nuts, fruit, Parmesan and a homemade vinaigrette.
—**SUSAN JONES** APPLETON, WI

START TO FINISH: 15 MIN.
MAKES: 16 SERVINGS (1 CUP EACH)

- 2 **packages (5 ounces each) spring mix salad greens**
- 2 **large apples, coarsely chopped**
- 1 **can (9¼ ounces) lightly salted cashews**
- 1 **package (5 ounces) dried cranberries**
- ½ **cup shredded Parmesan cheese**

VINAIGRETTE

- ⅔ **cup sugar**
- ½ **cup canola oil**
- ⅓ **cup cider vinegar**
- 1 **teaspoon ground mustard**
- 1 **teaspoon poppy seeds**
- 1 **teaspoon salt**

In a large bowl, combine the first five ingredients. In a small bowl, whisk vinaigrette ingredients until blended. Pour over the salad and toss to coat; serve immediately.

Nanny's Parmesan Mashed Potatoes get raves from my grandsons. That's all the endorsement I need! Sometimes I substitute red spuds with the skins on.
—**KALLEE KRONG-MCCREERY**
ESCONDIDO, CA

Nanny's Parmesan Mashed Potatoes

PREP: 20 MIN. • **COOK:** 20 MIN.
MAKES: 12 SERVINGS (¾ CUP EACH)

- 5 **pounds potatoes, peeled and cut into 1-inch pieces**
- ¾ **cup butter, softened**
- ¾ **cup sour cream**
- ½ **cup grated Parmesan cheese**
- 1¼ **teaspoons garlic salt**
- 1 **teaspoon salt**
- ½ **teaspoon pepper**
- ¾ **to 1 cup 2% milk, warmed**
- 2 **tablespoons minced fresh parsley**

1. Place potatoes in a 6-qt. stockpot; add water to cover. Bring to a boil. Reduce the heat; cook, uncovered, 10-15 minutes or until tender. Drain potatoes; return to pot and stir over low heat 1 minute to dry.

2. Coarsely mash potatoes, gradually adding the butter, sour cream, cheese, seasonings and enough milk to reach desired consistency. Stir in parsley.

TOP TIP

When I have extras left over from a big batch of homemade mashed potatoes, I freeze individual servings in muffin cups. Once they're frozen, I pop out each portion and store the spuds in resealable plastic freezer bags. During the week, I pull out as many servings as I need and heat them in the microwave.
—**GRETCHEN B.** SURPRISE, AZ

NANNY'S PARMESAN
MASHED POTATOES

SLOW COOKER
BACON-MUSHROOM
DRESSING

3. Cut or break gingerbread cake into ¾-in. pieces. In ten 12-oz. glasses or a 3-qt. trifle bowl, layer half of each of the following: cake, pumpkin mixture and whipped topping. Repeat layers. Refrigerate, covered, 4 hours or overnight. Top as desired.

Cherry Pear Pie

Dried sweet-tart cherries and mellow fresh pears go so well together in this prize-worthy pie topped with an almond streusel. I serve each slice with a scoop of cherry-vanilla frozen yogurt.
—TRISHA KRUSE EAGLE, ID

PREP: 30 MIN. • **BAKE:** 50 MIN. + COOLING
MAKES: 8 SERVINGS

Pastry for single-crust pie (9 inches)
FILLING
6 **cups sliced peeled fresh pears (about 5 large)**
½ **cup dried cherries**
4 **teaspoons lemon juice**
½ **teaspoon almond extract**
¾ **cup sugar**
¼ **cup cornstarch**

TOPPING
¾ **cup all-purpose flour**
⅓ **cup sugar**
⅓ **cup cold butter**
½ **cup sliced almonds**

1. Preheat oven to 375°. On a lightly floured surface, roll the pie pastry dough to a ⅛-in.-thick circle; transfer to a 9-in. pie plate. Trim the pie pastry dough to ½ in. beyond the rim of the plate; flute the edge. Refrigerate while preparing the filling.
2. In a large bowl, toss the pears and dried cherries with the lemon juice and extract. In a small bowl, mix the sugar and cornstarch; add to the pear mixture, tossing to coat. Transfer to the pastry-lined pie plate.
3. For the topping, in a small bowl, mix the flour and sugar; cut in butter until crumbly. Stir in the almonds. Sprinkle over filling.
4. Bake 50-60 minutes or until golden brown and the filling is bubbly. Cover the edge loosely with foil during the last 15 minutes if needed to prevent overbrowning. Cool on a wire rack.

CHERRY PEAR PIE

Make-Ahead Christmas Dinner

What a great gift—**easy recipes full of comfort and joy!** Assemble these updated classics on the night before Christmas or even sooner. Then enjoy **faster meal prep later,** giving you more time outside the kitchen to spend with family and friends.

PORK ROAST
WITH HERB RUB

EAT SMART

Pork Roast with Herb Rub

Marinating pork loin with herbs such as marjoram and sage gives it a mild, minty, out-of-this-world flavor. Everyone flocks to the table for a slice of this tender roast.
—**CAROLYN POPE** MASON CITY, IA

PREP: 5 MIN. + CHILLING
BAKE: 1¼ HOURS + STANDING
MAKES: 12 SERVINGS

- 2 **tablespoons sugar**
- 2 **teaspoons dried marjoram**
- 2 **teaspoons rubbed sage**
- 1 **teaspoon salt**
- ½ **teaspoon celery seed**
- ½ **teaspoon ground mustard**
- ⅛ **teaspoon pepper**
- 1 **boneless pork loin roast (4 pounds)**

1. Mix the first seven ingredients; rub over roast. Refrigerate at least 4 hours.
2. Preheat oven to 350°. Place roast on a rack in a shallow roasting pan, fat side up. Roast 1¼-1¾ hours or until a thermometer reads 145°.
3. Remove the roast from the oven; tent with foil. Let stand 15 minutes before slicing.
PER SERVING *4 ounces cooked pork equals 198 cal., 7 g fat (3 g sat. fat), 75 mg chol., 240 mg sodium, 2 g carb., trace fiber, 29 g pro.* **Diabetic Exchange:** *4 lean meat.*

SPINACH
PECAN S

MAKE-AHEAD
SPINACH MANICOTTI

2. Fill uncooked shells with ricotta cheese mixture; arrange over sauce. Pour the remaining sauce mixture over the top. Sprinkle with remaining mozzarella cheese and Parmesan cheese. Refrigerate, covered, overnight.

3. Remove from the refrigerator 30 minutes before baking. Preheat the oven to 350°. Bake, uncovered, 40-50 minutes or until the manicotti shells are tender.

FREEZE OPTION *Cover and freeze the unbaked casserole. To use, partially thaw in the refrigerator overnight. Remove from refrigerator 30 minutes before baking. Preheat oven to 350°. Bake casserole as directed, increasing time as necessary to heat through and for a thermometer inserted in center to read 165°.*

FAST FIX ▶
Quick Cranberry Sauce

My family loves this 10-minute cranberry sauce because the orange marmalade and Christmasy blend of spices make it stand out from ordinary versions.
—**LUCIA JOHNSON** MASSENA, NY

START TO FINISH: 10 MIN.
MAKES: 4 CUPS

- 2 cans (14 ounces each) whole-berry cranberry sauce
- 1 jar (12 ounces) orange marmalade
- 2 teaspoons orange juice
- 1 teaspoon ground cinnamon
- 1 teaspoon ground nutmeg
- ½ teaspoon ground cloves

In a large bowl, mix all ingredients. Refrigerate, covered, until serving.

QUICK CRANBERRY SAUCE

When I invite people to dinner, they often request a main dish of Make-Ahead Spinach Manicotti. It's just that good! I appreciate the convenience of prepping the night before.
—**CHRISTY FREEMAN** CENTRAL POINT, OR

FREEZE IT
Make-Ahead Spinach Manicotti

PREP: 20 MIN. + CHILLING • **BAKE:** 40 MIN.
MAKES: 7 SERVINGS

- 1 carton (15 ounces) whole-milk ricotta cheese
- 1 package (10 ounces) frozen chopped spinach, thawed and squeezed dry
- 1½ cups (6 ounces) shredded part-skim mozzarella cheese, divided
- ¾ cup shredded Parmesan cheese, divided
- 1 large egg, lightly beaten
- 2 teaspoons minced fresh parsley
- ½ teaspoon onion powder
- ½ teaspoon pepper
- ⅛ teaspoon garlic powder
- 3 jars (24 ounces each) spaghetti sauce
- 1 cup water
- 1 package (8 ounces) manicotti shells

1. In a large bowl, mix ricotta cheese, spinach, 1 cup mozzarella cheese, ¼ cup Parmesan cheese, egg, parsley, onion powder, pepper and garlic powder. In a large bowl, mix spaghetti sauce and water; spread 1 cup into a greased 13x9-in. baking dish.

FREEZE IT

Big-Batch Dinner Rolls

Homemade rolls are always in demand. For easier prep on the day of a special get-together, I make them in advance, partially bake and freeze. They quickly go from freezer to oven when guests are on the way—and soon we're all enjoying a basketful of goodness.
—**MARY JANE HENDERSON** SALEM, NJ

PREP: 25 MIN. + RISING • **BAKE:** 15 MIN.
MAKES: 4 DOZEN

- 2 packages (¼ ounce each) active dry yeast
- 1 cup warm water (110° to 115°)
- 2 cups warm 2% milk (110° to 115°)
- ½ cup shortening
- ¼ cup sugar
- 3 teaspoons salt
- 10 cups all-purpose flour

1. In a small bowl, dissolve the yeast in warm water. In a large bowl, combine the warm milk, shortening, sugar, salt, yeast mixture and 2½ cups flour; beat on medium speed until smooth. Stir in enough remaining flour to form a stiff dough.

2. Turn dough onto a floured surface; knead until smooth and elastic, about 6-8 minutes. Place in a greased bowl, turning once to grease the top. Cover with plastic wrap and let rise in a warm place until doubled, about 1½ hours.

3. Punch down dough. Turn onto a lightly floured surface; divide and shape into 48 balls. Place 2 in. apart on greased baking sheets. Cover with kitchen towels; let rise in a warm place until doubled, about 20 minutes.

4. Preheat oven to 375°. Bake 12-15 minutes or until golden brown.

FREEZE OPTION *Partially bake rolls at 325° for 10 minutes. Freeze cooled partially baked rolls in resealable plastic freezer bags. To use, bake the frozen rolls on greased baking sheets at 375° for 12-15 minutes or until golden brown.*

ROASTED BEEF TENDERLOIN

EAT SMART

Roasted Beef Tenderloin

Roast beef marinated overnight in spices and port wine makes a simply elegant main course for Christmas dinner or any holiday meal. A dash of hot sauce adds a little kick. Here's to a platter of good cheer!
—**SCHELBY THOMPSON**
CAMDEN WYOMING, DE

PREP: 10 MIN. + MARINATING
BAKE: 40 MIN. + STANDING
MAKES: 12 SERVINGS

- ½ cup port wine or ½ cup beef broth and 1 tablespoon balsamic vinegar
- ½ cup reduced-sodium soy sauce
- 2 tablespoons olive oil
- 4 to 5 garlic cloves, minced
- 1 teaspoon dried thyme
- 1 teaspoon pepper
- ½ teaspoon hot pepper sauce
- 1 beef tenderloin roast (3 pounds)
- 1 bay leaf

1. In a small bowl, whisk the first seven ingredients until blended. Pour ¾ cup marinade into a large resealable plastic bag. Add the roast and bay leaf; seal bag and turn to coat. Refrigerate 8 hours or overnight. Cover and refrigerate remaining marinade.

2. Preheat oven to 425°. Drain beef, discarding marinade and bay leaf in bag. Place roast on a rack in a shallow roasting pan. Roast 40-50 minutes or until meat reaches desired doneness (for medium-rare, a thermometer should read 145°; medium, 160°; well-done, 170°), basting occasionally with the reserved marinade. Remove the roast from the oven; tent with foil. Let stand 10 minutes before slicing.

PER SERVING *3 ounces cooked beef equals 193 cal., 8 g fat (3 g sat. fat), 49 mg chol., 257 mg sodium, 2 g carb., trace fiber, 25 g pro.* **Diabetic Exchanges:** *3 lean meat, ½ fat.*

Sweet Potato & Chipotle Casserole

Go beyond typical marshmallow-topped sweet potato casseroles. In this version, a sweet-and-spicy streusel nicely balances the zippy chipotle peppers. Everyone who tries it wants a second helping.
—DIANA MALACH VANCOUVER, WA

PREP: 45 MIN. • **BAKE:** 35 MIN.
MAKES: 18 SERVINGS (¾ CUP EACH)

- 6 pounds sweet potatoes, peeled and cubed (about 20 cups)
- 1 to 2 chipotle peppers in adobo sauce, finely chopped
- 1 cup heavy whipping cream
- 4 large eggs, beaten
- 1 teaspoon salt

TOPPING

- 1 cup packed brown sugar
- ¾ cup all-purpose flour
- ¾ teaspoon ground ginger
- ¾ teaspoon ground cumin
- ½ teaspoon ground cloves
- ¼ teaspoon cayenne pepper
- ⅓ cup cold butter
- 1½ cups chopped pecans

1. Preheat oven to 350°. Place sweet potatoes in a large stockpot; cover with water. Bring to a boil. Reduce the heat; cook, uncovered, 15-20 minutes or until tender.
2. Drain; return to the pot. Mash the potatoes with chipotle pepper to reach the desired consistency. Cool slightly. Stir in the heavy cream, eggs and salt. Transfer to a greased 13x9-in. baking dish (dish will be full).
3. For the topping, in a large bowl, mix the brown sugar, flour, ginger, cumin, cloves and cayenne; cut in the cold butter until crumbly. Stir in pecans. Sprinkle over the casserole. Bake, uncovered, 35-40 minutes or until a thermometer reads 160°.

⑤INGREDIENTS SLOW COOKER
Slow-Cooked Green Beans

These versatile slow-cooked green beans pair well with many different entrees.
—ALICE WHITE WILLOW SPRING, NC

PREP: 10 MIN. • **COOK:** 2 HOURS
MAKES: 12 SERVINGS

- 3 packages (16 ounces each) frozen french-style green beans, thawed
- ½ cup packed brown sugar
- ½ cup butter, melted
- 1½ teaspoons garlic salt
- ¾ teaspoon reduced-sodium soy sauce

Place the green beans in a 5-qt. slow cooker. In a small bowl, mix remaining ingredients; pour over the green beans and toss to coat. Cook, covered, on low 2-3 hours or until heated through. Serve with a slotted spoon.

SWEET POTATO & CHIPOTLE CASSEROLE

Yuletide Delights

Special sweets are a must during the holiday season. From cute cookies and rich fudge to a peppermint cheesecake and spiced trifle, this collection of **decadent desserts** will have your family, friends and Santa Claus covered. It's beginning to taste a lot like Christmas!

CREAMY PEPPERMINT PUNCH

(5) INGREDIENTS **FAST FIX**

Creamy Peppermint Punch

Kids of all ages go for the crushed candy rims on the glasses of my creamy punch. Don't care for eggnog? Simply substitute 4 cups of vanilla soy milk or plain milk.
—**LINDA FOREMAN** LOCUST GROVE, OK

START TO FINISH: 10 MIN.
MAKES: 16 SERVINGS (¾ CUP EACH)

　　Crushed peppermint candies,
　　　　optional
½　gallon peppermint ice cream,
　　　softened
1　bottle (1 liter) club soda, chilled
4　cups eggnog

1. If desired, moisten the rims of punch glasses with water. Sprinkle crushed peppermint candies on a plate; dip the rims of glasses in the crushed peppermint candies. Set the glasses aside.
2. Just before serving, combine the peppermint ice cream, club soda and eggnog in a 4-qt. punch bowl. Serve in the prepared glasses.
NOTE *This recipe was tested with commercially prepared eggnog.*

EAT SMART **(5) INGREDIENTS**

Mint Twist Meringues

In our house, meringues flavored with peppermint are a yuletide tradition.
—**CHERYL PERRY** HERTFORD, NC

PREP: 30 MIN. • **BAKE:** 40 MIN. + STANDING
MAKES: 2 DOZEN

2　large egg whites
½　teaspoon cream of tartar
¼　teaspoon peppermint extract
½　cup sugar
¼　cup crushed red and green mint
　　candies

1. Place egg whites in a small bowl; let stand at room temperature 30 minutes.
2. Preheat oven to 250°. Add cream of tartar and peppermint extract to the egg whites; beat on medium speed until foamy. Gradually add the sugar, 1 tablespoon at a time, beating on high after each addition until the sugar is dissolved. Continue beating until stiff glossy peaks form.
3. Cut a small hole in the tip of a pastry bag or in a corner of a food-safe plastic bag; insert a small star tip. Transfer the meringue to bag. Pipe 1½-in.-diameter cookies 2 in. apart onto parchment paper-lined baking sheets. Sprinkle with crushed candies.
4. Bake 40-45 minutes or until firm to the touch. Turn the oven off; leave the meringues in oven 1 hour. Remove from pans to a wire rack. Store in an airtight container.
PER SERVING *1 cookie equals 17 cal., trace fat (0 sat. fat), 0 chol., 5 mg sodium, 4 g carb., trace fiber, trace pro.*

MINT TWIST MERINGUES

MOLASSES CUTOUTS

FREEZE IT
Molasses Cutouts

Have fun cutting festive shapes from the dough and decorating the cooled cutouts with sprinkles. You just may have the most popular treats at your cookie swap!

—DEB ANDERSON JOPLIN, MO

PREP: 30 MIN. + CHILLING
BAKE: 10 MIN./BATCH
MAKES: ABOUT 3 DOZEN

- ⅔ cup shortening
- 1¼ cups sugar
- 2 eggs
- 2 tablespoons buttermilk
- 2 tablespoons molasses
- 3½ cups all-purpose flour
- 1 teaspoon salt
- 1 teaspoon baking soda
- 1 teaspoon baking powder
- 1 teaspoon ground ginger
- ½ teaspoon ground cloves
  Optional decorations: confectioners' sugar icing, colored sugar, sprinkles and nonpareils

1. In a large bowl, cream shortening and sugar until light and fluffy. Beat in the eggs, buttermilk and molasses. In another bowl, whisk the flour, salt, baking soda, baking powder, ginger and cloves; gradually beat into the creamed mixture.

2. Divide the dough in half. Shape each half into a disk; wrap in plastic wrap. Refrigerate 2 hours or until firm enough to roll.

3. Preheat oven to 375°. On a lightly floured surface, roll each portion of dough to ⅛-in. thickness. Cut with a floured 3-in. cookie cutter. Place 2 in. apart on greased baking sheets.

4. Bake 8-10 minutes or until edges begin to brown. Remove from pans to wire racks to cool completely. Decorate as desired.

FREEZE OPTION *Freeze undecorated cookies in freezer containers. To use, thaw cookies in covered containers and decorate as desired.*

CHRISTMAS
GINGERBREAD TRIFLE

Christmas Gingerbread Trifle

With contrasting colors and textures in the layers, trifles always make gorgeous desserts. This one is festive enough to be a holiday centerpiece! Sometimes I add a garnish of red and green M&M's and candy canes. When my niece first saw it, her eyes just lit up.

—CHERYL TOMPKINS KINGSVILLE, MO

PREP: 45 MIN. + CHILLING
MAKES: 14 SERVINGS

- 1 package (14½ ounces) gingerbread cake/cookie mix
- 2 cups cold 2% milk
- 2 cups cold eggnog
- 2 packages (3.4 ounces each) instant French vanilla pudding mix
- 1 package (5 ounces) gingerbread man cookies
- 1 carton (16 ounces) frozen whipped topping, thawed

1. Prepare and bake the gingerbread cake mix according to the package directions, using a 9-in. square baking pan. Cool completely on a wire rack. Cut cake into 1-in. cubes.

2. In a large bowl, whisk milk, eggnog and pudding mix 2 minutes. Let stand 2 minutes or until soft-set.

3. Arrange nine cookies around sides of a 4-qt. glass bowl, using a third of the cake cubes to stand cookies upright. Top with a third of the pudding and whipped topping. Repeat the layers. Top with remaining cake, pudding and whipped topping. Refrigerate trifle, covered, 4 hours or overnight.

4. Just before serving, top with the remaining cookies.

NOTE *This recipe was tested with commercially prepared eggnog.*

Double Chocolate Fudge

For us, Christmas means it's time to make fudge. If you think it's tricky to prepare, give my double chocolate version a try. You'll be pleasantly surprised!

—FLORENCE HASTY LOUISIANA, MO

PREP: 10 MIN. • **COOK:** 20 MIN. + CHILLING
MAKES: ABOUT 2½ POUNDS

- 1 teaspoon butter
- 1 package (12 ounces) semisweet chocolate chips
- 1 can (14 ounces) sweetened condensed milk, divided
- 1 cup chopped walnuts, divided
- 2 teaspoons vanilla extract, divided
- 1 package (11½ ounces) milk chocolate chips

1. Line a 9-in. square pan with foil; grease foil with butter.

2. In a large heavy saucepan, combine semisweet chocolate chips and ¾ cup sweetened condensed milk over low heat. Remove from heat; stir in ½ cup walnuts and 1 teaspoon vanilla. Spread into prepared pan.

3. In another saucepan, combine the milk chocolate chips and remaining sweetened condensed milk. Remove from the heat; stir in the remaining walnuts and vanilla. Spread over the first layer. Refrigerate, covered, 2 hours or until firm.

4. Using the foil, lift the fudge out of the pan. Remove the foil; cut the fudge into 1-in. squares. Store between layers of waxed paper in an airtight container.

Christmas Treat Garland

Sweeten your Noel decor with garlands starring chocolate-covered goodies. The best part: taking them down. *Mmm!* Grab a package of fudge-striped cookies or dipped pretzels at the grocery store, or dunk your own treats. When set, string them on ribbon. *Makes 1 garland.*

—*TASTE OF HOME* TEST KITCHEN

Crushed Peppermint Cheesecake

When we discovered peppermint Oreos, we knew they'd make an awesome crust for cheesecake. The cool, minty crunch combined with the creamy filling makes our favorite dessert even better.

—JEANNIE BURKHEAD PEQUOT LAKES, MN

PREP: 30 MIN. • **BAKE:** 70 MIN. + CHILLING
MAKES: 12 SERVINGS

- 20 **peppermint or mint creme Oreo cookies, finely crushed**
- 3 **tablespoons butter, melted**
- 5 **packages (8 ounces each) cream cheese, softened**
- 1 **cup sugar**
- 1 **cup (8 ounces) sour cream**
- 3 **tablespoons all-purpose flour**
- 2 **teaspoons peppermint extract**
- 4 **large eggs, lightly beaten**
- ½ **cup crushed candy canes or peppermint candies**
  Additional crushed candy canes or chopped Oreo cookies, optional

1. Preheat oven to 325°. Place a greased 9-in. springform pan on a double thickness of heavy-duty foil (about 18 in. square). Wrap the foil securely around the pan. In a small bowl, mix cookie crumbs and butter; press onto bottom and 1 in. up sides of prepared pan. Refrigerate 10 minutes.

2. In a large bowl, beat cream cheese and sugar until smooth. Beat in sour cream, flour and extract. Add eggs; beat on low speed just until blended. Remove 1½ cups of batter to a small bowl; stir in crushed candy canes.

3. Pour the plain batter over cookie crust. Drop the candy cane batter by tablespoonfuls over plain batter. Cut through batter with a knife to swirl. Place the springform pan in a larger baking pan; add 1 in. of hot water to larger pan.

4. Bake 70-80 minutes or until center is just set and top appears dull. Remove the springform pan from the water bath. Cool on a wire rack 10 minutes. Loosen the sides from the pan with a knife; remove foil. Cool 1 hour longer. Refrigerate overnight, covering when completely cooled.

5. Remove the rim from the pan. Top cheesecake with additional crushed candy canes if desired.

CRUSHED PEPPERMINT CHEESECAKE

FREEZE IT

Peppermint Twist Kisses

My dad is a big fan of these cookies tinted and shaped to look like candy. When I bake them at other times of year, I change the colors of the dough to suit the occasion.

—TRACI WYNNE DENVER, PA

PREP: 20 MIN. + CHILLING
BAKE: 10 MIN./BATCH
MAKES: 3 DOZEN

- 36 **candy cane kisses or milk chocolate kisses, unwrapped**
- ½ **cup butter, softened**
- ⅓ **cup sugar**
- ¼ **teaspoon salt**
- 1 **large egg yolk**
- ½ **teaspoon peppermint extract**
- ½ **teaspoon vanilla extract**
- 1¼ **cups all-purpose flour**
- 4 **to 8 drops red food coloring**

1. Freeze the kisses in a covered container for at least 1 hour. In a large bowl, cream butter, sugar and salt until light and fluffy. Beat in the egg yolk and extracts. Gradually beat the flour into creamed mixture.

2. Divide cookie dough in half; tint one portion red. Divide each half of dough into four portions and shape into 9-in.-long rolls. Place one red log next to one white log; twist gently to create one swirled roll. Roll gently until it becomes one log. Repeat with remaining dough. Wrap logs in plastic wrap; refrigerate 1 hour or until firm.

3. Preheat oven to 350°. Unwrap dough. Cut each log crosswise into nine slices; shape each slice into a ball. Place 1 in. apart on ungreased baking sheets. Flatten slightly with a glass.

4. Bake 10-12 minutes or until edges are lightly browned. Immediately press a kiss into the center of each cookie. Remove from pans to wire racks to cool.

FREEZE OPTION *Freeze the cookies, layered between waxed paper, in freezer containers. To use, thaw before serving.*

**Michelle Brooks'
Contest-Winning
Caramel Apple Crisp**
PAGE 239

Delectable Desserts

Cute-as-can-be cupcakes, special cookies, luscious cheesecakes, rich fudge...whatever treats please your family and friends most, you'll discover just the right recipes in this sweet chapter.

Peggy Walpert's Cola Cake with Strawberries & Cream PAGE 227

Marie Hattrup's Chocolate Mallow Drops PAGE 238

Angie Ricklefs' Crunchy Ice Cream Delight PAGE 226

CHERRY DEW DUMPLINGS

Crunchy Ice Cream Delight has been a family favorite for generations. For extra fun, double the butter and nuts, then sprinkle half on top.
—**ANGIE RICKLEFS** SIOUX CITY, IA

Crunchy Ice Cream Delight

PREP: 20 MIN. + FREEZING
MAKES: 15 SERVINGS

- 2 **tablespoons butter**
- ½ **cup slivered almonds**
- 1 **cup crushed Rice Chex**
- ½ **cup flaked coconut**
- ½ **cup packed brown sugar**
- ⅛ **teaspoon salt**
- 1 **carton (1¾ quarts) vanilla bean ice cream, softened if necessary**

1. Preheat oven to 375°. In a large skillet, melt the butter over medium heat. Add the almonds; cook and stir 2-3 minutes or until toasted. Stir in the Rice Chex, coconut, brown sugar and salt. Press onto the bottom of an ungreased 13x9-in. baking dish. Bake 5-6 minutes or until edges are golden brown. Cool 10 minutes; place in the freezer 30 minutes.
2. Gently spread ice cream over crust. Cover; freeze overnight. Cut into bars.

Cherry Dew Dumplings

I've never seen a recipe like this one, which combines dumplings and soda. Yum!
—**HEIDI SWOPE** TOLEDO, OH

PREP: 20 MIN. • **BAKE:** 35 MIN. + STANDING
MAKES: 16 DUMPLINGS

- 1 **package (8 ounces) cream cheese, softened**
- ½ **cup confectioners' sugar**
- 2 **tubes (8 ounces each) refrigerated crescent rolls**
- ⅓ **cup cherry pie filling**
- ½ **cup sugar**
- ½ **cup butter, melted**
- ¾ **cup Code Red Mountain Dew**

1. Preheat oven to 350°. In a small bowl, beat the cream cheese and confectioners' sugar until smooth. Unroll both tubes of dough; separate into 16 triangles. Place 1 tablespoon cream cheese mixture in center of each triangle; top with 1 teaspoon pie filling. Fold points of short side over filling; wrap remaining point around dumpling. Pinch the seams to seal.
2. Transfer the dumplings to a 13x9-in. baking dish. In a small bowl, mix the sugar and butter; pour over the dumplings. Pour the Mountain Dew around dumplings. Bake, uncovered, 35-40 minutes or until golden brown. Let stand 10 minutes before serving.

Vanilla Coffee Creamer

Coffee and dessert? Try this creamer! Split 1 vanilla bean lengthwise. Using the tip of a sharp knife, scrape seeds from the center into a small saucepan; add vanilla bean. Add one 14-ounce can sweetened condensed milk, 1 cup half-and-half cream and a dash of salt. Cook and stir over medium heat 5 minutes or until heated through. Remove from heat; let stand, covered, 15 minutes. Discard bean. Store in an airtight container in refrigerator up to 4 days. Stir before using. *Makes 2 cups.*
—**SHAUNA SEVER** SAN FRANCISCO, CA

APRICOT UPSIDE-DOWN CAKE

Cola Cake with Strawberries & Cream

Here in the South, we've been eating cola cake for decades. This easy version has strawberries, too. Chill it in the fridge, then enjoy a dreamy summer treat.
—PEGGY WALPERT FORT WORTH, TX

PREP: 25 MIN. • **BAKE:** 30 MIN. + COOLING
MAKES: 15 SERVINGS

- 2 **cups all-purpose flour**
- 1¾ **cups sugar**
- 1 **teaspoon baking soda**
- 1 **can (12 ounces) cola**
- ½ **cup butter, cubed**
- ½ **cup canola oil**
- ¼ **cup baking cocoa**
- 1½ **cups miniature marshmallows**
- 2 **eggs**
- ½ **cup buttermilk**
- 1 **teaspoon vanilla extract**

TOPPING

- 2 **cups sour cream**
- ½ **cup packed brown sugar**
- ½ **teaspoon vanilla extract**
- 3 **cups sliced fresh strawberries**

1. Preheat oven to 350°. Grease a 13x9-in. baking dish. In a large bowl, whisk the flour, sugar and baking soda. In a large saucepan, bring the cola to a boil; cook 7-9 minutes or until liquid is reduced to 1 cup. Stir in the butter, oil and cocoa; return to a boil, stirring occasionally. Remove from the heat; stir in the marshmallows until melted. Add to the flour mixture, stirring just until moistened.
2. In a small bowl, whisk the eggs, buttermilk and vanilla until blended; add to the flour mixture, whisking constantly. Transfer to the prepared dish. Bake 30-35 minutes or until a toothpick inserted in the center comes out clean. Cool completely in baking dish on a wire rack.
3. For topping, in a small bowl, mix sour cream, brown sugar and vanilla until smooth. Serve cake with topping and strawberries.

Banana Sundae Dessert

Indulge in all your favorite banana sundae toppings, from chocolate to cherries.

—CAROLINE WAMELINK

CLEVELAND HEIGHTS, OH

PREP: 25 MIN. + FREEZING
MAKES: 16 SERVINGS

- 1 package (12 ounces) vanilla wafers, crushed
- ½ cup butter, melted
- 2 tablespoons sugar
- 6 cups chocolate chip ice cream, softened if necessary
- 4 large firm bananas, sliced
- 2 jars (11¾ ounces each) hot fudge ice cream topping, divided
- 6 cups strawberry or cherry ice cream, softened if necessary
  Optional toppings: whipped cream, maraschino cherries, chopped walnuts, banana slices and colored sprinkles

1. In a bowl, mix wafer crumbs, melted butter and sugar; press onto bottom of a 13x9-in. dish. Freeze 15 minutes.
2. Spread chocolate chip ice cream over crust. Layer with the bananas and 1½ jars fudge topping (about 1½ cups). Freeze, covered, at least 30 minutes.
3. Spread the strawberry ice cream over the top. Freeze, covered, 6 hours or overnight.
4. Remove from freezer 10 minutes before cutting. Warm remaining fudge topping; drizzle over top. Serve with toppings as desired.

ENVELOPES
OF FUDGE

BANANA
SUNDAE
DESSERT

Named after a beloved theater here in Oxford, Mississippi, Hoka Cheesecake is truly addictive. Sometimes I top it off with a sprinkling of crust crumbs.
—**BETH ZIEGENHORN** OXFORD, MS

Hoka Cheesecake

PREP: 35 MIN. • **BAKE:** 50 MIN. + CHILLING
MAKES: 12 SERVINGS

- 2 **cups graham cracker crumbs**
- ¼ **cup sugar**
- ¼ **teaspoon ground cinnamon**
- ½ **cup unsalted butter, melted**

FILLING
- 3 **packages (8 ounces each) cream cheese, softened**
- 1 **cup sugar**
- ½ **cup unsalted butter, melted**
- 3 **tablespoons vanilla extract**
- 3 **large eggs, lightly beaten**

TOPPING
- ½ **cup sour cream**
- 2 **tablespoons sugar**
- 1 **tablespoon vanilla extract**

1. Preheat oven to 325°. In a small bowl, mix graham cracker crumbs, sugar and cinnamon; stir in the butter. Press onto bottom and 1 in. up sides of a greased 9-in. springform pan. Place on a baking sheet. Bake 10 minutes. Cool on a wire rack.

2. In a large bowl, beat the cream cheese and sugar until smooth. Beat in the butter and vanilla. Add the eggs; beat on low speed just until blended. Pour into the crust. Return the pan to the baking sheet.

3. Bake 45-50 minutes or until the center of the cheesecake is almost set. Let stand 5 minutes on a wire rack. In a small bowl, mix the sour cream, sugar and vanilla; spread over the top of cheesecake. Bake 5 minutes longer. Cool on a wire rack 10 minutes. Loosen the sides from pan with a knife. Cool 1 hour longer.

4. Refrigerate overnight, covering when completely cooled. Remove the rim from the pan.

BLUEBERRY RHUBARB
COUNTRY TART

Blueberry Rhubarb Country Tart

When your garden is bursting with fresh rhubarb, mix some of the stalks with blueberries for a rustic and bubbly tart.

—JEANNE AMBROSE MILWAUKEE, WI

PREP: 15 MIN. • **BAKE:** 40 MIN.
MAKES: 8 SERVINGS

  Pastry for single-crust pie
¾ cup sugar
¼ cup all-purpose flour
4 cups chopped fresh or frozen rhubarb, thawed
1 cup fresh or frozen blueberries, thawed
2 tablespoons 2% milk
1 tablespoon coarse sugar

1. Preheat oven to 400°. On a lightly floured surface, roll the dough into a 14-in. circle. Transfer to a parchment paper-lined baking sheet.
2. In a large bowl, mix sugar and flour. Add rhubarb and berries; toss to coat. Spoon filling over pastry to within 2 in. of edge. Fold the pastry edge over the filling, pleating as you go and leaving a 4-in. opening in center. Brush folded pastry with milk; sprinkle with coarse sugar. Bake 40-45 minutes or until crust is golden and filling is bubbly. Transfer tart to a wire rack to cool.

PASTRY FOR SINGLE-CRUST PIE
Combine 1¼ cups all-purpose flour and ¼ teaspoon salt; cut in ½ cup cold butter until crumbly. Gradually add 3-5 tablespoons ice water, tossing with a fork until the dough holds together when pressed. Wrap in plastic wrap and refrigerate 1 hour.
NOTE *If using frozen rhubarb, measure rhubarb while still frozen, then thaw completely. Drain in a colander, but do not press liquid out.*

Vanilla Sugar

Use this yummy flavored sugar as regular granulated sugar, discarding the vanilla bean as it loses its flavor. Place 2 cups sugar in an airtight container. Split 1 vanilla bean lengthwise; using the tip of a sharp knife, scrape the seeds into the sugar. Bury the vanilla bean in sugar. Cover; let stand for at least 24 hours. *Makes 2 cups.*

—JACKIE TERMONT RUTHER GLEN, VA

FREEZE IT
Ginger-Doodles

Both of my grandmothers spent time teaching me how to bake when I was a young child, and I've been baking ever since. My two brothers are huge fans of snickerdoodles, while I'm partial to gingersnaps. So I came up with a new cookie to make all three of us happy!

—BECKY TOTH HAVRE, MT

PREP: 25 MIN. • **BAKE:** 10 MIN./BATCH
MAKES: ABOUT 5 DOZEN

¾ cup butter, softened
1½ cups sugar, divided
½ cup packed brown sugar
1 large egg
½ cup maple syrup
3¼ cups all-purpose flour
1 teaspoon baking soda
¾ teaspoon ground cinnamon, divided
½ teaspoon ground ginger
¼ teaspoon salt
¼ teaspoon cream of tartar
¼ teaspoon ground nutmeg

1. Preheat oven to 350°. In a large bowl, cream the butter, ½ cup sugar and brown sugar until light and fluffy. Beat in egg and syrup. In another bowl, whisk flour, baking soda, ½ teaspoon cinnamon, ginger, salt, cream of tartar and nutmeg; gradually beat into the creamed mixture.
2. In a small bowl, combine remaining sugar and cinnamon. Shape the cookie dough into 1-in. balls; roll in the sugar mixture. Place 3 in. apart on ungreased baking sheets. Bake 10-12 minutes or until light brown. Remove to wire racks to cool.

FREEZE OPTION *Freeze the cookies in freezer containers. To use, thaw the cookies before serving.*

FREEZE IT
Brownies a la Mode

My husband and I sampled a dressed-up brownie at a restaurant and wanted to indulge at home. A from-scratch fudge sauce, vanilla ice cream and cherries take this dessert over the top!

—LISE THOMSON MAGRATH, AB

PREP: 20 MIN. • **BAKE:** 30 MIN. + COOLING
MAKES: 1½ DOZEN

1 cup butter, softened
2 cups sugar
4 large eggs
2 tablespoons canola oil
2 teaspoons vanilla extract
1 cup all-purpose flour
⅓ cup baking cocoa
FUDGE SAUCE
½ cup butter, cubed
2 cups sugar
½ cup baking cocoa
½ cup water
½ cup light corn syrup
1 teaspoon vanilla extract
½ teaspoon salt
  Vanilla ice cream and maraschino cherries

1. Preheat oven to 325°. Line a 13x9-in. baking pan with foil, letting ends extend up sides; grease the foil. In a large bowl, cream butter and sugar until light and fluffy. Add eggs, one at a time, beating well after each addition. Beat in oil and vanilla. In another bowl, whisk flour and cocoa; gradually beat into creamed mixture.
2. Spread into the prepared pan. Bake 30-35 minutes or until a toothpick inserted near the center comes out clean. Cool on a wire rack.
3. For fudge sauce, in a large saucepan, melt butter over medium heat. Stir in sugar, cocoa, water, corn syrup, vanilla and salt until blended. Bring to a boil. Cook, uncovered, 3-5 minutes or until sugar is dissolved and sauce is smooth, stirring frequently.
4. Lifting with foil, remove brownies from pan. Cut into eighteen 3x2-in. rectangles. Top each brownie with ice cream, fudge sauce and a cherry.

FREEZE OPTION *Securely wrap and freeze the cooled brownies in plastic wrap and foil. To use, thaw brownies at room temperature.*

PECAN TASSIES

FREEZE IT

Pecan Tassies

These cute little tarts shaped and baked in a miniature muffin pan always remind me of classic pecan pie. For festive color at Christmas, top each cooled tassie with half of a maraschino cherry.

—JOY CORIE RUSTON, LA

PREP: 25 MIN. + CHILLING • **BAKE:** 20 MIN.
MAKES: 2 DOZEN

- ½ cup butter, softened
- 3 ounces cream cheese, softened
- 1 cup all-purpose flour

FILLING

- 1 large egg
- ¾ cup packed brown sugar
- 1 tablespoon butter, softened
- 1 teaspoon vanilla extract
  Dash salt
- ⅔ cup finely chopped pecans, divided

1. In a small bowl, beat the butter and cream cheese until smooth; gradually beat in the flour. Refrigerate, covered, 1 hour or until firm enough to roll.

2. Preheat oven to 375°. Shape cookie dough into 1-in. balls; press evenly onto the bottom and up the sides of greased mini-muffin cups.

3. For filling, in a small bowl, mix egg, brown sugar, butter, vanilla and salt until blended. Stir in ⅓ cup pecans; spoon into pastries. Sprinkle with the remaining pecans.

4. Bake 20-25 minutes or until the edges are golden and filling is puffed. Cool in the pans 2 minutes. Remove to wire racks to cool.

FREEZE OPTION *Freeze the cooled cookies, layered between waxed paper, in freezer containers. To use, thaw in covered containers.*

FREEZE IT

Salted Toffee Cashew Cookies

Toffee, cashews and butterscotch chips together in one cookie? That sweet-salty combo is impossible to resist!

—CRYSTAL SCHLUETER NORTHGLENN, CO

PREP: 25 MIN. • **BAKE:** 10 MIN./BATCH
MAKES: ABOUT 5 DOZEN

- 1 cup butter, softened
- 1½ cups packed brown sugar
- 2 large eggs
- 1 teaspoon vanilla extract
- 2⅔ cups all-purpose flour
- 1 teaspoon salt
- 1 teaspoon baking soda
- 1½ cups chopped salted cashews
- 1 cup brickle toffee bits
- 1 cup butterscotch chips
  Salted whole cashews

1. Preheat oven to 375°. In a large bowl, cream butter and brown sugar until light and fluffy. Beat in eggs and vanilla. In another bowl, whisk flour, salt and baking soda; gradually beat into the creamed mixture. Stir in the chopped cashews, toffee bits and butterscotch chips.

2. Drop cookie dough by rounded tablespoonfuls 2 in. apart onto ungreased baking sheets. Press one whole cashew into each cookie. Bake 7-9 minutes or until golden brown. Cool on pans 2 minutes. Remove to wire racks to cool.

FREEZE OPTION *Freeze the cookies in freezer containers. To use, thaw cookies before serving.*

SALTED TOFFEE
CASHEW COOKIES

Easy Four-Layer Chocolate Dessert

I grew up on this cool, creamy, crunchy dessert. With rich layers on a walnut crust, it's a special treat. We drizzle chocolate syrup over each piece before serving.
—**KRISTEN JOHNSON** WAUKESHA, WI

PREP: 25 MIN. • **BAKE:** 15 MIN. + COOLING
MAKES: 15 SERVINGS

- 1 **cup all-purpose flour**
- ½ **cup cold butter**
- 1 **cup chopped walnuts, toasted, divided**
- 1 **package (8 ounces) cream cheese, softened**
- 1 **cup confectioners' sugar**
- 2 **cartons (8 ounces each) frozen whipped topping, thawed, divided**
- 2½ **cups 2% milk**
- 2 **packages (3.9 ounces each) instant chocolate pudding mix**
- 1 **cup semisweet chocolate chunks**
  Chocolate syrup

1. Preheat oven to 350°. Place flour in a small bowl; cut in the butter until crumbly. Stir in ½ cup nuts. Press onto bottom of an ungreased 13x9-in. baking dish. Bake 12-15 minutes or until light golden brown. Cool completely on a wire rack.

2. In a small bowl, beat cream cheese and confectioners' sugar until smooth; fold in one carton whipped topping. Spread over the crust. In a large bowl, whisk the milk and instant chocolate pudding mix 2 minutes. Gently spread over the cream cheese layer. Top with remaining whipped topping. Sprinkle with the semisweet chocolate chunks and remaining walnuts. Refrigerate until cold.

3. Cut into bars. Just before serving, drizzle with chocolate syrup.
NOTE *To toast nuts, bake in a shallow pan in a 350° oven for 5-10 minutes or cook in a skillet over low heat until lightly browned, stirring occasionally.*

2. Bake 35-40 minutes or until a toothpick inserted in the center comes out clean. Cool 10 minutes before inverting onto a serving plate. Serve warm with whipped topping.

Malted Milk Cake

This recipe calls for a 13x9 pan, but you could also make cupcakes in paper liners.
—**SUSAN SCARBOROUGH**
FERNANDINA BEACH, FL

PREP: 30 MIN. • **BAKE:** 20 MIN. + COOLING
MAKES: 15 SERVINGS

- 1 **cup butter, softened**
- 1 **cup sugar**
- 4 **large eggs**
- ½ **teaspoon butter flavoring, optional**
- 2⅓ **cups all-purpose flour**
- 1 **cup malted milk powder**
- 2 **teaspoons baking powder**
- ½ **teaspoon salt**
- ⅔ **cup whole milk**
- **FROSTING**
- ⅓ **cup butter, softened**
- 2¾ **cups confectioners' sugar**
- ⅓ **cup baking cocoa**
- ⅓ **cup whole milk**
- 1½ **cups coarsely crushed malted milk balls**

1. Preheat oven to 350°. Grease a 13x9-in. baking pan. In a large bowl, cream butter and sugar until light and fluffy. Add eggs, one at a time, beating well after each addition. The batter may appear curdled. If desired, beat in flavoring. In another bowl, whisk the flour, malted milk powder, baking powder and salt; add to the creamed mixture alternately with milk, beating well after each addition.

2. Transfer batter to prepared pan. Bake 18-22 minutes or until a toothpick inserted in center comes out clean. Cool completely in pan on a wire rack.

3. In a large bowl, beat butter until creamy. Beat in the confectioners' sugar and baking cocoa alternately with the milk until smooth. Spread frosting over the cake; sprinkle with crushed malted milk balls.

- **1 tablespoon water**
- **1 tablespoon lemon juice**
- **1 tablespoon honey**
- **½ teaspoon cornstarch**

BLUEBERRY SAUCE
- **1¼ cups fresh blueberries**
- **1 tablespoon water**
- **1 tablespoon lemon juice**
- **1 tablespoon honey**
- **½ teaspoon cornstarch**

1. Preheat oven to 350°. Place granola and walnuts in a food processor; pulse until fine crumbs form. Add butter and honey; pulse just until blended. Press onto bottom and up sides of a greased 9-in. pie plate. Bake 10-12 minutes or until lightly browned. Cool completely on a wire rack.

RED, WHITE AND BLUEBERRY ICE CREAM PIE WITH GRANOLA CRUST

2. Spread ice cream into the prepared crust. Freeze, covered, at least 2 hours.

3. In a small saucepan, combine the raspberry sauce ingredients. Bring to a boil. Reduce the heat to medium; cook, uncovered, 5-7 minutes or until thickened, stirring occasionally. Meanwhile, in another saucepan, repeat with the blueberry sauce ingredients.

4. Press each berry sauce through a fine-mesh strainer into a bowl; discard the seeds. Cool completely.

5. Transfer berry sauces to separate heavy-duty resealable plastic bags; cut a small hole in corner of each bag. Decorate the pie as desired. Freeze, covered, until serving. Serve with any remaining berry sauces.

FREEZE IT

Jeweled Thumbprints

When I moved here from Malta, a kind neighbor took me under her wing and baked cookies for me. Thumbprints with fruity preserves are specialties of hers.
—**MARIA DEBONO** NEW YORK, NY

PREP: 20 MIN. + CHILLING
BAKE: 15 MIN./BATCH + COOLING
MAKES: ABOUT 6 DOZEN

- **¾ cup butter, softened**
- **¾ cup confectioners' sugar**
- **1 large egg yolk**
- **½ teaspoon almond extract**
- **1¾ cups all-purpose flour**
- **½ cup raspberry or apricot preserves**

1. In a large bowl, beat butter and confectioners' sugar until blended. Beat in egg yolk and extract. Gradually beat in the flour. Refrigerate, covered, at least 2 hours or until firm.

2. Preheat oven to 350°. Shape cookie dough into ¾-in. balls. Place 1 in. apart on greased baking sheets. Press a deep indentation in the center of each with your thumb.

3. Bake 12-14 minutes or until edges are light brown. Remove from pans to wire racks. Fill each with ¼ teaspoon preserves; cool completely.

FREEZE OPTION *Freeze the unfilled cookies, layered between waxed paper, in freezer containers. To use, thaw the cookies in covered containers and fill with preserves.*

DARK CHOCOLATE
CROISSANT
BREAD PUDDING

Dark Chocolate Croissant Bread Pudding

Croissants make a yummy base for this rich, chocolaty bread pudding. I prefer dark chocolate, but semisweet or white work, too. If you'd like a little crunch, garnish with your favorite nuts.
—**JENNIFER TIDWELL** FAIR OAKS, CA

PREP: 15 MIN. + STANDING • **BAKE:** 40 MIN.
MAKES: 15 SERVINGS

- 8 **croissants, torn into 2-inch pieces**
- 1 **cup (6 ounces) dark chocolate chips**
- 8 **large eggs**
- 1 **cup sugar**
- 1 **tablespoon grated orange peel**
- 1½ **teaspoons ground cinnamon**
- ¼ **teaspoon ground nutmeg**
- ⅛ **teaspoon salt**
- 3 **cups 2% milk**
- 1 **cup orange juice**
- 2 **teaspoons vanilla extract**

1. Preheat oven to 350°. Place the croissants in a greased 13x9-in. baking dish; sprinkle with chocolate chips. In a large bowl, whisk eggs, sugar, orange peel, cinnamon, nutmeg and salt until blended. Stir in milk, orange juice and vanilla; pour over top. Let stand about 15 minutes or until bread is softened.
2. Bake, uncovered, 40-45 minutes or until puffed and golden brown; cover loosely with foil during last 10 minutes if top browns too quickly. Serve warm.

Homemade Vanilla Extract

I make my own vanilla as a gift for friends. It's easy! Split 6 vanilla beans lengthwise; place in a tall jar. Cover with 2 cups vodka. Seal jar tightly. Let stand in a cool dark place for at least 6 weeks, gently shaking the jar once a week. *Makes 2 cups.*
—**BECKY JO SMITH** KETTLE FALLS, WA

My family loves all sorts of cookies and bars—especially Raspberry-Chocolate Meringue Squares. They start with a buttery crust and end in airy delight!

—**NANCY HEISHMAN** LAS VEGAS, NV

RASPBERRY-CHOCOLATE MERINGUE SQUARES

WINTER FRUIT MACAROONS

Chocolate Mallow Drops

There's so much to love about these marshmallow-topped cookies, but the best part is the old-fashioned icing. I use it on chocolate cakes and cupcakes, too.

—**MARIE HATTRUP** SONOMA, CA

PREP: 35 MIN.
BAKE: 10 MIN./BATCH + COOLING
MAKES: ABOUT 3 DOZEN

- ½ cup butter, softened
- 1 cup sugar
- 1 large egg
- ½ cup 2% milk
- 1 teaspoon vanilla extract
- 1¾ cups all-purpose flour
- ½ cup baking cocoa
- ½ teaspoon baking soda
- ½ teaspoon salt
- ½ cup chopped pecans
- 18 to 22 large marshmallows, halved

ICING
- ¼ cup butter, cubed
- 2 ounces unsweetened chocolate, chopped
- 1 ounce semisweet chocolate, chopped
- 2 cups confectioners' sugar
- 3 to 6 tablespoons brewed coffee

1. Preheat oven to 375°. In a large bowl, cream butter and sugar until light and fluffy. Beat in the egg, milk and vanilla. In another bowl, whisk the flour, cocoa, baking soda and salt; gradually beat into creamed mixture. Stir in pecans.

2. Drop cookie dough by rounded tablespoonfuls 2 in. apart onto ungreased baking sheets. Bake 6 minutes. Press a marshmallow half onto each cookie, cut side down. Bake 2-3 minutes longer or until edges of cookies are set and marshmallows are softened. Remove from pans to wire racks to cool completely.

3. For the icing, in a microwave, melt the butter and chocolates; stir until smooth. Stir in confectioners' sugar and enough coffee to reach a drizzling consistency. Drizzle over the cookies. Let stand until set.

FREEZE IT
Winter Fruit Macaroons

Here's my take on one of my mother's favorite treats—macaroons. I make mine with sweetened condensed milk rather than egg whites. The dried fruit and nuts add winter-season appeal.

—**VERONICA MILLER** ALIQUIPPA, PA

PREP: 20 MIN. • **BAKE:** 10 MIN./BATCH
MAKES: ABOUT 7 DOZEN

- 1 can (14 ounces) sweetened condensed milk
- 2¼ cups flaked coconut
- 2¼ cups coarsely chopped dates
- 1½ cups coarsely chopped walnuts
- ¾ cup dried cherries
- ¾ cup dried cranberries
- ¾ teaspoon vanilla extract

1. Preheat oven to 350°. In a large bowl, mix all ingredients. Drop by tablespoonfuls 2 in. apart onto parchment paper-lined baking sheets.

2. Bake 8-10 minutes or until light brown. Cool on the pans 5 minutes. Remove to wire racks to cool. Store in an airtight container.

FREEZE OPTION *Freeze cookies, layered between waxed paper, in freezer containers. To use the cookies, thaw before serving.*

PRETZEL DESSERT

Vanilla White Chocolate Mousse

When I needed an easy dessert idea for my daughter's bridal shower, a co-worker came to the rescue. Her rich, smooth mousse looked simply elegant.

—MARINA CASTLE CANYON COUNTRY, CA

PREP: 20 MIN. + CHILLING
MAKES: 4 SERVINGS

- 1¼ cups heavy whipping cream, divided
- 2 tablespoons sugar
- 2 large egg yolks
- 7 ounces white baking chocolate, chopped
- 2 vanilla beans
  Toasted sliced almonds, optional

1. In a small saucepan, combine ¼ cup whipping cream and sugar; cook over medium heat until bubbles form around sides of pan.
2. In a small bowl, whisk a small amount of hot mixture into egg yolks; return all to pan, whisking constantly. Cook over low heat until the mixture is just thick enough to coat a metal spoon and a thermometer reads at least 160°, stirring constantly. Do not allow to boil. Immediately remove from heat. Stir in chocolate until smooth.
3. Split the vanilla beans lengthwise. Using the tip of a sharp knife, scrape seeds from the center into chocolate mixture; stir. Transfer to a large bowl; cool 10 minutes.
4. In a small bowl, beat the remaining cream until soft peaks form; fold into the chocolate mixture. Spoon into four dessert dishes. Refrigerate, covered, 1 hour before serving. If desired, sprinkle with almonds.

Pretzel Dessert

This always popular recipe makes a big batch in a 13x9 pan. That's fine with my family because any leftovers are just as yummy the next day!

—RITA WINTERBERGER HUSON, MT

PREP: 20 MIN. + CHILLING
MAKES: 16 SERVINGS

- 2 cups crushed pretzels, divided
- ¾ cup sugar
- ¾ cup butter, melted
- 1 package (8 ounces) cream cheese, softened
- 1 cup confectioners' sugar
- 1 carton (8 ounces) frozen whipped topping, thawed
- 1 can (21 ounces) cherry pie filling

1. In a large bowl, toss 1½ cups crushed pretzels with the sugar and melted butter. Press into an ungreased 13x9-in. dish.
2. In a large bowl, beat cream cheese and confectioners' sugar until smooth. Fold in whipped topping.
3. Spread half of the mixture over the pretzel layer. Top with the cherry pie filling; spread with the remaining cream cheese mixture. Sprinkle with the remaining pretzels. Refrigerate, covered, overnight before serving.

Contest-Winning Caramel Apple Crisp

My children and I prepare this together. We mix in a variety of apples to give the crisp a combination of flavors.

—MICHELLE BROOKS CLARKSTON, MI

PREP: 20 MIN. • **BAKE:** 45 MIN.
MAKES: 12 SERVINGS

- 3 cups old-fashioned oats
- 2 cups all-purpose flour
- 1½ cups packed brown sugar
- 1 teaspoon ground cinnamon
- 1 cup cold butter, cubed
- 8 cups thinly sliced peeled tart apples
- 1 package (14 ounces) caramels, halved
- 1 cup apple cider, divided

1. Preheat oven to 350°. In a large bowl, mix oats, flour, brown sugar and cinnamon; cut in butter until crumbly. Press half of the mixture into a greased 13x9-in. baking dish. Layer half of each of the following: apples, caramels and remaining oat mixture. Repeat layers. Drizzle ½ cup apple cider over top.
2. Bake, uncovered, 30 minutes. Drizzle with remaining apple cider; bake 15-20 minutes longer or until the apples are tender.

VANILLA WHITE CHOCOLATE MOUSSE

Banana Skillet Upside-Down Cake

I got my first cast iron skillet from my grandmother, and I've been cooking and baking with it ever since. This irresistible dessert uses both the stovetop and oven. Sometimes I add drained maraschino cherries and serve slices with ice cream.

—TERRI MERRITTS NASHVILLE, TN

PREP: 25 MIN. • **BAKE:** 35 MIN.
MAKES: 10 SERVINGS

- 1 package (14 ounces) banana quick bread and muffin mix
- ½ cup chopped walnuts
- ¼ cup butter, cubed
- ¾ cup packed brown sugar
- 2 tablespoons lemon juice
- 4 medium bananas, cut into ¼-inch slices
- 2 cups flaked coconut

1. Preheat oven to 375°. Prepare the banana bread batter according to the package directions; stir in walnuts.
2. In a 10-in. ovenproof skillet, melt butter over medium heat; stir in brown sugar until dissolved. Add lemon juice; cook and stir 2-3 minutes longer or until slightly thickened. Remove from heat. Arrange bananas in a single layer over brown sugar mixture; sprinkle with coconut.
3. Spoon the prepared batter over the coconut. Bake 35-40 minutes or until dark golden and a toothpick inserted in the center comes out clean. Cool 5 minutes before inverting onto a serving plate. Serve warm.

VANILLA BEAN CUPCAKES

FREEZE IT

Vanilla Bean Cupcakes

My young son loves all things vanilla, especially these flecked cupcakes spread with a homemade cream cheese frosting. Look for vanilla bean paste if you can't find the whole beans.

—ALYSHA BRAUN ST. CATHARINES, ON

PREP: 30 MIN. • **BAKE:** 20 MIN. + COOLING
MAKES: 1½ DOZEN

- ¾ cup unsalted butter, softened
- 1¼ cups sugar
- 2 large eggs
- 2 vanilla beans
- 2 cups cake flour
- 2 teaspoons baking powder
- ½ teaspoon salt
- ⅔ cup whole milk

FROSTING

- 1 package (8 ounces) cream cheese, softened
- 6 tablespoons unsalted butter, softened
- 1½ teaspoons vanilla extract
- 3 cups confectioners' sugar
  Assorted candies and coarse sugar

1. Preheat oven to 375°. Line 18 muffin cups with paper liners.
2. In a large bowl, cream butter and sugar until light and fluffy. Add eggs, one at a time, beating well after each addition. Split beans lengthwise; using the tip of a sharp knife, scrape seeds from center into creamed mixture. In another bowl, whisk flour, baking powder and salt; add to the creamed mixture alternately with milk, beating well after each addition.
3. Fill prepared cups three-fourths full. Bake 16-18 minutes or until a toothpick inserted in center comes out clean. Cool in the pans 10 minutes before removing to wire racks to cool completely.
4. In a large bowl, beat the cream cheese, butter and vanilla until blended. Gradually beat in the confectioners' sugar until smooth. Frost cupcakes. Decorate with candies and coarse sugar as desired. Refrigerate leftovers.
FREEZE OPTION *Freeze the cooled cupcakes in resealable plastic freezer bags. To use, thaw cupcakes at room temperature. Frost as directed.*

BANANA SKILLET UPSIDE-DOWN CAKE

Tiramisu Cheesecake Dessert

I wasn't always a big fan of the flavor of Italian tiramisu. Here's the recipe that changed my mind! It's one of my favorite treats to make during fall.

—**CHRISTIE NELSON** TAYLORVILLE, IL

PREP: 20 MIN. • **BAKE:** 40 MIN. + CHILLING
MAKES: 12 SERVINGS

- 1 **package (12 ounces) vanilla wafers**
- 5 **teaspoons instant coffee granules, divided**
- 3 **tablespoons hot water, divided**
- 4 **packages (8 ounces each) cream cheese, softened**
- 1 **cup sugar**
- 1 **cup (8 ounces) sour cream**
- 4 **large eggs, lightly beaten**
- 1 **cup whipped topping**
- 1 **tablespoon baking cocoa**

1. Preheat oven to 325°. Layer half of the vanilla wafers in a greased 13x9-in. baking dish. In a small bowl, dissolve 2 teaspoons instant coffee granules in 2 tablespoons hot water; brush 1 tablespoon mixture over the vanilla wafers.

2. In a large bowl, beat cream cheese and sugar until smooth. Beat in the sour cream. Add the eggs; beat on low speed just until blended. Remove half of the filling to another bowl. Dissolve the remaining instant coffee granules in the remaining hot water; stir into one portion of the filling. Spread over vanilla wafers.

3. Layer the remaining wafers over the top; brush with the remaining dissolved coffee granules. Spread with the remaining filling.

4. Bake 40-45 minutes or until the center is almost set. Cool on a wire rack 10 minutes. Loosen sides from dish with a knife. Cool 1 hour longer. Refrigerate overnight, covering when completely cooled.

5. To serve, spread with whipped topping. Dust with cocoa.

TIRAMISU CHEESECAKE DESSERT

Sherri Melotik's
Pan-Roasted Chicken
and Vegetables PAGE 250

On the Lighter Side

Whether a loved one has special dietary needs or you just want to eat healthier, rely on this chapter of delicious options. Each recipe includes nutrition facts to help you make the best choices for your family.

**Kayla Capper's
Sweet Potatoes with
Cilantro Black Beans**
PAGE 245

**Rachel Kimbrow's
Triple Tomato Flatbread**
PAGE 257

**Amy Lents'
Slow Cooker Beef Tips**
PAGE 255

GRILLED ANGEL FOOD CAKE
WITH STRAWBERRIES

EAT SMART 5 INGREDIENTS FAST FIX
Grilled Angel Food Cake with Strawberries

One night I goofed, accidentally baking a pound cake using the balsamic butter I save for grilling chicken. What a delicious mistake! Now I use the same idea for this summery grilled dessert. Give it a patriotic look with a drizzle of blueberry syrup.

—MOIRA MCGARRY PARKMAN, ME

START TO FINISH: 15 MIN.
MAKES: 8 SERVINGS

- 2 cups sliced fresh strawberries
- 2 teaspoons sugar
- 3 tablespoons butter, melted
- 2 tablespoons balsamic vinegar
- 8 slices angel food cake (about 1 ounce each)
  Reduced-fat vanilla ice cream and blueberry syrup, optional

1. In a small bowl, toss strawberries with sugar. In another bowl, mix the butter and vinegar; brush over the cut sides of cake.

2. Moisten a paper towel with cooking oil; using long-handled tongs, rub on the grill rack to coat lightly. Grill the cake, uncovered, over medium heat 1-2 minutes on each side or until golden brown. Serve cake with strawberries and, if desired, vanilla ice cream and blueberry syrup.

PER SERVING *1 cake slice with ¼ cup strawberries (calculated without ice cream and berry syrup) equals 132 cal., 5 g fat (3 g sat. fat), 11 mg chol., 247 mg sodium, 22 g carb., 1 g fiber, 2 g pro.* **Diabetic Exchanges:** *1½ starch, 1 fat.*

EAT SMART
Cool Summertime Oatmeal

Get a few more minutes of sleep in the morning—start your breakfast the night before! Here's a make-ahead recipe that lets you do just that. The next day, simply top your oatmeal however you prefer. My husband likes to add coconut.

—JUNE THOMAS CHESTERTON, IN

PREP: 10 MIN. + CHILLING
MAKES: 4 SERVINGS

- 1⅓ cups old-fashioned oats
- ¾ cup fat-free milk
- ¾ cup (6 ounces) reduced-fat plain yogurt
- ¼ cup honey
- 1 cup pitted fresh or frozen dark sweet cherries, thawed
- 1 cup fresh or frozen blueberries, thawed
- ½ cup chopped walnuts, toasted

1. In a small bowl, combine the oats, milk, yogurt and honey. Refrigerate, covered, overnight.

2. Top each serving with cherries, blueberries and walnuts.

NOTE *To toast nuts, bake in a shallow pan in a 350° oven for 5-10 minutes or cook in a skillet over low heat until lightly browned, stirring occasionally.*
PER SERVING *350 cal., 12 g fat (2 g sat. fat), 4 mg chol., 53 mg sodium, 55 g carb., 5 g fiber, 10 g pro.*

Wild Rice Pepper Salad

I've made this chilled salad countless times. In a small saucepan, bring ⅔ cup uncooked wild rice and 3 cups water to a boil. Reduce heat; cover and simmer for 1 hour or until rice is tender. Drain and place in a bowl. Refrigerate until chilled. Add 1 cup chopped green pepper, 1 cup chopped sweet red pepper, 1 cup sweet yellow pepper, ½ cup sunflower kernels, ⅓ cup chopped onion, ⅓ cup raisins and ½ cup Italian salad dressing; toss to coat. *Makes 6 servings.*

—DARLENE GIBBON MILNOR, ND

GRILLED LEEK DIP

Add red pepper and green onions; cook and stir 3-4 minutes or until tender. Stir in the black beans, salsa, corn, lime juice, creamy peanut butter, cumin and garlic salt; heat through. Stir in the cilantro.

3. With a sharp knife, cut an "X" in each sweet potato. Fluff the pulp with a fork. Spoon the bean mixture over the potatoes. If desired, sprinkle with additional cilantro.

PER SERVING *1 potato with ½ cup black bean mixture equals 400 cal., 6 g fat (1 g sat. fat), 0 chol., 426 mg sodium, 77 g carb., 12 g fiber, 11 g pro.*

EAT SMART **FAST FIX**
Quick Nicoise Salad
Like the traditional French salad Nicoise, my version has vegetables, tuna and eggs. Cooking the potato and beans together helps it come together quickly.
—**VALERIE BELLEY** ST. LOUIS, MO

START TO FINISH: 25 MIN.
MAKES: 4 SERVINGS (½ CUP DRESSING)

- 1 **pound red potatoes (about 2 large), cubed**
- ¼ **pound fresh green beans, trimmed**
- ½ **cup oil and vinegar salad dressing**
- ½ **teaspoon grated lemon peel**
- ¼ **teaspoon freshly ground pepper**
- 6 **cups torn romaine**
- 4 **large hard-cooked eggs, sliced**
- 3 **pouches (2½ ounces each) light tuna in water**
- 2 **medium tomatoes, chopped**

1. Place the red potatoes in a large saucepan; add water to cover. Bring to a boil. Reduce heat; cook, uncovered, 8-10 minutes or until tender, adding green beans during the last 2 minutes of cooking. Drain potatoes and beans; immediately drop into ice water. Drain and pat dry.

2. In a small bowl, combine salad dressing, lemon peel and pepper. Divide romaine among four plates; arrange potatoes, green beans, eggs, tuna and tomatoes over the romaine. Serve with dressing mixture.

PER SERVING *327 cal., 15 g fat (2 g sat. fat), 206 mg chol., 691 mg sodium, 27 g carb., 5 g fiber, 21 g pro.* ***Diabetic Exchanges:*** *3 lean meat, 2 vegetable, 2 fat, 1 starch.*

EAT SMART **5 INGREDIENTS**
Grilled Leek Dip
Smoky leeks from the grill make this dip stand out from the appetizer crowd. I've also used baby Vidalia onions.
—**RAMONA PARRIS** MARIETTA, GA

PREP: 10 MIN. • **GRILL:** 10 MIN. + CHILLING
MAKES: 20 SERVINGS (2 TABLESPOONS EACH)

- 2 **medium leeks**
- 2 **teaspoons olive oil**
- ½ **teaspoon salt, divided**
- ¼ **teaspoon pepper**
- 2 **cups (16 ounces) reduced-fat sour cream**
- 2 **tablespoons Worcestershire sauce**
  Assorted fresh vegetables

1. Trim and discard dark green portion of leeks. Brush leeks with oil; sprinkle with ¼ teaspoon salt and pepper. Grill leeks, covered, over medium-high heat 8-10 minutes or until lightly charred and tender, turning occasionally. Cool slightly; chop leeks.

2. In a small bowl, combine the sour cream, Worcestershire and remaining salt; stir in leeks. Refrigerate, covered, 2 hours before serving. Serve with fresh vegetables.

PER SERVING *2 tablespoons (calculated without vegetables) equals 43 cal., 2 g fat (1 g sat. fat), 8 mg chol., 93 mg sodium, 3 g carb., trace fiber, 2 g pro.*

EAT SMART **FAST FIX**
Sweet Potatoes with Cilantro Black Beans
As a vegan, I'm always searching for new dishes to enjoy and share. A main dish of loaded sweet potatoes went over especially big with my mom.
—**KAYLA CAPPER** OJAI, CA

START TO FINISH: 20 MIN.
MAKES: 4 SERVINGS

- 4 **medium sweet potatoes (about 8 ounces each)**
- 1 **tablespoon olive oil**
- 1 **small sweet red pepper, chopped**
- 2 **green onions, chopped**
- 1 **can (15 ounces) black beans, rinsed and drained**
- ½ **cup salsa**
- ¼ **cup frozen corn**
- 2 **tablespoons lime juice**
- 1 **tablespoon creamy peanut butter**
- 1 **teaspoon ground cumin**
- ¼ **teaspoon garlic salt**
- ¼ **cup minced fresh cilantro**
  Additional minced fresh cilantro, optional

1. Scrub the sweet potatoes; pierce several times with a fork. Place on a microwave-safe plate. Microwave, uncovered, on high 6-8 minutes or until tender, turning once.

2. Meanwhile, in a large skillet, heat the olive oil over medium-high heat.

For as long as I can remember, Mom treated us to Garden Tomato Salad. Now I fix it whenever a new veggie crop is ripe and ready to pick.
—SHANNON ARTHUR CANAL WINCHESTER, OH

BASIL GRILLED
CORN ON THE COB

GARDEN TOMATO SALAD

EAT SMART ⑤INGREDIENTS
Basil Grilled Corn on the Cob

Corn on the cob is a cherished summer favorite here in the Midwest. My recipe adds unexpected ingredients—fresh basil, cilantro and lemon juice—to give each bite even more seasonal appeal.

—**CAITLIN DAWSON** MONROE, OH

PREP: 15 MIN. + SOAKING • **GRILL:** 20 MIN.
MAKES: 4 SERVINGS

- 4 medium ears sweet corn
- 4 teaspoons butter, melted
- ¾ teaspoon salt
- ¼ teaspoon pepper
- 16 fresh basil leaves
- ½ medium lemon
- 2 teaspoons minced fresh cilantro

1. Place the corn in a 6-qt. stockpot; cover with cold water. Soak 20 minutes; drain. Carefully peel back corn husks to within 1 in. of bottoms; remove silk.

Brush butter over corn; sprinkle with salt and pepper. Press four basil leaves onto each cob. Rewrap corn in husks; secure with kitchen string.
2. Grill corn, covered, over medium heat 20-25 minutes or until tender, turning often. Cut the string and peel back the husks; discard basil leaves. Squeeze lemon juice over the corn; sprinkle with cilantro.
PER SERVING *125 cal., 5 g fat (3 g sat. fat), 10 mg chol., 489 mg sodium, 20 g carb., 2 g fiber, 4 g pro.* **Diabetic Exchanges:** *1 starch, 1 fat.*

EAT SMART FAST FIX ▶
Garden Tomato Salad

START TO FINISH: 15 MIN.
MAKES: 8 SERVINGS

- 3 large tomatoes, cut into wedges
- 1 large sweet onion, cut into thin wedges
- 1 large cucumber, sliced

DRESSING
- ¼ cup olive oil
- 2 tablespoons cider vinegar
- 1 garlic clove, minced
- 1 teaspoon minced fresh basil
- 1 teaspoon minced chives
- ½ teaspoon salt

In a large bowl, combine tomatoes, onion and cucumber. In a small bowl, whisk the dressing ingredients until blended. Drizzle over the salad; gently toss to coat. Serve immediately.
PER SERVING *1 cup equals 92 cal., 7 g fat (1 g sat. fat), 0 chol., 155 mg sodium, 7 g carb., 1 g fiber, 1 g pro.* **Diabetic Exchanges:** *1½ fat, 1 vegetable.*

FREEZE IT EAT SMART
Spinach & Feta Burgers

Ground turkey burgers have their fans, but we prefer these patties of lean ground beef mixed with spinach and feta cheese. They're great smothered with tzatziki sauce on toasted buns.

—**SUSAN STETZEL** GAINESVILLE, NY

PREP: 25 MIN. • **GRILL:** 15 MIN.
MAKES: 8 SERVINGS

- 1 tablespoon olive oil
- 2 shallots, chopped
- 2½ cups fresh baby spinach, coarsely chopped
- 3 garlic cloves, minced
- ⅔ cup crumbled feta cheese
- ¾ teaspoon Greek seasoning
- ½ teaspoon salt
- ¼ teaspoon pepper
- 2 pounds lean ground beef (90% lean)
- 8 whole wheat hamburger buns, split
  Optional toppings: refrigerated tzatziki sauce, fresh baby spinach and tomato slices

1. In a large skillet, heat the oil over medium-high heat. Add the shallots; cook and stir 1-2 minutes or until tender. Add the spinach and garlic; cook 30-45 seconds longer or until spinach is wilted. Transfer to a large bowl; cool slightly.

2. Stir the feta cheese and seasonings into the spinach. Add the beef; mix lightly but thoroughly. Shape into eight ½-in.-thick patties.

3. Grill the burgers, covered, over medium heat 6-8 minutes on each side or until a thermometer reads 160°. Grill buns over medium heat, cut side down, for 30-60 seconds or until toasted. Serve the burgers on buns with toppings if desired.

FREEZE OPTION *Place the patties on a plastic wrap-lined baking sheet; wrap and freeze until firm. Remove from pan and transfer to a resealable plastic freezer bag; return to freezer. To use, cook frozen patties as directed, increasing time as necessary for a thermometer to read 160°.*

PER SERVING *1 burger (calculated without optional toppings) equals 343 cal., 15 g fat (5 g sat. fat), 76 mg chol., 636 mg sodium, 25 g carb., 4 g fiber, 28 g pro. Diabetic Exchanges: 3 lean meat, 2 fat, 1½ starch.*

EAT SMART
Red Potato Salad with Lemony Vinaigrette

For healthier eating, we bypass the usual mayonnaise-based potato salads in favor of this one. Featuring red onion, Greek olives and a lemony vinaigrette, it doesn't sacrifice a bit of flavor.

—**ELIZABETH DEHART** WEST JORDAN, UT

PREP: 15 MIN. • **COOK:** 20 MIN. + CHILLING
MAKES: 12 SERVINGS (¾ CUP EACH)

- 3 pounds red potatoes, cubed (about 10 cups)
- ⅓ cup olive oil
- 2 tablespoons lemon juice
- 2 tablespoons red wine vinegar
- 1½ teaspoons salt
- ¼ teaspoon pepper
- 2 tablespoons minced fresh parsley
- 1 garlic clove, minced
- ½ teaspoon dried oregano
- ½ cup pitted Greek olives, chopped
- ⅓ cup chopped red onion
- ½ cup shredded Parmesan cheese

1. Place potatoes in a 6-qt. stockpot; add water to cover. Bring to a boil. Reduce the heat; cook, uncovered, 10-15 minutes or until tender. Drain; transfer to a large bowl.

2. In a small bowl, whisk oil, lemon juice, vinegar, salt and pepper until blended; stir in parsley, garlic and oregano. Drizzle over potatoes; toss to coat. Gently stir in olives and onion. Refrigerate, covered, at least 2 hours before serving.

3. Just before serving, stir in cheese.

PER SERVING *¾ cup equals 168 cal., 9 g fat (2 g sat. fat), 2 mg chol., 451 mg sodium, 20 g carb., 2 g fiber, 4 g pro. Diabetic Exchanges: 2 fat, 1½ starch.*

RED POTATO SALAD WITH LEMONY VINAIGRETTE

SPINACH & FETA BURGERS

SWEET & TANGY SALMON WITH GREEN BEANS

EAT SMART FAST FIX

Spicy Tomato Pork Chops

Pork simmered in tomato sauce is big at our house. Sometimes I sprinkle garlic powder or Creole seasoning, depending on what I have on hand, on the chops before browning them for extra zip.

—**HOLLY NEUHARTH** MESA, AZ

START TO FINISH: 30 MIN.
MAKES: 4 SERVINGS

- 1 tablespoon olive oil
- 4 boneless pork loin chops (5 ounces each)
- 1 large onion, chopped
- 1 can (8 ounces) tomato sauce
- ¼ cup water
- 2 teaspoons chili powder
- 1 teaspoon dried oregano
- 1 teaspoon Worcestershire sauce
- ½ teaspoon sugar
- ½ teaspoon crushed red pepper flakes

1. In a large skillet, heat the olive oil over medium heat. Brown the pork chops on both sides. Remove; keep warm. In same skillet, cook and stir onion until tender. Stir in remaining ingredients.
2. Return pork chops to the skillet. Bring to a boil. Reduce heat; simmer, covered, 15-20 minutes or until tender. Let stand 5 minutes before serving. Serve with sauce.
PER SERVING *1 chop with ⅓ cup sauce equals 257 cal., 12 g fat (3 g sat. fat), 68 mg chol., 328 mg sodium, 8 g carb., 2 g fiber, 29 g pro.* **Diabetic Exchanges:** *4 lean meat, 1 vegetable, 1 fat.*

EAT SMART
Sweet & Tangy Salmon with Green Beans

I'm always up for new ways to prepare salmon. In this recipe, a sweet sauce gives the fish and beans some barbecue tang. Even our kids love it!

—**ALIESHA CALDWELL** ROBERSONVILLE, NC

PREP: 20 MIN. • **BAKE:** 15 MIN.
MAKES: 4 SERVINGS

- 4 salmon fillets (6 ounces each)
- 1 tablespoon butter
- 2 tablespoons brown sugar
- 2 tablespoons reduced-sodium soy sauce
- 2 tablespoons Dijon mustard
- 1 tablespoon olive oil
- ½ teaspoon pepper
- ⅛ teaspoon salt
- 1 pound fresh green beans, trimmed

1. Preheat oven to 425°. Place fillets on a 15x10x1-in. baking pan coated with cooking spray. In a small skillet, melt butter; stir in brown sugar, soy sauce, mustard, oil, pepper and salt. Brush half of the mixture over salmon.

2. Place beans in a large bowl; drizzle with remaining brown sugar mixture and toss to coat. Arrange beans around fillets. Roast 14-16 minutes or until fish just begins to flake easily with a fork and green beans are crisp-tender.
PER SERVING *1 fillet with ¾ cup green beans equals 394 cal., 22 g fat (5 g sat. fat), 93 mg chol., 661 mg sodium, 17 g carb., 4 g fiber, 31 g pro.* **Diabetic Exchanges:** *5 lean meat, 1½ fat, 1 vegetable, ½ starch.*

Chunky Banana Cream Freeze

Indulge! Place 5 frozen peeled medium bananas, ⅓ cup almond milk, 2 tablespoons each finely shredded unsweetened coconut and creamy peanut butter, and 1 teaspoon vanilla extract in a food processor; cover and process until blended. Transfer to a freezer container; stir in ¼ cup chopped walnuts and 3 tablespoons raisins. Freeze for 2-4 hours before serving. *Makes 6 servings.*

—**KRISTEN BLOOM** APO, AP

ARTICHOKE
RATATOUILLE
CHICKEN

Artichoke Ratatouille Chicken

I loaded every fresh veggie I could find into my colorful chicken dish. Serve it by itself or over a bed of pasta.

—**JUDY ARMSTRONG** PRAIRIEVILLE, LA

PREP: 25 MIN. • **BAKE:** 1 HOUR
MAKES: 6 SERVINGS

- 3 **Japanese eggplants (about 1 pound)**
- 4 **plum tomatoes**
- 1 **medium sweet yellow pepper**
- 1 **medium sweet red pepper**
- 1 **medium onion**
- 1 **can (14 ounces) water-packed artichoke hearts, drained and quartered**
- 2 **tablespoons minced fresh thyme**
- 2 **tablespoons capers, drained**
- 2 **tablespoons olive oil**
- 2 **garlic cloves, minced**
- 1 **teaspoon Creole seasoning, divided**
- 1½ **pounds boneless skinless chicken breasts, cubed**

- 1 **cup white wine or chicken broth**
- ¼ **cup grated Asiago cheese**
  Hot cooked pasta, optional

1. Preheat oven to 350°. Cut the eggplants, tomatoes, peppers and onion into ¾-in. pieces; transfer to a large bowl. Stir in artichoke hearts, thyme, capers, olive oil, garlic and ½ teaspoon Creole seasoning.
2. Sprinkle chicken with remaining Creole seasoning. Transfer chicken to a 13x9-in. baking dish coated with cooking spray; spoon the vegetable mixture over the top. Drizzle wine over vegetables.
3. Bake, covered, 30 minutes. Uncover; bake 30-45 minutes longer or until the chicken is no longer pink and the vegetables are tender. Sprinkle with cheese. If desired, serve with pasta.
PER SERVING *1⅔ cups (calculated without pasta) equals 252 cal., 9 g fat (2 g sat. fat), 67 mg chol., 468 mg sodium, 15 g carb., 4 g fiber, 28 g pro.*
***Diabetic Exchanges:** 3 lean meat, 1 starch, 1 fat.*

Vanilla Meringue Cookies

These sweet little swirls are light as can be. They're all you need after a hearty dinner.

—**JENNI SHARP** MILWAUKEE, WI

PREP: 20 MIN. • **BAKE:** 40 MIN. + STANDING
MAKES: ABOUT 5 DOZEN

- 3 **large egg whites**
- 1½ **teaspoons clear or regular vanilla extract**
- ¼ **teaspoon cream of tartar**
  Dash salt
- ⅔ **cup sugar**

1. Place egg whites in a small bowl; let stand at room temperature 30 minutes.
2. Preheat oven to 250°. Add vanilla, cream of tartar and salt to egg whites; beat on medium speed until foamy. Gradually add the sugar, 1 tablespoon at a time, beating on high after each addition until the sugar is dissolved. Continue beating until stiff glossy peaks form, about 7 minutes.
3. Cut a small hole in the tip of a pastry bag or in a corner of a food-safe plastic bag; insert a #32 star tip. Transfer the meringue to bag. Pipe 1¼-in.-diameter cookies 2 in. apart onto parchment paper-lined baking sheets.
4. Bake 40-45 minutes or until firm to the touch. Turn off the oven (do not open oven door); leave the cookies in oven 1 hour. Remove from oven; cool completely on baking sheets. Remove cookies from paper; store in an airtight container at room temperature.
PER SERVING *1 cookie equals 10 cal., trace fat (0 sat. fat), 0 chol., 5 mg sodium, 2 g carb., 0 fiber, trace pro.*
***Diabetic Exchange:** Free food.*

VANILLA MERINGUE COOKIES

EAT SMART
Pan-Roasted Chicken and Vegetables

Here's a one-dish meal that tastes like it requires hours of prep work but takes just 15 minutes to get into the oven.

—SHERRI MELOTIK OAK CREEK, WI

PREP: 15 MIN. • **BAKE:** 45 MIN.
MAKES: 6 SERVINGS

- 2 **pounds red potatoes (about 6 medium), cut into ¾-inch pieces**
- 1 **large onion, coarsely chopped**
- 2 **tablespoons olive oil**
- 3 **garlic cloves, minced**
- 1¼ **teaspoons salt, divided**
- 1 **teaspoon dried rosemary, crushed, divided**
- ¾ **teaspoon pepper, divided**
- ½ **teaspoon paprika**
- 6 **bone-in chicken thighs (about 2¼ pounds), skin removed**
- 6 **cups fresh baby spinach (about 6 ounces)**

1. Preheat oven to 425°. In a large bowl, combine red potatoes, onion, olive oil, garlic, ¾ teaspoon salt, ½ teaspoon rosemary and ½ teaspoon pepper; toss to coat. Transfer to a 15x10x1-in. baking pan coated with cooking spray.
2. In a small bowl, the mix paprika and the remaining salt, rosemary and pepper. Sprinkle the chicken with the paprika mixture; arrange over the vegetables. Roast 35-40 minutes or until a thermometer inserted in the chicken reads 170°-175° and the vegetables are just tender.
3. Remove the chicken to a serving platter; keep warm. Top vegetables with spinach. Roast 8-10 minutes longer or until vegetables are tender and spinach is wilted. Stir vegetables to combine; serve with chicken.

PER SERVING *1 chicken thigh with 1 cup vegetables equals 357 cal., 14 g fat (3 g sat. fat), 87 mg chol., 597 mg sodium, 28 g carb., 4 g fiber, 28 g pro. Diabetic Exchanges: 4 lean meat, 1½ starch, 1 vegetable, 1 fat.*

HONEY-YOGURT BERRY SALAD

EAT SMART FAST FIX
Honey-Yogurt Berry Salad

I wanted my family to eat more fruit but not more sugary ingredients. So I began mixing fresh berries with plain yogurt, a little citrus and a touch of honey.

—BETSY KING DULUTH, MN

START TO FINISH: 10 MIN.
MAKES: 8 SERVINGS

- 1½ **cups sliced fresh strawberries**
- 1½ **cups fresh raspberries**
- 1½ **cups fresh blueberries**
- 1½ **cups fresh blackberries**
- 1 **cup (8 ounces) reduced-fat plain yogurt**
- 1 **tablespoon honey**
- ¼ **teaspoon grated orange peel**
- 1 **tablespoon orange juice**

In a 2-qt. glass bowl, gently mix the strawberries, raspberries, blueberries and blackberries. In a small bowl, mix yogurt, honey, orange peel and juice until blended. Just before serving, pour over berries.

PER SERVING *¾ cup equals 76 cal., 1 g fat (trace sat. fat), 2 mg chol., 23 mg sodium, 16 g carb., 4 g fiber, 3 g pro. Diabetic Exchange: 1 fruit.*

EAT SMART FAST FIX
Southwestern Sauteed Corn

My mother-in-law came up with this side dish one night for dinner. Everyone who tries it wants a second scoop.

—CHANDY WARD AUMSVILLE, OR

START TO FINISH: 20 MIN.
MAKES: 5 SERVINGS

- 1 **tablespoon butter**
- 3⅓ **cups fresh corn or 1 package (16 ounces) frozen corn**
- 1 **plum tomato, chopped**
- 1 **tablespoon lime juice**
- ½ **teaspoon salt**
- ½ **teaspoon ground cumin**
- ⅓ **cup minced fresh cilantro**

In a large nonstick skillet, heat butter over medium-high heat. Add corn; cook and stir 3-5 minutes or until tender. Reduce heat to medium-low; stir in the tomato, lime juice, salt and cumin. Cook 3-4 minutes longer or until heated through. Remove from heat; stir in cilantro.

PER SERVING *⅔ cup equals 104 cal., 3 g fat (2 g sat. fat), 6 mg chol., 256 mg sodium, 20 g carb., 2 g fiber, 3 g pro. Diabetic Exchanges: 1 starch, ½ fat.*

Pan-Roasted Salmon with Cherry Tomatoes

It sounds basic, but the chunky tomato sauce in this recipe is delicious. If I have white wine, I use that instead of chicken broth. The salmon fillets are great with asparagus — roast it alongside the fish.

—SWATI SHARAN HORSEHEADS, NY

START TO FINISH: 30 MIN.
MAKES: 4 SERVINGS

- 2 **cups cherry tomatoes, halved**
- 1 **tablespoon olive oil**
- ¼ **teaspoon kosher salt**
- ¼ **teaspoon pepper**

SALMON

- 4 **salmon fillets (6 ounces each)**
- ½ **teaspoon kosher salt**
- ¼ **teaspoon pepper**
- 1 **tablespoon olive oil**
- 2 **garlic cloves, minced**
- ¾ **cup reduced-sodium chicken broth**

1. Preheat oven to 425°. Place the cherry tomato halves in a foil-lined 15x10x1-in. baking pan. Drizzle with olive oil; sprinkle with salt and pepper. Toss to coat. Roast 10-15 minutes or until tomatoes are softened, stirring occasionally.

2. Meanwhile, sprinkle the fillets with salt and pepper. In a large ovenproof skillet, heat the oil over medium-high heat. Add the fillets; cook 3 minutes on each side. Remove from pan.

3. Add the garlic to pan; cook and stir 1 minute. Add broth, stirring to loosen browned bits from pan. Bring to a boil; cook 1-2 minutes or until the liquid is reduced by half. Stir in the roasted tomatoes; return the salmon to pan. Bake 5-7 minutes or until fish just begins to flake easily with a fork.

PER SERVING *1 fillet with 2 tablespoons tomato mixture equals 343 cal., 23 g fat (4 g sat. fat), 85 mg chol., 556 mg sodium, 4 g carb., 1 g fiber, 30 g pro. Diabetic Exchanges: 5 lean meat, 1½ fat, 1 vegetable.*

EAT SMART

Grilled Southwestern Steak Salad

Unlike me, my boyfriend isn't big on salads. Tossing in steak makes us both happy!

—YVONNE STARLIN HERMITAGE, TN

PREP: 25 MIN. • **GRILL:** 20 MIN.
MAKES: 4 SERVINGS

- 1 **beef top sirloin steak (1 inch thick and ¾ pound)**
- ¼ **teaspoon salt**
- ¼ **teaspoon ground cumin**
- ¼ **teaspoon pepper**
- 3 **poblano peppers, halved and seeded**
- 2 **large ears sweet corn, husks removed**
- 1 **large sweet onion, cut into ½-inch rings**
- 1 **tablespoon olive oil**
- 2 **cups uncooked multigrain bow tie pasta**
- 2 **large tomatoes**

DRESSING

- ¼ **cup lime juice**
- 1 **tablespoon olive oil**
- ¼ **teaspoon salt**
- ¼ **teaspoon ground cumin**
- ¼ **teaspoon pepper**
- ⅓ **cup chopped fresh cilantro**

1. Rub steak with salt, cumin and pepper. Brush poblano peppers, corn and onion with oil. Grill steak, covered, over medium heat or broil 4 in. from heat 6-8 minutes on each side or until meat reaches desired doneness (for medium-rare, a thermometer should read 145°; medium, 160°; well-done, 170°). Grill the vegetables, covered, 8-10 minutes or until crisp-tender, turning occasionally.

2. Cook pasta according to package directions. Meanwhile, cut corn from cob; coarsely chop peppers, onion and tomatoes. Transfer vegetables to a large bowl. In a small bowl, whisk lime juice, oil, salt, cumin and pepper until blended; stir in cilantro.

3. Drain pasta; add to the vegetables. Drizzle with the dressing; toss to coat. Cut steak into thin slices; add to salad.

PER SERVING *2 cups pasta mixture with 2 ounces cooked beef equals 456 cal., 13 g fat (3 g sat. fat), 34 mg chol., 378 mg sodium, 58 g carb., 8 g fiber, 30 g pro.*

PAN-ROASTED SALMON WITH CHERRY TOMATOES

DID YOU KNOW?

The heat-producing element in hot peppers is capsaicin. It is concentrated in the seeds and white membranes. Removing the seeds and trimming the membranes will lessen the heat.

EAT SMART
Parmesan Chicken with Artichoke Hearts

Chicken is endlessly versatile, and one of my favorite ways to prepare it is with artichokes. I add plenty of seasonings, Parmesan cheese and a lemony twist.

—**CARLY GILES** HOPUIAM, WA

PREP: 20 MIN. • **BAKE:** 20 MIN.
MAKES: 4 SERVINGS

- 4 **boneless skinless chicken breast halves (6 ounces each)**
- 3 **teaspoons olive oil, divided**
- 1 **teaspoon dried rosemary, crushed**
- ½ **teaspoon dried thyme**
- ½ **teaspoon pepper**
- 2 **cans (14 ounces each) water-packed artichoke hearts, drained and quartered**
- 1 **medium onion, coarsely chopped**
- ½ **cup white wine or reduced-sodium chicken broth**
- 2 **garlic cloves, chopped**
- ¼ **cup shredded Parmesan cheese**
- 1 **lemon, cut into 8 slices**
- 2 **green onions, thinly sliced**

1. Preheat oven to 375°. Place the chicken in a 15x10x1-in. baking pan coated with cooking spray; drizzle with 1½ teaspoons oil. In a small bowl, mix rosemary, thyme and pepper; sprinkle half over chicken.
2. In a large bowl, combine artichoke hearts, onion, white wine, garlic and the remaining oil and herb mixture; toss to coat. Arrange around chicken. Sprinkle chicken with cheese; top with lemon slices.
3. Roast 20-25 minutes or until a thermometer inserted in chicken reads 165°. Sprinkle with green onions.
PER SERVING *1 chicken breast half with ¾ cup artichoke mixture equals 339 cal., 9 g fat (3 g sat. fat), 98 mg chol., 667 mg sodium, 18 g carb., 1 g fiber, 42 g pro.* ***Diabetic Exchanges:*** *5 lean meat, 1 vegetable, 1 fat, ½ starch.*

EAT SMART
Orange-Glazed Pork with Sweet Potatoes

Warm up those chilly autumn or winter evenings with a pork tenderloin dinner. Sweet potatoes, tangy fruit and spices make it even more comforting.

—**DANIELLE LEE BOYLES** WESTON, WI

PREP: 20 MIN. • **BAKE:** 55 MIN. + STANDING
MAKES: 6 SERVINGS

- 1 **pound sweet potatoes (about 2 medium)**
- 2 **medium apples**
- 1 **medium orange**
- 1 **teaspoon salt**
- ½ **teaspoon pepper**
- 1 **cup orange juice**
- 2 **tablespoons brown sugar**
- 2 **teaspoons cornstarch**
- 1 **teaspoon ground cinnamon**
- 1 **teaspoon ground ginger**
- 2 **pork tenderloins (about 1 pound each)**

1. Preheat oven to 350°. Peel the sweet potatoes; core the apples. Cut potatoes, apples and orange crosswise into ¼-in.-thick slices. Arrange on a foil-lined 15x10x1-in. baking pan coated with cooking spray; sprinkle with salt and pepper. Roast 10 minutes.
2. Meanwhile, in a microwave-safe bowl, mix orange juice, brown sugar, cornstarch, cinnamon and ginger. Microwave, covered, on high for 1-2 minutes or until thickened, stirring every 30 seconds. Stir until smooth.
3. Place pork tenderloins over sweet potato mixture; drizzle with orange juice mixture. Roast 45-55 minutes longer or until a thermometer inserted in pork reads 145° and sweet potatoes and apples are tender. Remove from the oven; tent with foil. Let stand 10 minutes before slicing.
PER SERVING *4 ounces cooked pork with about 1 cup sweet potato mixture equals 325 cal., 5 g fat (2 g sat. fat), 85 mg chol., 467 mg sodium, 36 g carb., 3 g fiber, 32 g pro.* ***Diabetic Exchanges:*** *4 lean meat, 2 starch.*

EAT SMART
Spicy Roasted Sausage, Potatoes and Peppers

I love to share what I cook, and this hearty meal has quite a reputation around our town. People have actually approached me in public to ask for the recipe!

—**LAURIE SLEDGE** BRANDON, MS

PREP: 20 MIN. • **BAKE:** 30 MIN.
MAKES: 4 SERVINGS

- 1 **pound potatoes (about 2 medium), peeled and cut into ½-inch cubes**
- 1 **package (12 ounces) fully cooked andouille chicken sausage links or flavor of your choice, cut into 1-inch pieces**
- 1 **medium red onion, cut into wedges**
- 1 **medium sweet red pepper, cut into 1-inch pieces**
- 1 **medium green pepper, cut into 1-inch pieces**
- ½ **cup pickled pepper rings**
- 1 **tablespoon olive oil**
- ½ **to 1 teaspoon Creole seasoning**
- ¼ **teaspoon pepper**

1. Preheat oven to 400°. In a large bowl, combine the potatoes, andouille chicken sausage, onion, red pepper, green pepper and pickled pepper rings. Mix the olive oil, Creole seasoning and pepper; drizzle over potato mixture and toss to coat.
2. Transfer to a 15x10x1-in. baking pan coated with cooking spray. Roast 30-35 minutes or until vegetables are tender, stirring occasionally.
PER SERVING *1½ cups equals 257 cal., 11 g fat (3 g sat. fat), 65 mg chol., 759 mg sodium, 24 g carb., 3 g fiber, 17 g pro.* ***Diabetic Exchanges:*** *3 lean meat, 1 starch, 1 vegetable, 1 fat.*

TOP TIP

Don't have any Creole seasoning? Use common spices to make a tasty stand-in! The following spices may be substituted for 1 teaspoon Creole seasoning: ¼ teaspoon each salt, garlic powder and paprika; and a pinch each of dried thyme, ground cumin and cayenne pepper.

PARMESAN CHICKEN WITH
ARTICHOKE HEARTS

ORANGE-GLAZED PORK
WITH SWEET POTATOES

SPICY ROASTED SAUSAGE,
POTATOES AND PEPPERS

GOLDEN ZUCCHINI PANCAKES

GARLIC-HERB PATTYPAN SQUASH

EAT SMART
Golden Zucchini Pancakes

If you grow lots of zucchini, shred some to make these scrumptious golden brown cakes. You'll be glad you did! Flavored with minced garlic and oregano, the savory green-flecked pancakes are great dipped in warm marinara sauce.

—**TERRY ANN DOMINGUEZ** SILVER CITY, NM

PREP: 15 MIN. • **COOK:** 10 MIN./BATCH
MAKES: 8 ZUCCHINI PANCAKES

- 3 cups shredded zucchini
- 2 large eggs
- 2 garlic cloves, minced
- ¾ teaspoon salt
- ½ teaspoon pepper
- ¼ teaspoon dried oregano
- ½ cup all-purpose flour
- ½ cup finely chopped sweet onion
- 1 tablespoon butter
  Marinara sauce, warmed, optional

1. Place the zucchini in a colander to drain; squeeze well to remove excess liquid. Pat dry.
2. In a large bowl, whisk eggs, garlic, salt, pepper and oregano until blended. Stir in the flour just until moistened. Fold in zucchini and onion.
3. Lightly grease a griddle with the butter; heat over medium heat. Drop zucchini mixture by ¼ cupfuls onto the griddle; flatten to ½-in. thickness (3-in. diameter). Cook 4-5 minutes on each side or until golden brown. If desired, serve with marinara sauce.
PER SERVING *145 cal., 6 g fat (3 g sat. fat), 101 mg chol., 510 mg sodium, 18 g carb., 2 g fiber, 6 g pro.* **Diabetic Exchanges:** *1 starch, 1 fat.*

EAT SMART ⑤ INGREDIENTS FAST FIX
Garlic-Herb Pattypan Squash

I made this side dish with summer squash the first time I had a garden. Substituting pattypan squash works beautifully, too.

—**KAYCEE MASON** SILOAM SPRINGS, AR

START TO FINISH: 25 MIN.
MAKES: 4 SERVINGS

- 5 cups halved small pattypan squash (about 1¼ pounds)
- 1 tablespoon olive oil
- 2 garlic cloves, minced
- ½ teaspoon salt
- ¼ teaspoon dried oregano
- ¼ teaspoon dried thyme
- ¼ teaspoon pepper
- 1 tablespoon minced fresh parsley

Preheat oven to 425°. Place squash in a greased 15x10x1-in. baking pan. Mix the oil, garlic, salt, oregano, thyme and pepper; drizzle over the squash. Toss to coat. Roast 15-20 minutes or until tender, stirring occasionally. Sprinkle with parsley.
PER SERVING *58 cal., 3 g fat (trace sat. fat), 0 chol., 296 mg sodium, 6 g carb., 2 g fiber, 2 g pro.* **Diabetic Exchanges:** *1 vegetable, ½ fat.*

Fresh Berries with Lemon Yogurt

Here's a wonderful breakfast or dessert. In a small bowl, combine 2 cups sliced fresh strawberries, 1 sliced medium banana, 1 cup blueberries, ¼ cup limoncello and 1 tablespoon sugar; spoon into four dessert dishes. Whisk together ¾ cup plain yogurt and 3 tablespoons lemon curd; spoon over the fruit. *Makes 4 servings.*

—**SARAH VASQUES** MILFORD, NH

FRESH CORN &
POTATO CHOWDER

EAT SMART **SLOW COOKER**

Slow Cooker Beef Tips

With my busy schedule, I rely on a slow cooker all the time. I like to cook beef tips with portobellos and onion, then serve it all over mashed potatoes, rice or noodles.

—**AMY LENTS** GRAND FORKS, ND

PREP: 25 MIN. • **COOK:** 6¼ HOURS
MAKES: 4 SERVINGS

- ½ pound sliced baby portobello mushrooms
- 1 small onion, halved and sliced
- 1 beef top sirloin steak (1 pound), cubed
- ½ teaspoon salt
- ¼ teaspoon pepper
- 2 teaspoons olive oil
- ⅓ cup dry red wine or beef broth
- 2 cups beef broth
- 1 tablespoon Worcestershire sauce
- 2 tablespoons cornstarch
- ¼ cup cold water
  Hot cooked mashed potatoes

1. Place the mushrooms and onion in a 3-qt. slow cooker. Sprinkle beef with salt and pepper. In a large skillet, heat 1 teaspoon oil over medium-high heat; brown meat in batches, adding additional oil as needed. Transfer the meat to slow cooker.
2. Add the red wine to skillet, stirring to loosen browned bits from the pan. Stir in broth and Worcestershire sauce; pour over meat. Cook, covered, on low 6-8 hours or until meat is tender.
3. In a small bowl, mix the cornstarch and cold water until smooth; gradually stir into slow cooker. Cook, covered, on high 15-30 minutes or until gravy is thickened. Serve with the mashed potatoes.
PER SERVING *1 cup (calculated without mashed potatoes) equals 212 cal., 7 g fat (2 g sat. fat), 46 mg chol., 836 mg sodium, 8 g carb., 1 g fiber, 27 g pro. **Diabetic Exchanges:** 3 lean meat, ½ starch, ½ fat.*

EAT SMART
Fresh Corn & Potato Chowder

I've loved this tasty chowder ever since I was a child living in upstate New York.

—**TRACY BIVINS** KNOB NOSTER, MO

PREP: 15 MIN. • **COOK:** 25 MIN.
MAKES: 6 SERVINGS

- 1 tablespoon butter
- 1 medium onion, chopped
- 1 pound red potatoes (about 3 medium), cubed
- 1½ cups fresh or frozen corn (about 7 ounces)
- 3 cups reduced-sodium chicken broth
- 1¼ cups half-and-half cream, divided
- 2 green onions, thinly sliced
- ½ teaspoon salt
- ¼ teaspoon freshly ground pepper
- 3 tablespoons all-purpose flour
- 1 tablespoon minced fresh parsley

1. In a large saucepan, heat butter over medium-high heat. Add onion; cook and stir 2-4 minutes or until tender. Add potatoes, corn, broth, 1 cup half-and-half cream, green onions, salt and pepper; bring to a boil. Reduce the heat; simmer, covered, 12-15 minutes or until potatoes are tender.
2. In a small bowl, mix the flour and remaining half-and-half cream until smooth; stir into the soup. Return to a boil, stirring constantly; cook and stir 1-2 minutes or until slightly thickened. Stir in parsley.
PER SERVING *200 cal., 8 g fat (5 g sat. fat), 30 mg chol., 534 mg sodium, 26 g carb., 3 g fiber, 7 g pro. **Diabetic Exchanges:** 2 starch, 1½ fat.*

ITALIAN SAUSAGE AND
PROVOLONE SKEWERS

TARRAGON
ASPARAGUS

When we
didn't have
the buns for
our usual
sandwiches,
my husband improvised
and came up with a new
favorite—Italian Sausage
and Provolone Skewers.
—CINDY HILLIARD KENOSHA, WI

EAT SMART FAST FIX
Italian Sausage and Provolone Skewers

START TO FINISH: 30 MIN.
MAKES: 8 SERVINGS

- 1 **large onion**
- 1 **large sweet red pepper**
- 1 **large green pepper**
- 2 **cups cherry tomatoes**
- 1 **tablespoon olive oil**
- ½ **teaspoon pepper**
- ¼ **teaspoon salt**
- 2 **packages (12 ounces each) fully cooked Italian chicken sausage links, cut into 1¼-inch slices**
- 16 **cubes provolone cheese (¾ inch each)**

1. Cut the onion and peppers into 1-in. pieces; place in a large bowl. Add tomatoes, oil, pepper and salt; toss to coat. On 16 metal or soaked wooden skewers, alternately thread sausage and vegetables.
2. Grill, covered, over medium heat 8-10 minutes or until sausage is heated through and vegetables are tender, turning occasionally. Remove kabobs from the grill; thread one cheese cube onto each kabob.
PER SERVING *2 kabobs equals 220 cal., 13 g fat (5 g sat. fat), 75 mg chol., 682 mg sodium, 7 g carb., 2 g fiber, 20 g pro.* ***Diabetic Exchanges:*** *3 medium-fat meat, 1 vegetable.*

EAT SMART ⑤INGREDIENTS FAST FIX
Tarragon Asparagus

I grow purple asparagus and am always trying to fit it into my cooking. While experimenting, I discovered how good any type of asparagus is when grilled.
—SUE GRONHOLZ BEAVER DAM, WI

START TO FINISH: 15 MIN.
MAKES: 8 SERVINGS

- 2 **pounds fresh asparagus, trimmed**
- 2 **tablespoons olive oil**
- 1 **teaspoon salt**
- ½ **teaspoon pepper**
- ¼ **cup honey**
- 2 **to 4 tablespoons minced fresh tarragon**

On a large plate, toss the asparagus with the olive oil, salt and pepper. Grill, covered, over medium heat 6-8 minutes or until crisp-tender, turning occasionally and basting frequently with honey during the last 3 minutes. Sprinkle with the minced tarragon.
PER SERVING *76 cal., 4 g fat (1 g sat. fat), 0 chol., 302 mg sodium, 11 g carb., 1 g fiber, 2 g pro.* ***Diabetic Exchanges:*** *1 vegetable, ½ starch, ½ fat.*

CHICKEN TACOS WITH AVOCADO SALSA

Triple Tomato Flatbread

Tomatoes are the main reason I keep a vegetable garden. I created this fun and easy flatbread, which uses pizza dough, to showcase the different varieties I have.

—**RACHEL KIMBROW** PORTLAND, OR

START TO FINISH: 20 MIN.
MAKES: 8 PIECES

- 1 tube (13.8 ounces) refrigerated pizza crust
  Cooking spray
- 3 plum tomatoes, finely chopped (about 2 cups)
- ½ cup soft sun-dried tomato halves (not packed in oil), julienned
- 2 tablespoons olive oil
- 1 tablespoon dried basil
- ¼ teaspoon salt
- ¼ teaspoon pepper
- 1 cup shredded Asiago cheese
- 2 cups yellow and/or red cherry tomatoes, halved

1. Unroll and press the dough into a 15x10-in. rectangle. Transfer dough to an 18x12-in. piece of heavy-duty foil coated with cooking spray; spritz the dough with cooking spray. In a large bowl, toss the plum tomatoes and sun-dried tomatoes with the olive oil and seasonings.
2. Carefully invert the dough onto grill rack; remove foil. Grill, covered, over medium heat 2-3 minutes or until the bottom is golden brown. Turn; grill 1-2 minutes longer or until second side begins to brown.
3. Remove from grill. Spoon the plum tomato mixture over crust; top with cheese and cherry tomatoes. Return the flatbread to the grill. Grill, covered, 2-4 minutes or until the crust is golden brown and the cheese is melted.
PER SERVING *235 cal., 9 g fat (3 g sat. fat), 12 mg chol., 476 mg sodium, 29 g carb., 3 g fiber, 8 g pro. Diabetic Exchanges: 1½ starch, 1½ fat, 1 vegetable.*

Chicken Tacos with Avocado Salsa

My family has special dietary needs, and these zesty tacos suit everyone. For extra toppings, pile on jalapeno peppers, black olives, cilantro, onion or lettuce.

—**CHRISTINE SCHENHER** EXETER, CA

START TO FINISH: 30 MIN.
MAKES: 4 SERVINGS

- 1 pound boneless skinless chicken breasts, cut into ½-inch strips
- ⅓ cup water
- 1 teaspoon sugar
- 1 tablespoon chili powder
- 1 teaspoon onion powder
- 1 teaspoon dried oregano
- 1 teaspoon ground cumin
- 1 teaspoon paprika
- ½ teaspoon salt
- ½ teaspoon garlic powder
- 1 medium ripe avocado, peeled and cubed
- 1 cup fresh or frozen corn, thawed
- 1 cup cherry tomatoes, quartered
- 2 teaspoons lime juice
- 8 taco shells, warmed

1. Place a large nonstick skillet coated with cooking spray over medium-high heat. Brown chicken. Add water, sugar and seasonings. Cook 4-5 minutes or until chicken is no longer pink, stirring occasionally.
2. Meanwhile, in a small bowl, gently mix avocado, corn, tomatoes and lime juice. Spoon chicken mixture into taco shells; top with avocado salsa.
FREEZE OPTION *Freeze the cooled meat mixture in freezer containers. To use, partially thaw in refrigerator overnight. Heat through in a saucepan, stirring occasionally and adding a little water if necessary.*
PER SERVING *2 tacos equals 354 cal., 15 g fat (3 g sat. fat), 63 mg chol., 474 mg sodium, 30 g carb., 6 g fiber, 27 g pro. Diabetic Exchanges: 3 lean meat, 2 starch, 1 fat.*

EAT SMART FAST FIX

Corn, Rice & Bean Burritos

Stuff burritos with cheese, veggies and rice for a meatless meal everyone will enjoy.

—**SHARON BICKETT** CHESTER, SC

START TO FINISH: 30 MIN.
MAKES: 8 SERVINGS

- 1 tablespoon canola oil
- 1⅓ cups fresh or frozen corn, thawed
- 1 medium onion, chopped
- 1 medium green pepper, sliced
- 2 garlic cloves, minced
- 1½ teaspoons chili powder
- ½ teaspoon ground cumin
- 1 can (15 ounces) black beans, rinsed and drained
- 1½ cups cooked brown rice
- 8 flour tortillas (8 inches), warmed
- ¾ cup shredded reduced-fat cheddar cheese
- ½ cup reduced-fat plain yogurt
- 2 green onions, sliced
- ½ cup salsa

1. In a large skillet, heat the oil over medium-high heat. Add corn, onion and pepper; cook and stir until tender. Add garlic, chili powder and cumin; cook 1 minute longer. Add beans and rice; heat through.

2. Spoon ½ cup filling across center of each tortilla; top with cheese, yogurt and green onions. Fold the bottom and sides of tortilla over filling and roll up. Serve with salsa.

PER SERVING *1 burrito with 1 tablespoon salsa equals 326 cal., 8 g fat (2 g sat. fat), 8 mg chol., 500 mg sodium, 52 g carb., 4 g fiber, 13 g pro.*

CORN, RICE & BEAN BURRITOS

TURKEY SAUSAGE ZUCCHINI BOATS

EAT SMART

Turkey Sausage Zucchini Boats

When I worked in a school library, I would bring food for my co-workers to taste-test. They raved about this recipe.

—**STEPHANIE COTTERMAN**
WEST ALEXNDRA, OH

PREP: 30 MIN. • **BAKE:** 35 MIN.
MAKES: 6 SERVINGS

- 6 medium zucchini
- 1 pound lean ground turkey
- 1 small onion, chopped
- 1 celery rib, chopped
- 1 garlic clove, minced
- 1½ teaspoons Italian seasoning
- ¾ teaspoon salt
- ¼ teaspoon cayenne pepper
- ¼ teaspoon paprika
- 1 cup salad croutons, coarsely crushed
- 1 cup (4 ounces) shredded part-skim mozzarella cheese, divided

1. Preheat oven to 350°. Cut each zucchini lengthwise in half. Scoop out the pulp, leaving a ¼-in. shell; chop the pulp.

2. In a large skillet, cook the turkey, onion, celery, garlic and seasonings over medium heat 6-8 minutes or until turkey is no longer pink, breaking up turkey into crumbles. Stir in crushed salad croutons, ½ cup mozzarella cheese and zucchini pulp. Spoon into the zucchini shells.

3. Transfer shells to two ungreased 13x9-in. baking dishes; add ¼ in. water. Bake, covered, 30-35 minutes or until zucchini is tender. Sprinkle with the remaining cheese. Bake, uncovered, about 5 minutes or until cheese is melted.

PER SERVING *2 stuffed zucchini halves equals 240 cal., 11 g fat (4 g sat. fat), 63 mg chol., 556 mg sodium, 13 g carb., 2 g fiber, 23 g pro.* **Diabetic Exchanges:** *3 lean meat, 1 vegetable, ½ starch.*

Pan-Roasted Pork Chops & Potatoes

A one-ingredient marinade—Italian salad dressing—gives these pork chops plenty of flavor, and a crumb coating packs on the crunch. Brussels sprouts and potatoes make a complete dinner.

—**CHAR OUELLETTE** COLTON, OR

PREP: 20 MIN. + MARINATING
BAKE: 40 MIN. • **MAKES:** 4 SERVINGS

- 4 **boneless pork loin chops (6 ounces each)**
- ½ **cup plus 2 tablespoons reduced-fat Italian salad dressing, divided**
- 4 **small potatoes (about 1½ pounds)**
- ½ **pound fresh Brussels sprouts, trimmed and halved**
- ½ **cup soft bread crumbs**
- 1 **tablespoon minced fresh parsley**
- ¼ **teaspoon salt**
- ⅛ **teaspoon pepper**
- 2 **teaspoons butter, melted**

1. Place pork and ½ cup dressing in a large resealable plastic bag; seal bag and turn to coat. Refrigerate 8 hours or overnight. Cover and refrigerate remaining dressing.

2. Preheat oven to 400°. Cut each potato lengthwise into 12 wedges. Arrange the potatoes and Brussels sprouts on a 15x10x1-in. baking pan coated with cooking spray. Drizzle vegetables with remaining dressing; toss to coat. Roast 20 minutes.

3. Drain pork, discarding marinade. Pat pork dry with paper towel. Stir the vegetables; place pork over the top. Roast 15-20 minutes longer or until a thermometer inserted in pork reads 145°. Preheat broiler.

4. In a small bowl, combine the bread crumbs, parsley, salt and pepper; stir in butter. Top pork with crumb mixture. Broil 4-6 in. from heat 1-2 minutes or until bread crumbs are golden brown. Let stand 5 minutes.

NOTE *To make soft bread crumbs, tear bread into pieces and place in a food processor or blender. Cover and pulse until crumbs form. One slice of bread yields ½ to ¾ cup crumbs.*

PER SERVING *1 pork chop with 1 cup vegetables equals 451 cal., 16 g fat (5 g sat. fat), 87 mg chol., 492 mg sodium, 38 g carb., 5 g fiber, 38 g pro.* **Diabetic Exchanges:** *5 lean meat, 2½ starch, 2 fat.*

Roasted Curried Chickpeas and Cauliflower

Want to skip the meat? Enjoy a nutritious, warm-from-the-oven pan of goodness.

—**PAM CORRELL** BROCKPORT, PA

PREP: 15 MIN. • **BAKE:** 35 MIN.
MAKES: 4 SERVINGS

- 2 **pounds potatoes (about 4 medium), peeled and cut into ½-inch cubes**
- 1 **small head cauliflower, broken into florets (about 3 cups)**
- 1 **can (15 ounces) chickpeas or garbanzo beans, rinsed and drained**
- 3 **tablespoons olive oil**
- 2 **teaspoons curry powder**
- ¾ **teaspoon salt**
- ¼ **teaspoon pepper**
- 3 **tablespoons minced fresh cilantro or parsley**

1. Preheat oven to 400°. In a large bowl, combine potatoes, cauliflower, chickpeas, oil, curry powder, salt and pepper; toss to coat.

2. Transfer to a 15x10x1-in. baking pan coated with cooking spray. Roast 35-40 minutes or until vegetables are tender, stirring occasionally. Sprinkle with cilantro.

PER SERVING *1½ cups equals 339 cal., 13 g fat (2 g sat. fat), 0 chol., 605 mg sodium, 51 g carb., 8 g fiber, 8 g pro.* **Diabetic Exchanges:** *3 starch, 2 fat, 1 lean meat, 1 vegetable.*

PAN-ROASTED PORK CHOPS & POTATOES

ROASTED CURRIED CHICKPEAS AND CAULIFLOWER

**Pam Jefferies'
Deluxe Cheeseburger
Salad** PAGE 265

Cooking for Kids

Everyone from toddlers to teens will gobble up the family-friendly food in this special chapter. The bonus? Many of the recipes are so fun and easy to prepare, children will love helping you make them!

Ginger Burow's Brief Burritos
PAGE 262

Jennifer Stowell's Chili Dog Pizza
PAGE 274

Amber Willard's Fiesta Beef & Noodle Skillet *PAGE 266*

FROZEN BANANA
CEREAL POPS

Brief Burritos

My children never get tired of these beef-and-bean burritos. The bonus? It's a fuss-free recipe that goes together from start to finish in just 20 minutes, leaving some time for fun after dinner.
—**GINGER BUROW** FREDERICKSBURG, TX

START TO FINISH: 20 MIN.
MAKES: 8 SERVINGS

- 1 **pound ground beef**
- 1 **can (16 ounces) refried beans**
- 1 **can (10 ounces) diced tomatoes and green chilies, drained**
- ½ **cup chili sauce**
- 8 **flour tortillas (10 inches), warmed**
- ½ **cup shredded cheddar cheese**
- ½ **cup sour cream**

1. In a large skillet, cook the beef over medium heat 6-8 minutes or until no longer pink, breaking into crumbles; drain. Stir in beans, tomatoes and chili sauce; heat through.
2. Place about ½ cup meat mixture near the center on each tortilla; top with cheddar cheese and sour cream. Fold bottom and sides of tortilla over filling and roll up. Serve immediately.

TOP TIP

I often use leftovers from different dishes as an easy filling for burritos. I've filled flour tortillas with extras ranging from chili, chicken and beans to eggs with potatoes, tomatoes and onion from breakfast.
—**CARMEN HART** PRESCOTT VALLEY, AZ

⑤INGREDIENTS
Frozen Banana Cereal Pops

For a nutritious snack, we dip bananas in yogurt, roll 'em in cereal and pop 'em in the freezer. Ta-da! Fruit popsicles.
—**SCARLETT ELROD** NEWNAN, GA

PREP: 15 MIN. + FREEZING
MAKES: 8 POPS

- ¾ **cup (6 ounces) strawberry yogurt**
- 2 **cups Fruity Pebbles cereal**
- 4 **medium bananas, peeled and cut crosswise in half**
- 8 **wooden pop sticks**

1. Place yogurt and cereal in separate shallow bowls. Insert the wooden pop sticks through the cut side of bananas. Dip the bananas in yogurt, then roll in the cereal to coat. Transfer to waxed paper-lined baking sheets.
2. Freeze 1 hour or until firm. Transfer to resealable plastic freezer bags; return to the freezer.

Watermelon Pizza

Fruit pizza gets a whole new meaning! Load up watermelon wedges with the works for a fun summer snack. Juicy berries, sweet coconut, fresh mint and banana slices will help you keep cool with every refreshing bite. Or get creative with toppings such as kiwi slices, chopped nuts and drizzles of chocolate sauce to really make this colorful pie your own.
—**TASTE OF HOME** TEST KITCHEN

BROCCOLI, RICE AND
SAUSAGE DINNER

Stuffed PB&J French Toast Kabobs

Be a breakfast hero—turn peanut butter and jelly into French toast! For even more appeal, thread the pieces onto skewers.

—NICOLE MEYER ROSLYN, NY

START TO FINISH: 30 MIN.
MAKES: 4 SERVINGS

- ⅓ cup seedless strawberry jam
- 8 slices challah or egg bread (½ inch thick)
- 1 cup sliced fresh strawberries
- 1 teaspoon ground cinnamon
- ½ cup creamy peanut butter
- 5 large eggs
- ¾ cup 2% milk
- 5 tablespoons maple syrup, divided
- ¾ teaspoon vanilla extract
- 8 fresh strawberries, halved
  Additional maple syrup and sliced fresh strawberries

1. Spread the strawberry jam over four slices of bread. Top with sliced strawberries; sprinkle with cinnamon. Spread peanut butter over remaining bread; place over top.

2. Lightly grease a griddle; heat over medium heat. In a shallow bowl, whisk eggs, milk, 3 tablespoon maple syrup and vanilla until blended. Dip both sides of sandwiches in egg mixture, allowing each side to soak 10 seconds. Place the sandwiches on the griddle; toast 3-4 minutes on each side or until golden brown.

3. Transfer the sandwiches to a cutting board; brush the sandwiches with the remaining maple syrup. Cut sandwiches into quarters. On four metal or wooden skewers, alternately thread the French toast and halved strawberries. If desired, serve with additional syrup and strawberries.

Broccoli, Rice and Sausage Dinner

The first recipe my kids requested when they left home was this skillet supper of broccoli, smoked turkey sausage and rice. Serve it with sour cream to dollop on top.
~~ur teens like extra zip, pass around~~

Reduced-fat sour cream and
Louisiana-style hot sauce,
optional

1. In a large skillet, heat the oil over medium-high heat. Add the turkey sausage; cook and stir 2-3 minutes or until browned. Stir in the broccoli

STUFFED PB&J
FRENCH TOAST
KABOBS

Spaghetti Tacos

My son watches a show where the kids eat spaghetti tacos. As a joke, I made him his own. Now he wants them all the time!
—**MINDIE HILTON** SUSANVILLE, CA

PREP: 25 MIN. • **COOK:** 25 MIN.
MAKES: 6 SERVINGS

- 1 **can (15 ounces) tomato sauce**
- 1 **can (14½ ounces) diced tomatoes, undrained**
- 2 **teaspoons sugar**
- ¾ **teaspoon dried parsley flakes**
- ½ **teaspoon dried basil**
- ½ **teaspoon dried thyme**
- ½ **teaspoon pepper**
- ¼ **teaspoon garlic powder**
- ¼ **teaspoon onion powder**
- 12 **frozen fully cooked Italian turkey meatballs, thawed and quartered**
- 1 **package (13¼ ounces) whole grain thin spaghetti**
- 12 **taco shells**
- ¾ **cup shredded reduced-fat Italian cheese blend**
  Thinly sliced fresh basil, optional

1. In a large saucepan, combine the first nine ingredients; stir in meatballs. Bring to a boil. Reduce heat; simmer, covered, 20-25 minutes to allow the flavors to blend, stirring occasionally.

2. Meanwhile, in another saucepan, cook the spaghetti according to the package directions; drain and return to pan. Remove 1½ cups sauce from meatball mixture; add to spaghetti and toss to coat.

3. Heat the taco shells according to the package directions. Place ½ cup spaghetti in each taco shell; top with the meatball mixture and cheese. If desired, sprinkle with fresh basil.

CHOCOLATE & PEANUT BUTTER CRISPY BARS

For a dairy-free dessert, I came up with Chocolate & Peanut Butter Crispy Bars. My children and their friends always gobble them up, so I know I hit on something good!
—**DAWN PASCO** OVERLAND PARK, KS

SPAGHETTI TACOS

Ravioli Appetizer Pops

Like restaurant versions of fried ravioli? It's easy to fix at home with refrigerated pasta—and fun to serve on lollipop sticks! For dipping, use packaged sauces or whip up your favorite recipes.

—ERIKA MONROE-WILLIAMS SCOTTSDALE, AZ

PREP: 25 MIN. • **COOK:** 5 MIN./BATCH
MAKES: 3½ DOZEN

- ½ cup dry bread crumbs
- 2 teaspoons pepper
- 1½ teaspoons dried oregano
- 1½ teaspoons dried parsley flakes
- 1 teaspoon salt
- 1 teaspoon crushed red pepper flakes
- ⅓ cup all-purpose flour
- 2 large eggs, lightly beaten
- 1 package (9 ounces) refrigerated cheese ravioli
  Oil for frying
  Grated Parmesan cheese, optional
- 42 lollipop sticks
  Warm marinara sauce and prepared pesto

1. In a shallow bowl, mix the bread crumbs and seasonings. Place flour and eggs in separate shallow bowls. Dip the cheese ravioli in flour to coat both sides; shake off excess. Dip in egg, then in crumb mixture, patting to help coating adhere.

2. In an electric or large skillet, heat ½ in. of oil to 375°. Fry the ravioli, a few at a time, 1-2 minutes on each side or until golden brown. Drain on paper towels. If desired, immediately sprinkle with cheese. Carefully insert a lollipop stick into the back of each ravioli. Serve warm with marinara sauce and prepared pesto.

Loaded Pulled Pork Cups

Cheesy seasoned hash browns form the muffin-pan nests I load with pork, sour cream, bacon and more. Make, bake and collect the compliments.

—MELISSA SPERKA GREENSBORO, NC

PREP: 40 MIN. • **BAKE:** 25 MIN.
MAKES: 1½ DOZEN

- 1 package (20 ounces) refrigerated shredded hash brown potatoes
- ¾ cup shredded Parmesan cheese
- 2 large egg whites, beaten
- 1 teaspoon garlic salt
- ½ teaspoon onion powder
- ¼ teaspoon pepper
- 1 carton (16 ounces) refrigerated fully cooked barbecued shredded pork
- 1 cup (4 ounces) shredded Colby-Monterey Jack cheese
- ½ cup sour cream
- 5 bacon strips, cooked and crumbled
  Minced chives

1. Preheat oven to 450°. In a large bowl, mix hash browns, Parmesan cheese, egg whites and seasonings until blended. Divide hash browns among 18 well-greased muffin cups; press onto the bottoms and up the sides to form cups.

2. Bake 22-25 minutes or until edges are dark golden brown. Carefully run a knife around the sides of each cup. Cool 5 minutes before removing from pans to a serving platter. Meanwhile, heat the pulled pork according to the package directions.

3. Sprinkle cheese into cups. Top with pork, sour cream and bacon; sprinkle with chives. Serve warm.

TRAIL MIX BLONDIE BARS

Trail Mix Blondie Bars

These came out of a baking emergency! There was a potluck at my daughter's preschool, and I didn't have much in the kitchen. Muffin mix saved the day.

—JOSIE SHAPIRO SAN FRANCISCO, CA

PREP: 20 MIN. • **BAKE:** 15 MIN. + COOLING
MAKES: 2 DOZEN

- ¾ cup butter, cubed
- 1 package (14¾ ounces) chocolate chip quick bread and muffin mix
- ¾ cup graham cracker crumbs
- 2 large eggs, lightly beaten
- ½ cup salted peanuts
- ½ cup raisins
- ¾ cup milk chocolate M&M's
- ⅔ cup coarsely crushed miniature pretzels

1. Preheat oven to 350°. Grease a 13x9-in. baking pan. In a small heavy saucepan, melt butter over medium heat. Heat 5-7 minutes or until golden brown, stirring constantly. Remove from heat; cool slightly.

2. In a large bowl, combine chocolate chip quick bread mix, graham cracker crumbs, eggs and browned butter; stir just until blended. Stir in peanuts and raisins. Spread into the prepared pan. Top with M&M's and pretzels.

3. Bake 15-20 minutes or until center is set. Cool completely in pan on a wire rack. Cut into bars.

Snowman Beach Cups

Kids have the winter blahs? With a sweet spring-break setup, these frosty friends are sure to get smiles. Use cups of blue raspberry Jell-O for water, cookie crumbs for sand and candy for tubes and towels. Pipe faces and beachwear on marshmallows for snowmen. Then add cocktail umbrellas, and you'll have it made in the shade.

—*TASTE OF HOME* TEST KITCHEN

S'MORES CRISPY BARS

S'mores Crispy Bars

My aunt always brought a big pan of her special cereal bars to our family's summer cottage. Full of chocolate, marshmallows and graham crackers, the s'mores-style treats have the taste of summer.
—**BETSY KING** DULUTH, MN

PREP: 15 MIN. + COOLING
MAKES: 2 DOZEN

- ¼ cup butter, cubed
- 1 package (10½ ounces) miniature marshmallows
- 6 cups Rice Krispies
- 1½ cups crushed graham crackers
- 1 cup milk chocolate chips

FROSTING

- ¾ cup butter, softened
- 1 cup confectioners' sugar
- 1 jar (7 ounces) marshmallow creme

TOPPING

- ¼ cup crushed graham crackers
- 2 milk chocolate candy bars (1.55 ounces each)

1. In a 6-qt. stockpot, melt butter over medium heat. Add the marshmallows; cook and stir until melted. Remove from heat. Stir in cereal and crushed crackers. Fold in the chocolate chips. Press into a greased 13x9-in. baking pan. Cool to room temperature.

2. For frosting, in a small bowl, beat the butter and confectioners' sugar until smooth. Beat in marshmallow creme on low speed just until blended. Spread over bars. Sprinkle crushed crackers over frosting. Cut into bars. Break each candy bar into 12 pieces; place a piece on each bar.

Cheese & Mushroom Skillet Pizza

Indulge in a homemade crust—and still get dinner on the table in only 30 minutes! Friday pizza night just got even more fun, family-friendly and delicious.
—**CLARE BUTLER** LITTLE ELM, TX

START TO FINISH: 30 MIN.
MAKES: 4 SLICES

- 1 cup all-purpose flour
- 2 teaspoons baking powder
- 1 teaspoon dried oregano
- ½ teaspoon salt
- 6 tablespoons water
- 2 tablespoons plus 1 teaspoon olive oil, divided
- ½ cup pizza sauce
- 25 slices pepperoni
- 1 jar (4½ ounces) sliced mushrooms, drained
- 1 can (2¼ ounces) sliced ripe olives, drained
- 1 cup (4 ounces) shredded part-skim mozzarella cheese

1. Preheat broiler. In a small bowl, whisk flour, baking powder, oregano and salt. Stir in water and 2 tablespoons oil to form a soft dough. Turn onto a floured surface; knead 6-8 times. Roll into a 12-in. circle.

2. Brush bottom of a 12-in. ovenproof skillet with the remaining oil; place over medium-high heat. Transfer the dough to the pan; cook 2-3 minutes on each side or until golden brown. Remove from the heat. Spread with pizza sauce; top with pepperoni, mushrooms, olives and cheese.

3. Broil 3-4 in. from heat 3-5 minutes or until cheese is melted.

CHEESE & MUSHROOM SKILLET PIZZA

SKILLET NACHOS

2. Stir in the tomato juice, water, Worcestershire sauce and seasonings; bring to a boil. Add spaghetti. Reduce heat; simmer, covered, 9-11 minutes or until pasta is tender. Stir in beans; heat through. Top servings with sour cream and cheese.

FREEZE OPTION *Freeze the cooled pasta mixture in freezer containers. To use, partially thaw in refrigerator overnight. Heat through in a saucepan, stirring occasionally and adding a little water if necessary.*

EAT SMART | **⑤ INGREDIENTS** | **FAST FIX**

Strawberry-Carrot Smoothies

My children usually resist eating veggies. This five-minute fruit smoothie blends in nutritious carrot juice—but to my kids, it's just a super-delicious breakfast.
—**ELISABETH LARSEN** PLEASANT GROVE, UT

START TO FINISH: 5 MIN.
MAKES: 5 SERVINGS

- 2 **cups (16 ounces) reduced-fat plain Greek yogurt**
- 1 **cup carrot juice**
- 1 **cup orange juice**
- 1 **cup frozen pineapple chunks**
- 1 **cup frozen unsweetened sliced strawberries**

Place all ingredients in a blender; cover and process until smooth.
PER SERVING *1 cup equals 141 cal., 2 g fat (1 g sat. fat), 5 mg chol., 79 mg sodium, 20 g carb., 1 g fiber, 10 g pro. Diabetic Exchanges: 1 fruit, ½ reduced-fat milk.*

FAST FIX
Skillet Nachos

Mom gave me a fundraiser cookbook, and I've tried a number of the recipes. Hands down, the one I've used most is for beefy nachos prepared from start to finish in a skillet. At the table, offer popular toppings such as sour cream, tomatoes, jalapenos and lettuce.
—**JUDY HUGHES** WAVERLY, KS

START TO FINISH: 30 MIN.
MAKES: 6 SERVINGS

- 1 **pound ground beef**
- 1 **can (14½ ounces) diced tomatoes, undrained**
- 1 **cup fresh or frozen corn, thawed**
- ¾ **cup uncooked instant rice**
- ½ **cup water**
- 1 **envelope taco seasoning**
- ½ **teaspoon salt**
- 1 **cup (4 ounces) shredded Colby-Monterey Jack cheese**
- 1 **package (16 ounces) tortilla chips**
  Optional toppings: sour cream, sliced fresh jalapenos, shredded lettuce and lime wedges

1. In a large skillet, cook beef over medium heat 6-8 minutes or until no longer pink, breaking into crumbles; drain. Stir in the tomatoes, corn, rice, water, taco seasoning and salt. Bring to a boil. Reduce heat; simmer, covered, 8-10 minutes or until rice is tender and mixture is slightly thickened.

2. Remove from heat; sprinkle with cheese. Let stand, covered, 5 minutes or until the cheese is melted. Divide tortilla chips among six plates; spoon beef mixture over chips. Serve with toppings as desired.

FREEZE IT | **FAST FIX**
One-Pot Chilighetti

Need kid-pleasing food? Combining chili and spaghetti is a no-brainer!
—**JENNIFER TRENHAILE** EMERSON, NE

START TO FINISH: 30 MIN.
MAKES: 8 SERVINGS

- 1½ **pounds ground beef**
- 1 **large onion, chopped**
- 1 **can (46 ounces) tomato juice**
- 1 **cup water**
- 2 **tablespoons Worcestershire sauce**
- 4 **teaspoons chili powder**
- ½ **teaspoon salt**
- ½ **teaspoon ground cumin**
- ½ **teaspoon pepper**
- 1 **package (16 ounces) spaghetti, broken into 2-inch pieces**
- 2 **cans (16 ounces each) kidney beans, rinsed and drained**
  Sour cream and shredded cheddar cheese

1. In a 6-qt. stockpot, cook the beef and onion over medium-high heat 8-10 minutes or until beef is no longer pink and onion is tender, breaking up beef into crumbles; drain.

STRAWBERRY-CARROT SMOOTHIES

MEXI-MAC SKILLET

Simple Tomato Soup

On a day of bad weather when we were stuck in the house, I whipped up tomato soup using on-hand ingredients. Now my family requests it constantly! Whenever I send some with my daughter for lunch at school, I include extra for a friend who likes it just as much as we do.
— **LANAEE O'NEILL** CHICO, CA

START TO FINISH: 30 MIN.
MAKES: 8 SERVINGS

- 2 cans (14.5 ounces each) diced tomatoes with basil, oregano and garlic, undrained
- ¼ cup butter
- ½ cup finely chopped red onion
- 2 garlic cloves, minced
- 6 tablespoons all-purpose flour
- 1 carton (48 ounces) chicken broth
  Grated Parmesan cheese, optional

1. Place the tomatoes with juices in a blender; cover and process until pureed. In a large saucepan, heat the butter over medium-high heat. Add the onion; cook and stir until tender. Add garlic; cook 1 minute longer.
2. Remove from the heat; stir in the flour until smooth. Cook for 1 minute. Gradually whisk in the chicken broth. Add the pureed tomatoes; bring to a boil over medium heat, stirring occasionally. Reduce the heat and simmer for 20-25 minutes to allow flavors to blend. If desired, sprinkle with Parmesan cheese.

SIMPLE TOMATO SOUP

Mexi-Mac Skillet

I'm not sure who's a bigger fan of this recipe—my husband or me! He loves the taste, and I love how easy it is to prepare. I don't even have to precook the mac.
—**MAURANE RAMSEY** FORT WAYNE, IN

START TO FINISH: 30 MIN.
MAKES: 5 SERVINGS

- 1 pound lean ground beef (90% lean)
- 1 large onion, chopped
- 1 can (14½ ounces) diced tomatoes, undrained
- 1 can (8 ounces) tomato sauce
- 1 cup fresh or frozen corn
- ½ cup water
- 1¼ teaspoons chili powder
- 1 teaspoon dried oregano
- ½ teaspoon salt
- ⅔ cup uncooked elbow macaroni
- ⅔ cup shredded reduced-fat cheddar cheese

1. In a large nonstick skillet, cook beef and onion over medium-high heat 5-7 minutes or until the beef is no longer pink, breaking up beef into crumbles. Drain.
2. Stir in the tomatoes, tomato sauce, corn, water, chili powder, oregano and salt; bring to a boil. Stir in uncooked macaroni. Reduce the heat; simmer, covered, 15-20 minutes or until the macaroni is tender. Sprinkle with cheddar cheese.
PER SERVING *1 cup equals 283 cal., 11 g fat (5 g sat. fat), 55 mg chol., 716 mg sodium, 23 g carb., 4 g fiber, 25 g pro.* **Diabetic Exchanges:** *3 lean meat, 1 starch, 1 vegetable.*

FAST FIX
Pretzel-Coated Chicken Nuggets

Chicken nuggets are sure to please kids, but with a crushed pretzel crust, these appeal to adults, too. The crunchy bites can even make a tasty appetizer.

—**CARRIE FARIAS** OAK RIDGE, NJ

START TO FINISH: 30 MIN.
MAKES: 6 SERVINGS (½ CUP SAUCE)

- 2 large eggs
- ¼ cup 2% milk
- 3 cups buttermilk ranch or cheddar cheese pretzel pieces, finely crushed
- 1 cup all-purpose flour
- 1½ pounds boneless skinless chicken breasts, cut into 1-inch pieces
  Cooking spray

SAUCE
- ¼ cup Dijon mustard
- ¼ cup honey

1. Preheat oven to 425°. In a shallow bowl, whisk the eggs and milk. Place pretzels and flour in separate shallow bowls. Dip the chicken in flour to coat all sides; shake off excess. Dip in egg mixture, then in pretzels, patting to help coating adhere.
2. Place chicken on foil-lined baking sheets; spritz with cooking spray. Bake 12-15 minutes or until the chicken is no longer pink. In a small bowl, mix the Dijon mustard and honey. Serve with chicken.

PRETZEL-COATED
CHICKEN NUGGETS

FAST FIX
Mama Mia Meatball Taquitos

We love lasagna, but it takes too long on weekdays. My solution? Meatball taquitos!
—**LAUREN WYLER** DRIPPING SPRINGS, TX

START TO FINISH: 30 MIN.
MAKES: 6 SERVINGS

- 12 frozen fully cooked Italian turkey meatballs, thawed
- 2 cups (8 ounces) shredded part-skim mozzarella cheese
- 1 cup whole-milk ricotta cheese
- 1 teaspoon Italian seasoning
- 12 flour tortillas (8 inches)
  Cooking spray
  Warm marinara sauce

1. Preheat oven to 425°. Place Italian turkey meatballs in a food processor; pulse until finely chopped. Transfer to a large bowl; stir in the cheeses and Italian seasoning.

2. Spread about ¼ cup meatball mixture down center of each tortilla. Roll up tightly. Place on a greased 15x10x1-in. baking pan, seam side down; spritz with cooking spray.
3. Bake 16-20 minutes or until golden brown. Serve with marinara sauce.

DID YOU KNOW?

When a cheese maker separates milk or cream into curds and whey, the curds are used to make cottage cheese and the whey is used to make ricotta. That's why these cheeses, although similarly soft and mild in flavor, have such different textures. Both are considered "fresh" or unripened cheeses. Ricotta is a soft cheese that has a fine, moist, grainy texture. Cottage cheese is lumpier, whether the curds are small or large.

Lily Julow's
Honey-Mustard Brats
PAGE 279

Hot Off the Grill

When dinnertime's minutes away, take a fresh approach and head outdoors. From marinated meats to sizzling seafood, the grilled specialties in this chapter will get everyone fired up.

GRILLED LEMON-DILL SHRIMP

Dr Pepper Drumsticks

If you love Dr Pepper as much as I do, pour it into a homemade barbecue sauce for chicken drumsticks. Combined with bourbon, brown sugar, Worcestershire and more, the soda adds great flavor to the tender chicken.

—SHANNON HOLLE-FUNK VENEDY, IL

PREP: 20 MIN. • **GRILL:** 30 MIN.
MAKES: 6 SERVINGS

- 1 **cup ketchup**
- ⅔ **cup Dr Pepper**
- 2 **tablespoons brown sugar**
- 2 **tablespoons bourbon**
- 4 **teaspoons barbecue seasoning**
- 1 **tablespoon Worcestershire sauce**
- 2 **teaspoons dried minced onion**
- ⅛ **teaspoon salt**
- ¼ **teaspoon celery salt, optional**
- 12 **chicken drumsticks**

1. In a small saucepan, combine the first eight ingredients; if desired, stir in celery salt. Bring to a boil. Reduce heat; simmer, uncovered, 8-10 minutes or until slightly thickened, stirring frequently.
2. Moisten a paper towel with cooking oil; using long-handled tongs, rub on the grill rack to coat lightly. Grill the chicken drumsticks, covered, over medium-low heat 15 minutes. Turn; grill 15-20 minutes longer or until a thermometer reads 170°-175°, brushing occasionally with sauce.

EAT SMART **⑤ INGREDIENTS** **FAST FIX**

Grilled Lemon-Dill Shrimp

This delicious shrimp is one of my go-to recipes when I stare at the contents of my pantry and draw a blank. Cook up a box of angel hair pasta or spaghetti, and you're good to go. If you have veggies, add some of those, too—just grill them separately.

—JANE WHITTAKER PENSACOLA, FL

START TO FINISH: 30 MIN.
MAKES: 4 SERVINGS

- ¼ **cup olive oil**
- 1 **tablespoon lemon juice**
- 2 **teaspoons dill weed**
- 2 **garlic cloves, minced**
- ¾ **teaspoon salt**
- ½ **teaspoon pepper**
- 1 **pound uncooked shrimp (31-40 per pound), peeled and deveined**

1. In a large bowl, whisk the first six ingredients until blended. Reserve 3 tablespoons marinade for basting. Add the shrimp to the remaining marinade; toss to coat. Refrigerate, covered, 15 minutes.
2. Drain the shrimp, discarding any remaining marinade. Thread shrimp onto four or eight metal or soaked wooden skewers. Grill, covered, over medium heat or broil 4 in. from heat 2-4 minutes on each side, basting with the reserved marinade during the last minute of cooking.
PER SERVING *1 serving equals 221 cal., 15 g fat (2 g sat. fat), 138 mg chol., 578 mg sodium, 2 g carb., trace fiber, 19 g pro.* **Diabetic Exchanges:** *3 lean meat, 3 fat.*

Tender Pork Chops with Mango Salsa

The fruit salsa is so refreshing on these chops. In the refrigerator, marinate four 7-ounce bone-in pork loin chops in 3 tablespoons cider vinegar, 1 tablespoon salt-free grilling blend and 1 tablespoon olive oil for at least 2 hours. Discard marinade. Grill chops, covered, over medium heat for 4-5 minutes on each side or until a thermometer reads 145°. Let stand for 5 minutes before serving. Meanwhile, combine 2 chopped peeled mangoes, 1 cup chopped sweet onion, 1 seeded and finely chopped jalapeno pepper, 1 tablespoon lemon juice and 2 teaspoons honey. Serve with chops. *Makes 4 servings.*

—ANDREA RIVERA WESTBURY, NY

GRILLED CHICKEN, MANGO & BLUE CHEESE TORTILLAS

EAT SMART · FAST FIX

Grilled Chicken, Mango & Blue Cheese Tortillas

Here's a satisfying appetizer that could also make a light but delicious dinner.
—**JOSEE LANZI** NEW PORT RICHEY, FL

START TO FINISH: 30 MIN.
MAKES: 16 APPETIZERS

- 1 boneless skinless chicken breast (8 ounces)
- 1 teaspoon blackened seasoning
- ¾ cup (6 ounces) plain yogurt
- 1½ teaspoons grated lime peel
- 2 tablespoons lime juice
- ¼ teaspoon salt
- ⅛ teaspoon pepper
- 1 cup finely chopped peeled mango
- ⅓ cup finely chopped red onion
- 4 flour tortillas (8 inches)
- ½ cup crumbled blue cheese
- 2 tablespoons minced fresh cilantro

1. Moisten a paper towel with cooking oil; using long-handled tongs, rub on the grill rack to coat lightly. Sprinkle chicken with the blackened seasoning. Grill chicken, covered, over medium heat 6-8 minutes on each side or until a thermometer reads 165°.
2. Meanwhile, in a small bowl, mix yogurt, lime peel, lime juice, salt and pepper. Cool chicken slightly; finely chop and transfer to a small bowl. Stir in the mango and onion.
3. Grill the tortillas, uncovered, over medium heat 2-3 minutes or until puffed. Turn; top with the chicken mixture and sprinkle with blue cheese. Grill, covered, 2-3 minutes longer or until bottoms of tortillas are lightly browned. Drizzle with yogurt mixture; sprinkle with cilantro. Cut each tortilla into four wedges.
PER SERVING *1 wedge equals 85 cal., 3 g fat (1 g sat. fat), 12 mg chol., 165 mg sodium, 10 g carb., 1 g fiber, 5 g pro. Diabetic Exchanges: 1 lean meat, ½ starch.*

FAST FIX

Honey-Mustard Brats

Our honey-mustard glaze gives bratwurst a sweet and punchy flavor we love.
—**LILY JULOW** LAWRENCEVILLE, GA

START TO FINISH: 25 MIN.
MAKES: 4 SERVINGS

- ¼ cup Dijon mustard
- ¼ cup honey
- 2 tablespoons mayonnaise
- 1 teaspoon steak sauce
- 4 uncooked bratwurst links
- 4 brat buns, split

1. In a small bowl, mix the Dijon mustard, honey, mayonnaise and steak sauce.
2. Grill the bratwurst, covered, over medium heat 15-20 minutes or until a thermometer reads 160°, turning occasionally; brush frequently with the mustard mixture during the last 5 minutes. Serve on buns.

EAT SMART · FAST FIX

Ancho Garlic Steaks with Summer Salsa

The first time I tasted these, I was amazed at how well the blueberries and melon complement the peppery steak. It's fun to experiment with other fruits, too.
—**VERONICA CALLAGHAN** GLASTONBURY, CT

START TO FINISH: 30 MIN.
MAKES: 4 SERVINGS

- 2 boneless beef top loin steaks (1¼ inches thick and 8 ounces each)
- 2 teaspoons ground ancho chili pepper
- 1 teaspoon garlic salt

SALSA
- 1 cup seeded chopped watermelon
- 1 cup fresh blueberries
- 1 medium tomato, chopped
- ¼ cup finely chopped red onion
- 1 tablespoon minced fresh mint
- 1½ teaspoons grated fresh gingerroot
- ¼ teaspoon salt

1. Rub the steaks with chili pepper and garlic salt. Grill, covered, over medium heat or broil 4 in. from heat 7-9 minutes on each side or until the meat reaches the desired doneness (for medium-rare, a thermometer should read 145°; medium, 160°; well-done, 170°).
2. In a bowl, combine salsa ingredients. Cut the steak into thin slices; serve with the salsa.
NOTE *Top loin steak may be labeled as strip steak, Kansas City steak, New York strip steak, ambassador steak or boneless club steak in your region.*
PER SERVING *3 ounces cooked beef with ½ cup salsa equals 195 cal., 5 g fat (2 g sat. fat), 50 mg chol., 442 mg sodium, 10 g carb., 2 g fiber, 25 g pro. Diabetic Exchanges: 3 lean meat, ½ fruit.*

Whether you need something for a quick weeknight dinner or a cookout with friends, consider Cheddar Jalapeno Chicken Burgers with Guacamole. They'll kick your menu up a notch with Southwestern flavor.

—GABY DALKIN LOS ANGELES, CA

FAST FIX

Cheddar Jalapeno Chicken Burgers with Guacamole

START TO FINISH: 30 MIN.
MAKES: 4 BURGERS

- ½ cup finely chopped onion
- ⅓ cup finely shredded cheddar cheese
- ¼ cup minced fresh cilantro
- 2 garlic cloves, minced
- 2 teaspoons finely chopped jalapeno pepper
- 1 teaspoon ground cumin
- 1 teaspoon paprika
- ¾ teaspoon kosher salt
- ¼ teaspoon freshly ground pepper
- 1½ pounds ground chicken
- 4 hamburger buns, split
- ½ cup guacamole
  Optional toppings: sliced red onion, lettuce leaves, salsa and sour cream

1. In a large bowl, combine the first nine ingredients. Add ground chicken; mix lightly but thoroughly. Shape into four ¾-in. thick patties.

2. Moisten a paper towel with cooking oil; using long-handled tongs, rub on the grill rack to coat lightly. Grill the burgers, covered, over medium heat 7-8 minutes on each side or until a thermometer reads 165°. Serve on buns with guacamole and additional toppings as desired.

SPICY PEACH-GLAZED GRILLED CHICKEN

EAT SMART FAST FIX

Spicy Peach-Glazed Grilled Chicken

Simple chicken on the grill can't compare with this spicy-and-sweet treatment.

—KAREN SPARKS GLENDORA, CA

START TO FINISH: 25 MIN.
MAKES: 4 SERVINGS

- ½ cup peach preserves
- 3 tablespoons finely chopped seeded jalapeno pepper
- 1 tablespoon reduced-sodium soy sauce
- 1½ teaspoons chili garlic sauce
- 1 teaspoon spicy brown mustard
- 1 teaspoon olive oil
- ⅛ teaspoon plus ½ teaspoon salt, divided
- 4 boneless skinless chicken breast halves (6 ounces each)

1. For the glaze, in a small bowl, combine the first six ingredients; stir in ⅛ teaspoon salt. Reserve half of the glaze for serving.

2. Sprinkle the chicken breast halves with the remaining salt. Moisten a paper towel with cooking oil; using long-handled tongs, rub on grill rack to coat lightly. Grill the chicken breast halves, covered, over medium heat 5 minutes. Turn; grill 7-9 minutes longer or until a thermometer reads 165°, brushing the tops occasionally with the remaining glaze. Serve with reserved glaze.

NOTE *Wear disposable gloves when cutting hot peppers; the oils can burn skin. Avoid touching your face.*

PER SERVING *299 cal., 5 g fat (1 g sat. fat), 94 mg chol., 663 mg sodium, 27 g carb., trace fiber, 35 g pro.*

Beef and Blue Cheese Penne with Pesto

Want a healthier recipe that will please meat lovers? You found it!

—**FRANCES PIETSCH** FLOWER MOUND, TX

START TO FINISH: 30 MIN.
MAKES: 4 SERVINGS

- 2 **cups uncooked whole wheat penne pasta**
- 2 **beef tenderloin steaks (6 ounces each)**
- ¼ **teaspoon salt**
- ¼ **teaspoon pepper**
- 5 **ounces fresh baby spinach (about 6 cups), coarsely chopped**
- 2 **cups grape tomatoes, halved**
- ⅓ **cup prepared pesto**
- ¼ **cup chopped walnuts**
- ¼ **cup crumbled Gorgonzola cheese**

1. Cook the penne pasta according to the package directions.
2. Meanwhile, sprinkle steaks with salt and pepper. Grill steaks, covered, over medium heat or broil 4 in. from heat 5-7 minutes on each side or until the meat reaches desired doneness (for medium-rare, a thermometer should read 145°; medium, 160°; well-done, 170°).
3. Drain the penne pasta; transfer to a large bowl. Add the spinach, tomatoes, pesto and walnuts; toss to coat. Cut the steak into thin slices. Serve the pasta mixture with the beef; sprinkle with Gorgonzola cheese.
PER SERVING *532 cal., 22 g fat (6 g sat. fat), 50 mg chol., 434 mg sodium, 49 g carb., 9 g fiber, 35 g pro.*

Lime-Glazed Pork Chops

A simple but sensational four-ingredient glaze is the key to these tangy chops.

—**JACQUELINE CORREA** LANDING, NJ

START TO FINISH: 25 MIN.
MAKES: 4 SERVINGS

- ⅓ **cup orange marmalade**
- 1 **jalapeno pepper, seeded and finely chopped**
- 2 **tablespoons lime juice**
- 1 **teaspoon grated fresh gingerroot**
- 4 **bone-in pork loin chops (8 ounces each)**
- 4 **teaspoons minced fresh cilantro Lime wedges**

1. For the glaze, in a small saucepan, combine orange marmalade, jalapeno pepper, lime juice and grated ginger; cook and stir over medium heat 4-6 minutes or until marmalade is melted.
2. Moisten a paper towel with cooking oil; using long-handled tongs, rub on grill rack to coat lightly.
3. Grill the pork chops, covered, over medium heat or broil 4 in. from heat 6-8 minutes on each side or until a thermometer reads 145°, brushing with glaze during the last 5 minutes. Let stand 5 minutes. Sprinkle with cilantro; serve with lime wedges.
NOTE *Wear disposable gloves when cutting hot peppers; the oils can burn skin. Avoid touching your face.*
PER SERVING *286 cal., 8 g fat (3 g sat. fat), 86 mg chol., 85 mg sodium, 18 g carb., 0.55 g fiber, 34 g pro.* ***Diabetic Exchanges:** 4 lean meat, 1 fruit.*

BEEF AND BLUE CHEESE
PENNE WITH PESTO

CHICKEN ALFREDO WITH
GRILLED APPLES

Chicken Alfredo with Grilled Apples

If you've never grilled apples, here's a good reason to start! They go so well with the tender chicken, creamy Alfredo sauce, cheeses and splash of lemon in this main dish, which I created for a party.

—**RICHARD ROBINSON** PARK FOREST, IL

START TO FINISH: 25 MIN.
MAKES: 4 SERVINGS

- 4 **boneless skinless chicken breast halves (6 ounces each)**
- 4 **teaspoons chicken seasoning**
- 1 **large Braeburn or Gala apple, cut into ½-inch wedges**
- 1 **tablespoon lemon juice**
- 4 **slices provolone cheese**
- ½ **cup Alfredo sauce, warmed**
- ¼ **cup crumbled blue cheese**

1. Sprinkle both sides of chicken with the chicken seasoning. In a small bowl, toss apple wedges with lemon juice.
2. Moisten a paper towel with cooking oil; using long-handled tongs, rub on grill rack to coat lightly. Grill chicken, covered, over medium heat 5-8 minutes on each side or until a thermometer reads 165°. Grill apple wedges, covered, over medium heat 2-3 minutes on each side or until lightly browned. Top chicken with provolone cheese; cook, covered, 1-2 minutes longer or until cheese is melted.
3. Serve chicken with Alfredo sauce and apple. Sprinkle with blue cheese.
NOTE *This recipe was tested with McCormick's Montreal Chicken Seasoning. Look for it in the spice aisle.*

Lime and Sesame Grilled Eggplant

When I lived in Greece, I fell in love with eggplant. This recipe has an Asian twist.
—**ALLYSON MEYLER** GREENSBORO, NC

START TO FINISH: 20 MIN.
MAKES: 6 SERVINGS

- 3 **tablespoons lime juice**
- 1 **tablespoon sesame oil**
- 1½ **teaspoons reduced-sodium soy sauce**
- 1 **garlic clove, minced**
- ½ **teaspoon grated fresh gingerroot or ¼ teaspoon ground ginger**
- ½ **teaspoon salt**
- ⅛ **teaspoon pepper**
- 1 **medium eggplant (1¼ pounds), cut lengthwise into ½-inch slices**
- 2 **teaspoons honey**
- ⅛ **teaspoon crushed red pepper flakes**
  Thinly sliced green onion and sesame seeds

1. In a small bowl, whisk the first seven ingredients until blended; brush 2 tablespoons juice mixture over both sides of eggplant slices. Grill, covered, over medium heat 4-6 minutes on each side or until tender.
2. Transfer the eggplant to a serving plate. Stir honey and red pepper flakes into remaining juice mixture; drizzle over eggplant. Sprinkle with green onion and sesame seeds.
PER SERVING *50 cal., 2 g fat (trace sat. fat), 0 chol., 246 mg sodium, 7 g carb., 2 g fiber, 1 g pro. Diabetic Exchanges: 1 vegetable, ½ fat.*

PORTOBELLO FAJITAS

Portobello Fajitas

I serve my portobello mushroom fajitas family style so guests can build their own.
—**CAROLYN BUTTERFIELD** LAKE STEVENS, WA

START TO FINISH: 30 MIN.
MAKES: 4 SERVINGS

- 3 **large portobello mushrooms (about ½ pound)**
- 1 **large sweet red pepper, cut into strips**
- ½ **large sweet onion, sliced**
- ½ **cup fat-free Italian salad dressing**
- 2 **tablespoons lime juice**
- 4 **flour tortillas (8 inches), warmed**
- ½ **cup shredded cheddar cheese**
  Optional toppings: salsa, guacamole and sour cream

1. Remove and discard stems from mushrooms; with a spoon, scrape and remove the gills. Cut mushrooms into ½-in. slices and place in a large bowl. Add the pepper and onion; drizzle with Italian salad dressing and toss to coat. Let stand 10 minutes.
2. Transfer the vegetables to a lightly greased grill wok or open grill basket; place on grill rack. Grill, covered, over medium-high heat 10-12 minutes or until tender, stirring occasionally.
3. Drizzle vegetables with lime juice. Serve with tortillas, cheddar cheese and toppings as desired.
NOTE *If you do not have a grill wok or basket, use a disposable foil pan. Poke holes in the bottom of the foil pan with a meat fork to allow liquid to drain.*
PER SERVING *1 fajita (calculated without optional toppings) equals 282 cal., 8 g fat (4 g sat. fat), 15 mg chol., 664 mg sodium, 40 g carb., 4 g fiber, 10 g pro. Diabetic Exchanges: 2 starch, 1 medium-fat meat, 1 vegetable.*

Cajun Summer Vegetables

Give your veggies some zip! Place 2 each sliced medium yellow squash and zucchini, 1¾ cups sliced fresh mushrooms, ½ each medium yellow and red onions (sliced and separated into rings), 1 cup cherry tomatoes and ¼ cup sliced fresh carrots in a grill wok or basket. Grill, uncovered, over medium heat for 8-12 minutes or until tender, stirring frequently. Transfer to a bowl. Toss with 1 teaspoon Cajun seasoning. *Makes 6 servings.*
—**NANCY DENTLER** GREENSBORO, NC

GRILLED FLATBREAD
VEGGIE PIZZA

FAST FIX
Grilled Flatbread Veggie Pizza
We pile veggies onto flatbread and add mozzarella for a fun meatless entree.
—**DARLA ANDREWS** SCHERTZ, TX

START TO FINISH: 25 MIN.
MAKES: 4 SERVINGS

- 1 tablespoon butter
- ½ pound sliced baby portobello mushrooms
- 1 large green pepper, julienned
- 4 cups fresh baby spinach (about 4 ounces)
- ¼ teaspoon salt
- ⅛ teaspoon pepper
- 2 naan flatbreads or 4 whole pita breads
- 2 tablespoons olive oil
- ¼ cup prepared pesto
- 2 plum tomatoes, sliced
- 2 cups (8 ounces) shredded part-skim mozzarella cheese

1. In a large skillet, heat butter over medium-high heat. Add mushrooms and green pepper; cook and stir 5-7 minutes or until tender. Add the spinach, salt and pepper; cook and stir 2-3 minutes or until spinach is wilted.
2. Brush both sides of the flatbreads with oil. Grill the flatbreads, covered, over medium heat 2-3 minutes or until bottoms are lightly browned.

3. Remove from grill. Spread grilled sides with pesto; top with vegetable mixture, tomatoes and cheese. Return to grill; cook, covered, 2-3 minutes longer or until cheese is melted. Cut pizzas in half before serving.

EAT SMART **FAST FIX**
Tandoori Chicken Thighs
I spent time in India and love reminders of that vibrant culture. Tandoori chicken served with a tomato-cucumber salad and warmed naan makes a terrific meal.
—**CLAIRE ELSTON** SPOKANE, WA

START TO FINISH: 30 MIN.
MAKES: 4 SERVINGS

- 1 cup (8 ounces) reduced-fat plain yogurt
- 1 tablespoon minced fresh gingerroot
- 1 teaspoon ground cumin
- 1 garlic clove, minced
- ¾ teaspoon kosher salt
- ½ teaspoon curry powder
- ½ teaspoon pepper
- ¼ teaspoon cayenne pepper
- 4 boneless skinless chicken thighs (about 1 pound)

1. In a small bowl, mix the first eight ingredients until blended. Add the chicken to the marinade; turn to coat. Let stand 10 minutes.

2. Moisten a paper towel with cooking oil; using long-handled tongs, rub on the grill rack to coat lightly. Grill the chicken, covered, over medium heat 6-8 minutes on each side or until a thermometer reads 170°.
PER SERVING *193 cal., 9 g fat (3 g sat. fat), 78 mg chol., 333 mg sodium, 4 g carb., trace fiber, 23 g pro.* **Diabetic Exchanges:** *3 lean meat, ½ fat.*

EAT SMART **FAST FIX**
Grilled Tilapia with Pineapple Salsa
When I discovered this recipe years ago, it quickly became my favorite. The fresh, slightly spicy salsa is a terrific complement to the mild tilapia fillets.
—**BETH FLEMING** DOWNERS GROVE, IL

START TO FINISH: 20 MIN.
MAKES: 8 SERVINGS (2 CUPS SALSA)

- 2 cups cubed fresh pineapple
- 2 green onions, chopped
- ¼ cup finely chopped green pepper
- ¼ cup minced fresh cilantro
- 4 teaspoons plus 2 tablespoons lime juice, divided
- ⅛ teaspoon plus ¼ teaspoon salt, divided
  Dash cayenne pepper
- 1 tablespoon canola oil
- 8 tilapia fillets (4 ounces each)
- ⅛ teaspoon pepper

1. For the pineapple salsa, in a small bowl, combine the cubed pineapple, green onions, green pepper, cilantro, 4 teaspoons lime juice, ⅛ teaspoon salt and cayenne pepper. Refrigerate until serving.
2. Mix the canola oil and remaining lime juice; drizzle over the tilapia fillets. Sprinkle with the pepper and remaining salt.
3. Moisten a paper towel with cooking oil; using long-handled tongs, rub on grill rack to coat lightly. Grill the fish, covered, over medium heat or broil 4 in. from heat 2-3 minutes on each side or until fish just begins to flake easily with a fork. Serve with salsa.
PER SERVING *1 fillet with ¼ cup salsa equals 131 cal., 3 g fat (1 g sat. fat), 55 mg chol., 152 mg sodium, 6 g carb., 1 g fiber, 21 g pro.* **Diabetic Exchanges:** *3 lean meat, ½ fruit.*

FAJITAS
IN PITAS

heavy-duty foil (each about 18x12-in. rectangle). Drizzle with the olive oil; sprinkle with seasonings. Squeeze lemon juice over the top; place the squeezed wedges in packets. Fold the foil around mixture, sealing tightly.

2. Grill, covered, over medium heat 12-15 minutes or until fish just begins to flake easily with a fork, shrimp turn pink and potatoes are tender. Open foil carefully to allow steam to escape.

EAT SMART
Spicy Lemon Chicken Kabobs

Meyer lemons are the variety I like to use for these easy kabobs, but regular grilled lemons still add the signature smoky tang.
—**TERRI CRANDALL** GARDNERVILLE, NV

PREP: 15 MIN. + MARINATING
GRILL: 10 MIN.
MAKES: 6 SERVINGS

- ¼ cup lemon juice
- 4 tablespoons olive oil, divided
- 3 tablespoons white wine
- 1½ teaspoons crushed red pepper flakes
- 1 teaspoon minced fresh rosemary or ¼ teaspoon dried rosemary, crushed
- 1½ pounds boneless skinless chicken breasts, cut into 1-inch cubes
- 2 medium lemons, halved
  Minced chives

1. In a large resealable plastic bag, combine lemon juice, 3 tablespoons olive oil, white wine, red pepper flakes and rosemary. Add the chicken; seal the bag and turn to coat. Refrigerate up to 3 hours.

2. Drain the chicken, discarding the marinade. Thread the chicken onto six metal or soaked wooden skewers. Grill, covered, over medium heat 10-12 minutes or until no longer pink, turning once.

3. Place the lemons on the grill, cut side down. Grill 8-10 minutes or until lightly browned. Squeeze lemon halves over chicken. Drizzle with remaining oil; sprinkle with chives.

PER SERVING *1 kabob equals 182 cal., 8 g fat (2 g sat. fat), 63 mg chol., 55 mg sodium, 2 g carb., 1 g fiber, 23 g pro.* ***Diabetic Exchanges:*** *3 lean meat, 1 fat.*

FAST FIX
Fajitas In Pitas

For a weekend lunch with guests, we grill chicken and peppers to stuff inside warm pita pockets. Everyone loves it!
—**CLARA COULSON MINNEY**
WASHINGTON COURT HOUSE, OH

START TO FINISH: 25 MIN.
MAKES: 4 SERVINGS

- ½ cup mayonnaise
- 1 green onion, chopped
- 4 teaspoons Dijon mustard
- ¼ teaspoon pepper
- 3 boneless skinless chicken breast halves (6 ounces each)
- 2 medium sweet red peppers, halved and seeded
- 2 medium green peppers, halved and seeded
- 8 pita pocket halves, warmed
- 8 lettuce leaves

1. In a small bowl, mix mayonnaise, green onion, mustard and pepper; reserve ⅓ cup for assembling. Spread the remaining mixture over chicken and peppers.

2. Grill chicken and peppers, covered, over medium heat or broil 4 in. from heat for 5-6 minutes on each side or until a thermometer inserted in the chicken reads 165° and the peppers are tender. Cut chicken into ½-in. slices; cut peppers into 1-in. slices.

3. Spread the reserved mayonnaise mixture inside pita halves; fill with lettuce, chicken and peppers.

FAST FIX
Cajun Boil on the Grill

To feed the crowd at a family reunion, I made a huge batch of this Cajun boil.
—**ALLISON BROOKS** FORT COLLINS, CO

START TO FINISH: 30 MIN.
MAKES: 4 SERVINGS

- 1 package (20 ounces) refrigerated red potato wedges
- 2 salmon fillets (6 ounces each), halved
- ¾ pound uncooked shrimp (31-40 per pound), peeled and deveined
- ½ pound summer sausage, cubed
- 2 medium ears sweet corn, halved
- 2 tablespoons olive oil
- 1 teaspoon seafood seasoning
- ½ teaspoon salt
- ¼ teaspoon pepper
- 1 medium lemon, cut into 4 wedges

1. Divide potatoes, salmon, shrimp, sausage and corn among four pieces of

I do a lot of the prep for Summer Garden Pasta with Chicken Sausage in advance. When guests come for dinner, all I have to do is cook the penne and grill the meat.
—KARIE HOUGHTON MILTON, WA

SUMMER GARDEN PASTA WITH CHICKEN SAUSAGE

FAST FIX ▶
Summer Garden Pasta with Chicken Sausage

START TO FINISH: 30 MIN.
MAKES: 8 SERVINGS

- 3¼ cups uncooked mini penne pasta
- 1 package (12 ounces) fully cooked roasted garlic chicken sausage links or flavor of your choice
- 4 medium tomatoes, chopped (about 3 cups)
- 1 round (8 ounces) Brie cheese, cubed
- 1 cup shredded Parmesan cheese
- 1 cup loosely packed basil leaves, thinly sliced
- 3 garlic cloves, minced
- ½ teaspoon salt
- ½ teaspoon pepper
- ¼ cup olive oil

1. Cook the pasta according to the package directions. Meanwhile, grill sausages, covered, over medium heat or broil 4 in. from heat 7-9 minutes or until a thermometer reads 165°, turning occasionally. Remove the sausage from grill; cut into slices.
2. Drain the pasta; transfer to a large bowl. Stir in the sausage, tomatoes, cheeses, basil, garlic, salt and pepper. Drizzle with oil; toss to coat.

Rhubarb-Apricot Barbecued Chicken

Springtime brings back memories of the rhubarb that grew next to my childhood home. This recipe's my own creation.
—LAURIE HUDSON WESTVILLE, FL

PREP: 30 MIN. • **GRILL:** 30 MIN.
MAKES: 6 SERVINGS

- 1 tablespoon olive oil
- 1 cup finely chopped sweet onion
- 1 garlic clove, minced
- 2 cups chopped fresh or frozen rhubarb
- ¾ cup ketchup
- ⅔ cup water
- ⅓ cup apricot preserves
- ¼ cup cider vinegar
- ¼ cup molasses
- 1 tablespoon honey Dijon mustard
- 2 teaspoons finely chopped chipotle pepper in adobo sauce
- 5 teaspoons barbecue seasoning, divided
- 1¼ teaspoons salt, divided
- ¾ teaspoon pepper, divided
- 12 chicken drumsticks (about 4 pounds)

1. In a large saucepan, heat oil over medium heat. Add onion; cook and stir 4-6 minutes or until tender. Add garlic; cook 1 minute longer.

2. Stir in the rhubarb, ketchup, water, apricot preserves, vinegar, molasses, mustard, chipotle pepper, 1 teaspoon barbecue seasoning, ¼ teaspoon salt and ¼ teaspoon pepper. Bring to a boil. Reduce the heat; simmer, uncovered, 8-10 minutes or until rhubarb is tender.
3. Puree rhubarb mixture using an immersion blender. Or, cool slightly and puree in a blender. Reserve 2 cups sauce for serving.
4. Meanwhile, in a small bowl, mix the remaining barbecue seasoning, salt and pepper; sprinkle over chicken. Moisten a paper towel with cooking oil; using long-handled tongs, rub on grill rack to coat lightly. Grill chicken, covered, over indirect medium heat 15 minutes. Turn; grill 15-20 minutes longer or until a thermometer reads 170°-175°, brushing occasionally with the remaining sauce. Serve with the reserved sauce.

TOP TIP

When buying fresh rhubarb, look for stalks that are crisp and brightly colored. Tightly wrap fresh rhubarb in a plastic bag and store it in the refrigerator for up to 3 days.

FREEZE IT FAST FIX ▶
King Burgers

My husband and I think the sauce for this juicy burger tastes even better after being refrigerated overnight.

—MARY POTTER STERLING HEIGHTS, MI

START TO FINISH: 30 MIN.
MAKES: 6 SERVINGS

- 2 tablespoons butter
- ¼ cup mayonnaise
- 2 tablespoons prepared horseradish
- 2 tablespoons Dijon mustard
- ⅛ teaspoon salt
- ⅛ teaspoon pepper

BURGERS

- 1½ pounds ground beef
- ⅓ cup beef broth
- 2½ teaspoons hamburger seasoning, divided
- 6 hamburger buns, split
- 3 tablespoons butter, softened
  Toppings: shredded lettuce, sliced tomato and red onion

1. Cut the butter into six slices. Place butter on a small plate; freeze until firm. For the sauce, in a small bowl, mix the mayonnaise, horseradish, Dijon mustard, salt and pepper until blended.

2. In a large bowl, combine the beef, beef broth and 1½ teaspoons hamburger seasoning, mixing lightly but thoroughly. Shape into six patties. Place a butter slice in the center of each; shape beef around the butter slice, forming ¾-in.-thick patties. Sprinkle patties with the remaining hamburger seasoning.

3. Grill the burgers, covered, over medium heat 5-7 minutes on each side or until a thermometer reads 160°. Spread the buns with softened butter. Grill buns over medium heat, cut side down, for 30-60 seconds or until toasted. Serve the burgers on buns with sauce and toppings.

FREEZE OPTION *Place the patties on a plastic wrap-lined baking sheet; wrap and freeze until firm. Remove from pan and transfer to a resealable plastic freezer bag; return to freezer. To use, cook frozen patties as directed, increasing time as necessary for a thermometer to read 160°.*

SPICY BARBECUED CHICKEN

EAT SMART FAST FIX ▶
Spicy Barbecued Chicken

Here's one of our all-time favorite meals: zesty barbecued chicken, herbed corn on the cob and fresh coleslaw.

—RITA WINTRODE CORRYTON, TN

START TO FINISH: 30 MIN.
MAKES: 8 SERVINGS

- 1 tablespoon canola oil
- 2 garlic cloves, minced
- ½ cup chili sauce
- 3 tablespoons brown sugar
- 2 teaspoons salt-free seasoning blend, divided
- ¾ teaspoon cayenne pepper, divided
- 2 teaspoons ground mustard
- 2 teaspoons chili powder
- 8 boneless skinless chicken breast halves (4 ounces each)

1. In a small saucepan, heat oil over medium heat. Add the garlic; cook and stir 1 minute. Add chili sauce, brown sugar, 1 teaspoon seasoning blend and ¼ teaspoon cayenne pepper. Bring to a boil; cook and stir for 1 minute. Remove from heat.

2. In a small bowl, mix the mustard, chili powder and remaining seasoning blend and cayenne; rub over chicken breast halves. Moisten a paper towel with cooking oil; using long-handled tongs, lightly coat the grill rack.

3. Grill the chicken breast halves, covered, over medium heat for 4 minutes. Turn; grill 4-6 minutes longer or until a thermometer reads 165°, brushing tops occasionally with chili sauce mixture.

PER SERVING *179 cal., 5 g fat (1 g sat. fat), 63 mg chol., 293 mg sodium, 10 g carb., trace fiber, 23 g pro.* **Diabetic Exchanges:** *3 lean meat, ½ starch, ½ fat.*

KING BURGERS

BALSAMIC STEAK WITH
RED GRAPE RELISH

EAT SMART FAST FIX

Chicken with Peach-Cucumber Salsa

To keep our kitchen cool, we grill chicken and pass it with a minty peach salsa.

—**JANIE COLLE** HUTCHINSON, KS

START TO FINISH: 25 MIN.
MAKES: 4 SERVINGS

- 1½ cups chopped peeled fresh peaches (about 2 medium)
- ¾ cup chopped cucumber
- 4 tablespoons peach preserves, divided
- 3 tablespoons finely chopped red onion
- 1 teaspoon minced fresh mint
- ¾ teaspoon salt, divided
- 4 boneless skinless chicken breast halves (6 ounces each)
- ¼ teaspoon pepper

1. In a small bowl, combine peaches, cucumber, 2 tablespoons preserves, onion, mint and ¼ teaspoon salt.
2. Sprinkle chicken with pepper and remaining salt. Moisten a paper towel with cooking oil; using long-handled tongs, rub on grill rack to coat lightly. Grill chicken, covered, over medium heat 5 minutes. Turn; grill 7-9 minutes longer or until a thermometer reads 165°, brushing tops occasionally with remaining preserves. Serve with salsa.
PER SERVING *1 breast half with ½ cup salsa equals 261 cal., 4 g fat (1 g sat. fat), 94 mg chol., 525 mg sodium, 20 g carb., 1 g fiber, 35 g pro.* **Diabetic Exchanges:** *5 lean meat, ½ starch, ½ fruit.*

FAST FIX

Balsamic Steak with Red Grape Relish

A relish of red grapes, green onions and blue cheese gives this marinated steak an air of sophistication. Everything looks gorgeous and tastes just as good.

—**NAYLET LAROCHELLE** MIAMI, FL

START TO FINISH: 25 MIN.
MAKES: 4 SERVINGS

- 1 beef top sirloin steak (¾ inch thick and 1 pound)
- ¾ cup reduced-fat balsamic vinaigrette, divided
- 2½ cups seedless red grapes, halved
- 4 green onions, chopped (about ½ cup)
- ½ cup crumbled blue cheese
- ¼ teaspoon salt
- ¼ teaspoon coarsely ground pepper

1. Place steak in a large resealable plastic bag; add ½ cup balsamic vinaigrette. Seal the bag and turn to coat; let stand 10 minutes. Meanwhile, in a small bowl, toss the red grapes with the green onions and blue cheese.
2. Drain beef, discarding marinade. Sprinkle steak with salt and pepper. Grill steak, covered, over medium heat or broil 4 in. from heat 4-7 minutes on each side or until the meat reaches desired doneness (for medium-rare, a thermometer should read 145°; medium, 160°; well-done, 170°).
3. Cut steak into thin slices. Serve with grape relish and remaining vinaigrette.

Grilled Greek Fish

We love this! In a large resealable plastic bag, combine ⅓ cup lemon juice, 3 tablespoons olive oil, 2 tablespoons each minced fresh oregano and mint, 1 minced garlic clove, ½ teaspoon Greek seasoning and ½ teaspoon grated lemon peel. Add four 6-ounce tilapia fillets; seal bag and turn to coat. Refrigerate for 30 minutes. Drain and discard marinade. Grease grill rack. Grill tilapia, covered, over medium heat or broil 4 in. from the heat for 4-5 minutes on each side or until fish flakes easily with a fork. *Makes 4 servings.*

—**JUDY BATSON** TAMPA, FL

CHICKEN WITH
PEACH-CUCUMBER SALSA

**Danielle DeMarco's
Confetti Cake Batter
Cookies** PAGE 310

Easy Odds & Ends

Sample a little of this and a little of that in this bonus chapter of extra recipes. You'll discover everything from microwaved mainstays and canned treats to chicken dinners and birthday favorites.

**Juli Snaer's
Basil-Lemon Chicken**
PAGE 299

**Mary Shivers'
Southwest Shredded Pork Salad**
PAGE 293

**Mildred Fox's
Zucchini Frittata**
PAGE 305

Dinner Do-Overs

Day one: Use your slow cooker to make heaping helpings of a classic family supper. **Day two:** Get a jump on dinner by using the extra meat from the night before to fix something completely different but just as delicious. Mealtime becomes twice as nice!

TERIYAKI CHICKEN THIGHS

SLOW COOKER 🍲

Teriyaki Chicken Thighs

Here's a real slow-cooker sensation. Served over rice, the Asian-style entree always goes over big with my family.
—**GIGI MILLER** STOUGHTON, WI

PREP: 15 MIN. • **COOK:** 4 HOURS
MAKES: 8 SERVINGS

- 3 **pounds boneless skinless chicken thighs**
- ¾ **cup sugar**
- ¾ **cup reduced-sodium soy sauce**
- ⅓ **cup cider vinegar**
- 1 **garlic clove, minced**
- ¾ **teaspoon ground ginger**
- ¼ **teaspoon pepper**
- 4 **teaspoons cornstarch**
- 4 **teaspoons cold water**
  Hot cooked rice, optional

1. Place chicken in a 4- or 5-qt. slow cooker. In a small bowl, mix the sugar, soy sauce, cider vinegar, garlic, ginger and pepper; pour over the chicken. Cook, covered, on low 4-5 hours or until chicken is tender.

2. Remove the chicken to a serving platter; keep warm. Transfer cooking juices to a small saucepan; skim fat. Bring cooking juices to a boil. In a small bowl, mix cornstarch and cold water until smooth; stir into cooking juices. Return to a boil; cook and stir 1-2 minutes or until thickened. Serve with chicken and, if desired, rice.

FAST FIX ▶

Saucy Thai Chicken Pizza

Save some of your tender Teriyaki Chicken Thighs (below left) and give them a whole new look the next night. This Thai-inspired pizza recipe mixes the shredded meat with an Asian sauce and piles it onto a prebaked crust. Coleslaw mix, chopped peanuts, green onions and cilantro will finish off your dinnertime pie perfectly.
—**GIGI MILLER** STOUGHTON, WI

START TO FINISH: 25 MIN.
MAKES: 6 SLICES

- 1 **prebaked 12-inch pizza crust**
- 2 **cups shredded Teriyaki Chicken Thighs (recipe below left)**
- ½ **cup Thai peanut sauce**
- 1 **cup coleslaw mix**
- 1 **cup (4 ounces) shredded part-skim mozzarella cheese**
- 2 **green onions, thinly sliced**
- ¼ **cup chopped salted peanuts**
- 2 **tablespoons minced fresh cilantro**

1. Place the prebaked pizza crust on an ungreased 12-in. pizza pan or baking sheet. In a small bowl, combine the shredded chicken and Thai peanut sauce; spoon over the pizza crust. Top with the coleslaw mix and shredded mozzarella cheese.

2. Bake 10-12 minutes or until the mozzarella cheese is melted. Sprinkle with the green onions, peanuts and cilantro.

SAUCY THAI CHICKEN PIZZA

Green Chili Shredded Pork makes my hungry clan happy. We frequently have leftovers, but that's one of the reasons this is a mealtime favorite.
—MARY SHIVERS ADA, OK

GREEN CHILI SHREDDED PORK

FREEZE IT | **SLOW COOKER**

Green Chili Shredded Pork

PREP: 10 MIN. • **COOK:** 6 HOURS
MAKES: 8 SERVINGS

- 1 **boneless pork loin roast (3 to 4 pounds)**
- 1½ **cups apple cider or juice**
- 1 **can (4 ounces) chopped green chilies, drained**
- 3 **garlic cloves, minced**
- 1½ **teaspoons salt**
- 1½ **teaspoons hot pepper sauce**
- 1 **teaspoon chili powder**
- 1 **teaspoon pepper**
- ½ **teaspoon ground cumin**
- ½ **teaspoon dried oregano**
- 16 **flour tortillas (8 inches)**
  Optional toppings: chopped peeled mango, shredded lettuce, chopped fresh cilantro and lime wedges

1. Place pork in a 5- or 6-qt. slow cooker. In a small bowl, mix the apple cider, green chilies, garlic, salt, pepper sauce, chili powder, pepper, cumin and oregano; pour over the pork. Cook, covered, on low 6-8 hours or until meat is tender.

2. Remove the roast; cool slightly. Shred the pork with two forks. Return to slow cooker; heat through. Using tongs, serve the pork in tortillas with toppings as desired.

FREEZE OPTION *Place the shredded pork in freezer containers; top with the cooking juices. Cool and freeze. To use, partially thaw pork in the refrigerator overnight. Heat through in a saucepan, stirring occasionally.*

EAT SMART **FAST FIX**
Southwest Shredded Pork Salad

We have the perfect solution for a fridge full of extra shredded pork—this fabulous main-dish salad that tosses in black beans, tomato, onion and corn. Can't find cotija cheese? Simply substitute shredded mozzarella. Then just drizzle on the dressing of your choice and dig in!
—MARY SHIVERS ADA, OK

START TO FINISH: 20 MIN.
MAKES: 6 SERVINGS

- 6 **cups torn mixed salad greens**
- 3 **cups from Green Chili Shredded Pork (recipe below left), warmed**
- ¾ **cup canned black beans, rinsed and drained**
- 1 **medium tomato, chopped**
- 1 **small red onion, chopped**
- ½ **cup fresh or frozen corn**
- ½ **cup crumbled cotija or shredded part-skim mozzarella cheese**
  Salad dressing of your choice

Arrange salad greens on a large serving platter. Top with the shredded pork, black beans, tomatoes, red onion, corn and cheese. Serve with salad dressing.
PER SERVING *(calculated without dressing) equals 233 cal., 8 g fat (4 g sat. fat), 67 mg chol., 321 mg sodium, 12 g carb., 3 g fiber, 28 g pro.* **Diabetic Exchanges:** *4 lean meat, 1 vegetable, ½ starch.*

SOUTHWEST SHREDDED PORK SALAD

SLOW COOKER 🍲
Slow Cooker Pot Roast

I work full time but love to put together home-cooked dinners for my husband and son. It's such a comfort to get home and smell a simmering roast that I know will be fall-apart tender and delicious.

—**GINA JACKSON** OGDENSBURG, NY

PREP: 15 MIN. • **COOK:** 6 HOURS
MAKES: 6 SERVINGS

- 1 **cup warm water**
- 1 **tablespoon beef base**
- ½ **pound sliced fresh mushrooms**
- 1 **large onion, coarsely chopped**
- 3 **garlic cloves, minced**
- 1 **boneless beef chuck roast (3 pounds)**
- ½ **teaspoon pepper**
- 1 **tablespoon Worcestershire sauce**
- ¼ **cup butter, cubed**
- ⅓ **cup all-purpose flour**
- ¼ **teaspoon salt**

1. In a 5- or 6-qt. slow cooker, whisk water and beef base; add mushrooms, onion and garlic. Sprinkle the roast with pepper; transfer to slow cooker. Drizzle with Worcestershire sauce. Cook, covered, on low 6-8 hours or until meat is tender.

2. Remove roast to a serving platter; tent with foil. Strain cooking juices, reserving vegetables. Skim fat from cooking juices. In a large saucepan, melt butter over medium heat. Stir in flour and salt until smooth; gradually whisk in the cooking juices. Bring to a boil, stirring constantly; cook and stir 1-2 minutes or until thickened. Stir in cooked vegetables. Serve with roast.

NOTE *Look for beef base near the broth and bouillon.*

SLOW COOKER
POT ROAST

POT ROAST HASH

FAST FIX ▶
Pot Roast Hash

How's this for a hearty breakfast? It's so satisfying, you'll want to keep it in mind for dinner, too. In the morning, add some toast or a bowl of fresh fruit as a side dish. In the evening, put together a simple green salad instead. Either way, it's a meal you'll want again and again.

—**GINA JACKSON** OGDENSBURG, NY

START TO FINISH: 25 MIN.
MAKES: 5 SERVINGS

- 3 **cups frozen O'Brien potatoes**
- 2 **cups shredded meat from Slow Cooker Pot Roast (recipe above left)**
- ¾ **cup vegetables from Slow Cooker Pot Roast (recipe above left)**
- 1 **tablespoon butter**
- 5 **large eggs**
- ¼ **teaspoon salt**
- ¼ **teaspoon pepper**
  Minced chives

1. In a large skillet, cook the O'Brien potatoes according to the package directions; stir in the shredded meat and vegetables; heat through.

2. In another skillet, heat the butter over medium-high heat. Break the eggs, one at a time, into pan. Sprinkle with salt and pepper. Reduce the heat to low. Cook until the desired degree of doneness is reached. Serve eggs over hash; sprinkle with chives.

TOP TIP

When I have leftover beef or pork roast, I like using the meat to make barbecue sandwiches. I simply add barbecue sauce and a few drops of Worcestershire sauce, then scoop it onto buns and serve. Everyone enjoys this roast re-do.

—**PAULINE M.** FRANKLINTON, LA

Bean & Beef Slow-Cooked Chili

We always build up our chili with toppings like pico de gallo, red onion, cilantro and cheese. Save three cups to pile on nachos for an effortless supper tomorrow.

—**MALLORY LYNCH** MADISON, WI

PREP: 20 MIN. • **COOK:** 6 HOURS
MAKES: 6 SERVINGS (2¼ QUARTS)

- 1 **pound lean ground beef (90% lean)**
- 1 **large sweet onion, chopped**
- 3 **garlic cloves, minced**
- 2 **cans (14½ ounces each) diced tomatoes with mild green chilies**
- 2 **cans (15 ounces each) pinto beans, rinsed and drained**
- 2 **cans (15 ounces each) black beans, rinsed and drained**
- 2 **to 3 tablespoons chili powder**
- 2 **teaspoons ground cumin**
- ½ **teaspoon salt**

Optional toppings: sour cream, chopped red onion and minced fresh cilantro

1. In a large skillet, cook the beef, sweet onion and garlic over medium heat 6-8 minutes or until beef is no longer pink, breaking up beef into crumbles; drain.

2. Transfer the beef mixture to a 5-qt. slow cooker. Drain one can tomatoes, discarding liquid; add to slow cooker. Stir in the beans, chili powder, cumin, salt and remaining tomatoes. Cook, covered, on low 6-8 hours to allow the flavors to blend.

3. Mash beans to desired consistency. Serve with toppings as desired.

FREEZE OPTION *Freeze the cooled chili in freezer containers. To use, partially thaw chili in the refrigerator overnight. Heat through in a saucepan, stirring occasionally and adding a little water if necessary.*

DELUXE
WALKING NACHOS

Deluxe Walking Nachos

The kids will come running for this one! Chili leftovers get new life as an awesome filling for a handheld bag of walk-around nachos. Cut open each bag along one side, instead of across the top, making a larger opening so it's easier to fill and eat from.

—**MALLORY LYNCH** MADISON, WI

START TO FINISH: 20 MIN.
MAKES: 6 SERVINGS

- 6 **packages (1 ounce each) nacho-flavored tortilla chips**
- 3 **cups Bean & Beef Slow-Cooked Chili (recipe above left), warmed**
- **Optional toppings: shredded cheddar cheese, sour cream, chopped tomatoes and pickled jalapeno slices**

Cut open the tortilla chip bags. Divide the chili among the bags; add toppings as desired.

BEAN & BEEF
SLOW-COOKED CHILI

Quick Chicken

It's no surprise **chicken is such a winner** for dinner. This versatile bird is awesome piled on a pizza, stacked on sandwiches, served over pasta, tossed in a salad—you name it! And it's even better when the dish **gets to the table quickly** for your hungry family.

MY MOTHER'S LEMONY CHICKEN WITH BROCCOLI

My Mother's Lemony Chicken with Broccoli

Mom used to prepare super-succulent chicken mixed with broccoli for our family in Montana. Guests who joined us for supper couldn't stop raving.
—**JESSY DRUMMOND** SPRINGFIELD, TN

PREP: 15 MIN. • **COOK:** 20 MIN.
MAKES: 4 SERVINGS

- 1 pound boneless skinless chicken breasts, cut into 1-inch strips
- ½ teaspoon salt
- ¼ teaspoon pepper
- ½ cup all-purpose flour
- ¼ teaspoon garlic powder
- ¼ teaspoon paprika
- 1 large egg
- 3 tablespoons lemon juice, divided
- ¼ cup butter, cubed
- 1 cup chicken broth
- ½ teaspoon grated lemon peel
- 4 cups fresh broccoli florets
   Lemon wedges
   Hot cooked rice, optional

1. Sprinkle chicken with salt and pepper. In a shallow bowl, mix the flour, garlic powder and paprika. In another shallow bowl, whisk the egg and 1 tablespoon lemon juice. Dip the chicken in egg mixture, then in flour mixture; shake off excess.
2. In a large skillet, heat the butter over medium heat. Add the chicken; cook 4-6 minutes on each side or until no longer pink. Remove and keep warm. Add the chicken broth, lemon peel and remaining lemon juice to the skillet; bring to a boil. Stir in broccoli. Reduce the heat; simmer, covered, 8-10 minutes or until the broccoli is tender. Serve with chicken, lemon wedges and, if desired, rice.

FAST FIX
Bacon Chicken Chopped Salad

Here's one of the many reasons we look forward to tomato season. Chopped salads are simple to make and a great way to eat garden-fresh produce.
—**DONNA MARIE RYAN** TOPSFIELD, MA

START TO FINISH: 20 MIN.
MAKES: 6 SERVINGS (1 CUP DRESSING)

- 1 package (22 ounces) frozen grilled chicken breast strips
- 1 cup (4 ounces) crumbled blue cheese
- 3 tablespoons white wine vinegar
- 1 tablespoon water
- ⅛ teaspoon coarsely ground pepper
- ¼ cup canola oil
- 8 cups chopped romaine
- 3 medium tomatoes, chopped
- 6 bacon strips, cooked and crumbled

1. Heat chicken according to the package directions. Cool slightly; coarsely chop chicken.
2. For the dressing, place the cheese, vinegar, water and pepper in a small food processor; cover and process until smooth. While processing, gradually add oil in a steady stream.
3. In a large bowl, combine romaine, chicken, tomatoes and bacon. Serve with dressing.

BACON CHICKEN CHOPPED SALAD

CHEESY CHICKEN AND
LEEK PHYLLO PIE

Cheesy Chicken and Leek Phyllo Pie

In our house, potpie is so popular that it's a year-round staple. In spring, we use leeks, mushrooms and a lighter crust made of phyllo dough. If you don't have Gruyere, try Parmesan.

—ANDREA STEWART TORONTO, ON

PREP: 35 MIN. • **BAKE:** 30 MIN.
MAKES: 6 SERVINGS

- 6 tablespoons olive oil, divided
- 2 medium leeks (white portion only), thinly sliced
- 1 cup sliced fresh mushrooms
- 1 tablespoon all-purpose flour
- 1 cup chicken stock
- 1 can (5 ounces) evaporated milk
- 3 cups cubed cooked chicken
- ¾ cup plus 2 tablespoons shredded Gruyere cheese, divided
- 1½ teaspoons minced fresh thyme or
- ½ teaspoon dried thyme
- ½ teaspoon salt
- ½ teaspoon pepper
- 10 sheets phyllo dough (14x9-inch size)

1. Preheat oven to 350°. In a large skillet, heat 2 tablespoons oil over medium-high heat. Add leeks and mushrooms; cook and stir 3-4 minutes or until vegetables are tender. Stir in flour until blended; gradually stir in stock and milk. Bring to a boil, stirring constantly; cook and stir 3-4 minutes or until thickened. Stir in the chicken, ¾ cup cheese, thyme, salt and pepper.
2. Brush a 9-in. pie plate with some of the remaining oil. Place one sheet of phyllo dough into the prepared pie plate, allowing the ends to extend over edges of dish; brush with oil. (Keep the remaining phyllo covered with plastic wrap and a damp towel to prevent it from drying out.) Layer with seven additional phyllo sheets, brushing each layer with oil and rotating sheets to cover the pie plate. Transfer chicken mixture to crust.
3. Gently fold in the ends of the phyllo over filling, leaving an opening in the center. Crumble the remaining phyllo sheets over the filling; sprinkle with remaining cheese. Brush edges with remaining oil. Bake 30-35 minutes or until golden brown.

FAST FIX

Swiss Chicken Sliders

When some friends dropped by for a spur-of-the-moment bonfire, I created these mini sandwiches on the fly so we'd have something to eat. Bake until the cheese is nice and gooey!

—SARA MARTIN WHITEFISH, MT

START TO FINISH: 25 MIN.
MAKES: 6 SERVINGS

- ½ cup mayonnaise
- 3 tablespoons yellow mustard
- 12 mini buns, split
- 12 slices deli ham
- 3 cups shredded rotisserie chicken
- 6 slices Swiss cheese, cut in half

1. Preheat oven to 350°. In a small bowl, mix mayonnaise and mustard. Spread bun bottoms and tops with mayonnaise mixture. Layer bottoms with ham, chicken and Swiss cheese; replace the tops. Arrange in a single layer in a 15x10x1-in. baking pan.
2. Bake, covered, 10-15 minutes or until heated through and the Swiss cheese is melted.

SWISS CHICKEN SLIDERS

FAST FIX ▶

Chicken Club Pizza

A co-worker told me how she swaps in crescent rolls for pizza crust. I used that idea to turn an awesome sandwich into a pizza. For a cool topper, sprinkle on shredded lettuce after baking.
—SHERRI COX LUCASVILLE, OH

START TO FINISH: 30 MIN.
MAKES: 6 SLICES

- 1 tube (8 ounces) refrigerated crescent rolls
- 2 teaspoons sesame seeds
- ¼ cup mayonnaise
- 1 teaspoon dried basil
- ¼ teaspoon grated lemon peel
- 1 cup (4 ounces) shredded Monterey Jack cheese
- 4 ounces sliced deli chicken, cut into 1-inch strips
- 6 bacon strips, cooked and crumbled
- 2 plum tomatoes, thinly sliced
- ½ cup shredded Swiss cheese

1. Preheat oven to 375°. Unroll the crescent dough and separate into eight triangles; arrange in a single layer on a greased 12-in. pizza pan. Press onto the pan to form a crust and seal the seams; sprinkle with sesame seeds. Bake 8-10 minutes or until the edge is lightly browned.

2. In a small bowl, mix mayonnaise, basil and lemon peel. Spread over the crust; top with Monterey Jack cheese, chicken, bacon, tomatoes and Swiss cheese. Bake 8-12 minutes or until crust is golden and cheese is melted.

BARBECUED STRAWBERRY CHICKEN

CHICKEN CLUB PIZZA

When I want to impress, I put Barbecued Strawberry Chicken on the menu. It's easier to prepare than anyone would guess but always looks and tastes extra-special.
—BONNIE HAWKINS ELKHORN, WI

Barbecued Strawberry Chicken

PREP: 25 MIN. • **BAKE:** 15 MIN.
MAKES: 4 SERVINGS

- 2 tablespoons canola oil
- 4 boneless skinless chicken breast halves (6 ounces each)
- 2 tablespoons butter
- ¼ cup finely chopped red onion
- 1 cup barbecue sauce
- 2 tablespoons brown sugar
- 2 tablespoons balsamic vinegar
- 2 tablespoons honey
- 1 cup sliced fresh strawberries

1. Preheat oven to 350°. In a large ovenproof skillet, heat the oil over medium-high heat. Brown chicken on both sides. Remove from pan. In same pan, heat butter over medium-high heat. Add onion; cook and stir 1 minute or until tender.

2. Stir in the barbecue sauce, brown sugar, balsamic vinegar and honey. Bring to a boil. Reduce heat; simmer, uncovered, 4-6 minutes or until thickened. Return the chicken to the pan. Bake 12-15 minutes or until a thermometer reads 165°. Stir in the strawberries.

TURKEY ENCHILADA STACK

1. In a 9-in. microwave-safe pie plate, combine zucchini and onion. Microwave, covered, on high for 3-4 minutes or until tender; drain.

2. In a bowl, whisk the eggs, salt and pepper; stir in the cheddar cheese and ham. Carefully pour over the zucchini mixture. Microwave at 70% power for 8-9 minutes or until a knife inserted near the center comes out clean.
NOTE *This recipe was tested in a 1,100-watt microwave.*

EAT SMART **FAST FIX** ▸
Quick Asian Chicken Dinner

Craving Chinese food? Make your own version in less than half an hour.
—**CAROLYN ZIMMERMAN** FAIRBURY, IL

START TO FINISH: 25 MIN.
MAKES: 2 SERVINGS

- ½ **pound boneless skinless chicken breasts, cut into ½-inch strips**
- 1 **small onion, thinly sliced**
- 1 **tablespoon canola oil**
- 1 **cup frozen California-blend vegetables**
- ¾ **cup uncooked instant rice**
- ¾ **cup reduced-sodium chicken broth**
- 1 **tablespoon reduced-sodium soy sauce**

1. In a shallow 1-qt. microwave-safe dish, combine the chicken, onion and oil. Cover and microwave on high for 2 minutes.

2. Stir in the remaining ingredients. Cover and cook for 4-5 minutes or until the chicken is no longer pink and the rice is tender. Let stand, covered, for 5 minutes. Fluff rice with a fork.
NOTE *This recipe was tested in a 1,100-watt microwave.*
PER SERVING *1½ cups equals 356 cal., 10 g fat (1 g sat. fat), 63 mg chol., 591 mg sodium, 35 g carb., 2 g fiber, 29 g pro.* **Diabetic Exchanges:** *3 lean meat, 2 starch, 1½ fat, 1 vegetable.*

EAT SMART **FAST FIX** ▸
Turkey Enchilada Stack

As a child, my husband was a picky eater. My mother-in-law could always get him to devour this dish—so I knew it would be a safe bet on my own menus!
—**ASHLEY WOLF** ALABASTER, AL

START TO FINISH: 20 MIN.
MAKES: 4 SERVINGS

- 1 **pound lean ground turkey**
- 2 **cans (8 ounces each) no-salt-added tomato sauce**
- 3 **teaspoons dried minced onion**
- ½ **teaspoon garlic powder**
- ½ **teaspoon pepper**
- ¼ **teaspoon salt**
- 4 **whole wheat tortillas (8 inches)**
- ⅔ **cup shredded reduced-fat cheddar cheese**
  Optional topings: shredded lettuce, chopped tomatoes and reduced-fat sour cream

1. In a large skillet, cook turkey over medium heat until meat is no longer pink; drain. Stir in the tomato sauce, minced onion, garlic powder, pepper and salt; heat through.

2. In a microwave-safe 2½-qt. round or oval dish coated with cooking spray, layer one tortilla, about ¾ cup meat mixture and a scant 3 tablespoons cheese. Repeat layers three times. Cover; cook on high for 4-5 minutes or until the cheese is melted. Let stand for 5 minutes before cutting. Serve with toppings if desired.
NOTE *This recipe was tested in a 1,100-watt microwave.*
PER SERVING *1 piece (calculated without optional ingredients) equals 404 cal., 16 g fat (5 g sat. fat), 103 mg chol., 582 mg sodium, 31 g carb., 3 g fiber, 29 g pro.* **Diabetic Exchanges:** *4 lean meat, 2 starch, 1 fat.*

⑤ INGREDIENTS **FAST FIX** ▸
Zucchini Frittata

This is great for breakfast or any time at all. A little red pepper makes a pretty garnish.
—**MILDRED FOX** FOSTORIA, OH

START TO FINISH: 25 MIN.
MAKES: 4 SERVINGS

- 4 **cups finely chopped zucchini (3-4 medium)**
- 1 **small onion, chopped**
- 4 **large eggs**
- ¾ **teaspoon salt**
- ⅛ **teaspoon pepper**
- 1 **cup (4 ounces) shredded cheddar cheese**
- 1 **cup cubed fully cooked ham**

COUSCOUS & SAUSAGE-STUFFED
ACORN SQUASH

EAT SMART FAST FIX ▶

Pepper Steak with Potatoes

I added potatoes to one of my favorite Asian pepper steak dishes. Now it satisfies everyone in my house full of hungry guys.
—**KRISTINE MARRA** CLIFTON PARK, NY

START TO FINISH: 30 MIN.
MAKES: 6 SERVINGS

- 1½ **pounds red potatoes (about 5 medium), sliced**
- ½ **cup water**
- 1 **cup beef broth**
- 4 **teaspoons cornstarch**
- ⅛ **teaspoon pepper**
- 2 **tablespoons olive oil, divided**
- 1 **beef top sirloin steak (1 pound), thinly sliced**
- 1 **garlic clove, minced**
- 1 **medium green pepper, julienned**
- 1 **small onion, chopped**

1. Place the potatoes and water in a large microwave-safe dish. Microwave, covered, on high for 5-7 minutes or until tender.
2. Meanwhile, in a small bowl, mix the beef broth, cornstarch and pepper until smooth. In a large skillet, heat 1 tablespoon oil over medium-high heat. Add the beef slices; cook and stir 2-3 minutes or until no longer pink. Add the garlic; cook 1 minute longer. Remove from pan.
3. In same pan, heat the remaining oil. Add green pepper and onion; cook and stir until vegetables are crisp-tender. Stir the cornstarch mixture and add to the pan. Bring to a boil; cook and stir 1-2 minutes or until sauce is thickened. Add the potatoes and beef to the pan; heat through.
NOTE *This recipe was tested in a 1,100-watt microwave.*
PER SERVING *1 cup equals 277 cal., 10 g fat (2 g sat. fat), 55 mg chol., 179 mg sodium, 27 g carb., 3 g fiber, 23 g pro.* ***Diabetic Exchanges:*** *2 meat, 2 vegetable, 1 starch.*

FAST FIX ▶

Couscous & Sausage-Stuffed Acorn Squash

When I'm cooking for just two people, this comforting dinner of acorn squash, sausage and couscous is just the right size.
—**JESSICA LEVINSON** NYACK, NY

START TO FINISH: 25 MIN.
MAKES: 2 SERVINGS

- 1 **medium acorn squash (about 1½ pounds)**
- ¼ **teaspoon salt**
- ¼ **teaspoon pepper**
- 1 **tablespoon olive oil**
- 1 **medium onion, chopped**
- 2 **fully cooked spinach and feta chicken sausage links (3 ounces each), sliced**
- ½ **cup chicken stock**
- ½ **cup uncooked couscous**
  Crumbled feta cheese, optional

1. Cut the acorn squash lengthwise in half; remove and discard the seeds. Sprinkle squash with salt and pepper; place in a microwave-safe dish, cut side down. Microwave, covered, on high for 10-12 minutes or until tender.
2. Meanwhile, in a large skillet, heat the olive oil over medium heat. Add the onion; cook and stir 5-7 minutes or until tender and lightly browned. Add sausage; cook and stir 2-3 minutes or until lightly browned.

3. Add chicken stock; bring to a boil. Stir in couscous. Remove from heat; let stand, covered, 5 minutes or until stock is absorbed. Spoon over squash. If desired, top with feta cheese.

FAST FIX ▶

Apricot Brie

Your guests will never guess how little time you spent preparing an elegant appetizer of soft, creamy Brie over a spiced apricot sauce. Pair the cheese spread with slices of fresh-baked French bread.
—**ALICE GOGGIN** TRABUCO CANYON, CA

START TO FINISH: 20 MIN.
MAKES: 8 SERVINGS

- ½ **cup apricot preserves**
- 1 **tablespoon grated orange peel**
- 1 **tablespoon lemon juice**
- 1 **tablespoon orange juice**
- ⅛ **teaspoon ground cinnamon**
- 1 **round (8 ounces) Brie cheese**
  Sliced French bread

In a small microwave-safe bowl, combine the first five ingredients. Cook, uncovered, on high for 1 minute or until heated through. Pour into a shallow 3-cup microwave-safe serving dish. Place Brie cheese on preserves mixture. Cook 1-1½ minutes longer or until the cheese is softened. Serve with French bread.
NOTE *This recipe was tested in a 1,100-watt microwave.*

PEPPER STEAK
WITH POTATOES

Birthday Sprinkles

Here comes the happy! The party hits the table with these colorful cakes, pops, cookies, pretzels and more dressed up for fun. The cute sprinkle-filled treats are perfect for **brightening birthdays** but are such a snap to make, you'll want to fix them any ol' day of the week.

BIRTHDAY CAKE
FREEZER POPS

Chocolate Cupcakes

This classic recipe is simply unbeatable. Try sitting down with a big glass of milk and see if you can eat just one!

—MARLENE MARTIN
COUNTRY HARBOUR MINES, NS

PREP: 20 MIN. • **BAKE:** 15 MIN. + COOLING
MAKES: 16 CUPCAKES

- ½ cup butter, softened
- 1 cup sugar
- 1 large egg
- 1 teaspoon vanilla extract
- 1½ cups all-purpose flour
- ½ cup baking cocoa
- 1 teaspoon baking soda
- ¼ teaspoon salt
- ½ cup water
- ½ cup buttermilk
  Chocolate frosting and
  multi-colored sprinkles

1. In a small bowl, cream butter and sugar until light and fluffy. Beat in egg and vanilla. Combine the flour, cocoa, baking soda and salt; gradually add to creamed mixture alternately with water and buttermilk, beating well after each addition.

2. Fill paper-lined muffin cups two-thirds full. Bake at 375° for 12-15 minutes or until a toothpick inserted near center comes out clean. Cool for 10 minutes before removing from the pans to wire racks to cool completely. Frost the cupcakes and decorate with sprinkles.

CHOCOLATE
CUPCAKES

FREEZE IT
Birthday Cake Freezer Pops

While I was searching for birthday cake ice cream—my favorite flavor—I came up with these creamy pudding pops I can keep on hand. Now, instead of driving to the grocery store whenever a craving hits, I just head to my freezer!

—DAWN LOPEZ WESTERLY, RI

PREP: 20 MIN. + FREEZING
MAKES: 1½ DOZEN

- ⅔ cup sprinkles, divided
- 18 paper or plastic cups (3 ounces each) and wooden pop sticks
- 2 cups cold 2% milk
- 1 package (3.4 ounces) instant vanilla pudding mix

- 1 carton (8 ounces) frozen whipped topping, thawed
- 2 cups crushed vanilla wafers (about 60 wafers)

1. Spoon 1 teaspoon sprinkles into each cup. In a large bowl, whisk milk and pudding mix 2 minutes. Let stand 2 minutes or until soft-set. Stir in the whipped topping, crushed wafers and remaining sprinkles.

2. Cut a 1-in. hole in the tip of a pastry bag or in a corner of a food-safe plastic bag. Transfer mixture to bag. Pipe into the prepared cups. Top with foil and insert sticks through foil. Freeze until firm, about 4 hours. Let stand at room temperature 5 minutes before gently removing pops.

My kids say their special day is even more fun when I serve Birthday Cake Pancakes. I stack 'em up nice and high, then add melted vanilla frosting over the top to seal the deal delightfully.

—**DINA CROWELL** FREDERICKSBURG, VA

BIRTHDAY CAKE PANCAKES

FREEZE IT
Birthday Cake Pancakes

PREP: 15 MIN. + STANDING
COOK: 5 MIN./BATCH • **MAKES:** 6 SERVINGS

- 1 **cup pancake mix**
- 1 **cup yellow or white cake mix**
- 2 **eggs**
- 1½ **cups plus 1 tablespoon 2% milk, divided**
- 1 **teaspoon vanilla extract**
- ¼ **cup sprinkles**
- ¾ **cup vanilla frosting**
  Additional sprinkles

1. In a large bowl, whisk the pancake mix and cake mix. In another bowl, whisk eggs, 1½ cups milk and vanilla until blended. Add to dry ingredients, stirring just until moistened. Let stand 10 minutes. Fold in ¼ cup sprinkles.

2. Lightly grease a griddle; heat over medium heat. Pour the pancake batter by ¼ cupfuls onto the griddle, creating six large pancakes. Cook until bubbles on top begin to pop and the bottoms are golden brown. Turn; cook until the second side is golden brown. Repeat using 2 tablespoons batter, creating 12 medium pancakes, and 1 tablespoon batter, creating 18 small pancakes.

3. Place frosting and remaining milk in a microwave-safe bowl. Microwave, covered, on high for 10-15 seconds or until melted. To serve, stack one large pancake, two medium pancakes and three small pancakes on each plate; drizzle with frosting. Top with additional sprinkles.

FREEZE OPTION *Freeze the cooled pancakes between layers of waxed paper in a resealable plastic freezer bag. To use, place the pancakes on an ungreased baking sheet, cover with foil and reheat in a preheated 375° oven 5-10 minutes. Or, place a stack of three pancakes on a microwave-safe plate; microwave on high for 30-60 seconds or until heated through.*

NOTE *This recipe was tested with Aunt Jemima pancake mix.*

STRAWBERRY
MUFFIN CONES

NOTE *The cupcake cones are best served the same day they're prepared. Cupcakes can be baked in paper liners instead of ice cream cones.*

FREEZE IT
Confetti Cake Batter Cookies

My mom and I took up cake decorating as a hobby we could enjoy together. One day we decided to try using our favorite cake mix—funfetti—to make a basic dough for cutout cookies. Yum!

—**DANIELLE DEMARCO** BASKING RIDGE, NJ

PREP: 15 MIN + CHILLING
BAKE: 10 MIN./BATCH + COOLING
MAKES: ABOUT 2 DOZEN

- ½ **cup butter, softened**
- 2 **large eggs**
- 1 **teaspoon vanilla extract**
- 1 **package funfetti cake mix**

1. In a large bowl, beat the butter, eggs and vanilla until combined. Beat in the cake mix. Refrigerate, covered, 2 hours or until firm enough to roll.
2. Preheat oven to 350°. On a well-floured surface, roll the cookie dough to ¼-in. thickness. Cut with a floured 2½-in. cookie cutter. Place 1 in. apart on ungreased baking sheets. Bake 8-10 minutes or until set. Remove from the pans to wire racks to cool completely. Decorate as desired.
FREEZE OPTION *Transfer the cookie dough to a resealable plastic freezer bag; freeze. To use, thaw the dough in refrigerator until soft enough to roll. Prepare and bake cookies as directed; decorate as desired.*

Strawberry Muffin Cones

This is a such a fun way to serve cupcakes. I fill the ice cream cones with batter, then stand them inside muffin cups and bake. Children find the treats easy to eat—and adults say taking a bite makes them feel like a kid again! Dip the tops in chocolate and decorate for a festive finish.

—**BARB KIETZER** NILES, MI

PREP: 20 MIN. • **BAKE:** 20 MIN.
MAKES: 20 SERVINGS

- 2 **cups all-purpose flour**
- ½ **cup sugar**
- 2 **teaspoons baking powder**
- ½ **teaspoon baking soda**
- ½ **teaspoon salt**
- 2 **large eggs**
- ¾ **cup (6 ounces) strawberry yogurt**
- ½ **cup canola oil**
- 1 **cup chopped fresh strawberries**
- 20 **ice cream cake cones (about 3 inches tall)**
- 1 **cup (6 ounces) semisweet chocolate chips**
- 1 **tablespoon shortening**
  Colored sprinkles

1. In a large bowl, combine the first five ingredients. In another bowl, beat eggs, yogurt, oil and berries; stir into dry ingredients just until moistened.
2. Place cones in muffin cups; spoon 2 heaping tablespoons batter into each cone. Bake at 375° for 19-21 minutes or until a toothpick inserted near center comes out clean. Cool completely.
3. In a microwave, melt the chips and shortening; stir until smooth. Dip the muffin tops in chocolate; allow excess to drip off. Decorate with sprinkles.

Rich Buttercream Frosting

Just a few everyday ingredients come together for a creamy homemade frosting that's perfect for topping cupcakes, cakes and cookies. If you love making desserts, keep this recipe handy! In a large bowl, combine 1 cup softened butter, 8 cups confectioners' sugar, 6 tablespoons 2% milk and 2 teaspoons vanilla extract; beat until smooth (frosting will be thick). If desired, tint with food coloring. *Makes 5 cups.*
—*TASTE OF HOME* TEST KITCHEN

(5) INGREDIENTS

Ice Cream Birthday Cake

Colored jimmies instantly transform a plain dessert into a festive birthday treat.
—**BECKY HERGES** FARGO, ND

PREP: 50 MIN. + FREEZING
MAKES: 12 SERVINGS

- **4 cups birthday cake-flavored ice cream or flavor of your choice, softened if necessary**
- **1 funfetti cake mix (regular size)**
- **1 carton (8 ounces) frozen whipped topping, thawed**
  Sprinkles

1. Line a 9-in. round pan with plastic wrap. Spread ice cream into pan. Freeze 2 hours or until firm.
2. Prepare and bake the cake mix according to package directions, using two 9-in. round baking pans. Cool in pans 10 minutes before removing to wire racks to cool completely.
3. Using a serrated knife, trim tops of cakes if domed. Place one cake layer on a serving plate. Invert ice cream onto cake layer; remove plastic wrap. Top with remaining layer. Spread whipped topping over the top and sides of cake. Decorate with sprinkles as desired. Freeze 2 hours longer or until firm.

FAST FIX
Sparkling Pretzels

Pretzel rods coated with chocolate and sprinkles—what could be easier?
—**RENEE SCHWEBACH** DUMONT, MN

START TO FINISH: 30 MIN.
MAKES: ABOUT 2 DOZEN

- **8 ounces white baking chocolate, chopped**
- **1 package (10 ounces) pretzel rods**
  Colored sugar and sprinkles

In a microwave-safe bowl, melt white baking chocolate at 70% power for 1 minute; stir. Microwave at additional 10- to 20-second intervals, stirring until smooth. Dip each pretzel rod about halfway into melted chocolate; allow excess to drip off. Sprinkle with sugar and sprinkles. Place on waxed paper to dry.

TOP TIP

To dress up a chocolate layer cake from a packaged mix, I tuck a fruity surprise inside. I slice bananas and arrange them between the cake layers with the frosting. It takes very little time to do, and this dessert has become one of the most-requested birthday cakes at our house.
—**JOAN B.** ST. LOUIS, MO

ICE CREAM BIRTHDAY CAKE

Substitutions & Equivalents

EQUIVALENT MEASURES

3 teaspoons	=	1 tablespoon	16 tablespoons	=	1 cup
4 tablespoons	=	1/4 cup	2 cups	=	1 pint
5-1/3 tablespoons	=	1/3 cup	4 cups	=	1 quart
8 tablespoons	=	1/2 cup	4 quarts	=	1 gallon

FOOD EQUIVALENTS

GRAINS

Macaroni	1 cup (3-1/2 ounces) uncooked	=	2-1/2 cups cooked
Noodles, Medium	3 cups (4 ounces) uncooked	=	4 cups cooked
Popcorn	1/3 to 1/2 cup unpopped	=	8 cups popped
Rice, Long Grain	1 cup uncooked	=	3 cups cooked
Rice, Quick-Cooking	1 cup uncooked	=	2 cups cooked
Spaghetti	8 ounces uncooked	=	4 cups cooked

CRUMBS

Bread	1 slice	=	3/4 cup soft crumbs, 1/4 cup fine dry crumbs
Graham Crackers	7 squares	=	1/2 cup finely crushed
Buttery Round Crackers	12 crackers	=	1/2 cup finely crushed
Saltine Crackers	14 crackers	=	1/2 cup finely crushed

FRUITS

Bananas	1 medium	=	1/3 cup mashed
Lemons	1 medium	=	3 tablespoons juice, 2 teaspoons grated peel
Limes	1 medium	=	2 tablespoons juice, 1-1/2 teaspoons grated peel
Oranges	1 medium	=	1/4 to 1/3 cup juice, 4 teaspoons grated peel

VEGETABLES

Cabbage	1 head	=	5 cups shredded	Green Pepper	1 large	=	1 cup chopped
Carrots	1 pound	=	3 cups shredded	Mushrooms	1/2 pound	=	3 cups sliced
Celery	1 rib	=	1/2 cup chopped	Onions	1 medium	=	1/2 cup chopped
Corn	1 ear fresh	=	2/3 cup kernels	Potatoes	3 medium	=	2 cups cubed

NUTS

Almonds	1 pound	=	3 cups chopped	Pecan Halves	1 pound	=	4-1/2 cups chopped
Ground Nuts	3-3/4 ounces	=	1 cup	Walnuts	1 pound	=	3-3/4 cups chopped

EASY SUBSTITUTIONS

When you need...		Use...
Baking Powder	1 teaspoon	1/2 teaspoon cream of tartar + 1/4 teaspoon baking soda
Buttermilk	1 cup	1 tablespoon lemon juice or vinegar + enough milk to measure 1 cup (let stand 5 minutes before using)
Cornstarch	1 tablespoon	2 tablespoons all-purpose flour
Honey	1 cup	1-1/4 cups sugar + 1/4 cup water
Half-and-Half Cream	1 cup	1 tablespoon melted butter + enough whole milk to measure 1 cup
Onion	1 small, chopped (1/3 cup)	1 teaspoon onion powder or 1 tablespoon dried minced onion
Tomato Juice	1 cup	1/2 cup tomato sauce + 1/2 cup water
Tomato Sauce	2 cups	3/4 cup tomato paste + 1 cup water
Unsweetened Chocolate	1 square (1 ounce)	3 tablespoons baking cocoa + 1 tablespoon shortening or oil
Whole Milk	1 cup	1/2 cup evaporated milk + 1/2 cup water

Guide to Cooking with Popular Herbs

HERB	APPETIZERS SALADS	BREADS/EGGS SAUCES/CHEESE	VEGETABLES PASTA	MEAT POULTRY	FISH SHELLFISH
BASIL	Green, Potato & Tomato Salads; Salad Dressings; Stewed Fruit	Breads, Fondue, Egg Dishes, Dips, Marinades, Sauces	Mushrooms, Tomatoes, Squash, Pasta, Bland Vegetables	Broiled, Roast Meats; Meat & Poultry Pies; Stews; Stuffing	Baked, Broiled & Poached Fish; Shellfish
BAY LEAF	Seafood Cocktail, Seafood Salad, Tomato Aspic, Stewed Fruit	Egg Dishes, Gravies, Marinades, Sauces	Dried Bean Dishes, Beets, Carrots, Onions, Potatoes, Rice, Squash	Corned Beef, Tongue Meat & Poultry Stews	Poached Fish, Shellfish, Fish Stews
CHIVES	Mixed Vegetable, Green, Potato & Tomato Salads; Salad Dressings	Egg & Cheese Dishes, Cream Cheese, Cottage Cheese, Gravies, Sauces	Hot Vegetables, Potatoes	Broiled Poultry, Poultry & Meat Pies, Stews, Casseroles	Baked Fish, Fish Casseroles, Fish Stews, Shellfish
DILL	Seafood Cocktail; Green, Potato & Tomato Salads; Salad Dressings	Breads, Egg & Cheese Dishes, Cream Cheese, Fish & Meat Sauces	Beans, Beets, Cabbage, Carrots, Cauliflower, Peas, Squash, Tomatoes	Beef, Veal Roasts, Lamb, Steaks, Chops, Stews, Roast & Creamed Poultry	Baked, Broiled, Poached & Stuffed Fish; Shellfish
GARLIC	All Salads, Salad Dressings	Fondue, Poultry Sauces, Fish & Meat Marinades	Beans, Eggplant, Potatoes, Rice, Tomatoes	Roast Meats, Meat & Poultry Pies, Hamburgers, Casseroles, Stews	Broiled Fish, Shellfish, Fish Stews, Casseroles
MARJORAM	Seafood Cocktail; Green, Poultry & Seafood Salads	Breads, Cheese Spreads, Egg & Cheese Dishes, Gravies, Sauces	Carrots, Eggplant, Peas, Onions, Potatoes, Dried Bean Dishes, Spinach	Roast Meats & Poultry, Meat & Poultry Pies, Stews & Casseroles	Baked, Broiled & Stuffed Fish; Shellfish
MUSTARD	Fresh Green Salads; Prepared Meat, Macaroni & Potato Salads; Salad Dressings	Biscuits, Egg & Cheese Dishes, Sauces	Baked Beans, Cabbage, Eggplant, Squash, Dried Beans, Mushrooms, Pasta	Chops, Steaks, Ham, Pork, Poultry, Cold Meats	Shellfish
OREGANO	Green, Poultry & Seafood Salads	Breads; Egg & Cheese Dishes; Meat, Poultry & Vegetable Sauces	Artichokes, Cabbage, Eggplant, Squash, Dried Beans, Mushrooms, Pasta	Broiled, Roast Meats; Meat & Poultry Pies; Stews; Casseroles	Baked, Broiled & Poached Fish; Shellfish
PARSLEY	Green, Potato, Seafood & Vegetable Salads	Biscuits, Breads, Egg & Cheese Dishes, Gravies, Sauces	Asparagus, Beets, Eggplant, Squash, Dried Beans, Mushrooms, Pasta	Meat Loaf, Meat & Poultry Pies, Stews, Casseroles, Stuffing	Fish Stews, Stuffed Fish
ROSEMARY	Fruit Cocktail, Fruit & Green Salads	Biscuits, Egg Dishes, Herb Butter, Cream Cheese, Marinades, Sauces	Beans, Broccoli, Peas, Cauliflower, Mushrooms, Baked Potatoes, Parsnips	Roast Meat, Poultry & Meat Pies, Stews, Casseroles, Stuffing	Stuffed Fish, Shellfish
SAGE		Breads, Fondue, Egg & Cheese Dishes, Spreads, Gravies, Sauces	Beans, Beets, Onions, Peas, Spinach, Squash, Tomatoes	Roast Meat, Poultry, Meat Loaf, Stews, Stuffing	Baked, Poached & Stuffed Fish
TARRAGON	Seafood Cocktail, Avocado Salads, Salad Dressings	Cheese Spreads, Marinades, Sauces, Egg Dishes	Asparagus, Beans, Beets, Carrots, Mushrooms, Peas, Squash, Spinach	Steaks, Poultry, Roast Meats, Casseroles, Stews	Baked, Broiled & Poached Fish; Shellfish
THYME	Seafood Cocktail; Green, Poultry, Seafood & Vegetable Salads	Biscuits, Breads, Egg & Cheese Dishes, Sauces, Spreads	Beets, Carrots, Mushrooms, Onions, Peas, Eggplant, Spinach, Potatoes	Roast Meat, Poultry & Meat Loaf, Meat & Poultry Pies, Stews, Casseroles	Baked, Broiled & Stuffed Fish; Shellfish, Fish Stews

COOKING TERMS

AL DENTE An Italian term meaning "to the tooth." Used to describe pasta that is cooked but still firm.

BASTE To moisten food with melted butter, pan drippings, marinades or other liquid to add flavor and juiciness.

BEAT To rapidly mix with a spoon, fork, wire whisk or electric mixer.

BLEND To combine ingredients until just mixed.

BOIL To heat liquids until bubbles form that cannot be "stirred down." In the case of water, the temperature will reach 212°.

BONE To remove all meat from the bone before cooking.

BROIL To cook foods about 4 to 6 inches from a heat source.

COMBINE To place several ingredients in a bowl or container and mix thoroughly.

CREAM To beat ingredients together to a smooth consistency, usually in the case of butter and sugar for baking.

CRISP-TENDER A stage of vegetable cooking where the vegetables are cooked until they are crunchy yet tender enough to be pierced with a fork.

CUT IN To break down and distribute cold butter, margarine or shortening into a flour mixture using a pastry blender or two knives.

DASH A measurement less than ⅛ teaspoon that is used for herbs, spices or hot pepper sauce. This is not an accurate measurement.

DREDGE To coat foods with flour or other dry ingredients. Most often done with pot roasts and stew meat before browning.

DRIPPINGS The juices and melted fat that collect in the bottom of the pan as meat is cooked. The juices and some of the fat from the drippings can be used in gravies and sauces.

DUST To lightly sprinkle with confectioners' sugar, baking cocoa or flour.

FLAKE To separate foods into small pieces. The term is frequently used when describing the doneness of fish.

FLUTE To make a V shape or scalloped edge on pie crust using your thumb and fingers.

FOLD To incorporate several ingredients by careful and gentle turning with a spatula. Used generally when mixing beaten egg whites or whipped cream into the rest of the ingredients to keep the batter light.

COOKING TERMS

JULIENNE To cut foods into long thin strips much like matchsticks. Most often used for salads and stir-fry dishes.

KNEAD To work dough by using a pressing and folding action to make it smooth and elastic.

MARINATE To tenderize and/or flavor foods, usually meat or raw vegetables, by placing in a liquid mixture of oil, vinegar, wine, lime or lemon juice, herbs and spices.

MINCE To cut into very fine pieces. Often used for garlic or fresh herbs.

PARBOIL To boil foods, usually vegetables, until partially cooked. Most often used when vegetables are finished using another cooking method or chilled for marinated salads or dips.

PARTIALLY SET Describes the consistency of gelatin after it has been chilled for a short amount of time. Mixture should resemble the consistency of egg whites.

PINCH A measurement less than ⅛ teaspoon of a seasoning or spice that is easily held between the thumb and index finger. This is not an accurate measurement.

PROCESS To combine, blend, chop or puree foods in a food processor or blender.

PULSE To process foods in a food processor or blender using short bursts of power. This is accomplished by quickly turning the machine on and off.

PUREE To mash solid foods into a smooth mixture using a food processor, food mill, blender or sieve.

SAUTE To fry quickly in a small amount of fat, stirring almost constantly. Most often done with onions, mushrooms and other chopped vegetables.

SIMMER To cook liquids alone or a combination of ingredients with liquid just under the boiling point (180° to 200°). The surface of the liquid will have some movement and there may be small bubbles around the side of the pan.

SOFT PEAKS The stage of beating egg whites or heavy whipping cream when the beater is lifted from the mixture and the points of the peaks curl over.

STEAM To cook foods covered on a rack or in a steamer basket over a small amount of boiling water. Most often used for vegetables.

STIFF PEAKS The stage of beating egg whites or heavy whipping cream when the beater is lifted from the mixture and the points of the peaks stand straight up.

STIR-FRY To cook meats and/or vegetables with a constant stirring motion in a small amount of oil in a wok or skillet over high heat.

WARM To hold foods at a low temperature, usually around 200°, without further cooking.

General Recipe Index

This handy index lists every recipe by food category, major ingredient and cooking method, so you can easily locate the recipes that suit your needs.

✓*Recipe includes Nutrition Facts*

||||||||||||||||||||||||||||||||||||||||||||||||||||||||||||||||||||||||||||||

HERB HAPPY
GARLIC BREAD
PAGE 119

CRAB QUICHE WITH
HOLLANDAISE
PAGE 201

HOKA CHEESECAKE
PAGE 229

TANDOORI CHICKEN THIGHS
PAGE 284

COFFEE

Hazelnut Mocha Coffee, 161
Holiday Peppermint Mocha, 198
Homemade Irish Cream, 185

CONDIMENTS

Basil & Parsley Pesto, 302
Berry-Basil Limeade Jam, 302
Easy Apricot Jam, 303
Ginger Pear Freezer Jam, 301
Herb Mix for Dipping Oil, 186
Homemade Vanilla Extract, 236
Honey Blueberry Cobbler Jam, 300
Nutty Apple Butter, 168
Old-Fashioned Coney Hot Dog
   Sauce, 206
Quick Cranberry Sauce, 217
Refrigerator Jalapeno Dill Pickles, 300
Rhubarb-Cherry Chutney, 303
✓Slow-Cooked Peach Salsa, 301
Spinach-Basil Pesto, 83
Vanilla Coffee Creamer, 226
Vanilla Sugar, 231

COOKIES

(*also see Bars & Brownies*)
Acorn Treats, 208
Chocolate Mallow Drops, 238
Confetti Cake Batter Cookies, 310
Envelopes of Fudge, 228
Ginger-Doodles, 231
Jeweled Thumbprints, 235
✓Mint Twist Meringues, 220
Molasses Cutouts, 221
Pecan Tassies, 232
Peppermint Twist Kisses, 223
Red Velvet White Chip Cookies, 267
Salted Toffee Cashew Cookies, 232
✓Vanilla Meringue Cookies, 249
Winter Fruit Macaroons, 238

CORN

(*also see Corn Bread & Cornmeal*)
✓Basil Grilled Corn on the Cob, 246
✓Black Bean 'n' Corn Quesadillas, 91
✓Cheese Tortellini with Tomatoes and
   Corn, 104
Chicken, Asparagus & Corn
   Chowder, 55
✓Corn, Rice & Bean Burritos, 258
✓Fresh Corn & Potato Chowder, 255
Fresh Corn Omelet, 159
Green Chili Creamed Corn, 174
✓Southwestern Sauteed Corn, 250

CORN BREAD & CORNMEAL

✓Buttermilk Corn Bread, 145
Chicken Chile Relleno Casserole, 134
Cornmeal-Chive Drop Biscuits, 149
Jalapeno Hush Puppies, 147
Layered Corn Bread Salad, 20

CRANBERRIES

Apple Cranberry Cashew Salad, 213
Apricot Cranberry Chicken, 93
Cranberry Cream Cheese French
   Toast, 138
Cranberry Quick Bread, 144
Maple Cran-Apple Breakfast
   Pizza, 198
Nutty Cranberry Sticky Buns, 153
Quick Cranberry Sauce, 217
Sparkling Cranberry Kiss, 16

CUCUMBERS

✓Chicken with Peach-Cucumber
   Salsa, 288
Indian Cucumber Salad, 122
Refrigerator Jalapeno Dill Pickles, 300

DESSERTS

(*also see Bars & Brownies; Cakes &*
   Frosting; Candies; Cheesecakes;
   Cookies; Ice Cream, Sherbet &
   Sorbet; Pies & Tarts)
Birthday Cake Freezer Pops, 308
Campfire Peach Cobbler, 204
Caramel Fruit Dip, 68
Cherry Dew Dumplings, 226
Christmas Gingerbread Trifle, 222
Christmas Treat Garland, 222
Contest-Winning Caramel Apple
   Crisp, 239
Dark Chocolate Croissant Bread
   Pudding, 236
Dark Chocolate Pudding, 211
Easy Four-Layer Chocolate
   Dessert, 233
✓Fresh Berries with Lemon
   Yogurt, 254
Frozen Banana Cereal Pops, 262
Gingerbread & Pumpkin Cream
   Trifle, 215
Gingersnap Pear Trifles, 117
Hot Quick Banana Boats, 187
Instant Chocolate Pastries, 189
Italian Torte, 63
Peaches & Cream, 117
Peanut Butter Shakes, 69

Pot of S'mores, 206
Pretzel Dessert, 239
Strawberry Mousse Parfaits, 76
Ultimate Oreo Caramel Apples, 211
Vanilla White Chocolate Mousse, 239

DIPS & FONDUE

✓Avocado Bean Dip, 123
Brownie Batter Dip, 274
Caramel Fruit Dip, 68
✓Grilled Leek Dip, 245
Herb Mix for Dipping Oil, 186
✓Homemade Ranch Dressing & Dip
   Mix, 9
Jalapeno Hummus, 116
✓Loaded Baked Potato Dip, 16
Mocha Fondue, 189
Pretzel Mustard Dip, 64
Warm Feta Cheese Dip, 10

EGGS & EGG SUBSTITUTE

Breakfast Egg Casserole, 128
Breakfast Spuds, 161
✓Calico Pepper Frittata, 162
Cheese and Fresh Herb Quiche, 158
Cheesy Ham & Egg Sandwiches, 161
Chorizo & Egg Breakfast Ring, 197
Croque Madame, 199
Dutch Oven Cheesy Bacon & Eggs, 206
Egg Baskets Benedict, 161
Fresh Corn Omelet, 159
✓Garlic-Herb Mini Quiches, 190
Ham & Feta Omelet, 157
Mushroom-Avocado Eggs on Toast, 164
Pot Roast Hash, 294
✓Sausage and Egg Pizza, 158
Sausage & Sweet Potato Hash, 163
Sausage, Egg and Cheddar Farmer's
   Breakfast, 156
Scrambled Egg Bread, 205
Scrambled Egg Hash Brown Cups, 196

SCRAMBLED EGG
HASH BROWN CUPS
PAGE 196

SALMON VEGGIE PACKETS
PAGE 133

LEMON-BUTTER TILAPIA WITH ALMONDS
PAGE 85

DIJON PORK MEDALLIONS
PAGE 186

SAUCY THAI CHICKEN PIZZA
PAGE 292

**PORK & VEGETABLE SPRING ROLLS
PAGE 108**

WHITE BEAN
ARUGULA SALAD
PAGE 30

THAI CHICKEN TACOS
PAGE 59

CHICKEN & WAFFLES
PAGE 84

JALAPENO POPPER QUESADILLAS
PAGE 86

Alphabetical Recipe Index

This index lists every recipe in alphabetical order so you can easily find all of your favorites.

✓ *Recipe includes Nutrition Facts*

**CHEESY CHILI FRIES
PAGE 129**

DELUXE WALKING NACHOS
PAGE 295

**KING BURGERS
PAGE 287**

MINI MAC & CHEESE BITES
PAGE 15

PATIO PINTOS
PAGE 23

SOUTHWEST TURKEY LETTUCE WRAPS
PAGE 50

VANILLA BEAN CUPCAKES
PAGE 240